CULTURE AND BEHAVIOR

COLLECTED ESSAYS OF *Clyde Kluckhohn*

CULTURE
AND
BEHAVIOR

Edited by RICHARD KLUCKHOHN

The Free Press of Glencoe

Copyright © 1962 by The Free Press of Glencoe, A Division of
The Macmillan Company

PRINTED IN THE UNITED STATES OF AMERICA

For information, address:
The Free Press of Glencoe
A DIVISION OF THE MACMILLAN COMPANY,
   THE CROWELL-COLLIER PUBLISHING COMPANY
60 Fifth Avenue, New York 11

DESIGNED BY SIDNEY SOLOMON

Library of Congress Catalog Card Number: 61-14108

PREFACE

PROFESSOR KLUCKHOHN died suddenly of a heart condition on July 29, 1960, in Santa Fe, New Mexico. He left behind several unfinished manuscripts, out of one of which this volume developed. He had planned this book for some time as the first collection of his own essays to appear in print. It was planned with two purposes in mind, one of which was to make available in one place certain data and interpretations that were originally published in widely scattered sources. The second was to provide an integrated statement of his own theoretical premises, their development, and the interplay between them and his theoretical research. With the exception of "A Navaho Politician," all the selections presented were chosen by Professor Kluckhohn, and all have been at least partially revised by him. Passages contradicted by later knowledge have been omitted, save in those few cases in which the very error throws some light on the history of anthropology. Some revisions have been made in the interests of clarity and simplicity, and some extraneous passages have been omitted in order to preserve continuity of idea. The majority of the revisions were made by him, and I have made no substantive changes of any length. The introduction I wrote entirely, but based my text on some notes and an outline by Professor Kluckhohn.

Included in this volume is a complete and authoritative bibliography, the only one in print. This bibliography was compiled and prepared exclusively by Miss Lucy Wales, who also contributed extensively to the preparation of this volume.

I am deeply indebted to the Ford Foundation and to Harvard University for making available for completion of this book some of the funds from a grant given to Professor Kluckhohn and now administered by a committee composed of Professors J. O. Brew, Evon Z. Vogt, and Talcott Parsons. I am also indebted to Dr. Florence Kluckhohn, Professor Kluckhohn's literary executrix, for the release of the original manuscript for revision and completion. Last, I would like gratefully to acknowledge the assistance of Professor Brew, Director of the Peabody Museum, in making facilities and space available for the completion of this and other unfinished works.

Boston University   R. K.
January, 1962

CONTENTS

1 *INTRODUCTION*

by Richard Kluckhohn

Anthropology in Perspective

THE WORD "ANTHROPOLOGIST" means many things to many people, especially today; further, at different points in human history it has had an even wider scope of possible meanings and associations. To the "man in the street" the word more than probably will suggest a rather odd sort of person who is interested in odd savage customs from the more remote parts of the world. To the college student it will mean an instructor who teaches something akin to sociology, but limited to non-Western peoples for the most part. To members of many government agencies an anthropologist is a special sort of technician or scientist who can help them in sorting out practical problems involving American Indians, underdeveloped areas and their peoples, or any group whose way of life is very different from our own. Very recently the anthropologist has come into Madison Avenue as the man who may have a better key to the pocketbooks of America than the psychologist. Nor can even a member of the profession give an exact definition of what an anthropologist is. To say that anyone who studies mankind is an anthropologist would be fatuous, as social psychologists and neuroanatomists would be among the first to agree. To define him as one who studies his culture and its history would do double violence to the fact: on the one hand, by excluding physical anthropologists and, on the other, by including many historians and political scientists who disclaim anthropology. The usual rule of thumb is to define as an anthropologist any person who has taken a doctorate, or its equivalent, in a department of anthropology. Though useful in the main, this still excludes some, while it tells nothing about the scope of anthropology, its methods, or theoretical framework. These, however, are the very items that are so difficult to pin down, given the rather amorphous background and development of this discipline.

The nineteenth century was the formative period for anthropology, though its antecedents go back considerably further in time. Many have owned that Herodotus was the first anthropologist, owing to his detailed accounts of the customs and habits of peoples other than his own. In the same vein, Tacitus' *On Germany* could almost stand today as a preliminary report in a modern journal. The social philosophers of the eighteenth century contributed greatly to later developments in anthropology per se. In this, Lowie (1937, p. 10) cites Klemm:

Voltaire was the first to push aside dynasties, series of kings, and battles, and to seek what was essential, Culture, as it manifests itself in customs, faith, and governmental forms.

Nonetheless, it was in the nineteenth century that a series of interests, ideas, and endeavors came into rich being and interacted strongly with one another. One of these was the increasing amount of detailed collection of facts concerning many peoples throughout the world and the compilation of these facts by men such as Gustav Klemm. Another very significant development was the demonstration by Boucher de Perthes that man dates back into the Pleistocene Period. This not only laid the basis for anthropological archaeology, but also gave great impetus to the first great "school" of anthropology. The primary foundation of this school lay, however, upon the exposition of the theory of evolution by Darwin and others.

Another major development of the nineteenth century—albeit slighting the hardheaded, careful, and fact-collecting "anthropo-geography" of Bastian, then Ratzel, and their followers—was the beginning of the study of comparative law in England by Maine and McLennan, in Switzerland by Bachoffen, and here by the first American anthropologist, Lewis Morgan. Extensive inter-action between all of these major themes of anthropological in-vestigation occurred, and not a few hybrids were produced in the last decades of the century.

This is not a history of anthropology, however, so the exami-nation of a few examples of the scope of late nineteenth-century anthropological inquiry will be brief. In this period of flux and transition, Tylor and others propose evolutionary schemata, dis-cussing "primitive" systems as living fossils showing the stages all men must go through. Tylor also makes the first (quasi-) statistical study of cause and effect in social institutions. Franz Boas is beginning the detailed, unprejudiced field work that is later to become a hallmark of anthropology and to provide the ax with which to attack the evolutionary tree. Frobenius attempts to show linkage between Oceania and Africa. Interest in religion has become very important. The first edition of *The Golden Bough* is published; Rohde points out the importance of primitive religion and folklore; Usener is one of the first to use linguistic materials in treating religion; Marett is shortly to publish his monumental essays on religion. The great interest in primitive psychology, resuscitating Waitz in part, is just beginning. An-thropometry as a part of anthropology is just beginning; pre-historic archaeology is not yet a real part of anthropology; anthropological linguistics is unknown.

By the end of the nineteenth century, anthropology, as an over-all discipline, had become extremely broad in its range of inquiry. It did this not by continuing to build outward from a small beginning, as has been the case with some other disciplines, but rather by the fertile hybridization of many originally inde-pendent lines of development. In the ninth edition of the *En-cyclopaedia Britannica*, published shortly after the turn of the century, Tylor gave the following definition:

Anthropology . . . denotes the natural history of mankind. In the general classification of knowledge it stands as the highest section of zoology or the science of the animals, itself the highest section of biology or the science of living beings. To anthropology contribute various sciences, which hold their own independent places in the field of knowledge. Thus anatomy and physiology display the structure and functions of the human body, while psychology investigates the operations of the human mind. Philology deals with the general principles of language, as well as with the relations between the languages of particular races and nations. Ethics or moral science treats of man's duty or rules of conduct toward his fellow-man. Lastly, under the names of sociology and the science of culture, are considered the origin and development of arts and sciences, opinions, beliefs, customs, laws, and institutions generally among mankind, their course in time being partly marked out by the direct record of history, while beyond the historical limit our information is continued by inferences from relics of early ages and remote districts, to interpret which is the task of pre-historic archaeology and geology.

Anthropology then, was, at least in one major view, a kind of coordinating science with the purpose of determining human history. Others collected the facts, and still others made preliminary analyses, but it was the purpose of anthropology to realign all of these disparate efforts into a cohesive interpretation. For the most part, this all changed early in this century. Following the lead of Boas, and of many of the German school who had done so all along, it became of prime importance for the anthropologist to collect his own data. "Sociology and the science of culture" became the central core of anthropology. Prehistoric archaeology became, in this country at least, a major part of the field. The interest in primitive mentality continued and expanded, until many elements of psychology (and some psychologists themselves) became incorporated into the discipline. Physical anthropology became a coordinate branch in its own right, and, finally, anthropological linguistics came into its own, with many methods and interests markedly divergent from classical philology. Gradually there emerged, at least in the United States, the picture now typical of a university department of anthropology. On the continent, save in France, history remained the paramount concern until very recently, but the use of linguistics, archaeology, and physical anthropology was extensive. In

England and France, however, these latter three fields developed in large part independently of the main body of anthropology; the synchronic study and analysis of social institutions was the prime concern in America. Finally, both here and abroad the "subdisciplines" of social or cultural anthropology developed: culture and personality, defined as such in the early thirties but developing out of the old concern in primitive psychology; applied anthropology, born of the necessity of colonial administration and wartime need; subfields such as cultural history and social structure per se, which had never died abroad but had been neglected for a time here, and so on.

Anthropology as we know it today came about from an original mating of widely variant strains and then further expanded as a result of some rather selective inbreeding. At present it is both a science and a humanistic discipline, and it is concerned with both the synchronic and the diachronic approach. It treats both man the physical beast and man the social animal, and it does so both historically and analytically. Last, in recent years, it has chosen no longer to deal almost exclusively with non-Western or nonliterate peoples. This now raises the whole question of the relations between anthropology and the many other disciplines also included in one or more of these areas of investigation into the human animal.

Anthropology and Other Disciplines

No discussion of anthropology and its external relations can safely be made without at least mentioning the transactions between anthropologists and members of the various essentially "nonhuman" sciences. Indeed, physical anthropology often deals in "nonhuman" data and has worked closely, often along similar lines, with primatology and paleontology. Landsteiner and Levine, and the many others who pioneered in the refinement of blood-typing, have contributed as much to anthropology as to medicine. William Boyd, a professor of immunochemistry at

Boston University Medical School, has also been an editor of the *American Journal of Physical Anthropology* and has been a major contributor to the anthropological study of population genetics and its implications for the concept of race. Dobzhansky's or Sewell Wright's works are as important to the student as those of Weidenreich or Leakey. Studies in medical pathology largely prompted F. Clark Howell's excellent reappraisal of Neanderthal man.

Archaeology has also drawn heavily upon various sciences not primarily concerned with mankind. Geology is perhaps the most prominent, but nuclear physics (C^{14}, K^{40} dating) and astronomy (the disputed Zeuner dating system) have also played their parts. Soil chemistry has provided the relative dating system based upon fluorine absorption; botanists such as Mangelsdorf and others have made major contributions to human prehistory through their extensive work upon the antiquity and origin of various grains and other plants associated with human habitation. Moreover, the dividing line (if any need exist) between anthropological archaeology and classical archaeology is indeed hard to draw. European prehistoric archaeology is seldom incorporated into a department of anthropology, but by our definitions it is indeed anthropology and is also frequently more daring and provocative in its conclusions than our own. It is interesting to note here one curious hiatus that exists between anthropological archaeology and classical archaeology. The early civilizations of the Mediterranean "belong" to one field for the most part, while those of the New World "belong" to the other; both work on the civilizations of the Fertile Crescent and India, while each is largely behind the specialized field of early Sinitic history and prehistory.

Nonetheless, the major interactions (as opposed to transactions) between anthropology and other fields have occurred especially in the study of social behavior, and, since this is the major concern of this volume, I shall focus primarily upon these. A truism often forgotten in interdisciplinary discussions is that all those concerned with the whys and wherefores of human action, attitude, value, belief, and so on, have one fundamental, common basis: their data consist almost wholly of human behavior and its products, past and present. In any given collection of human beings, the sum total of all of their actual behaviors remains a constant; differences between the various fields occur in *which* and *how many* individual behaviors from the total group sum are recorded and studied, and in the paradigm presented in terms of which to explain those phenomena selected for study.

At the present time there are two main fields of inquiry which interact extensively with anthropology: sociology and psychology. Other disciplines have tended to follow their own lines of investigation. Economics, for instance, has for the most part devoted itself to the analysis of a special case of economic activity—Western European civilization. Only quite recently has economics turned to other systems, as it has become necessary to cope with important Asian economies, with the economic bases of underdeveloped nations, and with the "semi-artificial" economic system operative in many Communist countries. There is, however, the beginning of an interest among some economists in the analysis of *any* given economic system, and, in tune with this, anthropology has resuscitated and expanded the field of "primitive economics." An excellent example of the budding cooperation in this area is Polanyi, Arensberg, and Pearson's *Trade and Market in the Early Empires* (1957), another the forthcoming *Trade and Market in Africa*, edited by Paul Bohannan.

This area of cooperation is, however, only in the budding stage. Even less can be said of political science. True, political scientists have worked with anthropologists on various government projects, in Harvard's Russian Research Center, and in other area programs, but really mutual endeavor is yet to come. The anthropologist leaves the analysis of the major nations' political systems to the specialist in that area, and he, in turn, leaves to the anthropologist the peculiarities to be found in abstruse parts of the world.[1]

It is quite a different case with both sociology and psychology. With each there has been a long period of mutual interest, parallel development, and common endeavor. Particularly in the case of psychology, this is well demonstrated in later papers in

1. It is interesting, if disheartening, to note that Leach's brilliant volume, *Political Systems of Highland Burma* (1954), achieved little if any notice in any of the major journals of political science in this country.

this volume. In each field, however, the congruence with anthropological investigation has been quite different from that of the other. Let us, therefore, take a separate look at each.

PSYCHOLOGY[2]

The early interest in "primitive psychology" has been noted above. Labels were also confused in these early times. Rivers, nominally a psychologist, might well be called an anthropologist; Boas, on the other hand, wrote *The Mind of Primitive Man*. Much the same duality of interest can be attributed to Tylor, Marett, Hahn, Frazer, the Seligmanns, and many others. As time passed, the labels became more specific, but the two fields continued to work together. One essential difference became more pronounced and remains today the primary dividing line between the two. Psychology remained primarily concerned with the analysis of individual behavior and the explanation of factors causing that behavior; anthropology was concerned with the general behavior of a society and with the factors causing that behavior. Psychology called its causal construct "personality" and anthropology called its construct "culture." Yet, as Spiro (1951) has so succinctly pointed out, there is perforce a great deal of overlap in these two constructs, in that a large element in any given personality is that individual's *cultural heredity*, a modification of his *cultural heritage*. This has been stated by others in many ways, and, more important, has been tacitly recognized by most members of both fields. The anthropologist must be concerned with developments in psychology, as he is first dealing with individuals and their behavior (Sapir, 1938, p. 11):

In spite of all that has been claimed to the contrary, we cannot thoroughly understand the dynamics of culture, of society, of history, without sooner or later taking account of the actual interrelationships of human beings.

---

2. Here taken to mean clinical psychology, personality psychology, and psychiatry but to exclude most social psychology.

Or (Sapir, 1938, p. 10):

... this means ... that problems of social science differ from problems of individual behavior in degree of specificity, not in kind.

Conversely, many psychologists have realized that any system of personality dynamics or any system of personality measurement must be independent of any specific culture in order for either to be really valid. Erikson is one of the most widely known of those who have stressed the importance of cultural variation in understanding the individual. Sarason and Kaplan are well known, among others, for their analysis of psychometric materials from participants in cultures widely variant from our own.

The anthropological contributions to and uses of psychology have been many and varied. Perhaps the most significant has been the development of the unitary characterization of society, whether this be called "national character," *Weltanschauung* or "world-view," "basic" or "modal" personality, or what have you. All of these approaches to the characterization of a society as a whole presume that each and every member of that society possesses as an integrated part of his personality a substantial portion of the norms, values, and attitudes of his culture. Though not always stated as such, what this approach attempts is to present a picture of the "average" culture-bearing member of the society, *minus* all the idiosyncratic factors that vary from individual to individual. The model is, of course, a psychological one.

Another major utilization of psychology has appeared in what might be called the developmental approach to the acquisition of culture—in studies emphasizing the socialization techniques through which the growing person becomes enculturated. This emphasis may range from those studies in which it is the central theme, such as Whiting's *Becoming a Kwoma* (1941), through those in which it is a groundwork for later analysis, such as Du Bois' *People of Alor* (1944), to those many studies where socialization data is simply reported as part of the ethnographic data and is used only partially in the analysis of the culture; a good example of the last category is Holmberg's *Nomads of the Long Bow* (1950).

One cannot leave out the many types of data reported by anthropologists but utilized by psychologists. The most specific of these are the psychometric data collected by some ethnologists themselves, such as Du Bois, Gladwin, and J. Henry, or secured for them by a psychologist, as was the case with Kaplan's Navaho material. Another major fund of such material consists of personal documents and dreams. Finally, there is that large body of data of general ethnology, particularly that which focuses on mythology and religion, on which Freud himself and many others have drawn heavily.

Fairly recently, some anthropologists have undertaken the study of the setting of the psychotherapeutic process itself; the works of Caudill (1958), Henry (1954), and Devereaux (1944) are representative. Some anthropological work has focused directly on a particular personality syndrome in a given culture; examples are Whiting's work on Kwoma frustration (1944), Hallowell's on Saulteaux aggression (1940), and Devereaux's on Mohave orality (1947).

Inherent in these very few examples of anthropology's impingement on and utilization of psychology is the fact of the overwhelming impact upon anthropological theory and method of psychological (or psychiatric) theory and method. The whole area of study usually called "culture and personality" developed as much or more out of progress in psychology as it did out of anthropological progress. This general debt to psychology is too well known to need further documentation here. However, it might be well to point out that some psychologists have themselves worked essentially alone on non-Western peoples and in so doing have made contributions to ethnology, either by collecting new data themselves or by reinterpreting the data of others. Some examples of this are Porteus' work on several Australian groups (1931), Roheim's *Psychoanalysis and Anthropology* (1950), Kardiner's *The Individual and His Society* (1939), and Alexander Leighton's *My Name Is Legion*, subtitled "Foundations for a Theory of Man in Relation to Culture" (1959).

The other major mainstream of contact between these two fields lies in the many, and very productive, cooperative efforts by members of both. This cooperation has taken many forms;

joint field research, joint analysis of field data, combined departments within universities, addition of anthropologists to the
staffs of mental hospitals and to the staff of the National Institute
of Mental Health, and cooperative effort on government
and foundation committees. These are far too common and extensive to deserve any detailed explication here. Suffice it to say
that this pattern of joint effort is expanding consistently, at a
rate that perhaps exceeds that of development in either of the
fields alone. The contributions to date toward our general
understanding of human behavior have been great, and it is to
be expected that this will continue to be the case.

The pattern of relationships that emerges is, then, roughly as
follows. Anthropology and psychology have essentially different
final goals, one seeking to develop a theoretical framework that
can explain the observed regularities in the behavior of (fairly
large) groups of human beings, and the other seeking a similar
framework but with the understanding of individual behavior as
its end. The period of interaction between the two fields has
been quite a long one, and it is still increasing. Anthropology
has made factual contributions to psychology and has helped to
make possible, with substantial foundation, a generalization beyond the individual of Western civilization to the individual
per se, whatever his cultural background. Psychology, on the
other hand, has made fewer contributions of useful fact but
has been of great theoretical importance in helping the anthropologist deal with the mechanisms of the transmission of culture,
and with the problems resulting from cultural conflict as well.
Some very specific examples of anthropological contribution to
psychology and of joint endeavor follow in this volume (see
especially 1949g, 1946b, 1955g, 1951c).

SOCIOLOGY[3]

The relationship between this field and anthropology is more
difficult to delineate accurately, if only because one is denied the
heuristic device of separation in terms of final goals. Both fields
in this case are concerned with the analysis and explanation of

3. Here taken to include the majority of social psychology.

group behavior. A recent textbook in sociology (Broom and Selznick, 1955, p. 3) said of sociology:

Its long-run aim is to discover the basic structure of human society, to identify the main forces that hold groups together or weaken them, and to learn the conditions that transform social life.

And later (p. 5):

In many ways, anthropology and sociology have drawn closer together in recent years, particularly as anthropoligists have turned to the study of literate societies. A central emphasis on the analysis of culture, however, continues to characterize anthropological inquiry.

At the present time this consideration of emphasis upon culture, or the lack thereof, is certainly one way in which sociology and anthropology may be discriminated. There are also several other rough-and-ready generalizations that can be made on an empirical basis. For the most part, contemporary sociology deals almost wholly with Western societies, while anthropology has only recently added the analysis of these societies, or communities thereof, to its expanding list of societies from all other parts of the world. Traditionally, anthropological investigation has been for the most part of the participant observer type, while sociology, on the other hand, has used primarily the interview technique coupled with the collection of recorded empirical data. Anthropology has stressed a wholistic approach, while sociology has delved deeper into detailed studies of specific institutions within the society or focused on "problems" such as crime, divorce, and juvenile delinquency. None of these rather crude observations holds fully true of either field, but they help to highlight some of the more obvious differences.

In times past these two labels were much less valid than they are today. Weber and especially Durkheim, both early "sociologists," were very important in the development of anthropological theory. Mauss and Hubert are in much the same position, and Radcliffe-Brown could lay claim to either title— he worked primarily on non-Western peoples, but did not consider culture a terribly useful concept (though are his "social usages" very different from "cultural patterns"?). Going even further back in time, to Bachofen, Maine, Spencer, Morgan, Sumner, and others, either term could be applied.

Given this past debt and lack of any important division, it is surprising to note that today there is generally considerably less real interaction between anthropology and sociology than is the case with psychology. There are fewer joint publications, very few combined field studies. While there are a great many combined departments, the trend is for anthropology to become as separate in administration as it has often been in approach. Far fewer anthropologists publish in the *American Sociological Review* or the *American Journal of Sociology* than in *Psychiatry* or *Orthopsychiatry*.

At present there are within the rubric of sociology many subfields, often quite widely separated. However, another rough division can be made, separating "theoretical sociology," "statistical" or "methodological" approaches, research and methods dealing with small-group behavior, and the applied fields. Sometimes two or more of these areas are brought together; at other times they show little relation to each other—one can easily see the profitable collaboration in a work such as Parsons and Bales' *Family, Socialization, and Interaction Process,* but *Middletown* is a far cry from *The Social System.* There is in sociology at present no generally accepted over-all theoretical schema, such as the concept of culture provides for anthropology. If there is one general, uniting principle among the sociological subfields, it is a common concern with the delineation of social groups—the break-down of these groups into subgroups and individuals, the analysis of the roles of the smaller groups and/or individuals, the study of the processes and content of interaction within the group, and the delineation of the relative functions of the group and its component parts. Few empirical studies perform all of these functions, but some of the small-group studies come close (here much of what is sometimes classed administratively as social psychology is treated as part of greater sociology). Some theoretical frameworks do take account of all of these factors, and some go beyond, as is the case with Parsons' *(et al.)* "theory of action," which includes the "general theory of social systems," "personality theory, and some aspects of the theory of culture" (Parsons and Smelser, 1956, p. 5). Nonetheless, at least some of these elements are present in almost every work in sociology, theoretical or empirical. Much anthropological work would not come under any of these headings, save by a great deal of stretching of the imagination—this is true especially of works in religion, mythology, and material culture. Also, sociology is specifically marked by a very pervading, common absence of one concept, that of culture. It is frequently remarked upon, sometimes given lip-service, but it has never been a basic element either in the explanation of observed phenomena or in a major theoretical framework.

There are, of course, examples that fall between the fields, and scholars who share large elements of both, but these are fairly rare. Radcliffe-Brown's position has been noted, and, indeed, many English social anthropologosists and much of England social anthropology falls between the two fields—Leach, most of the time, is closer to Parsons than to Boas. French sociology is in much the same position, with regard to the two fields as practiced in the United States. W. Lloyd Warner is perhaps the best example of a living amalgamation of the two, but Redfield's debt to sociological theory and tradition is quite clear. Homans and Schneider's *Marriage, Authority, and Final Causes* (1955) is a brilliant example of the rare but sometimes highly stimulating collaborative effort.

In general, however, sociology remains quite distinct despite its focus on many of the behavioral systems also studied by anthropology. Far more than anthropology it remains specifically concerned with the structure of groups per se and the details of interaction within these groups. Sociology brings to bear quite a different battery of theoretical tools and uses a widely different methodology, be this the compilation and statistical analysis of large amounts of data on a large sample of people or the manipulation of small groups behind one-way mirrors. It makes more use by far of empirical generalization for predictive purposes. Still, there are few anthropologists working on Western communities and even fewer sociologists working on non-Western ones.

This situation will, of course, change as further time passes and each field broadens the base of its research. But it is most unlikely that any general amalgamation will take place in the foreseeable future, though it is hoped that there will be an increase in the borrowings from each by the other. In the words of Kroeber and Parsons (1958, p. 583):

It will undoubtedly be most profitable to develop both lines of thinking and to judge them by how much each increases understanding. Secondly, . . . we may in time expect to learn in which area each type of conceptualization is the more applicable and productive. By some such procedure, we should improve our position for increasing understanding of the relations between the two.

Summary

In general, the major differences between social anthropology and the other social sciences is that anthropology was born of intercultural variation, while all the others were originally concerned with one or another type of intracultural variation, and most have remained there until the present, or at least the recent past. The first of the other fields to work extensively with data from disparate cultures was psychology (clinical psychology and psychiatry). This fact, coupled with a largely developmental approach, and the basic similiarities between the concepts of culture and personality, these have tended to bring these two fields into a closer relationship than social anthropology shares with any other field. Psychology and anthropology also share a primary utilization of a limited number of cases, but go into great depth with these, whereas sociology and social psychology do not for the most part use this method.

While these two fields have attempted to deal with man in the general sense, all the rest have concerted their efforts on Western man—with a frequent exception in the case of the various studies on the Far East, and more recently India and the Middle East. This pattern is now changing, and, as anthropologists are beginning extensive work on various aspects of Western man, political scientists, economists, sociologists, and others are beginning work on non-Western materials. Generally speaking all social sciences other than anthropology and personality psychology (clinical psychiatry) have developed principles, axioms, and "laws" that are not dependent upon a developmental and causal concept such as that of culture or personality. It will be very interesting to observe the results as these and other fields move into traditionally anthropological areas, and vice versa, and it is to be expected that many fresh insights will be provided by both "sides," as it were; but, in the main, it is probable that the methodological and theoretical similarities between anthropology and psychology will serve to maintain closer cooperation between these fields than any of the others. Nor is it expected that *major* change will be effected in anthropology by multicultural research on the part of other social sciences; it is redundant to say that personality psychology is dependent upon the concept of personality, but anthropology, especially in the United States, *is* dependent upon the concept of culture.

REFERENCES

Bohannan, Paul (Sr. Ed.) (1962), *Trade and Market in Africa*. Evanston, Ill.: Northwestern University Press.

Broom, Leonard, and Philip Selznick (1955), *Sociology*. Evanston, Ill.: Row, Peterson & Company.

Caudill, William (1958), *The Psychiatric Hospital as a Small Society*. Cambridge: Harvard University Press.

—— (1944), "The Social Structure of a Schizophrenic Ward and Its Therapeutic Fitness," *Journal of Clinical Psychopathology*, 6:231-265.

George, Devereaux, (1947) "Mohave Orality," *Psychoanalytic Quarterly*, 16:519-546.

Du Bois, Cora (1944), *People of Alor*. Minneapolis: University of Minnesota Press.

Hallowell, A. Irving (1940), "Aggression in Saulteaux Society," *Psychiatry*, 3:395-407.

Henry, Jules (1954), "The Formal Structure of a Psychiatric Hospital," *Psychiatry*, 17:139-151.

Holmberg, Allan R. (1950), *Nomads of the Long Bow*. Washington, D.C., Smithsonian Institution, Institute of Social Anthropology, Publication No. 10.

Homans, George C., and David M. Schneider (1955), *Marriage, Authority, and Final Causes*. New York: The Free Press.

Howell, F. Clark (1952), "Pleistocene Glacial Ecology and the Evolution of 'Classical Neanderthal' Man," *Southwestern Journal of Anthropology*, 8:377-410.

Kardiner, Abram (1939), *The Individual and His Society*. New York: Columbia University Press.

Kroeber, Alfred L., and Talcott Parsons (1958), "The Concepts of Culture and or Social System," *American Sociological Review*, 23:582-583.

Leach, E. R. (1954), *Political Systems of Highland Burma*. Cambridge: Harvard University Press.

Leighton, Alexander (1959), *My Name Is Legion*. New York: Basic Books.

Lowie, Robert H. (1937), *The History of Ethnological Theory*. New York: Holt, Rinehart, Winston.

Lynd, Robert S., and Helen Merrell Lynd (1929), *Middletown*. New York: Harcourt, Brace and Company, Inc.

Parsons, Talcott (1951), *The Social System*. New York: The Free Press.
_____ and Fred Bales (1955), *Family, Socialization, and Interaction Process*. New York: The Free Press.
_____ and Neil J. Smelser (1956), *Economy and Society*. New York: The Free Press.

Polanyi, Karl, Conrad M. Arensberg, and Harry W. Pearson (1957), *Trade and Market in the Early Empires*. New York: The Free Press.

Porteus, Stanley (1931), *The Psychology of a Primitive People*. New York: Longmans, Green and Company.

Roheim, Geza (1950), *Psychoanalysis and Anthropology*. New York: International Universities Press.

Sapir, Edward (1948), "Why Cultural Anthropology Needs the Psychiatrist," *Psychiatry*, 1:7-12.

Spiro, Melford (1951), "Culture and Personality, the Natural History of a False Dichotomy," *Psychiatry*, 14:19-46.

Tylor, Edward B. (1875-1889), "Anthropology," *Encyclopaedia Britannica*, ninth edition.

Whiting, John (1941), *Becoming a Kwoma*. New Haven: Published for the Institute of Human Relations by Yale University Press.
_____ (1944), "The Frustration Complex in Kwoma Society," *Man*, 44:140-144.

2 THE CONCEPT
OF CULTURE

THE LAWYER: At the last meeting of this little discussion group of ours, we got into an argument about "culture" as a technical term in anthropology—exactly what anthropologists mean by it and whether the concept is useful or not. The big dictionaries and even the anthropological books in the club library didn't help us out very much. We did gather that the anthropological conception carries with it an implication of human interference, of something being added to or altered from a state of nature. But we found ourselves wishing that we could ask questions that might clear up points which were side-stepped or not discussed in these formal statements. We therefore prevailed upon you gentlemen to come here and let us put you on the spot.

THE HISTORIAN: Was I right in insisting last time that the

1945b Reprinted by permission of the publishers from Clyde Kluckhohn and W. H. Kelly, "The Concept of Culture," in *The Science of Man in the World Crisis*, edited by Ralph Linton. New York, Columbia University Press, pp. 78-105.

anthropologist's conception of culture is much more inclusive than the historian's?

FIRST ANTHROPOLOGIST: Yes. To anthropologists a humble cooking pot is as much a "cultural" product as is a Beethoven sonata.

THE BUSINESSMAN: I am relieved to hear that. For my wife a person who has "culture" is someone who can talk about Debussy, T. S. Eliot, Picasso, and those people.

THE HISTORIAN: The anthropological concept, I believe, derives directly from eighteenth-century thought. Giovanni Vico, for example, pointed out that the social world is the work of man; human customs are neither directly derivable from human biology nor divinely ordained and revealed.

THE LAWYER: Do anthropologists apply the term "culture" to our civilization? Isn't there a difference between "culture" and "civilization"?

SECOND ANTHROPOLOGIST: To most anthropologists, a civilization is simply a special type of culture—namely, a complex or "high" culture. Or one can properly follow the etymological meaning of the term and say that a civilization is a culture of a people who live in cities. People who have lived in cities have invariably possessed a complex way of life and have almost always had a written language.

Perhaps it would also be well to state for the record that anthropologists have never followed another distinction that certain sociologists have made between culture and civilization. This usage discriminates between "civilization" as comprising the sum total of human "means" and "culture" as constituting the collectivity of human "ends."

THE PHILOSOPHER: Am I correct in inferring that anthropologists would insist that the concept "culture" is applicable to all human behavior?

FIRST ANTHROPOLOGIST: Decidedly. Many educated people seem to have the notion that "culture" applies only to exotic ways of life or to societies where relative simplicity and relative homogeneity prevail. Some sophisticated missionaries, for example, will use the anthropological conception in discussing the special modes of living of South Sea Islanders but seem amazed at the idea that it could be applied equally to the inhabitants of

New York City. And social workers in New York City will talk about the "culture" of a colorful and well-knit immigrant group but boggle at applying it to the behavior of staff members in the social service agency itself.

THE ECONOMIST: A moment ago you used the term "society." This brings me to a point which I have found confusing in certain recent more or less popular writings of anthropologists. Sometimes the terms "culture" and "society" seem to have been used as synonyms.

FIRST ANTHROPOLOGIST: There would be fairly general agreement in our profession that this is undesirable. The terminology that has attained almost complete acceptance among us can be put simply, though not altogether precisely, as follows: A "society" refers to a group of people who have learned to work together; a "culture" refers to the distinctive ways of life of such a group of people.

THE PHILOSOPHER: In my language, then, "a culture" is an abstraction, whereas "a society" is not?

THIRD ANTHROPOLOGIST: That is certainly correct in the sense that you can see the individuals who make up a society, while you never see "culture." However, that statement must not be made to imply that the processes of inference and abstraction are not involved in many of the specific problems of deciding where one society leaves off and another begins. Some anthropologists assert that such problems can always be resolved by sufficiently detailed observation of the frequencies with which human beings in a defined territory interact. This is doubtless a valid operation by which to decide what individuals constitute "a society," but we should be deluding ourselves if we pretended that reasoning were not as necessary as observation to the delimitation of society.

SECOND ANTHROPOLOGIST: I can't agree with your first statement that culture is never observed directly. What does an anthropologist actually do when he is working in the field? Yes, he sees the human organisms who make up a society. He not only sees them but also their behavior. He likewise sees the objects they have made and all the alterations they have produced in their natural environment. What the anthropologist does is to record the distinctive ways of behaving that he sees and characteristic products of behavior (artifacts, and the like). These constitute the culture of that group.

THIRD ANTHROPOLOGIST: You have correctly described what anthropologists actually do in the field. I assume, of course, that your "ways of behaving" include verbal behavior, and especially statements made by the people as to how things are done and how they "should" be done. But field notes on what members of a group have done and said are only the raw data of the anthropologist. Before he can state the distinctive regularities (i.e., the "ways"), he necessarily abstracts from what he has actually heard and observed. Both "society" and "culture" are conceptual constructs or "models." In each case, although by somewhat different operations, the anthropologist adds to or subtracts from his immediate perceptions.

THE LAWYER: I can see that we are getting into deep water. Lest some of us laymen flounder, I wonder if it wouldn't be wise to give us more background before we enter into a highly specialized discussion. I wonder if one of you won't treat us for a few minutes as an undergraduate class to which you are expounding the mysteries of "culture" for the first time.

FIRST ANTHROPOLOGIST: I hate to show myself in such pedantic colors, but I must confess that I came prepared for just such a contingency. Here are some pages from an introductory lecture. Perhaps you will allow me to read them slowly, just as they stand:

The concept of culture is made necessary by the observed fact of the plasticity of human beings. Newborn members of different groups are taught to carry out "the same" acts in an almost infinite variety of different ways. It is virtually impossible to discover a single act which is carried out in precisely the same manner by the members of all societies. Even such apparently biological processes as sneezing, walking, sleeping, and making love are stylized. If human beings—in spite of all the constitutional differences that prevail among individuals—can be taught to think, feel, believe, and act in certain ways that are approximately the same for whole groups, this must mean an alteration of a mode of behavior we must assume would have occurred had the teaching not taken place. Further, if whole groups or societies learn to do certain things in a more or less uniform fashion, we can make some sort of a general statement concerning the group. This kind of learned

behavior, which, in its specific aspects, is common to a group of people, transmitted by the older generation to its offspring, or transmitted in some portion by any member of one group to a member or members of another group, is called "culture." This is one of the primary concepts of anthropologists. It is a technical term, and no simple dictionary definition will do for our purposes. It is never used, for example, to imply "high" or "low" attainments; nor does it designate the stage of civilization of any race or group; nor the activities in any particular field, such as music, art, or literature.

One way to comprehend the meaning of this concept is to analyze the behavior of a particular individual. A good example is the simple matter of eating a meal. Suppose we imagine that we are witnessing a family of southern Arizona Indians sitting around their campfire fifty years ago and eating their evening meal. The man in whom we are interested is the head of the family, and he is sitting on the ground near a big pot of food. He is hungry and dips into the pot with his hands and eats a mixture of boiled rabbit meat and corn meal, pouring it directly from his scooped fingers into his mouth. Once in a while he gives some of it to a small child sitting near him. He belches occasionally as he eats, asks his wife to bring more wood for the fire, wipes his mouth with the back of his hand, and finally finishes the meal by washing his mouth out with water and spitting it out on the ground nearby.

By studying this sequence of acts it is possible to separate out certain dimensions that spring from interrelated but distinct factors. The first of these is the *biological;* the man is eating because all organisms must eat to keep alive; it is part of his nature to do so, and the whole procedure of this event, no matter how it may differ in details of style from similar events in other societies, springs from fundamental biology.

The *social* dimension can be isolated next. The man gives food to a child; he asks his wife to put wood on the fire. So long as our attention is directed to the circumstances of the age differences between the man and the child and the sex differences between the man and his wife, we are still making biological abstractions from our complete observations. But when our selective interest becomes focused upon the sheer fact of interaction between two pairs of human beings (man-child; husband-wife) our abstractions have a social rather than a biological frame of reference.

But now, if our attention turns to the *mode* in which either the biological or the social acts (or biosocial events) are carried out, we are isolating a *cultural* dimension of behavior. Let us look at the whole sequence of observations from this point of view. The man is sitting on the ground, eating a mixture of rabbit meat and corn meal, wipes his lips with the back of his hand, and washes his mouth out with water.

All these things, and many others, identify him as belonging to a *particular* society. Other people in his group eat their meals this same way, and they have learned to do so because they are members of that group. Other individuals, in other societies, sit at a table to eat, use knives and forks, consider it unforgivable to belch in public; they use aluminum pots in which they cook, and china dishes to hold their food. Clearly, when one looks at the details of daily living of peoples who have had diverse histories, speak their own tongues, and follow their own religions, there is an exuberant—almost infinite—variation in the styling and patterning of activities that subserve the same general biological, psychological, economic, and other "functions." These styles and patterns are not "given" either by human biology or by constants in the process of social interaction. They are created and transmitted by men. And groups differ as regards when, from whom, and under what sanctions comparable modalities of talking and acting are learned.

Because of certain common usages, you may find the distinction which has been drawn between the "social" and the "cultural" rather confusing, but—take my word for it—this differentiation is important and useful. Perhaps the following lucid statement by Sanford Winston will clarify the matter for you:

"The social and the cultural are intimately related; nevertheless they are not the same. . . . The social interaction which takes place between two individuals comes under the category of the social insofar as it pertains to their reactions to one another as individuals. But where their behavior is affected by the patterned ways of behavior existent in the society of which they are a part, their own *social* behavior is influenced by a *cultural* factor. The introduction, the tipping of the hat, and other formalized rules of politeness, the business of courtship and the channeled ways of behavior toward each other of man and wife, are all examples of patterned (i.e., cultural) ways of behaving. The interaction is social, but it is affected by the cultural; it may largely coincide or . . . it may veer away from the patterned ways of behavior laid down by a given society."

Finally, there is the part of this Indian's behavior which is typical of this one man as an individual rather than as a member of his group. The way he holds his food, the speed with which he eats, the tone of his voice when he speaks to his wife, the way he fishes around for the last bit of rabbit—insofar as each of these "mannerisms" betrays a difference from norms characteristic in his group for a man of his age and position. This aspect of his behavior may be called *idiosyncratic*. This idiosyncratic dimension of behavior seems to be partly the result of learning that has occurred through circumstances peculiar to this one individual and partly innate (the consequences of factors of physical heredity).

Two important matters must be emphasized in connection with this analysis. The first of these is that any act is a whole in the concrete, observable world. By abstraction we have broken down this behavior into these aspects for purposes of analytic understanding. All of these dimensions of behavior (idiosyncratic, cultural, social, and biological) are interdependent; that is, as one is altered, the others are likewise affected. But if we see behavior in its multidimensionality, we are less likely to have an oversimple picture of the "forces" that determine these acts.

The second thing is to point out that we have been using the term "culture" rather loosely. Culture is not, strictly speaking, the visible act, the speech, or the product of these things. It is a *way* of thinking, feeling, believing. It is the knowledge stored up (in memories of men, in books and objects) for future use—patterns for doing certain things in certain ways, not the doing of them. We study the overt behavior, the speech and gestures and activities of people, and the tangible results of these things, such as tools, houses, cornfields, and what not. It has been customary in lists of "culture traits" to include such things as watches or lawbooks. This is a convenient way of thinking about them, but we must remember that they, in themselves, are nothing but metals, paper, and ink. What is important is that some men know how to make them, while others set a value on them, are unhappy without them, direct their activities in relation to them, or disregard them.

Culture, then, is one facet of human life. It is that part which is learned by people as the result of belonging to some particular group, and is that part of learned behavior which is shared with others. It is our social legacy, as contrasted with our organic heredity. It is the main factor which permits us to live together in a society, giving us ready-made solutions to our problems, helping us to predict the behavior of others, and permitting others to know what to expect of us.

"Culture"—as manifested in the concrete through culture surrogates —regulates our lives at every turn. From the moment we are born until we die there is constant conscious or unconscious pressure upon us to follow certain types of behavior that other men have created for us. Some paths we follow willingly, others we follow because we know no other way, and still others we deviate from or go back to most unwillingly. Mothers of small children know how unnaturally most of this comes to us—how little regard we have, until we are "culturalized," for the "proper" place, time, and manner for certain acts such as eating, defecating, sleeping, getting dirty, and making loud noises. But by more or less adhering to a system of related designs for carrying out all the acts of living, for thinking, believing, and feeling, a group of men and women feel themselves linked together by a powerful chain of sentiments. Ruth Benedict gave an almost complete definition of the concept when she said, "Culture is what binds men together."

THIRD ANTHROPOLOGIST: I like what you have just read us. Tentatively, however, I would raise some queries:

1. Isn't the universal dimension left out? I would assert flatly that every man is, in certain respects, (a) like all other men, (b) like some other men, and (c) like no other man.

2. Isn't your "social" dimension merely a special case of a wider category that we might call "situational," which would include perduring influences from the physical environment and historical accidents?

3. In turn, are the resultants from membership in a particular group to be subsumed entirely under the "cultural" dimension?

THE PSYCHOLOGIST: Before we get involved in overly ambitious conceptual schemes, I suggest we focus upon culture as such. Let me see if I can translate the gist of what has been said into my own terms. "Culture" means the totality of social habits.

FIRST ANTHROPOLOGIST: I would certainly say that social habits, and the alterations brought about in the nonhuman environment through social habits, are the raw data of the anthropologist. However, "habit" is too neutral a term. It would be more exact to say "socially valued habits," for a group is never affectively indifferent to its culture.

THE PSYCHOLOGIST: I suppose that aspect of psychology which is most intimately related to "culture" is what we today call "learning theory." Wouldn't you agree that the transmission of culture can be understood only insofar as learning and teaching are understood?

FIRST ANTHROPOLOGIST: Yes, inasmuch as all human beings of whatever "races" seem to have similar nervous systems and biological equipment generally, we would anticipate that the basic processes of learning are very similar if not identical among all groups. We therefore look to the psychologist to inform us about the laws of learning. On the other hand, we can show that *what* is learned, from whom learning takes place, and when the learning of certain skills usually occurs varies according to culture. Also, I should like to point out that there is one danger in speaking of culture as being "taught." "Teaching" is not limited, as in the popular sense, to conscious instruction. Individuals learn—"absorb" more nearly suggests, in nontechnical language, the process—much of their culture through imitation of both the "matched-dependent" and "copying" types. Take, for example, those gestures and expressive movements ("motor habits") that are observed as characteristic of certain groups. Every anthropologist regards these as cultural phenomena, and yet only in dancing schools, armies, and the like is explicit instruction as to posture, and so forth, given.

THE PSYCHOLOGIST: If I am not mistaken, C. S. Ford (1942, p. 557) has defined culture as consisting of "traditional ways of solving problems" or "of learned problem solutions." Stable cultures, I suppose, pass on answers to specific problems that the groups in question have encountered in their histories rather than universally valid general principles.

THIRD ANTHROPOLOGIST: It is true that any culture is, among other things, a set of techniques for adjusting both to the external environment and to other men. Insofar as Ford's statement points to this fact, it is helpful, but it will not do as a synoptic definition. For cultures create problems as well as solve them. If the lore of a people states that frogs are dangerous creatures, or that it is not safe to go about at night because of were-animals or ghosts, threats are posed that do not arise out of the inexorable facts of the external world. This is why all "functional" definitions of culture tend to be unsatisfactory: they disregard the fact that cultures create needs as well as provide a means of fulfilling them.

THE PSYCHIATRIST: In fact, my profession has always tended to think of culture as something which was repressive to the "natural" nature of man, as something which produced needless neuroses by demands and thwartings during the process of molding individuals into shapes uncongenial to their native temperament. Freud, writing to Einstein, defined culture as a system of defenses consisting of "a progressive displacement of instinctual aims and a restriction of instinctual impulses," and leading to "a strengthening of the intellect, which is beginning to govern instinctual life, and an internalization of the aggressive impulses, with all its consequent advantages and perils."

FIRST ANTHROPOLOGIST: These statements are important. But they seem to me somewhat incomplete and one-sided. First, culture is *both* fulfilling and frustrating. Second, while all cultures constrict and regulate the impulse life of human beings, most of the cultural process falls into the "nonrational" rather than into the strictly "rational" category.

FOURTH ANTHROPOLOGIST: I have held my peace, but at this point I really must protest. Where is this "culture" which you talk about as "doing" this and that? If anthropology is to become a natural science, it must deal only in empirical and observable entities. In spite of the fact that most archaeologists, ethnologists, and social anthropologists still feel that "culture" is their master concept, I maintain we would get further if we stuck to human interaction with other humans and with the natural environment. You can see those things, but has any of you ever seen "culture"?

FIRST ANTHROPOLOGIST: I freely admit that to say "culture" does something is an inexact or metaphorical way of speaking. But this is merely a convenient shorthand expression in place of the long-winded though admittedly more precise "the human representatives of the group that share this culture do thus and so." As for "seeing," your admired natural scientists have never seen "gravity" or "evolution." And yet they find the introduction of these concepts indispensable for making the facts intelligible and for predicting them. "Culture" is an abstract generalizing concept, as essential to the understanding and prediction of events in the human world as is gravity to the understanding and prediction of events in the physical world.

SECOND ANTHROPOLOGIST: I accept and use the concept "culture," but I shy away from these high abstractions. I think it is better to stick to a more traditional definition, such as, "Culture is that complex whole which includes artifacts, beliefs, art, all the other habits acquired by man as a member of society, and all products of human activity as determined by these habits."

FIRST ANTHROPOLOGIST: That is all right as a descriptive statement of what students of culture investigate. But as a definition I find it both awkward and unacceptable on logical grounds. It seems awkward because the enumeration is incomplete, and experience shows that in definitions by enumeration those elements which are not explicitly stated tend to be forgotten even though they be implied. You, for example, have not even mentioned language. The definition also fails in neatness because the entities listed are at such widely varying levels of abstraction —everything from abstract beliefs to concrete artifacts.

THIRD ANTHROPOLOGIST: I would file two other objections. First, the definition is too intellectualistic. One gets no hint that people are other than affectively neutral toward their culture. This is just a list of culture content. Except, possibly, for the single word "whole," there is no indication that culture has organization as well as content.

FOURTH ANTHROPOLOGIST: Why must you insist on introducing these mystical expressions? Science must remain at the level of what may be seen and measured.

THIRD ANTHROPOLOGIST: No whole will be understood merely by describing, however fully, each part. There is always the question of arrangement, of emphasis, of intensity.

THE ECONOMIST: How about "social heredity" as a brief abstract definition of culture?

THIRD ANTHROPOLOGIST: This definition has been widely current and has been of much utility in drawing attention to the fact that human beings have a social as well as a biological heritage. The principal drawbacks in this conception of culture are that it implies too great stability of culture and too passive a role on the part of man. It suggests that man gets his culture as he gets his genes—without effort and without resistance. It tends too much to make us think of the human being as what Dollard has called "the passive porter of a cultural tradition." Men are, as Simmons has recently reminded us, not only the carriers and the creatures of culture—they are also creators and manipulators of culture. "Social heredity" suggests too much of the dead weight of tradition.

THE PSYCHIATRIST: Yes, culture is not merely a "given." Really, in a strictly literal sense, it is not a "given" at all—it is only available. Indeed, Ortega y Gasset has defined culture as "that which is sought." The phrase "social legacy" perhaps avoids some of these difficulties, but even this is hardly satis-factory. One wants a definition which points to the fact that the irreducible datum of the social scientist is the individual and his behavior. From the angle of individual psychology, no defi-nition of culture is adequate that does not make us aware of the active role of the individual as regards his culture and of the fact that he has an impulse life.

THE BUSINESSMAN: Much of what has been said was mildly diverting as an exhibition in logical adroitness, but frankly I still don't see why anybody bothers about "culture" at all.

FIRST ANTHROPOLOGIST: Well, one of the interesting things about human beings is that they try to understand themselves and their own behavior. While this has been particularly true of Europeans in recent times, there is no group which has not developed a scheme or schemes to explain man's actions. I would claim that the concept of culture is essential to such under-standing.

SECOND ANTHROPOLOGIST: I would phrase the case a little differently. Science is concerned with all observable phenomena, including man himself and his behavior. "Culture" is a con-venient descriptive category for organizing our objective reports on the behavior characteristic of specified human groups.

THE PHILOSOPHER: It strikes me that the last two statements contain the key to much of our apparent disagreement. For some anthropologists "culture" is primarily a descriptive concept; for others it is primarily an explanatory concept. We suspect also that this central distinction is very closely related to another problem, which has not been raised explicitly tonight but which is often puzzling to the nonanthropologist—namely, the shift of discourse from "culture" in general to "a culture." So-called definitions are always constructed from a point of view—which is all too often left unstated. Not all definitions are substantive—that is, "descriptive." Nor is "explanatory" the only other alter-native. Some of the definitions which have been partially stated or implied have been "functional"; others may be characterized as epistemological; that is, they have been intended to point toward the type of phenomena from which we gain our knowl-edge of "culture." There is also the point that some definitions look toward the actions of the individual as the starting point of all assertions, whereas others, while perhaps admitting these as ultimate referents, depart from abstractions referable to groups. However, the distinction between "explanatory" and "descriptive" seems to be central.

THE LAWYER: That makes sense to me. We have opened up a good deal of ground this evening, but I for one would like to pursue various matters further, perhaps along more systematic lines, as indicated by our philosopher. Perhaps you anthropologists could be persuaded to join us in another session?

THIRD ANTHROPOLOGIST: It would seem worthwhile to me. I, for one, should like to organize my ideas, perhaps writing out some of the more crucial ones. I propose that we begin next time with the general "explanatory" notion.

Part II: "Culture" as an Explanatory Concept

THIRD ANTHROPOLOGIST: *By "culture" we mean those historically created selective processes that channel men's reactions both to internal and to external stimuli.*

SECOND ANTHROPOLOGIST: That is certainly an "analytical abstraction" all right.

THIRD ANTHROPOLOGIST: That is precisely the idea: that, with this concept, certain aspects of the concrete phenomena may be analyzed out, and thus whole events may be better "explained" and predicted.

FIRST ANTHROPOLOGIST: Your statement at least avoids the difficulty lurking in those definitions of culture that employ the phrase "acquired by man as a member of society." That phrase seems to suggest that "culture" as an explanatory concept refers *only* to dimensions of the behavior of individuals resultant upon their membership in a particular society (either through birth or through later affiliation). But "culture" also helps us to understand such processes as "diffusion," "culture contact," and "acculturation."

FOURTH ANTHROPOLOGIST: Even I find some merit in the explanatory definition proposed. You at least make some concessions to a behavioristic approach when you speak of "reactions" and "stimuli."

THIRD ANTHROPOLOGIST: Naturally I would agree that any concept or proposition in behavioral science must be ultimately referable back to human behavior. Even when we deal with distribution of "culture traits," we must remember that we are dealing with products of human hands, with traces left by human activity.

FOURTH ANTHROPOLOGIST: But why did you find it necessary to include "*internal stimuli*"?

THIRD ANTHROPOLOGIST: When a man eats, he is reacting to an internal "drive"—namely, hunger contractions consequent upon the lowering of blood sugar, and so forth—but his precise reaction to these internal stimuli cannot be predicted by physiological knowledge alone. Whether a healthy adult "feels hungry" twice, three times, or four times a day, and the hours at which these "feelings" recur, is influenced by cultural habits. *What* he eats is of course limited by sheer objective availability, but it is also partly regulated by culture. It is a biological fact that some types of berries are poisonous, but it is a cultural fact that, a few generations ago, most Americans considered tomatoes to be poisonous and refused to eat them. On the other hand, milk, which we regard as a healthful and pleasing food, is regarded by certain peoples of the earth as either dangerous or disgusting. Such selective, discriminative use of the biological (and other) aspects of the environment is characteristically cultural. In a still more general sense, too, the process of eating is channeled by culture. Whether a man eats to live, lives to eat, or eats and lives is partly individual idiosyncrasy, but there are also cultural correlations.

SECOND ANTHROPOLOGIST: Why do you use the word "reaction" instead of the more straightforward "action"?

THIRD ANTHROPOLOGIST: Because "reaction" comes nearer to conveying the feeling tone that is associated with all selective designs for living.

FOURTH ANTHROPOLOGIST: I am partially convinced, but I must once more come back to my question: Why did you introduce this unseen "culture"?

THIRD ANTHROPOLOGIST: There is no human being, if he be even a few weeks old, who reacts completely freshly to any stimulus situation. Few human responses can be explained entirely through even the most complete knowledge of the individual's biological equipment and private experience up to that point and the objective facts of the given situation.

FOURTH ANTHROPOLOGIST: But where does "culture" come from? You seem to invoke it as a kind of *deus ex machina.*

THE HISTORIAN: History is a sieve. Isn't each culture a pre-cipitate of history? Cultures preserve those aspects of the past which, usually in altered form, live on in the present. Each culture is surely a cumulative historical product.

BIOLOGIST: Does this mean that culture consists of those ways of meeting situations that prove to have survival value?

THIRD ANTHROPOLOGIST: This is a large and important part of the truth. The process of culture may well be regarded as something added to man's innate biological capacities, which provides instruments that enlarge or may even substitute for biological functions and which to a limited degree compensate for biological limitations—as in insuring that the biological fact of death does not always mean that what the dead individual has learned is lost to his group or even to humanity at large.

Nevertheless, I believe this to be a dangerously misleading formulation unless it is properly explained and qualified. In the first place, it is an observed fact that most groups elaborate certain aspects of their culture far beyond maximal relative utility or survival value. In other words, not all culture is adaptive—in the sense of promoting sheer physical survival. At times, indeed, it does exactly the opposite. We must bring in the concept of adjustment—that is, lowering of tension—as well as that of adaptation. In the second place, aspects of culture that once directly promoted survival may persist after they have ceased to have survival value. An analysis of contemporary Navaho culture will disclose many features that cannot possibly be construed as adaptations to the total environment in which Navahos now find themselves. However, it is altogether likely that these represent survivals, with modifications that have occurred during the centuries, of cultural forms that were

adaptive in one or another environment in which certain ancestors of the contemporary Navaho lived prior to entering the
Southwest.

FIRST ANTHROPOLOGIST: In other words, you are saying that
no way of reacting is taken over by a group unless it has direct
adaptive or adjustive value for individuals as such (or as constituting a group) *at the time the design for living becomes cultural.*

THIRD ANTHROPOLOGIST: That seems plausible at any rate—a
good working hypothesis. However, my main point here is that
when dealing with culture as an explanatory concept, one must
always be alive to time perspective and favor the idea of "limitation of possibilities." It is usually wise to think of a specified
factor as *influencing* (rather than as *determining*) an outcome.
There are no "determinants" as palpable, dissectable elements;
there are only processes that result in determination. In discussing culture as an explanatory concept, we must always favor
interactive rather than descriptive notions. As Boas so often
insisted, we cannot account for complex historical changes by
any neat formula. While many patterned ways of reacting
unquestionably represent almost inevitable responses to an
external environment in which the group lives or once lived,
there are certainly also many cases where the inexorable conditions of action merely limit the possibility of response rather
than eventually compelling one and only one mode of adaptation. These "choices" are probably themselves determined—if
we imagine a frame of reference wide enough to encompass all
possible types of factors. But behavioral science today cannot
deal with so many variables. Hence, so far as a theoretical
system of manageable scope is concerned, these "choices" must
be treated as "accidents of history."

Let me give an example or two. In a society where the chief
has great power, one particular chief happens to be born with
an endocrine imbalance that brings about certain unusual (to
that group) idiosyncrasies in personality. By virtue of his position, he is able to bring about certain modifications in the way
of life of his group (say, in the religion) that are congenial to
his "temperament." It may be argued, and it may be true, that
no amount of authority could insure the persistence of such
alterations unless they somehow had adjustive or adaptive value

for more than a single individual. I do not believe that the empirical evidence bearing on this problem has been sufficiently
analyzed to permit a definite answer to the question. But what
is certain is that such a circumstance has been known to be
followed by relatively temporary or relatively enduring changes
in group designs for living—sometimes primarily in the form of
strong "reaction formations." The fact of the chief's position
and all that was consequent upon it is not an "accident" from
the point of view of the cultural system. The unusual temperament is, however, due to an "accident of the genetic process."

Or suppose that in the same group a chief dies a relatively
young man, leaving an infant as his successor. This has been
observed rather frequently to result in a marked crystallization
of two factions around two rival older relatives, each of whom
has about equally valid claims to act as "regent." Through these
circumstances a complete and lasting splitting off of two groups
takes place. Each group thereafter has pursued its own separate
destiny, and the end result is the formation of two distinguishable
variants of what was at one time a more or less homogeneous
culture. Now, to be sure, it is likely that the original factional
lines had their bases in "economic," demographic, or other
"external" conditions. Yet, had it not been for the "accidental"
death of the first chief in his early maturity, the society might
have indefinitely continued intact as an equilibrium of opposed
tendencies. In short, the form and the mesh of the "sieve which
is history" must be seen as shaped not only by the total "environment" at any given point in time but also by individual "psychological" and "accidental" factors.

FIRST ANTHROPOLOGIST: Could we then say that culture
includes all those ways of feeling, thinking, and acting that are
not inevitable as a result of human biological equipment and
process and/or objective external situations?

THIRD ANTHROPOLOGIST: My objection to that definition
would be, first, that it defines culture as a "residual category"—
which is logically undesirable—and, second, that I believe it is
better to mention explicitly the time dimension as indicated by
the phrase "historically created."

HISTORIAN: This suggests also the cumulative nature of
culture.

THIRD ANTHROPOLOGIST: Yes, provided we remember that in another sense culture is not exactly "cumulative." A culture, in its totality, at any given point in time has likewise the property of uniqueness. That is why it is essential to include the word "selective" in any definition.

THE BIOLOGIST: So far tonight this has been almost a private party for anthropology. You have gone a little too fast for me—largely because you have talked in a jargon with which I am not familiar. I would like more evidence, set in a framework to which I am accustomed. It seems to me still that I can interpret human behavior satisfactorily in terms of the old categories of heredity and environment.

THE LAWYER: I can see that there has been a selection of possible modes of behavior and that these selections then may become established in a group, but aren't you overemphasizing this aspect? It seems to me that, in common-sense terms, if we understand human nature, and if we then make our interpretation in the light of the concrete situation at hand, we get along very well.

FIRST ANTHROPOLOGIST: No. If you will look beyond the records of our own time and place, you will find that the matter is not so simple. There are certain recurrent and inevitable human problems, and the ways in which man can meet them are limited by his biological equipment and by certain facts of the external world. Anthropologists have perhaps in recent years been too much preoccupied with the diversity found upon the earth and have neglected the basic similarities. But, apart from these important but very general resemblances, the conception of one single, unchanging "human nature" is a reassuring fiction of folklore. When it comes to details, there are "human natures." For example, old age is a situation to which all human beings who live long enough must adjust. But we find that in some human societies the old, regardless of their particular achievements, are entitled to respect and to authority. In other societies we find that the old, again regardless of individual differences, are ordinarily treated with relative indifference or active contempt. In still other societies whether or not an aged person is treated with deference or with neglect seems to depend mainly on his personality and achievements. Thus we see that, though age is a biological fact, it is always socially defined. This fact that "human nature" has some (though not unlimited) plasticity is the widest and the most certain induction which anthropologists can derive from the cross-cultural record.

THE BIOLOGIST: But is this really "plasticity"? Or are these differences the result of different strains of biological heredity?

FIRST ANTHROPOLOGIST: There is abundant proof that not all the variations, at any rate, are so determined. For instance, Victorian Englishmen were as restrained and prudish as Elizabethan English were boisterous and bawdy. Yet the genetic composition of the English population seems to have been substantially identical in the two periods.

THE ECONOMIST: You spoke of situations as being "socially defined." Isn't this just another way of saying that one aspect of the environment is social? Isn't, then, "cultural" just another and needless word meaning "social"?

THIRD ANTHROPOLOGIST: I think not. "Socially defined" means "defined by or within a group." "Social" always means "having to do with human interaction." But it says nothing as to the *manner* of that interaction. As Winston says, "Human relationships involve not only social interaction; they also involve patterned ways of behaving." There are universal social processes, just as there are universal biological processes. Such are for example, the division of labor, subordination, and superordination. But the precise *forms* that these processes take are myriad, and these *forms* are cultural. Let us take an instance where, as so often, biological and social facts are intertwined. In many human groups the physically weak have been, almost without qualification, at a disadvantage. In some groups, however, there have been effective deterrents against the strong taking advantage of the weak. Bullying has been punished by social disapproval and hence has actually been relatively rare. In a few societies privileged positions have tended to be given to certain types of the physically weak or to certain types of the psychologically "abnormal."

Just as sociobiological situations or purely social situations can be stylized, so also some purely biological situations are stylized. Take vomiting, for example. Vomiting is a biological event, and it can be produced by causes that are solely biological. But in other cases, although individual differences in neurological equipment and in previous experience play their part, the event sequence that would lead up to vomiting could never be predicted purely on the basis of biological knowledge. For instance, Americans who have eaten rattlesnake have been known to vomit upon being told what they had been fed; since rattlesnake meat is digestible and nutritious, the vomiting was produced by some extrabiological factor.

Similar illustrations could be given for other biological processes, such as weeping or fainting. Such biological processes are also caught in a cultural web. Here is a telling example. The newborn infant excretes whenever tensions in the bladder and colon reach a degree of intensity. Before long, however, biological rhythms have surrendered to superimposed conventions. Most human beings in good health defecate only once or twice during a day. This ordinarily occurs at culturally preferred times within the twenty-four hour cycle, and in many human groups only at designated places and under defined conditions as to who else may or may not be present. So interesting and so vital is the interrelation of the biological and the cultural dimensions of human behavior that some anthropologists feel the study of these connections to be the distinctive feature of anthropology.

THE PSYCHOLOGIST: Isn't this just a kind of "conditioning"?

THE BIOLOGIST: Yes, couldn't we call it simply "environmental conditioning"?

FIRST ANTHROPOLOGIST: A very particular sort of "conditioning." No group deliberately sets out to train its children to vomit under certain circumstances. This result, rather, is a kind of incidental by-product of a style of life or of some aspect of such a style of life. Certainly, also, it must be admitted that this process is a result of the "environment" in the wider sense. It is not, incidentally, that I deny the categories of heredity and environment. Far from it. I do insist that they are very abstract categories. I also believe that this familiar dichotomy has the effect of perpetuating what we would all now recognize to be a false question—namely, the issue as to whether a particular event or quality was caused by heredity *or* environment. We now know that in very few cases as far as an individual is concerned, and in almost no cases so far as nations or tribes are concerned, can the innate factors alone or the surroundings alone be said to determine the course of action.

THIRD ANTHROPOLOGIST: The naive—and very powerful—view is that we have individual organisms (they can be seen) and that they exist in an external world (which can also be seen and described). This is the view which common sense takes, and it is very hard to shake oneself out of this apparently sound formula. But it won't cover the phenomena. The *awareness* of the external environment is too selective. Put down various groups of adults who have been trained in different social traditions on a deserted island. What they "see" initially in their surroundings will not be identical at all. Nor will, of course, the techniques by which they try to adjust themselves to this environment. Between culturalized organisms and their surroundings there exists, as it were, a screen which is none the less "real" for being inferred rather than perceived directly by the senses. This screen is "culture."

SECOND ANTHROPOLOGIST: The screen is, in some sense, a part of the environment of action. What happens in human history follows upon an extraordinary, complicated, and constantly continuing interaction of inherited predispositions and potentialities with the pressures and challenges of environing situations (biological, physical, social, and cultural).

FIRST ANTHROPOLOGIST: It is useful to isolate these four dimensions of the environment by abstraction. I have written out a statement about this so that I could express myself precisely:

Depending upon the type of data with which the scientist is dealing and upon the type of problem he is trying to solve, various break-ups of the milieu are indicated. If the focus is primarily upon the individual's differences from other individuals, then the total environment needs to be resolved into:

  1. those portions common to the subject and to all human beings

  2. those that tend to be shared with all members of the subject's society

  3. those shared only with certain subgroups (e.g., age and/or sex categories)

4. those that are in some sense private to the given subject

When the eye is upon the group (as is usually the case with the anthropologist), a major distinction to be drawn is that between the natural and the human environment—the physical and biological world as "given" by "nature" and as directly or indirectly modified by the action of man. This differentiation is made central by the geographer. A slightly different but related division is more congenial to the psychologist. This is between those forces of the environment which are impersonal (inanimate objects and conditions, flora and fauna) as contrasted with those forces which are mediated through persons.

THE PHILOSOPHER: Where does "culture" come in?

FIRST ANTHROPOLOGIST: There are cultural dimensions to both the human and nonhuman or personal and impersonal environments. In fact, I prefer a segregation that slices the pie a different way, abstracting out those aspects due to "culture" whether expressed in human interaction or in modifications of the natural landscape, domestication of plants or animals, or alterations of the wildlife balance. Separate the unaltered natural surroundings into the *physical environment* (the world of nonliving matter) and the *biological environment* (flora and fauna, including bacteria and viruses to which man is host). The human environment may be broken down (by abstraction) into the *social* environment and the *cultural* environment. On the one hand, there are those features of human life that are contingent upon the numbers of individuals involved, the relative size, strength, and intelligence of different individuals, the geographical position of the groups in question relative to other human groups, and other factors—all those features of human interaction which depend ultimately upon the "givens" of the natural or biological environments but are expressed in social processes may be termed the social environment.

On the other hand, there are those features of the environment which, rather than being "given" by factors external to man, seem, as it were, to involve some element of human arbitrariness. Those aspects of the environment which are determined, not by external factors as manifested in immediate situations, but by those selective forces from the past which live on in the present may be called the "cultural environment."

THE PSYCHOLOGIST: I wonder if you could translate all this into the slightly different conceptual scheme in which I am accustomed to work. In trying to understand a single concrete act on the part of an individual I have found it helpful to ask these questions:

1. What are the innate endowments and limitations of the individual?

2. What has his total experience been prior to the act we are studying?

3. What is his immediate situation?

FIRST ANTHROPOLOGIST: No one of these variables can be elucidated in a completely satisfactory manner without introducing the concept "culture":

1. Except in the case of newborn babies and of individuals born with clear-cut structural or functional abnormalities, we can observe "innate endowments" only as modified by cultural training. In hospitals in New Mexico where Zuñi Indian, Navaho Indian, Spanish-American, and Anglo-American babies are born it is possible, using the Moro Startle Response Test, to classify the newly arrived infants as hyperactive, average, and hypoactive. The norms were worked out in New York City hospitals, and the distributions for the two Indian groups (and especially the Zuñi) tend almost to fall outside the hyperactive category. My point here, however, is not concerned with this interesting variability in population genetics, but rather with the consequences of cultural training. Take a Navaho baby and an Anglo baby both of whom, at birth, fall into the hyperactive category. Then observe them again at the age of two years. The same Navaho child will no longer seem hyperactive—*as compared with the Anglo child*. The Navaho child *is* likely to seem given to quick and restless movement as compared with other Navaho two-year-olds.

2. A purely "objective" description of the individual's experience doesn't get us very far. His interpretation of these events is indispensable, and his description will be made, at least in part, in terms of standards and expectations current in his group. Losing a mother tends to *mean* one thing in one society, quite a different thing in another society.

3. Naturally, the immediate situation as well as past experience

is reacted to, not in purely rational or objective fashion, but in terms of the situation as meaningfully defined by the participant. Almost no human situations are viewed in ways that are *altogether* the resultant of the individual's idiosyncratic personality. Culture is—among other things—a set of ready-made definitions of the situation that each participant only slightly retailors in his idiomatic way.

THE BIOLOGIST: May we get back to some examples?

THIRD ANTHROPOLOGIST: If we are to begin at the beginning, we start off, I suppose, with the basic observation of the diversity of human behavior. How shall we explain it? At the level of the individual it is well known that individuals who have exactly the same genes (identical twins) but who are brought up apart may, although manifesting some striking resemblances in behavior as well as appearance, nevertheless exhibit different moral codes, life goals, and fundamental assumptions. Perhaps these data, however, seem to require only the explanatory abstractions of the impersonal and social environments to account for the observed differences.

Yet another familiar class of observations respecting individuals does not seem so easily taken care of without the culture concept. A few years ago a young man of American parentage who had been reared in a Chinese family from infancy paid his first visit to America. Reporters commented not only upon his apparently complete bewilderment in the American way of life, but also upon the fact that his walk, arm and hand movements, and facial expression were "Chinese—not American." They insisted that one had to fix one's attention upon his blond hair and blue eyes to convince oneself that he was of white stock at all. Here the point is that an individual's acts and attitudes not only failed to resemble those of his own close relatives in this country, but that they resembled those of all members of an alien physical group and contrasted with those of all other members of his own biological group.

To take a less dramatic but better-known illustration, a third-generation Italian, unless he has been reared in the Italian colony of a large American city, shows "social habits" that resemble those of "Old Americans" much more closely than those of residents of Italy. The influence of the various domestic environments in which these Italian-Americans grew up was not so powerful but that we can recognize common tendencies in all of them which ally them to other "Americans."

The variations and similarities that obtain between groups of human beings must also both be clarified. Groups of the same strain of physical heredity show great differences in behavioral norms, and groups of unquestionably different strains show great similarities. It has been remarked by many observers in the Japanese relocation centers that Japanese who have been born and brought up in this country, especially those who were reared apart from any large colony of Japanese, resemble their white neighbors in all behavioral characteristics much more closely than they do their own Japanese relatives who had grown up in Japan and them immigrated to this country.

THE PSYCHOLOGIST: This proves that human beings can learn from each other—and we knew that already. What proof is there that if all white Americans were wiped out, the Japanese-American wouldn't eventually revert to designs for living highly similar to those characteristic of the Japanese of Japan?

THIRD ANTHROPOLOGIST: Obviously, there can be no certain answer to such a hypothetical question. But note carefully that the concept of culture as I have phrased it in no way denies the possible importance of innate factors. It does not assert the patent absurdity that the behavior of all Japanese (of Japan) or the behavior of all white Americans is minutely identical. It says merely that the behavior of each group, though showing much individual variation, still shows certain common tendencies within the one group that contrast sharply with those within the other group. Since the common tendencies of the American group are also to a perceptible degree exhibited by large numbers of individuals of Japanese racial stock—although it is not claimed that their behavior shows precisely the same modalities as the white Americans—it is argued that these shared trends may be attributed to the presence and influence of communicable designs for living.

THE ECONOMIST: But there is also the factor of environment —in the usual popular sense. Perhaps if Japan were depopulated and colonized by white Americans, these would, within a certain number of generations, develop social definitions of the situation that would hardly be distinguishable from those characteristic of the Japanese today.

THIRD ANTHROPOLOGIST: Although there are interesting and complicated interdependencies between the physical-biological environment and the social-cultural environment, I think some instances will show that the cultural is a dimension that must not be neglected. First of all, you must admit that the natural environments of the United States are very various, and yet the Americans of the arid Southwest and of rainy Oregon still behave in ways that are easily distinguishable from inhabitants of the Australian desert, on the one hand, and from those of verdant England, on the other.

Tribes like the Pueblo and the Navaho, living in substantially identical natural and biological environments, still manifest very different ways of life. The English who live in the Hudson Bay region and those who live in British Somaliland still share common designs for living. It is true, of course, that the different natural environments are responsible for observable alterations. But the striking fact is that, in spite of the tremendous differences in the physical environment, shared designs for living still persist.

The inhabitants of two not very distant villages in New Mexico, Ramah and Fence Lake, are both of the so-called Old American physical stock. The rocky tablelands, the annual rainfall and its distribution, and the flora and fauna surrounding the two villages hardly show perceptible variations. The density of population and the distance from a main-traveled highway are similar in the two cases. Still, even the casual visitor immediately notices distinctions: there are characteristic differences in dress; the style of the houses and the plan of the villages is different; there is a saloon in one town and not in the other. A completion of this catalog would conclusively demonstrate that distinct patterns of life prevail in the two settlements. Why? Primarily because the two villages represent variants of the general Anglo-American social traditions. They have somewhat different cultures. Perhaps it would be better to say that these are two sub-cultures of generalized American Culture.

THE PHILOSOPHER: There are two questions upon which I

must pin you down. The first is: Where is the locus of culture—
in society or in the individual?

THIRD ANTHROPOLOGIST: Asking the question that way poses
a false dilemma. "Culture" is an abstraction. Hence culture as a
concrete, observable entity does not exist anywhere—unless you
wish to say that it exists in the "minds" of the men who make
the abstractions, and this is hardly a problem that need trouble
us as scientists. The objects and events from which we make our
abstractions do have an observable existence. But culture is like
a map. Just as a map isn't the territory itself, but an abstract
representation of the territory, so also a culture is an abstract
description of trends toward uniformity in the words, acts, and
artifacts of human groups. The data, from which we come to
know culture, then, are not derived from an abstraction such as
"society" but from direct observable behavior and behavioral
products. Note, however, that "culture" may be said to be
"supra-individual" in at least two nonmystical, perfectly empirical senses:

1. Artifacts as well as individuals show the influence of culture.

2. The continuity of a culture never depends upon the continued existence of any particular individuals unless the whole
culture-bearing group be wiped out.

THE PHILOSOPHER: Very good. Now my second question: Can
"culture" ever be said to be the cause of anything?

THIRD ANTHROPOLOGIST: Not in any very strict or exact way
of speaking. In the first place, I would always question the
advisability of using the term "cause" in social-science theory.
Too much of an unidirectional force is implied. Even to say
"culture determines" is an inexact and elliptical way of speaking,
justified perhaps in certain circumstances by the convenience of
brevity. Inexact, however, it is, because no concrete phenomenon
is ever completely and solely determined by culture. Sometimes,
to be sure, culture may be the "strategic factor"; that is, the
crucial element that proximately determines that a given act
tends to be differently carried out in one group than in another
or that the act is somehow now what we would anticipate from
a knowledge of the physical and biological forces operative.
But "cultural determinism" in any simple or literal sense is as

objectionable as any other class of unilateral determinism, such as "geographical determinism" or "economic determinism."

Although, in the concrete, the influence of culture is always mediated by persons or by books or other artifacts, one is nevertheless justified in speaking of a culture as a determinant of events when discourse is being carried on at a high level of abstraction—provided one keeps in mind the degree of abstraction. The point may become clearer from an analogy—though all analogies, including this one, are tricky. Suppose a man who has an infectious disease that is thought to be due to a virus enters a city and communicates his illness to others. What "causes" the epidemic—the man or the virus? Either answer is equally correct, depending upon the conceptual scheme within which one is working. We should be too close to reifying an abstraction if we were to say that, in similar fashion, either men or things can become "hosts" to culture. Also, this metaphor, like the definition of culture as "social heredity," implies too passive a relationship between men and culture—as if culture were a microorganism acquired casually and unknowingly by contact. And yet the analogy remains intriguing. It is less misleading than "social heredity." Genes are acquired in immutable form at birth, whereas microorganisms may change with the host and in time—as do cultures.

SECOND ANTHROPOLOGIST: Your analogies are very slippery. Let's get back to stubborn and irreducible fact. As Eugen Fischer used to say: "Culture always walks on two legs."

THE PSYCHOLOGIST: Of course, a cultural *agent* is always involved. A cultural dictum is an abstraction.

FIRST ANTHROPOLOGIST: Science must always be *based* upon events in all their concreteness but does not consist of an inventory of such events. Science is not so much a body of knowledge as a mode of taking account of experience. To do this effectively, it cannot be timid about employing constructs. The human mind can know "reality" only as sieved through an a priori net. Correspondence, however, between logical constructs and nature is not surprising, since the mind is itself a product of nature.

THIRD ANTHROPOLOGIST: The main differences between nineteenth-century science and contemporary science is that scientists realize today that they cannot, in any literal sense, "describe reality." They can construct models that bear a relation to "objective fact." The scientist is more inventor than discoverer.

The history of science shows that too stringent a focus upon specific parts can lead into at least as grievous errors and dead ends as attention to more abstract and embracing wholes. Field theory in physics demonstrated that causality often does not work between little bits of stuff but only between large patterns of activity. Lashley proved the pattern of communal excitation in the brain; one gets satisfactory laws for the brain only by considering the whole and ignoring the parts of which it is made up.

Obviously, it is factual that "culture walks on two legs" and that only cultural agents *act*. For certain purposes of research and analysis such propositions must be in the forefront of consciousness. On the other hand, preoccupation with the concrete and specific must not become obsessive, for there are regular cultural processes that we shall understand more quickly and more fully if we do not bog down in the examination of every dimension of each concrete act. Remember that linguistics thrives by being completely anonymous and impersonal, with a minimum of reference to its carriers and their psychology, and by dealing with the relations of specific forms, without serious concern for their specific productive causes.

THE PHILOSOPHER: Could you relate what you have just said to the arguments over the proposition of Spengler, Sorokin, and others that cultures have their own independent laws of growth and decay?

THIRD ANTHROPOLOGIST: Anthropologists have probably been too hasty in their complete rejections of these theories. The theories have, to greater or lesser degree, been phrased so unfortunately that condemnations of them as "mystical" or "metaphysical" could be given plausibility. But an anthropologist who really wishes to understand these interpretations can "translate" them into his own conceptual scheme so that, if the levels of abstraction are kept straight, they seem to merit partial acceptance or at least careful re-examination.

For, while no culture is "superorganic" in the sense that it would continue to "exist" after all the human beings who shared it had died and all the nonhuman manifestations of that culture had been destroyed, a culture that is a going concern still has properties that exhibit some independence from the other forces with which the culture is in interaction. One of the diagnostic features of a culture is its selectivity. Most specific needs can be satisfied in a wide variety of ways, but "the culture selects" only one or a very few of the organically and physically possible modes. "The culture selects" is, to be sure, a metaphorical way of speaking. The *original* choice was necessarily made by an individual and then followed by other individuals (or it wouldn't have become culture). But, from the angle of those individuals who later learn this bit of culture, the existence of that element in a design for living has the *effect* of a selection that was not made by these human beings as a reaction to their own particular situation but rather a choice made by individuals long gone that still tends to bind contemporary actors.

Such a selective awareness of the natural environment, such a stereotyped interpretation of man's place in the world, is not merely inclusive—by implication it also excludes other possible alternatives. Because of the "strain toward consistency" in cultures, such inclusions and exclusions are meaningful far beyond the specific activity which is overtly involved. Just as the "choice" of an individual at a crucial epoch may commit him in certain directions for the rest of his life, so likewise, the original bents, trends, and "interests" that become established in the designs for living of a newly formed society tend to channel a culture in some directions as opposed to others. Subsequent variations in the culture—both those that arise internally and those that are a response to contact with other cultures or to changes in the natural environment—are not random. In some sense, at least, there may be a "cultural orthogenesis"—analogous to Sapir's "drift" in language.

THE LAWYER: Before we break up, will one of the anthropologists summarize our discussion of culture as an explanatory concept?

SECOND ANTHROPOLOGIST: We have concentrated upon culture as one of the conceptual instruments that help us to analyze and understand human acts. The fact that we have not talked about the other explanatory function of the concept—"culture" as a way of formulating data about the spread of distinctive objects and ideas, as making intelligible various observed "presences" and "absences"—is doubtless because this general notion is more easily grasped.

FIRST ANTHROPOLOGIST: In brief, we have argued that human action is framed by four universal dimensions:

1. The biological potentialities and limitations of the human species and the distinctive hereditary make-up of particular individuals and groups.

2. The external nonhuman environment.

3. The social environment.

4. A precipitate from past events that has taken its character at any given moment partially as a consequence of the first three dimensions as they existed when those events occurred and partially as a consequence of the selective force of an historical precipitate (culture) that already existed when a given past event occurred.

THIRD ANTHROPOLOGIST: There can be no basic disagreement with those four propositions. Nevertheless, let me propose an alternative schema that in fact cuts across the one you have given but seems to me to bring some gains in precision and in economy of expression. First, I should prefer to speak of a dimension of "*constitution*" rather than of one of "biological heredity." The individual's physiological make-up at a given time—and that is what is pertinent—is a product of influences emanating both from the germ plasm and from influences derived from the environment (diet, presence of endemic diseases, drugs, and the like). Second—and this may surprise you—I would merge culture in a wider category: *group membership*. Culture is not the only influence that bears with approximate constancy upon all members of a relatively stable, organized group. What of climate, locations, topography? In the case of the smaller societies living in homogeneous physical environments there are presumptive grounds for allowing importance to these factors. Then, as has been suggested, membership in a group carries with it exposure to a generalized social environment. The individual must adjust to the presence or absence of other human beings in specified numbers and of specified age and sex. The density of population affects the actual or potential number of face-to-face relationships available to each person. Finally, there is *situation:* circumstances that are not standard for a whole group nor for a culturally defined segment of it such as those who occupy particular statuses (men and women, age grades, priests, parents, and the like).

Let me give some examples. Most families in a tribe or band live quite close to each other. But one or more families live at the periphery of the tribal territory and at such a distance from their neighbors that interaction rates are diminished. A culture may define approved behavior in a dyad or a triad; yet such small groups have properties that are inherent—cross-culturally —in the dyadic or triadic situation. Likewise, the "accidents" belong to the category of "situation." Unique events of special significance occur in the histories of peoples and of particular individuals that are not predictable, not "foreordained" by biology, physical environment, culture, or social environment. Illustrations for the history of a group have already been mentioned. For the individual, take the child's losing a parent by death or divorce, birth order in a family, chance exposure to an infectious disease, adventitious but momentous contacts with others.

Schematically and incompletely:

Constitutional. Genetic, environmental, cultural (because culture as well as environment influences nutritional level; culture also conditions "medical" treatment, child training practices, and so on).

Group Membership. Culture (accumulated knowledge, values, roles, and other aspects), physical environment (if reasonably homogeneous), social environment, biology (population genetics; exposure to disease, and so on, insofar as this is the result of membership in a group as opposed to the vicissitudes of the life histories of particular individuals).

Situation. The things "that just happen to people"—unique and significant events in the history of the group.

THE ECONOMIST: I see advantages in this scheme. From one point of view, however, I do see loss as well as gain. As a statistician would say, you have "confounded" the very dimensions (biological, environmental, social, cultural) that we set out to isolate. The relative merits of the two kinds of abstraction depend upon the immediate purpose in hand. So let me, at the risk of seeming stubborn, recur to a small issue—the distinction between the social and the cultural. I am now convinced that the cultural cannot be eliminated. But can't the social? Or would it not be advisable to speak of the "sociocultural"?

THIRD ANTHROPOLOGIST: There is something to be said for this last alternative. The concrete social (that is, interactive) behavior observed among human beings must in most cases be assumed to be the combined product of biological and cultural influences. Usually, then, the "social" and the "cultural" are inextricably intermingled in observable acts.

However, some social acts are not culturally patterned. This is one reason for retaining a distinct "social" dimension. Another arises out of one certainly valid aspect of Durkheim's position. If we postulate that all ongoing human behavior must be in some sense "functional," we must posit social collectivities as the referents of some behavior systems, for these cannot be explained as meeting needs (biological or "psychological") of isolated human organisms. In other words, "society," like "culture," is an "emergent" with properties not altogether derivable from a summation of even the fullest kind of knowledge of the parts. Indeed—to go back to the framework of "determination" —it seems likely that culture itself may be altered by social as well as by biological and natural environmental forces. A plurality of individuals (of such and such numbers, and the like) continually interacting together produces something new, which is a result not merely of previously existing cultural patterns but also of the sheer fact of social interaction. "Cultural change" likewise has its social dimension. Suppose that two random samples of, say, 5,000 and 500 persons from a society with a clear-cut culture are set down on islands of identical environment (but of areas varying proportionately with the sizes of the two groups). After some generations one could anticipate that the cultures of the two populations would have become recognizably distinct—partly as a result of "historical accidents," but also as accommodations to the contrasting number of actual and potential face-to-face relationships. Patterns for human adjustment which were suitable to a society of 500 would not work equally well in the society of 5,000, and vice versa. Thus, we must regard the environment of interaction (abstracted from the cultural patterning that prevails in it) as one of the determiners of alterations in the system of designs for living.

THE PHILOSOPHER: A final question. Nothing has been said of

the relationship of symbols to culture. I seem to remember that Bain has defined culture as "all social behavior mediated by symbols."

SECOND ANTHROPOLOGIST: This definition is inacceptable for three reasons:

1. Culture is not behavior but an abstraction from behavior.

2. Not all social behavior is culturally patterned, and culture is not manifested exclusively in interaction.

3. Culture is mediated by signs as well as by symbols. This is not, of course, to deny the crucial importance of symbols to culture. Some designs for living (notably language) can be expressed and transmitted only through symbols.

FIRST ANTHROPOLOGIST: While I follow your objections to Bain's definition, I do not think we should let them obscure the tight nexus between symbols and culture. I'll content myself with quotations from two well-known anthropologists. Malinowski once said, "Symbolism is that modification of the human organism which allows it to transform physiological drive into cultural value." Leslie White gives this definition: "Culture is the name of things and events dependent upon symbolling considered in an extrasomatic context."

THE LAWYER: May I sum up? Culture as an explanatory concept is useful both in analyzing actions of human beings (whether considered as individuals or groups) and in elucidating geographical distributions of artifacts or forms of behavior and historical sequences.

Along substantive lines, I would rephrase the definition offered: *By "culture" we mean those historically created definitions of the situation which individuals acquire by virtue of participation in or contact with groups that tend to share ways of life that are in particular respects and in their total configuration distinctive.*

Part III: "Culture" as a Descriptive Concept

THE PHYSICIAN: I had to miss the first two sessions, but let me see if I can apply what I learned from the transcript. Can we say that "culture" in general as a descriptive concept means the accumulated treasury of human creation: books, paintings, buildings, and the like; the knowledge of ways of adjusting to our surroundings, both human and physical; language, customs, and systems of etiquette, ethics, religion, and morals that have been built up through the ages?

FIRST ANTHROPOLOGIST: In referring to culture as "a store-house of adjustive responses" and as "a human creation," you strike notes upon which we would all now agree. But, in my opinion, the objections to an enumerative definition and to a definition that lists, in part, concrete phenomena still stand.

SECOND ANTHROPOLOGIST: I also now share the view that, even at a descriptive level, culture must be considered as an abstraction. Even a "culture trait" is, in a sense, an "ideal type." Take, for instance, alarm clocks: no two are ever exactly alike; some are large, some small; some work perfectly, and others don't; some are shiny and some are painted in soft colors. If we examined minutely enough several clocks that have just been produced by the same factory, we should find that even these show small differences.

THE BUSINESSMAN: Let me take this idea a little further. "Bank" is a general term applying to all the specific institutions that conduct certain types of financial transactions. Doesn't "culture," then, as a descriptive concept mean the sum of all such generalizations?

FIRST ANTHROPOLOGIST: I would prefer to say "a summation of all the ideas for standardized types of behavior."

THIRD ANTHROPOLOGIST: The notion of defining culture, in a descriptive sense, as a set of blueprints for action (including feeling, of course) is very attractive. And it is probably sound, provided that it is clearly realized that such a statement is made from the standpoint of the observer, the student of culture, rather than from that of the participant in culture. For the participant much of culture is unverbalized and probably in a still wider sense implicit.

THE PSYCHIATRIST: I agree. I have always protested against such statements as "culture consists of ideas," because we know well from comparative psychiatry that there is also such a thing as "culturally standardized unreason."

FIRST ANTHROPOLOGIST: Yes. While a great deal of culture is

cognitive and is cognitively transmitted, the place of feeling
bulks enormously.

THE ECONOMIST: Perhaps we need three categories: rational,
irrational, and nonrational.

FIRST ANTHROPOLOGIST: Quite. In Pareto's terms, some of
culture is "logical," some is "illogical," but probably the highest
proportion is "nonlogical."

THIRD ANTHROPOLOGIST: May we then give the following
substantive definition: *By "culture" we mean all those historically created designs for living, explicit and implict, rational,
irrational, and nonrational, that exist at any given time as potential guides for the behavior of men.*

THE LAWYER: I have only one question: Why is it necessary
to say "at any given time"?

FOURTH ANTHROPOLOGIST: Because culture is constantly being
created and lost. No definition must suggest that culture is
static.

SECOND ANTHROPOLOGIST: Does "designs for living" mean
that you intend the concept to include only "theory"—that is,
the ways in which things "ought" to be done or felt?

THIRD ANTHROPOLOGIST: No. "Design" denotes both "theory"
and "practice." "Design" is meant to designate both "behavioral
patterns" and "ideal patterns." Remember that culture is always
a conceptual construct. The anthropologist not only observes
that people say (or otherwise indicate) that they have certain
standards for behavior, violations of which are punished by great
or small sanctions. He equally notes that even disapproved behavior sequences tend to fall into certain modalities. From the
observer's standpoint it is as if people were unconsciously adhering to certain "blueprints" or "designs" also for conduct that
is prohibited or indifferent from the standpoint of shared "moral"
norms.

THE PHILOSOPHER: Now I only wonder how you are going
to make the transition from "culture" to "a culture." No physicist speaks of "a gravity."

FIRST ANTHROPOLOGIST: Surely when the physicist "explains"
the falling of certain concrete bodies at a given time and place,
he must—if he is to be precise as to details—get beyond the gen-

eral principle of gravity. He must describe the particular field of gravity that affected those bodies at just that time. Similarly, "a culture" is just a convenient short expression for "a special field of that force known as culture."

THE LAWYER: But you are making an explanatory concept of "a culture."

SECOND ANTHROPOLOGIST: "A culture" may be used in either the descriptive or the explanatory sense, or both. The descriptive usage carries explanatory overtones.

THE PHILOSOPHER: To the extent, I suppose, that description of recurrent responses of one group contrast with those of other groups to "the same" situation; therefore the sheer description suggests: "Ah, this particular pattern of behavior cannot be determined by the special genes of this group nor by the unique features of the environing situation. It must be cultural." Let me give a small, concrete, and simple-minded illustration. When Americans meet, they shake hands. Japanese bow. The "intent" is the same in both cases. And Japanese-Americans shake hands as "naturally" as other Americans. The characteristic variations in response must be traced to those historically derived regularities in behavior that distinguish Japanese from Americans.

THIRD ANTHROPOLOGIST: In the strict sense, we can designate patterns of and for behavior as pertaining to a culture only when there are two or more objectively possible and functionally effective means or modes of satisfying a desire or carrying out an activity and a given group exhibits a consistent and stylized preference for one path to the goal among alternatives that are —from the observer's point of view—all open. For example, to say that a people living on the sea catch and eat fish is not—if one wants to be precise—a statement about their culture. One gets into the cultural realm only when one reports in detail how they catch fish and prepare them, which fish and modes of preparation are preferred, what fish or parts thereof are not eaten, and the like.

THE PHYSICIAN: You said "patterns of and for behavior." A certain tribe believes that the world is flat. Mustn't that notion be ascribed to their culture? But is it a "pattern of or for behavior"?

THIRD ANTHROPOLOGIST: In the sense that this cognitive assertion is expectable in that culture. The phrase "patterns of and for" is economical—you must read some extensions into it.

THE LAWYER: May we have a definition of "a culture," in the descriptive sense?

FIRST ANTHROPOLOGIST: *"A culture" is an historically derived system of explicit and implicit designs for living that tends to be shared by all or specially designated members of a group.*

THIRD ANTHROPOLOGIST: That satisfies me. The word "system" does a lot of work in that definition. It suggests abstraction. It directly implies that a culture is organized, that it is selective.

THE PSYCHOLOGIST: I suppose a rat psychologist would say that the models constructed by anthropologists for each separate culture provide the specifications for the various human mazes.

THE ECONOMIST: Why did you use the word "group" rather than the more familiar "society"?

FIRST ANTHROPOLOGIST: Because, to have the maximum usefulness, the generic idea should be applicable to social units both larger and smaller than those to which the term "society" is ordinarily applied. Thus, we need to speak of "Islamic culture," in spite of the fact that various Mohammedan peoples interact with each other less intensively than they do with other non-Islamic societies. Also, it is useful to speak of the subcultures of cliques and of relatively impermanent social units, such as, for example, members of summer camps.

THE PHYSICIAN: Let me pose you an example. Take an "institution" like the Komsomol that is found in various Communist countries. Do we refer these "patterns of and for behavior" to "Communist culture"?

FIRST ANTHROPOLOGIST: For comprehensiveness I would say it was necessary to operate on two levels here. The pattern that tends to be found in all Communist countries is referable to a generalized Communist culture. But the differences—and there are some—would be ascribed to the various national cultures: Polish, Albanian, and so on.

THE PSYCHOLOGIST: I like the word "tends." Some of us have in the past felt cheated because we have been assured that studying a culture would give us the common ground against which various personality figures emerged. Our own investigations along this line seem to indicate that it was misleading to depict any single background as being in any literal sense "common" to all members of any group.

SECOND ANTHROPOLOGIST: Anthropologists are quite aware that even in small, nonliterate societies no person knows fully or knows about "all" of that culture. The probability of knowledge and use of a specific cultural trait will vary according to the number of systematic and random alternatives that culture offers and the extent to which the given behavior is culturally standardized at all.

FIRST ANTHROPOLOGIST: Just as "tends" reminds us that no individual thinks, feels, or acts precisely as the "design" indicates that he will or should, so also "specially designated" is a reminder that not all of the "blueprints" that constitute a culture are meant to apply to each and every individual. There are sex differentials, age differentials, class differentials, prestige-group differentials, and others.

THIRD ANTHROPOLOGIST: It seems to me that you have enunciated two related but separate propositions. It is important that we should not mix them. First, there is the proposition that the sharing is tendency rather than fact. As L. K. Frank puts it, what we can actually observe is the "idiomatic version of each personality's utilization of cultural patterns." And he goes on to make a useful analogy, something along these lines: Thereby we can abstract the regularities and uniformities and likewise observe the personality distortions and skewings, as we have learned to observe the statistical regularities of a gas but also recognize and acknowledge the irregular and nonconforming behavior of individual molecules of that gas.

Second, there is the proposition of the compartmentalization and segmentation of a culture. While each individual's utilization of pattern is idiomatic, some sets of patterns are always felt as appropriate for certain categories of individuals. A background of culture is to be regarded as approximately constant—not for every individual in all groups that have some continuity and functional wholeness—but rather for those who occupy the same set of statuses or perform about the same roles within the total group.

THE PSYCHIATRIST: That is not the end of the story. Two

Americans grew up in New York City. Both are wealthy, upper-class lawyers. I could specify further, but grant me that the cultural heritage of these two men is, to a first approximation, the same. It does not follow at all that the culture that each has internalized approaches identity. They had parents of different temperaments and varying interests. Their own temperaments and peculiar life experiences motivated them to select and weigh from the "common" cultural heritage.

FIRST ANTHROPOLOGIST: Of course. The culture "built in" to persons varies along role and status lines and also by individuality. Yet it remains true that at least in those groups which have some historical continuity and which are generally called "societies" all individuals tend, in spite of idiosyncratic phrasings, to share interpretations of the external world and man's place in it. To some degree every individual is affected by this common "view of life." A culture is made up of overt, patterned ways of behaving, feeling, and reacting. But it also includes a characteristic set of unstated premises or hypotheses that vary greatly in different societies. Thus, one group unconsciously assumes that every chain of actions has a goal and that when this goal is reached, tension will be reduced or disappear. To another group, thinking based upon this assumption is meaningless—they see life, not as a series of purposive sequences, but as made up of experiences that are satisfying in and of themselves rather than as means to ends.

THE PHILOSOPHER: Are you saying that each culture is integrated about certain dominant interests and in accord with certain postulates and assumptions?

THIRD ANTHROPOLOGIST: No culture can be regarded as a completely integrated system. Most cultures, like most personalities, can be regarded as permeated by apparent contradictions. But, to greater or lesser extent, every way of life that is not in the process of rapid dissolution is a structure—not a haphazard collection of all the different physically possible and functionally effective ways of satisfying biological needs, but an interdependent system with all its traits and patterns segregated and arranged in a manner that is felt as appropriate. Even in cultures that do not approach complete integration one may detect certain recurrent themes in a variety of specific contexts.

THE PSYCHOLOGIST: Are you talking about what some anthropologists have called the "absolute logics" of a people or about what others refer to as "the logic of the sentiments"?

THIRD ANTHROPOLOGIST: Both. Every people not only has a sentiment structure that is to some degree unique but also a more or less coherent body of distinctive presuppositions about the world. This last is really a borderland between reason and feeling. Perhaps in a certain ultimate sense the "logic" of all peoples is the same. But their premises are certainly different.

THE PHILOSOPHER: Do you mean the conscious, the stated premises—what a logician would call the "postulates"—or the unstated premises, "assumptions"?

THIRD ANTHROPOLOGIST: There are both cultural postulates and cultural assumptions. Some of the most critical premises of any culture are often unstated, even by the intellectuals of the group. Likewise, some basic categories of "thinking" are implicit—save, perhaps, to a tiny minority in rationally sophisticated societies.

FOURTH ANTHROPOLOGIST: If the premises and the system of categories are unconscious, how are they transmitted?

FIRST ANTHROPOLOGIST: In part through the *language*. Linguistic morphology preserves and transmits the unformulated philosophy. For example, Dorothy Lee (1940, p. 357) has shown that among the Trobriand Islanders ". . . the sequence of events does not automatically fall into the mould of causal or telic relationship." Because of the mould that grammar imposes upon their "thinking" these people find certain types of communication with Europeans difficult, since Europeans talk in causal terms.

The morphology of any language inevitably begs far-reaching questions of metaphysics and of values. A language is not merely an instrument for communication and for rousing the emotions. Every language is also a device for categorizing experience. The continuum of experience can be sliced very differently. We tend all too easily to assume that the distinctions which Indo-European languages (or our own particular language) force us to make are given by the world of nature. As a matter of fact, comparative linguistics shows plainly that talking demands unconscious conceptual selection. No human organism can respond to all the kaleidoscopic stimuli that impinge upon it from the external world. What we notice, what we talk about, what we feel as important, is in some part a function of our linguistic patterns. Because these linguistic habits tend to remain as unquestioned "background phenomena," each people tends to take its fundamental categories, its unstated basic premises, for granted. It is assumed that others will "think the same way," for "it's only human nature." When others face the same body of data but come to different conclusions, it is seldom brought out that they might be proceeding from different premises. Rather, it is inferred that they are "stupid" or "illogical" or "obstinate."

FOURTH ANTHROPOLOGIST: How does it happen that different peoples have different systems of categories?

FIRST ANTHROPOLOGIST: A language is one aspect of a culture. Therefore, we must refer to the "accidents of history" and to all the other forces that we mentioned as producing the forms of culture. Each individual tends to classify his experiences along the lines laid down by the grammar to which he is habituated, but the grammar itself is a cultural product. Dorothy Lee (1938, p. 89) has made this point very well:

True enough, the thought of the individual must run along its grooves; but these grooves, themselves, are a heritage from individuals who laid them down in an unconscious effort to express their attitudes toward the world. Grammar contains in crystallized form the accumulated and accumulating experience, the *Weltanschauung* of a people.

THIRD ANTHROPOLOGIST: There is another angle to the perpetuation of cultural organization, particularly at the implicit level. This is the culturally prescribed system of child training. If all adults have been subjected to about the same deprivations and frustrations during socialization, they are likely to see life in somewhat the same terms. Roheim (1942, p. 164) says: ". . . the dominant idea of a culture may be an addiction but it is always a system formation that can be explained on the basis of the infantile situation." Margaret Mead deals with the relation of "infantile traumas" to the one or more focal points in each culture under the conception of "plot in culture."

FOURTH ANTHROPOLOGIST: Although partially won over, I am still unhappy about this phrase "implicit culture."

THIRD ANTHROPOLOGIST: A conception of this order is made necessary by certain eminently practical considerations. Programs of the British Colonial Services or of our own Indian Service that have been carefully thought through for their continuity with the cultural inventory and with the overt cultural patterns nevertheless fail to work out. Intensive investigation does not reveal major flaws in the set-up at the technological level. The program is sabotaged by resistance that must be imputed to the manner in which members of the group have been conditioned by their implicit designs for living to think and feel in ways which were unexpected by the administrator.

FIRST ANTHROPOLOGIST: Students of culture change are also agreed that the way in which a group accepts, rejects, or readapts borrowed elements cannot be fully understood in terms of direct and explicit functions. The process is also related to the cultural structure, including those portions of it that are implicit. Even after the content of the culture of a group of American Indians has become completely European, its way of life still somehow retains a distinctive flavor—as if the "container" remained "aboriginal."

THIRD ANTHROPOLOGIST: We would freely admit that conceptual instruments objective enough and precise enough to deal with the patterning of implicit culture are only beginning to be evolved. The importance of tacit cultural premises and categories is probably obvious enough. But the sheer statement of the presence and absence of these (and of all other features of culture, whether implicit or explicit) is not enough. The full significance of any single element in a cultural design will be seen only when that element is viewed in the total matrix of its relationship to other elements—and, indeed, to other designs. Naturally, this includes accent, or emphasis, as well as position. Accent is manifested sometimes through frequency, sometimes through intensity. The indispensable importance of these questions of arrangement and emphasis may be driven home by an analogy. Take a musical chord made up of three notes. If we are told that the three notes in question are B, D, and G, we receive information. But it alone will not enable us to predict the type of sensation that the playing of this chord is likely to evoke in us or in others. We need many different sorts of relationship data. Are the notes to be played in that or some other order? What duration will each receive? How will the emphasis, if any, be distributed? We also need, of course, to know whether the chord will be played in the key of C or in the key of B-flat minor, and whether the instrument is to be a piano or an accordion.

FIRST ANTHROPOLOGIST: "Explicit culture" and "implicit culture" are polar concepts; that is, it is not possible to say in every case without hesitation or qualification that a given cultural phenomenon belongs to explicit or to implicit culture. Some data fall unequivocally into one or the other of these two categories, but others tend only toward one pole or the other. Nevertheless, the making of this discrimination helps enormously to keep us alive to the varying levels of abstraction and to remind us whether we are talking in terms that might be present in the consciousness of cultural participants or in terms that have been introduced by the observer. Herskovits has said that a culture may be thought of "as a kind of psychological iceberg of whose totality but a small portion appears above the level of consciousness."

THE ECONOMIST: Are you implying that the implicit culture exists in the unconscious of participants?

FIRST ANTHROPOLOGIST: No. In the first place, I am not using psychoanalytic language. By "unconscious" I mean here only the Watsonian sense of "not verbalized" or "not habitually verbalized"—the unstated premises, for example. However, "implicit culture" encompasses more than can properly be referred to the categories of "present" or "not present" in the consciousness of cultural participants. In every culture there are certain pervasive principles or "orderings." Participants—unless they be behavioral scientists—are not aware of the very existence of these, and hence they do not impinge upon either the conscious or unconscious mental life of participants. The task of discovering the general "laws" of a culture is undertaken by specially trained investigators. Although the methods will probably be quite different, the problem is rather similar to that of factor analysis. The aim is to isolate certain "loadings" in the materials, certain clusters that persistently turn up.

THIRD ANTHROPOLOGIST: *Explicit culture*, then, includes all those features of group designs for living that might be described to an outsider by participants in the culture. Actually, the field worker could get his basic data as much or more from observation, from qualified participation, or from listening to informal conversations as from asking members of the group questions about their ways of life. The basic differentiae of explicit culture are:

1. Maximal conscious awareness (implying some capacity to verbalize on the part of the participants).

2. Limitation of the scientist's role in constructing his conceptual model of the culture to first order abstractions, neglecting variations and details that seem to be irrelevant to the central tendencies which are to be taken as representing the design itself.

To avoid confusion, it should be noted that the basic data from which the anthropologists abstract explicit culture encompass manifestations of "feeling" and "thought" and are in no sense restricted to objects and acts in the narrow behavioristic sense. In other words, "explicit" does *not* draw the line which "objective" is supposed to draw from the "subjective."

Implicit culture designates that sector of the culture of which the members of the group are unaware or minimally aware. This means, unquestionably, that the anthropologist describing implicit culture cannot hope to approach as nearly the function of a relatively precise, relatively passive instrument as he does when describing explicit culture. His role is more active; he necessarily "puts something in" to the data. Whereas the trustworthiness of an anthropologist's portrayal of explicit culture depends upon his receptivity, his completeness, and his detachment as a recorder, and upon the skill and care with which he makes his inductive generalizations, the trustworthiness of his conceptual model of the implicit culture stands or falls with the balance achieved between sensitivity of creative imagination and freedom from preconception. In this sense, implicit culture *is* more "subjective" than explicit culture.

THE PSYCHOLOGIST: Let me come back to one question about "a culture" that remains foggy for me. In a general way, I can understand that one can properly speak at different levels of abstraction. One may contrast "European culture" with "Islamic culture," but in other contexts "French culture" is also opposed to "German culture." But how far does this go, and what are the exact operations by which the anthropologist decides whether he is dealing with two distinct cultures? To be concrete, should one speak of "northern French culture" and "southern French culture"? of "rural or peasant French culture" versus "metropolitan French culture"? of "the culture" of Auvergne or Brittany? Or are these all variants or subcultures of generalized French culture?

THIRD ANTHROPOLOGIST: If we slightly paraphrase a definition offered by Lévi-Strauss, we get the conceptual essence: A culture is a set of patterns of and for behavior prevalent among a group of human beings which, from the point of view of the research at hand and of the scale on which it is being carried out, presents, in relation to other such sets, significant discontinuities. But the principal piece of unfinished business is to work out a set of standard operations by which one can establish "significant" discontinuities. In many instances language is a sufficient, though rough and ready, indicator. On the other hand, to say that the cultures of the French-speaking Belgium and of Quebec were French subcultures would surely obscure some pertinent phenomena. Conversely, the cultures of Pakistan and Iran are in many respects variants of generalized Islamic culture, in spite of the fact that the languages of these cultures are not Arabic. Neither language nor political unit is an altogether satisfactory criterion of cultural differentiation, though each is meaningful. If what has been said earlier about language is approximately correct, two or more groups who speak the same language will share many features of both cultural content and cultural organization. And no political unit will long endure unless a high proportion of its citizens accept cultural anthropology, I think we should explore the linguistic analogies as far as we can. Isn't Western culture an abstraction many of the same cognitive and evaluative premises.

FIRST ANTHROPOLOGIST: As in most matters of theory in

on about the same level as the Indo-European linguistic phylum and "Latin culture," comparable to, say, the Germanic language family? When one comes to the distinction between "language" and "dialect," the linguists have a rigorous criterion: If there is mutual intelligibility, then they are dialects of the same language. I suggest that this should be a paradigm for our drawing the lines between "distinct cultures" and "subcultures of one culture." When people from two groups, despite perceptible variation in the details of their life-ways, nevertheless share enough basic assumptions so that they can communicate—in the broadest sense of that term—comfortably, then their cultures are only variants of a single culture.

SECOND ANTHROPOLOGIST: Another linguistic parallel may be instructive. Brugmann argued that only uniquely shared innovations constitute a basis for positing distinct units. However, he found a number of instances where features that did not appear to be attributable to Proto-Indo-European were shared by two or more of the principal branches of Indo-European. He then invoked the criterion of quantity. A sizable number of innovations at all linguistic levels is decisive as far as distinctiveness is concerned.

FOURTH ANTHROPOLOGIST: Wait a minute. You say "at all linguistic levels." Does this mean that we can't say, for instance, that Navaho culture is distinct from generalized Apache culture unless we can point to a distinctly Navaho social invention in all sectors of culture: religion, social organization, economy, and so on?

FIRST ANTHROPOLOGIST: This would get us into impossible trouble. I would maintain, rather, that we should accept as decisive any *fundamental* change. For example, when the Romance languages were evolving from Latin, there was a shift from vowel quantity to vowel accent. I would be content to say that once this new principle was established in a linguistic community, it alone would be enough to make the determination: This speech is no longer a dialect of Latin, but a new language.

SECOND ANTHROPOLOGIST: Applying your illustration to non-linguistic culture, would you not then have to conclude that shift in residence pattern was in and of itself enough to complete the transition from subculture to independent culture? Or is it possible for groups with radically different economies to have "the same culture"? I would think not, except possibly in the case of large nation-states that are transected by numerous subcultures.

THIRD ANTHROPOLOGIST: We just don't know enough yet, either empirically or theoretically, to agree upon what is "fundamental." My own hunch is that the highest common factors in the distinctiveness of a culture reside in the core values and the "primitive" cognitive assumptions. In making up my mind as to whether two designs for living were distinct or merely variants, I would always like to have answers to such questions as the following:

1. What are the ultimate criteria of "truth" and "falsity"? In revelation or in custom or in rational knowledge?

2. What are the attributes of a "good" person?

3. What is desirable in experience and in what rank order?

I suspect that to get to the significant structure points in cognitive and value systems we shall have to go beyond the phenomenologically "given," to "translate" into abstract categories that are valid cross-culturally. Published arguments about whether or not a myth is "Oedipal" bog down in futile disputes: Must every theme in the story as told by Sophocles reappear? (If so, we might as well forget the category.) Will three themes be enough—and can they be any three? Or will an implication of mother-son incest or a hint of parricide do? On the other hand, Lévi-Strauss' (1955) "translation" of the meaning of the Oedipus myth frees us from the impasse of counting traits in all their specificity and directs the inquiry to psychological regularities embodied in variable cultural dress: ". . . the overrating of blood relations is to the underrating of blood relations as the attempt to escape autochthony is to the impossibility to succeed in it."

THE LAWYER: May I once more presume to give a stark summary? As a descriptive concept, culture means "models of historically derived modalities of and for behavior, explicit and implicit." Descriptive culture deals first and foremost with particulate, whole cultures. Anthropologists also comparatively describe selected aspects (aesthetic, religious, or whatever) of a series of particulate cultures.

The concept of "a culture" is used over a wide range of abstractions. The dividing line between "a culture" and a "sub-culture" or "cultural variant" has not yet been firmly staked out. Some leads for further thinking have been given.

Part IV: The Utility of the Concept "Culture" in Its Various Senses

THE BUSINESSMAN: All this is not without interest, but it does seem awfully abstract and remote from everyday affairs. I'd like to interject a practical question: What good is this concept so far as the contemporary world is concerned? What can you do with it?

FIRST ANTHROPOLOGIST: First and foremost, I would insist that its use lies in the aid the concept gives to man's endless quest to understand himself and his own behavior. For example, this relatively new idea makes some of the questions that trouble one of the most learned and acute thinkers of our age, Reinhold Niebuhr, seem pseudo-problems. In his book, *The Nature and Destiny of Man* (1941-1943), Niebuhr argues that the universally human sense of guilt or shame and man's capacity for self-judgment necessitate the assumption of supernatural forces. But these facts are susceptible of self-consistent and relatively simple "explanation" in purely naturalistic terms through the concept of culture. Social life among humans never occurs without a system of "conventional understandings" that are transmitted more or less intact from generation to generation. Any individual is familiar with some of these, and they constitute a set of standards against which he judges himself. To the extent that he fails to conform he experiences discomfort, because the intimate conditioning of infancy and childhood put great pressure on him to internalize these norms and his unconscious tendency is to associate withdrawal of love and protection or active punishment with deviation. This and other issues that have puzzled philosophers and scientists for countless generations become fully or partially understandable by means of this fresh conceptual instrument.

But if your interest is in action rather than thought, the principal claim which can be made for culture is that it helps us toward *predicting* human behavior. One of the reasons that such prediction has not been very successful thus far has been that it has been carried out, for the most part, on the naive assumption of a minutely homogeneous "human nature." In the framework of this assumption all human thinking proceeds from the same premises; all human beings are motivated by the same needs and goals. But in the cultural framework we see that, while the ultimate logic of all peoples may be the same (and thus communication and understanding possible), the thought proc- esses depart from radically different premises—especially un- conscious or unstated premises. But those who have the cultural outlook are more likely to look beneath the surface and bring the culturally determined premises to the light of day. This may well not bring about immediate agreement and har- mony, but it will at least facilitate a *more* rational approach to the problem of "international understanding" and to diminish- ing friction between groups within a nation.

The concept of culture also encourages paying attention to the more concrete aspects of ways of life other than our own. It suggests, for example, the usefulness of knowledge of alien "customs" if we wish to foresee how a foreign people will behave in a certain situation and of respect for these same cus- toms if we wish to get along with that foreign people.

A culture is not only a reticulum of patterned means for satis- fying needs, but equally a network of stylized goals for individual and group achievement. If we need to predict human action, we mustn't assume that the effect motivations in all human groups are the same. Even the primary drives, such as hunger and sex, though biological "givens," are subtly modified and channeled by culture. What kind of food or what type of sexual experience will be most striven after cannot be predicted through biological knowledge alone. There exist for every human group "secondary drives." Among us, for example, the "need" felt for cars or radios often goads individuals even harder than that for sexual satisfaction.

Every culture is also a structure of expectancies. If we know a culture, we know what various classes of individuals within it expect from each other—and from outsiders of various categories. We know what types of activity are held to be inherently gratifying.

SECOND ANTHROPOLOGIST: One great contribution of the concept of culture is that of providing some persons with some detachment from the conscious and unconscious emotional values of their own culture. The phrase "some detachment" must be emphasized. An individual who viewed the designs for living of his group with complete detachment would almost certainly be disoriented and unhappy. But I can prefer (that is, feel affectively attached to) American manners while at the same time perceiving certain graces in English manners that are lacking or more grossly expressed in ours. Thus, while unwilling to forget that I am an American and hence have no desire to ape English drawing room behaviors, I can still derive a lively pleasure from association with English people on "social" occasions. Whereas, if I have no detachment, if I am utterly provincial, I am likely to regard English manners as utterly ridiculous, uncouth, perhaps even immoral. With that attitude I shall certainly not get on well with the English, and I am likely to resent bitterly any modification of our manners in the English or any other direction. Such attitudes clearly do not make for international understanding, friendship, and cooperation. They equally make for too rigid a social structure. Anthropological documents and anthropological teachings are valuable, therefore, in that they tend to emancipate individuals from an overly perfervid allegiance to every item in the cultural inventory. The person who has been exposed to the anthropological perspective by incongruity is more likely, on the one hand, to "live and let live" both within his own society and in his dealings with members of other societies; on the other hand, he will probably be more flexible in regard to needful changes in social organization to meet changed technological structure and changed economies.

THIRD ANTHROPOLOGIST: In a way, I would say that the most important implication of "culture" for action is the profound truth (so frequently overlooked by every sort of "social planners") that you can never start with a clean slate so far as human beings are concerned. No human being or group of human beings can ever freshly see the world in which they move. Every human is born into a world defined by already existing cultural patterns. Just as an individual who has lost his memory is no longer "normal," so the idea of a society's—at any point in its history—becoming completely emancipated from its past culture is inconceivable. This is one source of the tragic failure of the Weimar constitution in Germany. In the abstract, it was an admirable document; but it failed miserably in actual life, partly because it provided for no continuity with existent designs for acting, feeling, and thinking. The constitution departed from the untenable assumption that in human affairs it is possible to start with a clean slate.

Finally, as the word "design" in our definition implies, every culture has organization as well as content. This fact carries with it the highly practical warning to administrators and lawmakers that a "custom" that it is desired to abolish or change cannot be isolated. Any change may have repercussions in areas of behavior where they are least expected.

While serious anthropologists disavow all messianic pretensions and make no claim that "culture" is any "philosopher's stone" that will end all problems, nevertheless the explanatory concept does carry an overtone of legitimate hope to troubled men. What men have created they can destroy or change. "Systematically modified human behavior" would almost do as a definition of culture. One must remember, of course, at the same time that planned culture change is immensely difficult—even when the pre-existing culture is taken into account—and always involves unanticipated consequences. As for destruction, some cultures or culture-parts are much more vulnerable than others. Certain cultures have proven immensely resistant. Neither the Austro-Hungarian empire nor the Nazis nor—thus far—the Communists have been able to exterminate the Polish culture. The basic proposition remains, however: With wisdom and with patience constructive improvement of cultures is possible in principle.

Both human appetites and consummatory responses can—within limits—be modified.

SECOND ANTHROPOLOGIST: I would be content for some time to come if we could just foresee a little better—and therefore prepare ourselves a little better—for those changes which go on in cultures without rational intention or plan. No culture is a completely self-sealing system. Alterations, major or minor, are constantly occurring consequent upon contacts with other cultures and new environmental pressures, and possibly in terms of systematic properties inherent in each cultural system. Anthropology will be very useful if it can only forecast with some accuracy that a specified type of alteration will be followed by other changes of such and such dimensions.

Part V: Review

THE BUSINESSMAN: In my language, you people have convinced me of three main points:

1. Man is one; cultures are many. Human nature has both mutable and immutable aspects.

2. Some things people do for biological reasons. Others they do in the exercise of their intelligence. The cultural sphere bears a relation to both human biology and to human reason but is not identical with either and may interfere with both.

3. As culture varies, so will many features of behavior.

But I should be grateful for a more technical summary from the anthropologists. What propositions about culture do you regard as essential upon which there is almost unanimous consensus? First, please review for me quickly in what culture consists.

THIRD ANTHROPOLOGIST: Part of culture consists in norms for and modalities in behavior. Another part consists in ideologies justifying or rationalizing certain ways of behaving. Finally, every culture includes broad general principles of selectivity and ordering ("highest common factors") in terms of which patterns of and for behavior are potentially reducible to parsimonious generalizations.

FIRST ANTHROPOLOGIST: Culture is a phenomenal process that occurs in space and time. Almost all behavior is selective. But human behavior is selective in the special sense that there exist historically created and man-made standards of selectivity: Conventional premises and concepts that are communicated (whether by explicit verbalization or in other ways) within the group and culturally transmitted and culturally induced needs and wants.

THIRD ANTHROPOLOGIST: That seems to me to cover the essence of the explanatory notion. A culture is a complex yet unitary pattern, characterized as much by its organization as by its content and having implicit as well as explicit dimensions.

THE PHILOSOPHER: Ought not disagreements or incomplete agreements to be mentioned in a summary?

SECOND ANTHROPOLOGIST: These would reduce to phrasings and shadings. I see what is meant by "implicit culture" and grant its significance. I shan't feel comfortable in using the term until the idea has been formulated with greater clarity and until the operations by which an "implicit culture" can be defined have been specified with greater rigor.

Perhaps the philosophers (like Bidney) have to continue to worry about the locus of culture and the ontological status of culture. I don't believe these questions are any longer problems for us. There is, however, a wide spectrum of opinion among anthropologists as to how abstract formulations of culture should be and as to whether a culture should be regarded as a "logical construct" or "model" rather than as a descriptive synthesis of observed reality.

FIRST ANTHROPOLOGIST: I think, after all, something remains of the "locus" problem. It is false to assert that a culture is *nothing but* a logical construct of patterns or forms that exist only in the minds of behavioral scientists. A culture—certainly its explicit portion—is also internalized in the participant individuals. No one person has internalized it all, but a composite —except for perhaps those interrelations and purely formal properties inferred by the analyst of the implicit culture—exists in the total group as well as being manifested in its artifacts. Possibly we should follow the general semanticists and "index" "Culture$_1$" the logical construct produced by the anthropologist and "Culture$_2$," the norms internalized in individuals as exhibited by patterned regularities in abstracted elements of their behavior.

THE LAWYER: Have comparative studies been made of series of definitions of culture to see how much agreement and variation there is?

THIRD ANTHROPOLOGIST: Kroeber and Kluckhohn (1952a) analyzed several hundred definitions and statements about culture by anthropologists and others. Apart from occasional bizarre definitions, they found that the major variability in definitions rested (a) in what properties of culture were stressed and (b) in how explicitly comprehensive a definition was. They also point to historical fashions in the definition of culture. They state that most behavioral scientists now formulate the concept of culture approximately as follows:

Culture consists of patterns, explicit and implicit, of and for behavior acquired and transmitted by symbols, constituting the distinctive achievement of human groups, including their embodiments in artifacts; the essential core of culture consists of traditional (i.e., historically derived and selected) ideas and especially their attached values; culture systems may, on the one hand, be considered as products of action, on the other as conditioning influences upon further action.

3 THE POSITION

OF Bc 51

THE PECOS CLASSIFICATION has been used in the distributional analyses but not in the description of Bc 51. In other words, it has been used only when others had assumed the responsibility for the assignment of a site or a part of a site to a particular category in the Pecos classification. The reluctance to assign a label to Bc 51 is not to be understood as based upon a conviction that the Pecos classification has not been useful in the development of Southwestern archaeology. But close study of the recent literature seemed to show some equivocation on certain issues of classification and suggested that an unqualified assignment of this site might lead some later comparative student to make equations not altogether justified by the facts. The data from Bc 51 bring out particular classificatory difficulties sufficiently sharply that a fairly extended discussion will perhaps be profitable.

1939a Reprinted by permission of the publisher from Clyde Kluckhohn and Paul Reiter, *Preliminary Report on the 1937 Excavations, Bc 50-51, Chaco Canyon, New Mexico.* Univeristy of New Mexico Bulletin, Anthropological Series 3, No. 2.

At first glance the matter may appear to be simple enough. Roberts has, on several occasions during the 1930's, published lists of traits diagnostic of the various Anasazi subdivisions, and these lists have been widely accepted. One might think, then, that it was merely a question of determining whether the material from a given site conformed to a particular set of specifications. But if one is working with a specific assemblage of data and endeavoring to follow out operations which are precisely defined, a number of questions arise: Is it absolute presence or absence of the criteria which count or merely pre-dominance—or does the answer to this question vary in the case of various traits? To what extent must the culture or "culture period" check with the majority of the diagnostics? Are certain of the criteria indispensable and others not? That is, suppose eight criteria are taken as diagnostic of Pueblo I in the Chaco, and suppose it is agreed that at least six of these must conform (so far as there is evidence available on the trait in question), will we still call a site Pueblo I if six of the eight criteria are found indubitably associated with a masonry type or a pottery complex which has been accepted as diagnostic of Pueblo II? Cases of this general sort are not unknown to experience.

Observation of the actual operations of archaeologists suggests that in many cases the classification of a site is actually made on the basis of pottery complex or architectural style (including masonry type). If this fact is explicitly stated, the procedure may well be the most convenient and quite unobjectionable. If, however, there is assertion or implication that the classification has been made on the basis of total culture complex, this is misleading, for what occurs is that other culture elements found associated with the critical pottery complex or architectural style are simply dragged in after the crucial step has been taken. If we are really operating with pottery or masonry-architectural complexes (or a combination of these two) only, it would be in the interests of clear thinking to bring this circumstance into the open, either through terminology or explicit statement. It seems possible that classificatory operations based solely upon these apparently somewhat more sensitive and more consistent criteria would be the most useful. The associated culture elements (not used in cultural classification) could then be studied apart from the prejudice of a question-begging nomenclature, and, after the trends toward uniformity had been unequivocally ascertained, the operations for definition truly in terms of total culture complex could be rigorously set up.

It would, then, be necessary to clarify the proportion of traits otherwise regarded as diagnostic of, let us say, Pueblo II, that could be admitted *seriatim* in a Pueblo I site. It would, likewise, be imperative to state whether any criteria are to be weighted as of greater importance and which differentiae are to be applied first. Because, as in physical anthropology, two investigators can use the same diagnostic traits in making a classification and yet get different results, depending on the order in which they are applied (with resultant eliminations), it follows that the relative significance to be attached to positive and negative evidence would have to be specified.

Finally, there is the vexatious "time problem." Are tree-ring dates to have a part in our assignment, and, if so, how important a place? Roberts (1935, p. 33) has written: "It should be emphasized that these designations apply to the complex and not to a single element or series of years." He appears to adhere quite consistently to this position. For example, he has recently (1938a, p. 61) insisted that a particular Chaco masonry type (Slab Base Rubble) is both Basket Maker III and Pueblo I (i.e., he rejects masonry type as a binding criterion), for "Judd's report on this house and the published pictures of the pottery *and other objects* found in the structure clearly indicate that it belongs to the Pueblo I period."[1] Even here, though, the use of the word "period" suggests that the time factor, as well as culture complex, enters in. And Roberts has elsewhere (1938b, p. 80) indicated that he realizes that terminology of this sort tends to acquire "a time connotation as well as a descriptive meaning." Southwestern archaeologists, undoubtedly, continually write and speak of "Pueblo II times" or "the Pueblo I period." As a matter of fact, while most Southwestern archaeologists seem to give verbal assent to Roberts' proposition that the Pecos classification is merely a descriptive categorization of assemblages of traits, evidence is not lacking that dating slips in as a covert criterion. Indeed, within the last few years a few archaeologists, apparently dis-

---

1. The italics in this and other quotations are mine.

turbed by the lack of objectivity of other procedures, avowedly classify sites primarily by their tree-ring dates. For example, we find Baldwin (1939, p. 314) writing ". . . it was occupied from about 1150 to 1320 A.D., *thus* belonging to Pueblo III . . . and the early part of Pueblo IV."

In short, some archaeologists at present use the labels of the Pecos classification in accord with pottery or architectural complexes found present, others endeavor to take account of total culture complexes, and still others make the distinctions primarily on the basis of tree-ring and documentary dates—with multitudinous ill-defined combinations of these three alternatives. The real difficulty is that the criteria are not consistently used. Either they are mingled (in a manner that is not made explicit) or one set is used on one occasion and a different set on another. Hence, various questions are begged by the assignment of such labels. A worker gets no (or an inadequate number of) tree-ring dates at a given site but labels it Pueblo I. Experience shows that comparative students are all too likely to assume that the culture of this site can be chronologically equated with that of undated sites, perhaps in quite different regions. The converse error is, perhaps, less frequent but also occurs. It is probably true that the more competent professional Southwestern archaelogists are fully aware that Pueblo II has dates that range over a wide spread in various areas, but archaeologists specializing in other regions and ethnologists are more likely to fall into the fallacy of "one culture complex, one period." Thus Elsie Parsons, in her recently published work on Pueblo religion (1939, p. 10), writes without qualification, "In the archaeological period called Pueblo II and dated about 875 to 1000 . . . ." The fact of the matter is that one may find sites assigned to Pueblo II dated by archaeologists from as early as 715 to as late as 1144. The facts of Southwestern archaeology should surely not be presented in a terminological form resulting in misconceptions of this sort on the part of experts in related fields. Unfortunately, Roberts, in one of his surveys for the nonspecialist (1935, p. 25), does not help matters when he states that Pueblo II dates approximately from ". . . 875 to 950, longer in the peripheral districts." It is true that elsewhere in his article (p. 21) he says, "While the progression of stages infers a certain degree of contemporaneity between sites of the same horizon, it does not, necessarily, mean that they will fall within identical chronological dates." Nevertheless, it seems certain that the reader whose primary professional interest is not Southwestern archaeology would gain an impression that the spread of dates for particular culture complexes is considerably less than is in fact the case.

Until one is prepared to say relatively unequivocally, "When I say 'Pueblo II,' I mean a culture distinguished by the presence of the following traits . . . , by the absence of the following . . . , by the relative preponderance of such and such traits as opposed to such and such others in proportions which approach statistical constancy" or "When I say 'Pueblo II,' in a given area, I mean sites or distinguishable portions of sites that give no dates earlier than . . . and no dates later than . . . ," misunderstanding will result unless any assignment of the labels of the Pecos classification is guarded and unless the basis or bases for such assignment is made fully overt. In the case of sites where tree-ring dates or widely varying masonry or pottery styles indicate the likelihood that more than one culture complex is represented, the need for assurance that the various features of the inventory were truly associated in the usage of a particular people becomes particularly urgent. Association in the refuse mound or room fill of such a site may well be at least once removed from the actual historical complex. Even in cases where articles are found indubitably grouped with a single burial or on the floor of a room, the possibilities of error from heirloom pieces or intrusion have been underestimated, and, on close examination, the quantitative basis for some generalizations appears hopelessly inadequate.

So much for a consideration of these problems in the abstract. Let us now look at Bc 51 facts in the light of them. An archaeologist who casually inspected the site and the material from it would be likely to describe it as a Pueblo II site. If one were able to analyze the intellectual operations performed in making such an assignment, they would also certainly reduce themselves to two or perhaps three. First of all, since Bc 51 is not, on the one hand, "a great terraced communal house of many rooms" nor, on the other hand, of slab construction, there would be an unwillingness to assign it either to Pueblo III or Basket

Maker III. In the second place, the pottery types that are generally the most numerous in rooms and kivas (Exuberant Corrugated and Escavada Black on White) are types that competent pottery specialists have considered to be diagnostic of Pueblo II. A third general consideration might also enter into the judgment. Certain types of complexity and elaboration of material culture usually associated with such Chaco Pueblo III sites as Pueblo Bonito were not found here. There are, on the other hand, certain traits present that would seem fairly definitely to rule out Basket Maker III and, possibly, Pueblo I.

But now let us examine the matter with somewhat greater attention to detail. Suppose, to start with, we use Roberts' widely accepted "Survey of Southwestern Archaeology" (1935) in trying to decide whether this is a Pueblo I or a Pueblo II site. In five of his sets of diagnostic traits (Sandals, Basketry, Textiles, Weapons, "Other Traits") no features are listed that set off Pueblo I from Pueblo II; this leaves Crania, Pottery, and Houses. Roberts suggests that round crania are proportionately more numerous in Pueblo I sites. However, recent and as yet unpublished research by Dr. George Woodbury and Dr. Carl Seltzer indicates that no clear-cut distinction can be made between the crania of sites that have been assigned to Pueblo I or to Pueblo II. And so we are left with Pottery and Houses as diagnostic criteria.

So far as published evidence goes, the conviction that Escavada preceded such types as Gallup and Chaco Black on White in predominant popularity rests on the data from a single site (Hawley, 1934), except that the latter types gain in prominence in the upper levels at Bc 50, Bc 51, and Leyit Kin. We can probably grant that the available data indicate that Escavada is a type of somewhat earlier popularity. Dr. Hawley's Escavada Pottery Complex seems quite certainly to be later than the Red Mesa Pottery Complex and earlier than other pottery complexes found in the Chaco. But is there satisfactory evidence that the Escavada Pottery Complex may be regarded as determinant for a total culture complex? Reserve on this point seems proper. It would be hard to make an unimpeachable case for clear differentiation of the inventory of artifacts associated with the Red Mesa Pottery Complex. And the prominence of Exuberant and

Escavada must not obscure the fact that types the floruit of which is given a Pueblo III provenience by Dr. Hawley and trade types assigned in their indigenous areas to dates usually considered to be Pueblo III are present in appreciable numbers in more than one locus and on more than one level. Also, we must be vigilant against an infinite regression in reasoning here. If, because a Pottery Complex appears to precede one or more later Pottery Complexes associated with the great communal houses typical of Pueblo III in the Chaco, we take the first Pottery Complex as the determinant of Pueblo II in the Chaco, it is mere tautology to cite these pottery types as *additional* evidence for a site being Pueblo II. It has been so defined.

Turning to "Houses," Bc 51 does not altogether conform to Roberts' list (1935, p. 11) if one takes it literally. He says, "These dwellings . . . contained from six to fourteen rooms." Bc 51 has more than nineteen rooms. Roberts writes, "Usually at the south or southeast side, detached from the building, was a subterranean ceremonial chamber." One kiva at Bc 51 was at the southwest side, another at the northeast, but, after all, Roberts has qualified here by "usually." Kivas 3, 4, and 5 are not detached from the building, although kiva 5 may have been when built. Land contours may, of course, account for certain variations. There are six kivas at Bc 51. It is more than plausible that not all of these were used simultaneously, but it hardly seems likely that only one was used during a single time interval. This is not written with a view to carping at Roberts' excellent summary, but it seems worthwhile to point out the difficulties when one attempts to apply the minutiae of definitions with precision. Residually, at least, Bc 51 is Pueblo II in house type.

Small difficulties and reservations aside, this much seems certain and important: If we do label Bc 51 as a Pueblo II site, *we are so doing on the basis of two sets of criteria* (Pottery and Houses) *alone.* It is not an assignment on the basis of total cultural complex except, perhaps, in a grossly negative way (that we did not find atlatls or objects of European manufacture, for example.)

To be sure, some of the problems which have been raised disappear if we adopt the newer terminology suggested by Roberts and say simply that this is a Developmental Pueblo site.

A number of workers have pointed out that Pueblo I and Pueblo II were, perhaps, the most dubious categories in the Pecos classification, and the very fact that so few sites have been assigned by their excavators to Pueblo II suggests that this complex may have been an ill-defined or needless category. At best, it has been treated in practice as something between a Platonic Idea and a residual category.

Even, however, if we call Bc 51 Developmental Pueblo, difficulties connected with the time issue remain. The only tree-ring dates obtained from this site fall relatively late, within the time interval during which the large structures across the canyon, almost invariably assigned to Pueblo III, seem to have been occupied. It is only fair to recall that these dates came from a room that had been partially refaced with masonry of a type assigned by Hawley to Pueblo III. It is possible, indeed, that they represent merely the reoccupation of a single room in Bc 51 by persons from across the canyon. On the other hand, even the date of 922+, obtained from Bc 50, is as late as that of cutting dates of logs from Pueblo Bonito, Chetro Ketl, and other "Pueblo III" Chaco sites. The possibility may be granted that logs of earlier dates from the Great Pueblo sites might represent reused logs obtained from abandoned sites of different architectural type. In any case, however, the principal period of occupation of most Bc 51 superstructure rooms falls materially later than 922. In Hawley's opinion "sometime between 975 and 1045" would be a fair estimate as the building period for Bc 51. Unless various supposedly trade pottery types (such as Sunset Red and McElmo) appear in the Chaco considerably earlier than in their putatively indigenous areas, Bc 51 must have been extensively occupied *at least* as late as about 1000.

In short, a minimum statement would be that human beings were almost certainly living in Chetro Ketl and Pueblo Bonito during at least part of the time that Bc 51 was occupied. Now we do not as yet have a complete report on any of the Great Pueblo Chaco ruins, and it would be a mistake to assume too readily that the cultural remains from, say, Pueblo Bonito are altogether homogeneous. Nevertheless, Pueblo Bonito and other Chaco sites of similar architectural type are commonly taken (without qualification) as typical Pueblo III or Great Pueblo.

In other words, during a certain time interval the cultures on the north side of Chaco Canyon were Great Pueblo, while the (at least partially) contemporary ones about a mile away on the south side were Developmental Pueblo.

If this be so, either our definitions fail somehow to correspond to the historical actualities or there is some rather special explanation. One possibility of the latter sort suggests itself. In looking at all of the facts from Bc 50-51, one is presented with two general alternatives of interpretation. There may, on the one hand, have been essentially continuous occupation from the time of the pithouse dwellers forward. The development may have been unbroken and largely autochthonous, and those who last lived in the northern rooms of Bc 51 may have been the lineal descendants, culturally and physically, of the carriers of the Lino Gray pottery complex at Bc 50-51. Some of the archaeologists with whom the writer has discussed the evidence prefer this as the most economical hypothesis. They would also favor the view that there was continuity between the cultures that seem to have existed side by side, for a time, on the north and south sides of the canyon. Apart from architecture-masonry and, perhaps, pottery types, the cultural differences between Chaco Great Pueblo and Developmental Pueblo sites appear, so far as present knowledge takes us, to reduce themselves largely to the greater richness in cultural inventory of the former and to the presence of certain articles (such as the well-known Bonito mosaics) implying a culture of greater complexity where there were more resources and more specialization of labor. On this view, the inhabitants of Bc 51 were either "poor relations" or conservatives who refused to adopt the "progressive" architectural styles of their congeners across the canyon.

This may well be the correct interpretation. But, while there is no proof that Bc 50-51 was not continuously inhabited, there is equally certainly no proof that it was. And it is well known that abandoned habitation sites in the Southwest have often been later reoccupied by quite distinct peoples. Let us therefore boldly develop an alternative hypothesis. Speculation in science is dangerous when it is not clearly designated as such. But frank speculation is sometimes valuable in preventing the closure of the mind to the range of equally possible interpretations of a given set of facts. And if alternative explanations are admitted at a given stage in research, the next stage of investigation will (or should) be planned broadly enough to test the choice. Whereas, if the only possibility envisioned is that which first occurs, the range of investigation may be so narrowed that the advance of knowledge is retarded.

Let me start with a statement that can hardly rise above the level of personal opinion. In terms of what we know about Pueblo cultures, both archaeologically and ethnologically, it does not seem to me altogether plausible, at the moment, that the people who lived in the sites on the south side of the canyon were carriers of precisely the same cultural tradition as the inhabitants of the great communal houses. The very circumstance that the "small house sites" seem to be almost entirely on the *south* side of the canyon may itself be significant. At least, the contemporaneity of the two architectural styles militates against either a purely developmental or a purely physiographic explanation of the localization of the two architectural types. It is possible that at farming colonies one would find certain of the more valuable articles unrepresented, but are these sites far enough away to be farming colonies of the sort known among the modern Pueblo? Moreover, the fact of the numerous ceremonial chambers and the fact that virtually all of the non-perishable artifacts necessary for existence have been found would seem to make possible the inference that the dwellers led an essentially independent life. I am aware, of course, that the material cultures of the modern Hopi towns of First and Third Mesas, for example, are not identical in all particulars. But I know of no case where different contemporaneous villages of the same "tribe" had differing major architectural and masonry styles or such marked disparity in richness of total cultural inventory.

Another guess than that the inhabitants of Bc 51 were the "poor relations" of the people who were the carriers of the Pueblo III culture might be that they were (perhaps in part) migrants from another region, representatives of a related but somewhat less advanced cultural heritage drawn to the Chaco by the prosperity of its inhabitants, or, conceivably, by the reputation for magnificence and power of their ceremonialism or by the protection that these populous towns could offer (or by a combination of any or all of these factors). If we may judge at all from documented Pueblo history, such a movement in a time of stress or trouble is altogether in accord with the configuration of Pueblo behavior patterns. Roberts and others have suggested migrations to the Chaco from southwestern Colorado from fairly early times on. Dutton (1938, p. 94) has suggested this interpretation for Unit III at Leyit Kin. Such a possibility for Bc 51 gains slightly in credibility from the fact that McElmo and other wares, supposedly indigenous to that region, appear to be appreciably more prominent at Bc 51 than at Chetro Ketl, the only Chaco Great Pueblo site from which the pottery has been reported in detail. This is sheer speculation, but it is speculation that will permit of some testing in the light of future evidence. Surely, the apparently synchronous presence within less than a mile of one another of sites that would be assigned to Great Pueblo and Developmental Pueblo requires explanation. The almost contiguous presence of migrants from some distance presents no circumstance contrary to what we know of Pueblo history. In fact, the Laguna group at Isleta, the Tewa on First Mesa, and the plausibility of Keresan-speakers in the Jeddito Valley make it altogether conceivable that the inhabitants of Bc 51 may even have spoken a different language from the dwellers in, say, Pueblo Bonito.

Probably the single fact of greatest general import that has emerged thus far from the Bc 50-51 excavations is that the various stages recognized by the Pecos classification (and very commonly referred to as "periods") do not, necessarily, represent separate and clear-cut time periods, *even in the same geographical locality*. Here it can hardly be merely a question of a brief overlap. Tree-ring dates and pottery types both make it almost certain that cultures that most archaeologists would designate as Developmental and Great Pueblo existed for a considerable time within a very short distance of one another.

In view of this fact (and of other difficulties that have been mentioned), one is inclined to wonder whether the Pecos classification has not, after all, outlived its major usefulness. That it has been useful in the ordering and systematization of the multifarious data of Southwestern archaeology no sensible person would question. But we must remember, as Whitehead has so often reminded us, that a classification is, at best, "a half-way house." A classification is useful so long as the facts fall without violence into it. As soon, however, as their greater bulk, greater complexity, or greater subtleties of discrimination make the classification a Procrustean bed into which the maimed and helpless facts are forced, the classification should be abandoned or radically modified. As Kidder (1936, p. xviii, ftnt. 3) has observed, ". . . our investigation has now reached a point at which formal classifications, such as the Pecos nomenclature are not only of lessening value, but are often, as in the present case, positively misleading." At very least the Pecos classification should take explicit account of the differing periods of development in different areas and of varying genetic sequences in various regions of Anasazi culture. To be sure, the concrete difficulties that have been pointed out here arise out of the facts from but a single locality.

The Colton (1939) classification would have the great advantage (for the situation under discussion) of not exaggerating the distinctions between Bc 50-51 and Leyit Kin on the south side of Chaco Canyon and Pueblo Bonito and Chetro Ketl, almost directly opposite on the north and almost certainly lived in during the same period that considerable portions of the smaller sites were occupied. Under the Pecos classification one is compelled to assign the two sets of cultures to utterly different categories. This seems a distortion of the facts. Under Colton's system, they would, presumably, be classified merely as different foci of the Chaco branch. This distinction would be analogous to that between modern Pueblo "tribes." Since, for all of the impressive differences in architecture-masonry and in some other features, the two sets of inventories show such an overwhelming number of artifacts and articles of substance in common that this terminology would seem to adhere more closely to the contrast given by the data. This is congruent with one of the generalities that appeared from the distributional analyses: cultural similarities and continuities in the same geographical area are most impressive. In addition to some striking differences, the number of close parallels between the artifacts of Shabik'eshchee and Bc 51 is rather amazing when one comes to total them up. The Colton system will also, doubtless, make it easier for us to keep clearly in mind the fact that single sites do not necessarily represent a single time interval or a single homogeneous culture. Our minds are prone to utilize tags that relegate inconvenient complexities into the background. It is so easy to say "Pueblo Bonito is a Pueblo III site" and be done with it. The "component" and "focus" terminology seems likely to bring out more clearly the probably somewhat intricate cultural history of such sites than does the unilinear and limited set of categories of the Pecos classification.

That Bc 50 (superstructure at least), Bc 51, and Leyit Kin (Units I and II at least) would be considered simply as components of a single focus appears probable. It seems likely that some rooms at Bc 50 were built before most of Bc 51, and there is no proof that any rooms in the two mounds were ever lived in during precisely the same years. But of cultural differences that appear to be consistent and significant there are few. Almost all distinctions are of this sort: no twilled ring baskets were found in Bc 51 and no coiled baskets in Bc 50; no awls of class 1a were found in Bc 51, although several were found in Bc 50; one object of antler was found in Bc 51; the palettes found in Bc 50 were larger. The proportion of extended burials may be significantly higher in Bc 51.

Now, clearly, such variations depend so much on negative evidence and upon accidents of the sampling process that no case for cultural differentiation can be built upon them. Perhaps the evidence affords some slight indication of variation in cultural fashions that may well be correlated with the hypothesis that the period of floruit of Bc 51 was somewhat later than that of Bc 50. But an archaeologist would be hard put indeed to distinguish random samples of the objects found at the two mounds. Almost the only contrast that seems perfectly clear-cut and indicative of a distinct cultural pattern is the consistent presence of turkey bones behind the fire screens in all of the kivas of Bc 50. The range of variation, with respect to Leyit Kin, appears slightly greater, perhaps because of its possibly more heterogeneous character. But the same general conclusion applies.

Throughout this section emphasis has been laid—probably overmuch—upon terminology and classification. A classificatory nomenclature is indispensable if we are not to become lost in a welter of isolated facts. This consideration must not, however, be allowed to obscure the all important fact that we are dealing with the products of the activity of human beings. Human activity notably fails to exhibit exceptionless uniformities. In concluding this discussion of the position of Bc 51, stress should be laid upon the range of diversity exhibited within this limited collection of material. Consider the kiva plans. How far, in respect of individual features, do they rigidly conform to a single pattern? Even the southward orientation of the ventilator shafts—which Dr. Kidder (p. 597) has considered "a most stringent ceremonial requirement" within the San Juan area—is far from constant. Surely all classifications can but, at best, express modal tendencies and must be used purely heuristically, with constant awareness that they are most crude categorizations of the human acts we are trying to reconstruct.

BIRD AND MAMMAL

REMAINS

Bird and Mammal

BONES OF ALL THE MAMMALS and birds found at Bc 50 were also found at Bc 51; in addition, a few bones of elk *(Cervus canadensis)*, ground squirrel *(Citellus tridecemlineatus parvus)*, hawk *(Buteo* sp.—probably Red-Tailed), and scaled quail *(Callepepla squamata)* were discovered. The percentages of the 3,824 identifiable bone remains were so extraordinarily similar (save for appreciably greater representation of the golden eagle) that publication of the tabulation does not seem worth while.

The distribution of the bones offers some features of interest. Less than 500 identifiable pieces came from the refuse mound. Metaposials (especially metatarsals) and teeth of deer and antelope were especially prominent, along with a fair number of rabbit pelves and some deer and antelope ribs. Some bird and

1939a Reprinted by permission of the publisher from Clyde Kluckhohn and Paul Reiter, *Preliminary Report on the 1937 Excavations, Bc 50-51, Chaco Canyon, New Mexico.* University of New Mexico Bulletin, Anthropological Series 3, No. 2.

mammal bones came from the fill of all rooms, but the northern rooms yielded very few, and a number of these were bones of rodents that were very possibly not food remains. Only rooms 16, 17, 19, 20, 21, and 23 afforded more than thirty identifiable bones. It was in these rooms and in the kivas that this class of remains were concentrated. From room 16 (sub) alone came more than 900, nearly 90 per cent rabbit pelves, scapulae, and long bones but with a few deer long bones, ribs, and vertebrae. (Could this collection of rabbit bones possibly be connected with a communal rabbit hunt?) More than a third of the total (1,419) bird and animal bones came from kiva 3, with close to 20 per cent being of deer and antelope. This greater percentage for these two animals (average in the whole collection of 11.9 per cent) was maintained in all the kivas. From this fact (plus the generally larger representation of animal bones in the kivas) it is tempting to infer ritual feasting in the kivas (possibly of men's societies, conceivably connected with hunting?). The antelope skull in the ventilator tunnel of kiva 1 is possibly a relic of such a feast, but one also recalls the careful preservation of the skull after ritual hunting in certain modern pueblos.

Turkey remains (both bones and shells) were also prominent in all kivas, although not found between fire screen and ventilator as in Bc 50. However, only two rooms failed to give evidence of the turkey, and bones and shells were also frequently found in the refuse mound, although there was no evidence of the burial of these birds. The precise function of the turkey in Pueblo culture remains obscure. Elsie Parsons has recently suggested that possibly the turkey was once a sacrificial bird, as in Mexico. It is not eaten by some present-day Pueblos.

A Note on Comparative Distribution

From a survey of the literature it would appear that Southwestern archaeologists have been rather cavalier in documenting this class of remains. Out of 112 reports (which reported rather fully on most classes of objects found) seventy-four failed completely to list mammal and bird remains. In many of the others the information was rather incomplete and imprecise. Hibben,

M. R. Harrington, Mera, and Steward are honorable exceptions in that they go beyond stating the presence of the bird or mammal and give exact figures on relative representation.

To be sure, the record—so far as we know it at present—appears to be a comparatively complacent one. Jackrabbit, rabbit, and deer seem, as Hough has observed, to have been rather consistently the staple animal foods of the prehistoric inhabitants of the Southwest. Prairie dog and other rodents, some antelope, and fewer mountain sheep bones are also reported in almost all cases. Elk remains were discovered in four Chaco sites, in the Piedra region, on Mesa Verde, at Winona Village, and in the Chama Valley ("possibly"); bison at several Texas sites, Pecos, southwestern New Mexico, the Swarts ruin, a cave at the rear of the Tularosa cliffhouse, the Mogollon region, Snaketown, and sites in the Great Salt Lake area. At first glance these occurrences of the rarer animals seem to reflect only geographic position. Several of the cases, however, perhaps mean either a different physical environment at the time in question or the equally important cultural fact of hunting expeditions to distant points.

Recent detailed studies of the hunting methods of contemporary Southwestern peoples have clearly demonstrated how much social and ceremonial organization enters into the procurement of the birds and animals they eat or otherwise use. Relative figures from different sites or proportions of remains of animals that are more difficult to capture or that could presumably only be obtained at a distance would, taken in the context of other data, sometimes permit of guarded comparative inferences on social organization. Similarly, only when numbers are recorded in full can we make other than impressionistic comparisons as to the relative importance of hunting in the basic economy of various cultures or periods. Haury has suggested that the Mogollon peoples relied more heavily on game than did the Pueblo, and the Hohokam less than either of these. Haury has also observed that deer bones bulked less large at Snaketown than in pueblo sites. Guernsey and Kidder found deer and antelope bones rare in their northeastern Arizona sites, with mountain sheep quite common.

The possibility also exists that presence or consistent absence of animal remains would aid in establishing cultural similarities or continuities through tie-ups with ritual prohibitions or observances. Bear hunting, for example, is practiced for food at Jemez, and bear paws are part of the equipment of Keresan medicine societies. But the killing of bears is strictly forbidden at Isleta, and bears were probably killed by the Hopi only under necessity, although their emergence legend refers to the eating of bear flesh as a normal practice. Ruling out a few reported occurrences from cave sites, I have noted bear remains only from Pueblo Bonito and Chetro Ketl, the Riana Ruin, and Awatovi. (Fewkes thought that this bear skeleton represented a carcass awaiting consumption at the time the town was burned.) Mountain lion, parts of which are also used ritually by present-day Pueblos, has also been reported but seldom from excavations: claws from Pueblo Bonito, bones from northeastern Arizona and from an Apache Creek site in the Upper Gila area. To what extent this negative evidence rests upon lack of full identification or publication of remains is an interesting question.

As to bird remains, turkey and Golden Eagle bones have been discovered in the vast majority of later sites. Turkey remains were relatively scarce at Snaketown, and Haury questions whether the bird was domesticated by the carriers of Hohokam and Mogollon cultures. Most authorities seem to feel that the introduction of the domesticated turkey is a fairly definite culture-period diagnostic. My colleague, Dr. Brew, informs me that, although turkey bones are very plentiful in later sites on Alkali Ridge, they do not appear in the earlier levels. Whether the turkey and other birds whose remains are found rather frequently were generally eaten remains a disputed question. The smaller birds identified most often have bright-colored plumage, and the fondness of contemporary Pueblos for their feathers is well known. Hargrave, however, apparently has evidence that turkey, quail, hawks, owls, coots, and robins were eaten in the Flagstaff region.

Burial of birds and animals is also an interesting feature of this class of evidence. The burial of dogs, macaws, and turkeys is too familiar to require citation. Morris has reported the burial of a badger. The eagle cemeteries of the modern Hopi are well known, but I have not discovered archaeological documentation.

5   *NAVAHO WOMEN'S*

KNOWLEDGE OF THEIR

SONG CEREMONIALS

O NE ASPECT OF INVESTIGATION in ethnology and
social anthropology that has been (at least until
rather lately) scandalously neglected is that of
participation. We have been too often content with purely formalized descriptions that give, in effect, simply the ideology of
the culture—perhaps as conceived by a very few informants.
The highly significant question of "goodness of fit" between
theory and practice has almost entirely been passed over. A
male Indian of a particular tribe is supposed to follow such and
such patterns of behavior toward relatives whom he calls by
such and such a kinship term. It is very interesting and very
important to know this, but we can hardly hope to attain an
intellectual grasp of the behaviors in question unless we also
have concrete data indicating what proportion of the actual
individuals in the tribe in question follow out more or less the

1938b Reprinted by permission of the publishers from Clyde Kluckhohn,
"Navaho Women's Knowledge of Their Song Ceremonials," *El
Palacio*, Vol. 45, pp. 87-92.

letter of the theory, what proportion deviate somewhat (and in what directions), and what proportion disregard the ideal patterns almost entirely. We have too many statements of the form "The Navaho do thus and so." Now such rough-and-ready generalizations have little scientific meaning unless we are given controls—some indication of how many concrete observations formed the basis for such statements of uniformities. We require abundant documentation in roughly this form: "Under such and such specified conditions I observed (or was told by so and so) that Navahos A, B, C, . . . , X acted thus, while Navahos 1, 2, 3, . . . , 38 responded to the relevant stimulus in this slightly different fashion."

In short, if we are to deal with the highly meaningful question of participation in a way that is reducible to actual human behaviors, generalizations must be given a quantitative basis. In respect to any particular phase of behavior the range of variation, the frequency distributions, and something crudely equivalent to the "standard deviation" of statistics must be indicated—even though in many cases the data can perhaps provide only the roughest of first approximations to these categories. In a paper entitled "Participation in Ceremonials in a Navaho Community" (1938c) I attempted to supply this sort of information for the Ramah Navaho in so far as "ceremonial" practice is concerned. To some extent "Navaho Classification of Their Song Ceremonials" (1938a) by Wyman and myself does the same thing as far as "ceremonial" theory is concerned. But there is at least one important gap that prevents this study from being considered as an adequate treatment of the distribution of "ceremonial" knowledge among the Ramah Navaho: The data were gathered almost exclusively from male informants. To be quite candid, at the time of writing the monograph with Wyman I would have been able to make almost wholly unsubstantiated guesses as to the extent to which the women of the Ramah band would have been able to show independently the knowledge we recorded for their husbands, sons, and kinsmen.

During this past summer, therefore, I took occasion to question systematically on this point forty different women and twenty unmarried girls (out of a total of roughly ninety married women and 120 unmarried girls in this group). Ten of the

women were putatively past fifty years of age, twenty were
between roughly fifty and thirty, and ten were probably under
thirty. The girls were all probably less than eighteen years of
age and more than seven. I believe I am justified in stating that
the individuals interviewed represent a fair sample from the
points of view of economic status, geographical location, and
relation to male ceremonial practitioners. The interviews were
carried out on three successive days in widely separated hogans.
Hence the possibility that results were materially influenced by
women who had been questioned "talking the matter over" with
women yet to be questioned is virtually excluded. Procedure
was formulated, not with the hope of throwing light on subtleties of psychology (the variations in affect toward various
ceremonials), but rather in the direction of answering simple
questions on the basis of straightforward and standardized
interrogation. Each woman or girl was interviewed alone or in
the presence of other women only (the latter was the case in
nearly 90 per cent of instances). If other women were present,
they were requested not to participate in the discussion. The
person being questioned was asked first to name all ceremonials
of which she remembered ever having heard; she was given as
much time as she wished to complete her list. She was then asked
if she could group any or all of these into larger or smaller
categories and to mention any sort of affiliations she believed
existed between any two or more ceremonials. Finally, after her
remarks on this subject were concluded, the observer mentioned
to the informant every ceremonial appearing in the table that
she had failed to list and asked if she had perhaps heard of it
after all.

The general statements that can be made after an inductive
analysis of the resultant data may be expressed quite briefly.
(The point of reference throughout is the "Summary Classification" published in Wyman and Kluckhohn.) The average number of ceremonials mentioned by the women is seventeen (out
of fifty-eight possibilities), the modal number is fifteen (five
cases), and the range is between seven and thirty-one. If the
women and the girls are lumped, the mean drops to eleven. No
girl named more than ten ceremonials, and the average for girls
is six. Girls strongly tended to name merely the ceremonials

most frequently performed by and for members of this group. It is likely, however, that these figures are somewhat lower than the actual facts warrant because of excessive shyness on the part of most of the young girls questioned.

There is, in general, distinct correlation between number of ceremonials listed and age group. The mean for the ten women who were more than fifty is twenty-seven; that for the group between thirty and fifty, sixteen; that for the youngest group, eleven. In only two individual instances are there exceptions to this general trend. The evidence likewise indicates correlation between number listed and close relationship to male ceremonial practitioners. In all save three cases the highest rankings within each age group were all attained by wives or daughters of singers. For all practical purposes, no girls and no women, except members of the oldest age group and wives and daughters of singers, showed any knowledge of the system of classification of ceremonials that male members of the group had evidenced. Only two women, presumably past sixty and married to singers, showed other than very rudimentary familiarity with classification and principles of classification. There is a much sharper break between ceremonial knowledge of men and women in respect to affiliations of ceremonials than in respect to awareness of existence of ceremonials.

The mentioning of the names of other ceremonials (in Navaho) by the investigator did not greatly alter the figures, although the mean for all women rose from seventeen to twenty. There are some rather uniform tendencies in the ceremonial knowledge of which women professed complete ignorance even after it had been disclosed. No woman appeared to have heard of Prostitution Way, Way to Remove Somebody's Paralysis, or Gesture Dance. Only three women had heard of Earth Way, four of Awl Way, and six of Mountain Peak Blessing Way. None had heard of more than two branches of Night Way. Women were (as might have been anticipated) particularly weak on knowledge of war and hunting ceremonials. Women tended to be vague on the existence of male and female (and other) branches of all save the most common chants. In general, women showed less familiarity than men of the same grades with extinct or obsolescent ceremonials. In sum, and broadly speaking, their knowledge did not extend to the more esoteric peripheries. On the other hand, it should be mentioned that one old woman mentioned "*Big* Hand-Trembling Way" for the first time in my experience, and subsequent investigation revealed this to be a fairly well-established locution. Another woman of middle age (the daughter of an old singer) gave valuable and hitherto unknown information on the affiliations of Reared in Earth Way.

By and large, the knowledge of ceremonial theory on the part of Navaho women in this area fits very well with the facts on participation by women in ceremonial practice. There are no women singers and curers in this group. Nor do women join in the singing or assist in the making of sandpaintings, although both of these practices have been observed elsewhere in the Navaho country on the part of women who were neither singers nor curers (nor learning to be). Participation by women of the Ramah region in both the theory and practice of their "religious" system is markedly less (age group for age group) than participation by men. Nevertheless, they are by no means completely ignorant of ceremonial ideology. Their knowledge is, in fact, somewhat more impressive than their participation, which is limited to attendance at ceremonials and to carrying out hand-trembling divination.

6 SOME SOCIAL AND PERSONAL ASPECTS OF NAVAHO CEREMONIAL PATTERNS

"AN ACCUMULATION OF MINUTE DETAILS, however silly it may appear, is the only correct means to reach the fundamental truths."—*Letter of A. F. Bandelier to L. H. Morgan, February 28, 1874.*

Here and there in the published literature on Navaho ceremonials one finds a suggestive detail or an illuminating general statement bearing on the relationship of ceremonial organization to social organization, but as yet no systematic analysis of any body of data from this point of view. This paper will supplement my "Participation in Ceremonials in a Navaho Community" (1938c) in the direction of providing an account of the "religious" behaviors of the Ramah Navaho. The treatment will center upon the learning of ceremonials, the family and clan affiliation of practitioners, their teachers, patients, and those

1939d Reprinted by permission of the publishers from Clyde Kluckhohn, "Some Personal and Social Aspects of Navaho Ceremonial Patterns," *Harvard Theological Review,* Vol. 32, pp. 67-82.

attending ceremonials, but it will be convenient to incorporate also a few details bearing on individual status.

No circumstance reflects more dramatically the interdependence of the ceremonial and social organization than the fact that if a singer or curer sings over his own wife, their future relationship is perforce governed by the rules regulating the behavior between men and women of the same clan. Nor is this simply theory. In the Ramah cases where a singer did sing over his own wife the marriage was immediately and permanently dissolved. Just because it is so unusual, so "dangerous," for a man to sing over his own wife, such a ceremonial is thought of as unusually potent. When, therefore, a singer's wife is seriously or chronically ill and other singers have treated her without success, her own husband may, as a last desperate attempt, agree to conduct a ceremonial himself. Medical ethics in our society dictate, of course, that a physician not treat the members of his own immediate family. But it is not an altogether analogous practice that operates here, for a man frequently sings over his own children and over the children of his sisters. Moreover, there is the further prescription that a singer may not later marry a woman who has at any time been his patient, and I have no record of any case where this occurred. Indeed, the Navahos recognize the general principle involved. One informant (12)[1] stated, "After a man has sung over someone, those two must act afterward just like two people in the same clan."[2] Highly similar remarks were volunteered by five other informants. Several informants affirmed that this held for diagnosis also, but I have three cases where husband or wife diagnosed for the other partner without separation ensuing. My inference, on the basis of general knowledge of the culture, is that the theory is applicable, but that, since diagnosis is regarded as somewhat less serious business, the principle is violated more lightly.

---

1. The numbers referring to informants are the same as those used in Wyman and Kluckhohn (1938a) and as used in subsequent publications and in this book.

2. One is reminded of the fact that curing societies in many Pueblos add to their membership the individuals whom they treat. Dr. Elsie Clews Parsons has called my attention to the fact that at Zuñi marriage with ceremonial fathers and their families is forbidden.

Ceremonial Practitioners

There are four singers, two practitioners of Blessing Way who are not singers, and thirteen "curers" in the area at present. There are also sixteen diagnosticians, but, since this rite is not transmitted by formal instruction, it is not necessary to deal with them further at this point.

To be noted here is the fact that all six of the principal ceremonialists are related biologically and by clan in a variety of different dimensions. Dick, Bidaga, and Sam are full brothers. Jake is the son of the father's clan sister of these three brothers, and Jake's father is a fellow clansman of their mother. Solao's father was the biological brother of the paternal grandmother of the three brothers and therefore also a fellow clansman and biological relative of Jake. Rafael's father was also from this same clan and likewise a biological relation of Jake's. Rafael's mother was later Jake's wife. Similarly, as will be seen later, most of the curers are closely related to each other and to the principal ceremonialists in ways that will be specified.

The Learning of Ceremonials

Let me now take up a detailed case history of the learning of ceremonials by members of this group. I present these data rather fully, because no comparable set has been published and because they not only constitute a basis for inductions as to social and ceremonial interconnections but are also pertinent to other ethnological questions.

Dick Pino (1) is about sixty years old and is a member of Clan 37.[3] About thirty-five years ago he began to learn the

---

3. The numerals refer to the list in Reichard (1928) and are used to avoid expensive typesetting of phonetic characters. The differentiation of clans rather than their names would seem to be in point here, and the interested specialist can check very readily. This work of Reichard's also contains (p. 146) some useful data on the learning of ceremonials.

Chiricahua Apache Wind Way from his father's clan sister's son (Clan 22—same as informant's father, of course) who lived north of Gallup but practiced frequently in the Ramah area. It was about five years before he was considered competent to conduct the ceremonial himself. The learning was carried out mainly through attendance upon the teacher when he was singing in the Ramah region (and twice by assisting the singer near the latter's own home), but there were also a number of occasions when the teacher gave him private and individual instruction. Gradually he was given more important responsibilities as an assistant. Parts of the ceremonial that he had learned completely he conducted independently as a "curer." The singer conducted the ceremonial over the learner four times, twice in winter and twice in summer. This is called "for the purpose of making him holy." One informant (2) stated that where there were male and female versions of a ceremonial the prospective singer ought to have both sung over him, even though he planned to sing but the one himself. Finally, on one occasion, when the old teacher was approached by one of those present at the last night of a Chiricahua Apache Wind Way to sing for a member of the latter's family, the singer said, "Why don't you get this younger man here who has been helping me? He can do it all right now."

Dick Pino does not remember precisely what he paid for his instruction and training but said it included "one horse, some money, things at different times. Then I paid him what I got the first time I sung by myself—you always have to do that, and I gave him part of what I got every time after that for quite a while."

Excerpts from two discussions of learning by singers will supplement the above case history. Jake (2) observed:

The singer knows which of these who are following him around know things. Sometimes he will ask them questions and take what they say. The people who come to the sing hear this. Sometimes the singer tells the people that a man who is helping him knows it all. So the people decide to ask him to sing for that. . . .

When you learn a chant from a man, you must always keep it exactly like you were taught. Each man must follow his own teacher exactly all his life. That's why you see different singers doing things

a little bit different. Every man is sticking to what his teacher
taught him.

You get lots of practice. Even when your teacher sings over you,
you sing along with it yourself. Every other time [in chants, not
in Blessing Way rites] the patient just keeps still and lets the singer
and the others sing for him. But when a man is learning, he sings
even when he is a patient. That way, pretty soon he gets so that
when he sings one song, another comes right up in front of him. It's
just like when you are riding along, looking a long ways. First one
thing comes up, then another. That's the way they learn it.

The following remarks are from comments of Solao (3):

You can learn a sing by parts. You can learn just a few songs and
part of the story. You can just get the medicine without the songs.
Lots of people do it that way. Some singers will give the songs without the story. It really isn't right, though. The story always goes
with the songs and the medicines. That's the only way you can
remember it all just like it's supposed to be.

There is actually a good deal of informal learning of songs,
medicines, and parts of ceremonial behaviors. Indeed, many of
the adult men of this group, whether singers or curers or not,
have varying amounts of such knowledge and are in demand as
"helpers." In general, however, anyone who attempts to conduct
ceremonials without having entered into a somewhat formalized
teacher-learner relationship meets with disapproval on the part
of recognized practitioners and distrust on the part of people
generally.

The material presented thus far is so representative of the
practice and theory of learning and acceptance that hereafter
I shall mention only important divergences from these patterns.
The only general qualification to be made is that in the case of
learning "blackenings" (portions of Evil Way ceremonials in
which the patient's body is blackened) or other excerpts from
ceremonials the practice is that the teacher conducts the ceremonial over the learner only once. (Statements as to the theory
here involved were conflicting, being mainly apparent rationalizations after the facts.)

At about the time he began to sing the Chiricahua Apache
Wind Way Dick Pino started to learn the Life Way, Female

Shooting Branch; Evil Way, Female Shooting Branch; and Shooting Way, Female Branch (including the Upper Regions Side and Dark Circle of Branches Phase), together with various supplementary ceremonies from a biologically unrelated singer of Clan 35 who lived in the Two Wells region but also practiced frequently near Ramah. This singer's clan is, however, "linked" to Dick's. After about three years Dick Pino was called upon to conduct Life Way, but it was "about seven years before I started to do the other two by myself." Once again Dick made no pretence at remembering exactly the fees and "royalties" he had paid, saying:

That old man taught me for little because he was a very good friend. I gave him a horse and a bridle and a few other little things, I don't remember what. After I started to sing by myself I gave him some blankets.

At various times (thirty to fifteen years ago) Dick learned many of the songs of Blessing Way from his father. He has not learned the whole ceremonial systematically, but he knows enough to conduct the girl's adolescence rite. Twelve years ago Dick Pino learned the blackening forms of Moving Up Way and of Evil Way, Male Shooting Branch, from his mother's brother. Learning these required only attendance at "eight or ten" performances of the ceremonials and "a few hours extra with my maternal uncle alone." No fee was paid except for conducting the ceremonials over the learner once. Future statements that no fee was paid are to be understood as "no fee other than that for the ceremonial or ceremonials conducted by teacher over learner."

Jake (2) is about eighty-five years old and is a member of Clan 22. When he was in his early twenties, he learned Flint Way, Female Branch, and two blackenings from his mother's brother (the same who taught Dick Pino Chiricahua Apache Wind Way). He began to practice the blackenings within about two years, but it was about ten years before he knew the legend and all the songs of Flint Way properly.

Some people can learn the songs, some can't. Finally my maternal uncle took a dry ear of corn, and every time he sings one song he takes off a kernel and puts it in a cup. Then he got an unmarried girl who was related to me to grind these kernels up into mush. He put this in a medicine basket and let it cool. Then he sung and while he was singing he put some of that mush in my mouth. He did this four times while he sang a special song. Then he made me eat the rest of the mush as fast as I could with all five fingers. After that I didn't have much more trouble.

He paid no fee. When he was "nearly forty," he acquired Evil Way, Female Shooting Branch, and Life Way, Female Shooting Branch, from the same singer of Clan 35 who also taught Dick Pino these ceremonials. Jake learned them in "just two or three years" but only learned part of the legends. He paid "a lot" but was unable to be specific.

Solao (3) is a member of Clan 18 and must be very close to ninety years old. When he was about thirty-five, he learned Flint Way, Male Branch, from a man of Clan 17 (this is "linked" to Clan 18) who lived in the Two Wells Area; he paid "a horse, ten sheep, and some cash." At roughly the same period he learned Blessing Way from an unrelated man (Clan 35) who lived near Tohaci, paying two deerskins, a pair of moccasins, and some silver. Some five years later he learned a blackening from an unrelated man, paying a pair of pants, a deerskin, and some money.

The fourth singer in the area, Sam Pino (4), is the younger brother of Dick Pino. He learned the Chiricahua Apache Wind Way from the same man who taught Dick, and Sam paid comparable fees. Sam is at present studying the Shooting Way, Female Branch, with Dick and frequently assists him. He gives his older brother a basket or some other gift from time to time.

Practitioners of Blessing Way are not strictly "singers," because the Blessing Way rite does not include chanting to a rattle. Nevertheless, those who can conduct a complete Blessing Way are regarded as full-fledged ceremonialists—in contrast to the "curers," who can carry out only portions of chants or rites. In addition to Solao, there are two practitioners of Blessing Way. Bidaga (5) learned the rite from his father and paid no fee. Rafael (16) learned from his father's younger brother, who lived near Mariana Lake but stayed with Rafael for nearly a year while teaching Rafael. Besides food and clothing during this period, Rafael gave his uncle five unbroken horses and a Navaho rug.

Coming now to the curers (with whom I shall deal more summarily), Jaciano (6), Margadito (5), and Julio (17) are all sons of Jake and members of Clan 51a, but none of them has learned all the "medicine" of their father. Jaciano acquired Evil Way, Female Shooting Branch; Life Way, Female Shooting Branch; and one blackening from Jake, paying no fees. In addition, he has learned the nine-day form of the Shooting Way, Female Branch, from an unrelated member of Clan 32 who lives near Crownpoint. He has also just finished learning the Chiricahua Apache Wind Way. He began his studies with a deceased member of the Ramah group (Clan 35) and finished with a teacher (a fellow clansman and distant biological relative) who lives near Thoreau. Margadito has learned from his father portions only (and no legends) of the Shooting Way, Female Branch; Life Way, Female Shooting Branch; and one blackening. Julio has learned only a part of the Shooting Way, Female Branch. Neither Julio nor Margadito made any payment to their father, who was their only teacher. Richard Pino (34) has learned most of the Chiricahua Apache Wind Way; part of the Shooting Way, Female Branch; and one blackening from his father's brother (Dick Pino) and has paid no fees. Jose Martin (13), a member of Clan 35, has learned part of the Life Way, Female Shooting Branch, from Jake, who is unrelated to him but is a clan relative of Jose's wives. He has also learned two sandpaintings (and attendant songs and ceremonials) of the Shooting Way, Female Branch, from an unrelated member of his wife's father's clan (22) who lives in the Two Wells Country. Two half brothers (same mother and their fathers were brothers)—Oyez (22), Clan 22, and Frank Navaho (23), Clan 22 —have learned portions of Hand-Trembling Way from the latter's father, Clan 17, who lives in the Danoff region; neither made any payment. Sellio (18), Clan 51a, learned portions of the Life Way, Female Shooting Branch, from a deceased, unrelated member (Clan 35) of the Ramah group. The teacher's clan is that of Sellio's wife. Sellio paid him the horse that he received for conducting his first ceremonial. Felipe (8), Clan 51a, learned part of the Chiricahua Apache Wind Way from a brother living near Thoreau (the same who taught Jaciano).

Felipe paid his brother the fees for his first ceremonials. For the same consideration he learned a blackening from a brother of Jake (Felipe's father was the son of Jake's sister; Jake's wives were the sisters of Felipe's mother) who lived near Crownpoint. Patricio Garcia (19), Clan 18, learned the same blackening from Felipe (his sister's husband) and paid him his first fees. Frank Martin (20), Clan 37, learned a blackening from a deceased maternal uncle of his mother and taught this blackening to an affinal relative, George Beaver (21), Clan 1, who turned over his first fees. Acho (24) has learned part of the Shooting Way, Female Branch, without any formalized relation to any teacher but simply by "picking it up from his stepfather, Dick Pino." Dick commented upon this:

A year ago I was singing Shooting Way, Female Branch over at Sam's place. That boy, he was there but he got scared and started to shake. He went out and went away. He got worse during the night —got stiff, his arms bent in, his hands shut tight, his legs twisted. Two men went over and brought him back inside where I was singing. They put him beside Calladito's son whom I was singing over. Then he got better. . . . People who start singing that way without studying with a singer and paying him, they always get sick. If they don't get sick right away, they get sick when they get older and have to straighten that up themselves. The best way is to learn from a singer the right way.

These are the facts from this area. There are two questions of theory that, while having little or no bearing on the interpretation of this particular set of data, are relevant to our general understanding. A number of practitioners remarked that in the past some ceremonials were connected with particular clans. For example, seven informants independently mentioned (and four independently disagreed) that only men from clans whose names include "water" were supposed to do Blessing Way. Three others referred chants of the God-Impersonators Subgroup to the "red" clans (most especially members of Clan 20). One singer (cc—from near Tohaci) commented on the virtual disappearance of correlation between clan and ceremonial:

The trouble is that singers teach their songs to their sons no matter what clan they belong to. So things get all mixed up and aren't the way they were meant to be.

To some very slight extent other factors of selection are operative. A person who has narrowly escaped being struck by lightning is held to be peculiarly qualified to learn the chants (especially the Shooting chants) for which the lightnings are considered etiological factors.

SUMMARY

The data on the teacher's relationship to the learner (by individuals rather than total number of ceremonials) are shown in Table I. Neither the interview data nor the table is decisive as to whether the learner most often affiliates himself with a teacher on the basis of previous personal connection or on the basis of interest in a particular ceremonial, but both sources of information strongly suggest that the former prevails more frequently.

TABLE I

Father	6
Father's brother	3
Other biological relatives in father's clan . . .	3
Stepfather	1
Mother's brother	3
Biological relative in own clan	1
Member of linked clan	2
Affinal relative (including wife's clansmen and wife's father's clansmen)	5
Unrelated	6

Generalizations that may be inferred from the above table do not necessarily apply to other groups of Navaho, but, lacking comparative information, let us at least draw some conclusions for the Ramah Navaho.

1. Close biological-sociological relationship appears to be a determinant of the transmission of ceremonial knowledge in more than three cases out of four.

2. The father's side is more prominent than the mother's.

3. Payment for instruction, like payment for ceremonials, varies with kinship and other factors. The nearest approach to a stand-

ard fee is in the case of learning a blackening or some other portion of a ceremonial where (unless the teacher was a father or a mother's brother) the payment was uniformly the first fee received by the learner. Although some payment is regarded as prerequisite to the efficacy of a ceremonial, no payment is required from father or mother's brother for ceremonial instruction.

4. There is little indication that clan, as such, is a factor of importance in the initiation of the teacher-learner relationship. However, informants commented to the effect that after the ceremonial has been learned, the two individuals stand to each other in a relationship "something like clan."

5. Ceremonials not infrequently are learned from persons to whom there is no biological or formalized sociological relationship. To questions of the sort, "From whom does one learn a ceremonial?" replies follow this general pattern: "From anyone. Usually from a relative, but it can be from anyone."

Divination

A rather striking feature of Navaho culture to which attention has never been explicitly drawn is the contrast between the manner in which ceremonials are learned and the manner in which the practice of hand-trembling divination is begun.[4] The former falls into the "priestly" tradition—there is formal instruction in a system of abundant lore. The latter falls into the "shamanistic" tradition—there is no formal instruction and a minimum of lore; it is a question of a direct "gift." It is also interesting that while

---

4. On this general question, cf. Goodwin (1938, p. 37 and *passim*). In the lore of Navaho chants there are but a few hints of direct contact with the supernatural of the shamanistic type. Hill (1938, p. 74) in discussing the Rain Chant gives one of the most striking of these: "During a ceremony, the individuals in a hogan were supposed to sit and think hard, stare straight ahead, and be very quiet. If the chanter was performing the ceremony in the right manner some one of the audience would get a vision pertaining to the chanter and his objective. This would be a sign that the ceremony was being properly conducted and that it would be successful."

only nine of the sixteen who sometimes do hand-trembling are women, actually they carried out nearly 80 per cent of the diagnoses of which I have record.

None of the singers in this society also practice divination. Of the thirteen curers only two do motion-in-the-hand, and of these one has diagnosed but once in two years and the other has carried on but a single ceremonial during this time and is just barely recognized as a curer. It seems fairly clear that a different temperamental selection operates for the two specialties. I have also a decided impression that the community feels that both professions ought not to be practiced by the same person.

Since persons doing divination by hand-trembling have no teacher, we cannot attempt to discover relationships to social organization in the manner that we utilized in the case of the singers and curers. But study of the data nevertheless reveals a very pertinent tendency. Eleven of the sixteen fall into four fraternities: two brothers, two brothers, three sisters, three sisters and a brother. Two other diagnosticians are married to two of the sisters of the last-named fraternity. Moreover, the first-named pair are the sons of a dead sister in this fraternity who also did hand-trembling. In other words, half of the diagnosticians are closely associated with a single family group (which, incidentally, is that of the singer, Jake). Two of the remaining women diagnosticians are daughter and maternal aunt-foster mother. In sum, out of the sixteen there is but a single one who is not closely related to at least one other diagnostician. That the culture seems to recognize a tendency for the capacity to be associated with family lines seems indicated by the following:

RICHARD PINO'S WIFE (30): About eight years ago a singer from over near Thoreau came to sing Life Way, Female Shooting Branch, for the son of Antonio's sister. My older sister had done hand-trembling and figured out that he should come and that he should sing this, but the boy was very sick and didn't get better. So my youngest sister did motion-in-the-hand and said the same singer should do Flint Way, Male Branch, which he also knew. But the boy still didn't get better. So one day while he was doing medicine the singer stopped singing and said to me: "This isn't doing and good. I don't think we've got the right way yet. Your sisters can do hand-trembling. I think you can do it too. Sometimes people who just start to do hand-trembling find things out easier than people who have been doing it for a long time." So he put medicine on my hand and sang several Hand-Trembling Way songs and put corn meal on my hand. While he was singing my hand started to shake.

It will perhaps be enlightening to follow out case histories of the circumstances under which these sixteen individuals first began to "shake." Five diagnosticians became conscious of their powers under conditions of solitude—either out herding sheep or in the hogan alone at night. Some actual statements are psychologically interesting:

CRAZY WOMAN (25): A long time ago I was out herding sheep by myself. I lay down and went to sleep a little while. I got up and felt bad. I didn't think like I used to—I felt like I was drunk or something. It seemed like somebody was talking to me, but I didn't see anyone. The voices told me to go some place and I started to go and then my hand and arm started to shake. I couldn't stop it. Then I thought of something my father had lost and it quit. I went and told my father and I was right. After that people started coming to me to find things they'd lost or for me to tell them what singer to get and what sing to have.

YOUNGER SISTER OF 25 (26): I had just had a baby about twenty days before. I was pretty sick and sometimes my mind was about gone. One night I was all alone with my little baby. Pretty soon I felt like someone was with us—grown people and babies. I ran out of the hogan and hollered to these people. I started to do hand-trembling. My mind was all gone. My relatives got the fat singer of Hand-Trembling Way from Danoff, and he straightened me up so I could do hand-trembling all right. He put pollen on my arm and sung for me and said I could do it for the people from then on.

GOLASTICO (9): When I was about fifteen I lay down in the shade at noon one day and took a nap. I was alone. I had been out all morning with the sheep. All of a sudden I woke up and my arm was shaking hard and I couldn't stop it for about fifteen minutes. I told people about that, but it was three years before anybody asked me to find out what was making them sick.

MARIO, YOUNGER BROTHER OF 9 (27): I was out looking for horses alone. When the sun got hot I went to sleep under a tree. I woke up faint and in a daze. Right away my hand started to shake.

All of these accounts (except possibly the third) fit very nicely into the picture of shamanism (in the narrow sense).

Julio (17) was seized with a violent attack of hand-trembling while watching his sister (28) perform diagnosis. In the remaining eleven cases the onset of hand-trembling occurred while the individual either was attending a ceremonial (seven instances) or was the patient in a ceremonial (four instances). The attack occurred in four cases while the patient was sitting on the sandpainting and singing was going on, in seven cases simply during singing. In five cases the ceremonial in question was one or the other of two forms of Hand-Trembling Way (no other ceremonial occurs more than once in a list). I suggest the possibility that this second pattern of acquiring hand-trembling is a secondary development and represents a kind of linking up of the shamanistic form of "religious" behavior with the "priestly" form. That the connection is strongly felt is shown (among other ways) by the fact that one diagnostician —Juanita (15)—scarcely dares enter a hogan where a ceremonial is being carried on lest uncontrollable arm-quivering ensue. Another evidence is that diagnosticians feel that they must have ceremonials at intervals, regardless of any recognized illness. Jake (2) said of his son-in-law Salamon (35):

He doesn't like to do hand-trembling any more. He's afraid he is getting sick from doing it too much without being sung over.

A number of informants (13, 2, 1, 6, 15) stated or inferred that Hand-Trembling Way ceremonials were the cure par excellence for "hand-trembling sickness." This theory is, I suspect, of comparatively recent origin. But cognitive association between the rite of divination and the ceremonial is also evidenced by the circumstance that (at least in the Ramah and Danoff-Two Wells areas) singers of Hand-Trembling Way do not sing other ceremonials, although in far the greater number of cases in these areas a singer who knows a whole ceremonial also conducts parts at least of others. (Systematic inquiry during the summer of 1938 among a large number of informants in various parts of the Navaho country revealed only a single case—near Pine Springs—of a singer of Hand-Trembling Way who sang other full ceremonials. Certainly a trend toward a uniformity is indicated here, although no informant seemed aware of it as a matter of theory.)

Most of the case histories of the second pattern reveal also a kind of ceremonial sanction for the inborn gift. A few examples will serve:

JUANITA (15): I was very sick. Dick Pino was singing Chiricahua Apache Wind Way for me. When the people were all singing the last night, I felt a trembling in my chest and it got heavier and heavier. Next I felt my upper arm moving. My breath was tied up. Then I started to do hand-trembling. So the singer put pollen on my hand and arm and sang a few Hand-Trembling Way songs.

SOLAO'S WIFE (32): My stomach and legs were all swollen up. They decided to have Hand-Trembling Evil Way for me. The second day, when the doctor had me sit on the sandpainting and started to sing, my hand shook a little. Each day after that, when I got on the painting, it shook a little more. The last night they made a painting on buckskin. When I sat on that and the doctor sang, my hand shook hard and wouldn't stop. So he put pollen on it and sang special songs and said after that I could help people when they asked me.

MRS. BIG (33): About twenty years ago I was very sick and lay in bed and couldn't do anything. They put up Mountain Top Way for me. My sister's husband was the singer. The first time they put me on a sandpainting, my hand shook a little bit. But it kept getting worse each time. The people decided about me then and decided to do the right thing for me so I could do hand-trembling for the people. My sister's husband put corn pollen on my hand and sang a few Hand-Trembling Way songs for me so I could do hand-trembling all I want. If you are going to do hand-trembling right, people have to sing and pray for you.

RICHARD PINO (34): Eighteen years ago one of Antonio's boys went crazy part of the time; they were singing Hand-Trembling Way for him. One night I was helping with the sandpainting. While I was moving my arm up and down, somebody said it looked broken out. I looked at it and it looked drawn out big. After the boy sat on the sandpainting and they started singing, my arm started shaking. So they sang over me too and gave me the regular medicine of the sing and put pollen on my hand so I could do it right.

SUMMARY

1. In this Navaho band diagnosticians tend to be, as a matter of observation, concentrated in certain biological lines and family groups. There is some slight evidence that at least the

biological aspect of this generalization finds a place in cultural theory. There is no evidence whatsoever that clan, as such, influences the distribution of hand-trembling diagnosticians in this population.

2. There are two principal patterned ways of acquiring hand-trembling divination. Each reflects a different underlying concept of relation to the supernatural from that which prevails, in general, as regards the ceremonials and manner of learning ceremonials. But the second perhaps represents a bridge across a fundamental dichotomy of Navaho religion.

Social Relationships between Patients and Practitioners

To what extent do clan and family ties influence the choice of a singer, curer, or diagnostician? I have studied the relevant data, but, since their interpretation seems quite straightforward in all except trifling particulars and since they are not otherwise informative, I shall present only the results of analysis. After stating the widest generalizations that the facts permit, I shall enlarge somewhat upon various aspects of these generalizations and make certain qualifications.

Aside from personal likes and dislikes and interfamily feuds (and these considerations appear to have played an extremely small role during the period of my study), the determining factors in the choice of a practitioner appear to be close relationship by blood or marriage, geographical propinquity, and specialized knowledge on the part of practitioner. To a considerable extent the economic question of the fees that must be paid is a kind of master factor conditioning the significance of these three: the related practitioner charges less; the fee is to some extent a function of the distance the practitioner must travel; and the specialist with a reputation for unusual knowledge commands higher payments in Navaho society, as in our own. These implications must constantly be borne in mind, but it will be useful to treat the three factors named as abstracted from the very significant economic context.

The relative importance of these three factors varies with other circumstances. In the case of minor illnesses and somewhat perfunctory brief ceremonials, geographic propinquity would appear to be the dominant determinant. If a curer lives a few miles away, his services will be secured even though the patient's own father is a leading singer but lives thirty miles away. When full ceremonials, on the other hand, are in question, it is relationship[5] that stands out. Roughly one-third of the ceremonials of the singers were for persons closely related to them by either blood or marriage. This is, of course, in part simply a function of the facts that the Ramah band is small and mainly endogamous and that relatives tend to be concentrated in particular localities. But, with only three exceptions, persons closely related by blood or marriage to a singer called upon that singer for a full ceremonial, regardless of distance, unless the diagnostician had specifically advised a ceremonial not known to that singer. Putting it another way, the data show that a singer almost invariably conducts the ceremonials that are held over his children, the children of his sisters, and his grandchildren (and the husbands and wives of these three groups), and usually those held over his brothers and sisters and their wives or husbands and children. Persons closely related to a curer frequently called upon an unrelated singer but very seldom indeed upon an unrelated curer. Actually, the practice of a number of curers is practically limited to their own blood, clan, and affinal relatives. They are not sufficiently recognized for outsiders to have any confidence in them.

When illness is chronic or critical, the importance of both of these first two factors is materially diminished. Then there is a strong tendency to seek out the man (with little regard for relationship or for distance involved) who either knows some

---

5. Mainly close familial relationship. But there is some evidence that, other things being equal, a diagnostician or singer in the same clan as the patient is preferred to an outsider. Of the two local singers most in demand, Dick Pino (1) is a member of the clan (37) most numerous in the area, but Jake (2) belongs to a clan (22) that has but fifteen representatives in this area. Of the five practitioners most frequently called in from the outside, three are from the first and third most populous clans (37 and 35) in the area, the fourth is from Clan 22, and the fifth is from a clan (20) that has but three representatives here.

ceremonial that is unknown to any member of the Ramah group
but may alone, it is felt, cure the illness. The additional factor
of social prestige undoubtedly enters into the choice of an outside singer in certain cases. This factor is more difficult than
the others to document with full precision. Documentation consists, in the first place, in the fact that (with only three
exceptions, each of which was a case of critical or persistent
illness) the very expensive outside singers have been imported
by the few families in this region who are really prosperous. In
the second place, numerous statements of this order provide
documentation:

RICHARD PINO (34): The Antonios ought to have an Enemy Way
for the people. Everybody knows that. But they're too stingy.

SAM (4): Balthazar had a Night Way down at Carro Alto five
years ago. And everybody in that outfit has been bragging about it
ever since.

ANTONIO's WIFE (36): That singer we got from Crownpoint to do
Shooting Way, Male Branch, for me knew so much he had to have
five men help him. Nobody else around here could have paid him.

Still another point should be mentioned. It appears to be generally accepted as part of Navaho theory that the more that is
paid for a ceremonial, the more effective it is likely to be.

I have been speaking specifically of singers and curers. The
same principles apply in all three situations to the selection of
a diagnostician: "When people live all together you don't pay
much for doing hand-trembling—just pay a little corn pollen or
an arrowhead." (58) But if local diagnosticians and singers have
failed, the next step is very often that of calling in an outside
diagnostician—and usually one who can do star-gazing or listening (methods of divination not practiced by any member of the
Ramah band).

Thus far we have neglected the complication that in the
greater number of cases the choice of a singer is not direct but
is mediated through the advice of a diagnostician. It is simply a
matter of record that diagnosticians (except perhaps in severe
cases) tend very definitely to recommend in the first instance
singers and curers who are either neighbors or relatives of the
patient or both. It seems fairly evident that they are adhering

to a social pattern that is in large part unconscious but never-theless constrains the choice. The question as to whether there is connivance (or at least some kind of unformalized understand-ing) between particular diagnosticians and particular singers or curers at once presents itself, and I have examined the facts very carefully from this point of view. There is little support for the hypothesis that such arrangements exist. In the main, the leading diagnosticians have recommended the various singers and curers in a way that does not suggest partiality. It is true that the three daughters, the son, and the son-in-law of Jake who are diagnosticians tend strongly to recommend Jake, his sons Marga-dito and Jaciano, and his son-in-law Richard Pino as singers. But an examination of the cases where this was done shows that by far the greater number of the patients were also members of this extended family group. And, apart from these four diagnosticians, the records of those who have diagnosed often enough to provide a fair sample evidence primarily an adherence to the principles of relationship, geographic propinquity, and specialization, and secondarily a disposition to recommend one singer about as often as another and to show no marked prefer-ence for a particular curer.

There is one instance (involving the first introduction of a certain outside singer to this community) where connivance seems plain. During the autumn of 1936 an old woman from north of Gallup came down into the Ramah country to pick piñons. Finding in Solao's wife (32) a fellow member of Clan 35, she stayed for some time with that extended family. When the diagnosis of the illness of one of the grandchildren presented some difficulties, she volunteered to do hand-trembling. Her recommendation was that her own son be summoned to do Eagle Way. This advice was followed, and the singer has be-come something of a fashion in the region. Eagle Way had not been carried out there for some time, but after the ceremonial for the Solao group, Bluebird (10) immediately received two invitations to conduct the ceremonial for members of two other families. Professional engagements in his own area prevented immediate acceptance, but it was arranged that he should return in about six weeks. (I have, incidentally, data on ceremonials being arranged for a longer period than this in advance.)

Particularly in the case of singers from the outside, advantage is often taken of the presence of a singer in one's own immediate vicinity to ask him to come back "after shearing" or "after the lambs have been sold," for example. I know of cases where an outside singer has collected several such somewhat indefinite advance requests. More than once when such a singer has returned (without the invitation's having been renewed at the actual time by the sending of an intermediary), at least one of the families involved have greeted him with some such statement as: "We aren't quite ready for you yet. Come back again in about two weeks." On the other hand, when such a postponement occurs, it is likely (in my observation) that some other family that has been considering having a ceremonial for one of its members will give the singer an opportunity to fill in this idle time (often at something less than his usual fee). Last summer Bluebird performed Eagle Way twice and a Mountain Top Way excerpt once in this area (on the recommendation of local diagnosticians). There is abundant evidence that, from time to time, different outside singers become locally popular. Then a case goes badly, and they cease to be invited.[6] On the other hand, at least two outside singers have enjoyed a sustained popularity in this area for twenty years or more.

Instances of this sort where the diagnostician's position is utilized to personal or familial advantage undoubtedly occur. Theoretically, the diagnostician can consider any singer or curer he knows and any ceremonial (or supplementary ceremony, such as a specific sandpainting at additional expense). And the diagnostician could clearly (so far as actual manipulation is concerned) control the issue of the rite of diagnosis. Actually, however, this theoretically sweeping jurisdiction over ceremonial practice is sharply limited by several circumstances. First of all, the diagnostician normally discusses the alternatives with the family group before he carries out hand-trembling in their presence. If he suggests that he might "think about" a

6. It is too often forgotten that the Navaho expects results—or at all events not bad results—from their singers. A singer who consistently has failures loses his practice. Of course, a considerable degree of rationalization of failure is part of the system. It is my impression that the limit of toleration of rationalization is markedly less for the singer from outside.

nine-night Mountain Top Way during the hand-trembling, they are almost certain to say that it is useless because they couldn't afford it in any case. In the second place, choice is restricted by the fact that particular etiological factors tend to be associated with particular ceremonials. Further, it is clear from the data that the diagnostician, with extremely few exceptions, limits himself to the culturally expected alternatives. Finally, it is not merely that the diagnostician is limited by the expressed wishes of the particular family and by the choices institutionalized in the culture. The family often on their own responsibility reject in whole or in part the advice of the diagnostician. This is a matter that I did not systematically investigate in the field, but in connection with other topics I noted eight instances in which a kind of informal family council vetoed the recommendations of a diagnostician and either called in another diagnostician or made their own independent selection of singer or ceremonial or both.

SUMMARY

1. The principal factors (all markedly interdependent with economic situation) influencing the choice of a practitioner are close biological-sociological relationship, geographical propinquity, and professional reputation of the practitioner. The relative importance of these factors varies with the circumstances that have been specified, but they are listed in what is probably the modal diminishing order of importance. Clan, as such, appears to be a determinant to only a very slight degree.

2. The recommendations of diagnosticians are decidedly patterned and are also conditioned by the circumstances of the particular case.

Social Relationships between Patients and Assistants or Spectators at Ceremonials

The singer usually has a first assistant and several other helpers. The relationship of the first assistant is significant in respect to

the singer rather than to the patient. Sometimes the singer takes
with him to the ceremonial a member of his extended family
group who has had some experience and training. Dick (1) and
Jake (2) are quite occasionally accompanied by their sons-in-
law. These two men are not trying to learn the ceremonials.
Usually, however, the first assistant is a son, a sister's son, or a
brother of the singer. Similarly, a singer will occasionally turn
over to those whom he has trained (particularly if they be his
own or his sisters' children) the carrying out of the "repeats" of
his ceremonials. The patient cannot properly get someone else
to finish the cycle of four if the original singer is still alive. But
that the singer is privileged to transfer the responsibility to a
nonpupil and nonrelative is shown in that Jake has twice trans-
ferred it to Dick on the ground that "he could help the sick
person more." In these cases, in addition to the routine calico
and baskets, Dick was paid a share of the original fees by Jake.

Sometimes one of the singer's pupils or former pupils will
not come until the last day or two of the ceremonial, and the
first assistant until then (if not a relative whom the singer has
brought along) is some member of the patient's family—often
the father if the patient is a young person. The secondary assistants (helpers) are provided by the patient's family. They are
usually members of the extended family group, but neighbors
are sometimes asked to help. In general, the only qualification
is that they should have some knowledge of ceremonial procedure—specifically, no one ought to be an assistant who has not
himself or herself had at least one ceremonial. (But persons may
otherwise assist at their own risk—it does not affect the efficacy
of the ceremonial.[7] However, those who have themselves had
the ceremonial seem definitely to be preferred as assistants and
helpers, and in Shooting Way chants preference is given to those
who have narrowly escaped death by lightning. In only one
case is a particular social relationship to the patient demanded.
The man or woman who assists the patient in the ceremony of

7. In this paper I follow the practice used in Wyman and Kluckhohn
(1938a): any general statement such as this may be assumed to rest on a
minimum of four independent testimonies, not contradicted by any member of the group. Where a statement is documented by less than four informants or where there are discrepancies, names or numbers of informants
have been cited.

the bath must be a member neither of the patient's clan nor of the biological family. It is particularly interesting that this ceremony is singled out, in view of the fact that in many pueblos (especially in the West) "the head is bathed in yucca suds by a person who stands in some special social or ceremonial relation to the subject" (usually, Dr. Parsons writes me, the father's sister or ceremonial father's sister—not a member of the person's clan nor of his household). For calling my attention to another parallel I must thank Dr. A. H. Gayton: commonly in Central California the person who assists receives, as here, the basket as a perquisite. My records show only one case where this requirement was violated.

Those present (other than patient, singer, and necessary assistants) until the final day of a ceremonial are almost invariably limited to members of the patient's immediate family group and perhaps a few neighbors. Spectators gather during the final day, reaching a maximum during the concluding all-night singing. Study of the lists of those present suggests that kinship and geographical propinquity are the two principal determinants of attendance.[8] Only one fact that is at all remarkable emerges— namely, that paternal relatives are about 15 per cent more numerous in the lists than maternal relatives. Since this is true in spite of the fact that the residence system is still more matrilocal than patrilocal, it may be significant. At the very least, it affords demonstration of the bilateral character of kinship reciprocities.

That there are expected reciprocal behaviors stands out very clearly both in word and act. Juanita (15) complained bitterly that her maternal niece and foster daughter, who lives a few miles away, had not come to assist her in cooking for the spectators during the final day and night of a Chiricahua Apache Wind Way. She remarked, "When they've got something going on up at their place, I always go up and help." Close relatives who live at a distance are often sent for (especially if they know

---

8. In the case of singers on ceremonials new to the region, "curiosity" enters as an additional factor of importance. Perhaps one should also mention friendship, but (often with the exception of a single close friend among younger people) friends are usually selected from among kinfolk and neighbors.

the songs) to help with the singing during the final night. Many statements make it clear that there is social pressure upon brothers and sisters, uncles and aunts, and other relatives of the patient to aid by their presence and by gifts of food and money. The principal penalty for failure to do so is, of course, similar behavior when circumstances are reversed. To a lesser extent the same pattern of reciprocity applies to neighbors (the two categories are seldom mutually exclusive here).

SUMMARY

1. The sociological relationship of the principal assistant is usually to the singer, that of the other assistants and spectators to the family of the patient. Paternal relatives are present in somewhat greater numbers than maternal relatives.
2. Patterned reciprocal behaviors between relatives and neighbors are in evidence.

Discussion

This paper has demonstrated some features of the interdependence of social and ceremonial organization in a Navaho band. Perhaps most of the points established could have been predicted a priori, but—feeling as I do that the neglect of the obvious has been a cardinal flaw of sociological and anthropological research—I am not disposed to apologize for this inductive analysis of highly specific data. I do, however, realize acutely that I have touched only upon some of the more outstanding relationships. Such a subtlety, for example, as the social personality of the singer deserves extended discussion. As a lead for other workers to check, I submit three tentative generalizations which are imperfect inductions from scattered observations in my field notes:

1. During the intervals between ceremonial procedures (and

to a degree even during some of these procedures) the singer is expected to joke and maintain a jocular mien.

2. Becoming a singer is probably the principal mechanism for the "circulation of the elite" (in the Paretian sense) in Navaho society as a whole.

3. The singer is expected to be more than usually hospitable and to give liberally to friends and relatives, particularly perhaps to old people, the fees and presents that he receives. Yet there is a considerable degree of ambivalence of feeling toward the singer. Apparently singers who are either too prosperous or who have too many failures are suspected of witchcraft. This may explain in large part a fact that more than one observer has commented upon: Singers in Navaho society, while seldom terribly poor, are not in general as well off as might be anticipated in view of the substantial increments to their income. In this group, Dick (1) and Jake (2) both have an extraordinary number of economic dependents, and the former is actually poor by the standards of the community.

A singer whose hair is turning or has turned white is particularly liable to suspicion. Occasionally one hears a tale of collusion between singer and diagnostician involving witchcraft.

It is clear that an individual could seldom arrange to have a ceremonial carried out unless he had "economic" cooperation from the members of his immediate and extended family groups. These "economic" reciprocities involved in ceremonial behaviors are, like the "social," rather fully patterned and somewhat intricate both in operation and in their effects. Ceremonials act to some degree as "economic" levelers. Those regarded as well-off or well-to-do feel, as has been pointed out, social pressure to give the more elaborate and more expensive ceremonials. Conversely, the acquisition of ceremonial knowledge is recognized not only as an avenue to the attainment of economic security but also as a means of economic mobility. If poor parents have a son who is regarded as being unusually alert and as having a good memory, friends will often say:

You ought to have your boy learn so and so's chant. Then, later on, he'd be able to help you all out. He would give you a lot of the things that people gave him for singing for them.

Summary

The summaries at the close of each section have provided generalizations on specific points from particulate data. These generalizations can be subsumed only in terms of the broadest tendencies:

1. Clan, as such, influences ceremonial life slightly. The existence of such a unit of social differentiation is, however, evident at certain points.[9]

2. Bilateral biological-sociological close relationship stands out as a signally important determinant of various ceremonially oriented behaviors. The local subgroup also plays a role of importance.

3. There is abundant demonstration that ceremonial structure is patterned with reference to social structure.

4. Most of the ceremonial knowledge of this group derives from three deceased individuals (especially the two principal teachers of Dick Pino and Jake Bagan).

---

9. In the main, however, it seems to me that this analysis bears out Dr. Parsons' generalization (1936, p. 229) that "Navaho clanship is dissociated with Navaho ceremonialism." There are, nevertheless, a few evidences of connection. For example, in Enemy Way we are told (Haile, 1938, p. 219) that a person from the patient's clan is usually chosen to go after the scalp "because he will do it free of charge."

7 NOTES
ON NAVAHO
EAGLE WAY

AGLE WAY IS ONE of the least known of Navaho chants. Wyman and I (1938a, pp. 189, 14-111, *passim*) have recently published a little general information, and Newcomb (1940) has published a version of the chant legend. The ceremonial appears to be obsolescent. I have never had a definite and specific report of a full five-night performance in recent years, and, so far as I know, I am the only field worker who has witnessed even an excerpt. I am in no position to write a comprehensive discussion of this chant, but I happen to have certain materials that ought to be spread upon the record for the use of other students. Since I do not expect to do further field work on the subject of Navaho ceremonials, it would serve no purpose to hold these data until some fabled day when they might be "complete." During the summer of 1937 two informants, one of them a curer knowing excerpts of Eagle Way, volunteered to tell me episodes from the

1941b Reprinted by permission of the publishers from Clyde Kluckhohn, "Notes on Navajo Eagle Way," *New Mexico Anthropologist*, Vol. 5, pp. 61-64.

chant legend. Both were obtained through an interpreter (David Skeet of Two Wells), and I shall give them exactly as he rendered them, except that I have translated some terms that he left in Navaho. To have put them into "better English" would be to distort the data as received, and our interest in these materials is a scientific interest, not a literary one. During the same summer I saw an excerpt of Eagle Way (lasting several hours) performed about twenty-five miles south of Ramah, New Mexico. My notes on this excerpt will be organized according to the plan set forth in Kluckhohn and Wyman.

Episodes from the Eagle Way Chant Legend

The first of these was told me by Jake, a singer of the Ramah area who was more than eighty years old. Jake (2) does not give any part of Eagle Way but had been told this episode by a curer from Punta de Malapais who did give Eagle Way excerpts:

This is the story of the eagle and the bee and it happened many years ago. There used to be people on the earth going around to look for eagle nests to see if some young ones in it. First this man found a eagle nest with two little ones in it. He killed those two. He begin to look around for some more. Found another nest with two. He did this two more times. Killed two out of each nest. After he killed the last ones a big eagle came along and asked this man why he killed these young ones. He sure mad about that. Didn't like for him to do all that. Told him he should let those young ones go and says, "Come with me! Let's go up in the heaven." The other man says he didn't want to go up in the heaven with an eagle. The eagle kept saying that and so he made up his mind and went up in the heaven with the eagle.

Both went up in heaven through the sky. Sky opened up big enough so they could get through. Place they come to is some kind of place up there. He notice there is a house like this one we're in but a long one. It was on the east side, and half of it was blue and the other yellow. There were other houses on south and west and north. Those houses are different colors from half to the other half. They got down in the middle of these houses. The east house was the house that the eagle people owned it. The south house was owned by some other kind of birds—ayash. The west by buzzard. On the fourth side were all these small eagles [hawks].

They put the man in the house on the east. Get him to learn, put him on the job to learn Eagle Way. Got him started so he started to learn. Got it all learned, every bit of it—every song and every pray. When he learn all these songs and prays, next year after that one of these eagles says want to go to war. Got enemies close to the east side from there. This man who learned the Eagle Way says he wants to go along. From this time this man who learned the song had a friend who started to go with him [Big Fly]. All the eagles they want to go along, but Big Fly says go see Spider first. Spider has a house on one side. The man went down there and asked Spider, but Spider says he better not go. Well, he wanted to go just the same even if Spider says no. He wants to go pretty bad. Thinks there is a lot of fun in it. All these four different direction houses, the people in them, they get together and start to go. Finally the man went along. The enemies had a place down here on the east side. They came to the place. They found it was house of Big Wasp. These were their enemies. They come pretty close and the wasps came out of their houses and heading for these other bunch. They fight quite a while there and the wasps whip all the eagles and all the rest. Eagles full of stings in their feathers. Right into their bodies. This man, he just kept watching behind. Well, they got back to their place. This man thought he could kill these wasps by himself. The next day he didn't say a word about it to the eagles. Just started off, started to going over. Big Fly says break up some of these rabbit brush. Can use some for whip. Then he went over there and Big Fly says must keep chewing all the time on this rabbit brush. When they got close, the wasps start to get after him. He started to blow on it, start to kill it. Kept doing that on the wasp until he kill all of them. At last there came a great big one out of the house and that was the boss of all. Blow some on him—get him down until he can't do anything. Didn't kill him—just kinda weaken it up. Start to go home with it, carrying that bee. Come back to that house where the eagle people was. Heard a lot of talk going on inside, talking about him. Some already know he gone back to enemy. Says that man sure killed. Can't do anything by himself. That's what they all saying. The man walk in with that wasp—drop him before all these people and say, "Here's your enemy. That's all that's left. I whip them all. I kill them all." But the people all got up and say, "That's our enemy. I hope that's truth." That's what the eagle says. But they find out that it is true. Well, they kill that last one.

Next day they want to go—they have some more enemies another place. They all wanted to go over there and fight that enemies, so they all started and got there. And that was another kind of wasp—the yellow wasp. Again this man who whipped the wasps stood behind the eagles and watched how they fought. [Here the story was repeated practically as above except for substitutions of names.]

Next day they want to go out again. Goe some more enemies—the flat rocks. These flat rocks will start to fight. After they got out there to that place the wind starts first and then flat rocks start flying around. Hit eagles in head. After quite a lot got hit, they went home. The man made up a club of cedar. Peeled it off and smoothed it up. [Here the story again repeated itself essentially, with a final big rock (instead of a big wasp) being left and subdued.]

Next day the eagles want to go over to another place. These enemies were called "Sticking Plants Moving Around." The wind blows these weeds around and sticks them to the meat of the eagles. The man used a fork stick to fight them. He piled all these weeds except one together and burned them. The one big one he took back to show the Eagles just like he had the boss of all the other enemies.

When he got rid of all these enemies, "That's the end," the man says. After that this man begin to think he wants to go down where he used to be, but he has no way to go back. Someone came along and gave him a sunbeam, and he can stand on this sunbeam. In a minute he came right down on top of one Mountain. Came back to his old place, and a little while after that, just a short time, he got sick of this place where he has been on account of what he did up there, killing these animals.

In the sky he had married an Eagle Woman. Without that head men would not have taught him Eagle Way. He had left her in the sky, but she had taught him all the Eagle Way songs. Now on earth he had another wife and her people put up Eagle Way for this man. He told them how to do it, but Big Fly helped. The life of each one of the four enemies [the chiefs] had gone into evil spirits and bothered him. This man's body and face were painted just like man who goes into pit to trap eagles get painted. He got well on that.

An Eagle Way practitioner (gd) living near Gallup told the following story:

Eagle Way chant began with Sky White Tail and Sky Yellow Tail.[1] They lived in the north part of the Navaho country at a place

---

1. The reference is to a type of eagle and a type of hawk, respectively.

called Water Crosses. Sky White Tail arose out of the water that comes from the east. Sky Yellow Tail came up from the water that comes from the north. Sky White Tail's mother was fish. Sky Yellow Tail's mother was otter. They met at Water Crosses, and Sky White Tail said, "My younger brother." The other one said, "My older brother." They were brothers after this.

They were little children. Then the White Wind came and dressed Sky White Tail up. He grew at the same time. When White Wind finished dressing Sky White Tail up, Sky White Tail was full grown. Yellow Wind came and did it same way to Sky Yellow Tail. Both winds were Edge-of-the-Water Winds.

First thing the brothers faced to the east and looked for something they could go with. Saw nothing. Also south, west, and north. Saw nothing. East again, then south again. They saw something making a crooked line. Wondered what it was. Soon they knew it was lightning. Sky White Tail said, "I'll get that one to move me around for my trip." They also saw something that was hanging down. That was a rainbow. Sky Yellow Tail said that will be his. Both started walking toward these things.

They started to walk a little way. Came on something lying right in their way. Two things. One white and straight. One yellow and crooked. Sky White Tail said, "Don't look at these things. I am going to jump on this one. you jump on that one." These two things moved very fast to a piece of rock. Around rock with wings. The two eagle people got off on top of that rock. Noticed one side to it had a door. Started for that door. As they got near, the door opened. They went in and saw a man and a woman. They looked almost the same. One was white, other yellow from neck and shoulders up. The one with white neck called Sky White Tail to come over and shake hands with him and sit by him. The other called the other the same way, saying, "Come here, my maternal grandchild."

The white-necked one said to both, "I am your father." He said, "Of course, you don't know how you came and how you were raised. I put you over there." The white-necked one said, "I have a home. I want you to go there with me. From now on you will be used by the Indians. Some will talk one language, some another. You are the eagle people. Your feathers will be used by these Indians. Now we will go eat."

They started to take a step but didn't move. Room shook. Could hear thunder noise, "di-l." White-necked eagle put up wings and moved them back and forth. Woman just prayed. The white-necked one said, "We are doing something and not noticing it." He told the people to bow their heads and not look around. "This white rock is flying now. The thunder is the one that makes it fly. We are flying to the east." As they flew around, the white-necked one told them they were going over Pelado Peak, Mount Taylor, the San Francisco Mountains, and the La Plata Mountains.

After a while they looked around and the door was open. Just as soon as door opened, brothers noticed they were right on top of the rocks where they had been before. This was near Toadlena. There the white-necked one gave them a good talk. Said this rock was his body and all the different Indians would go by it. It is a rock shaped like an eagle with tail towards north. "If we hadn't met together and come here, there wouldn't be any Indians on earth. But now the tribes of Indians will be spread out."

On the floor of this room was a pelt made of eagle feathers. He told Sky White Tail and Sky Yellow Tail to sit on this pelt. The woman sang. White-necked one gave his name to Sky White Tail; the woman gave her name to Sky Yellow Tail. White-neck told Sky White Tail and Sky Yellow Tail to stay by this rock always. "If you travel in the air, go way up in the four directions, but remember where this rock is. Always come back to this rock. This is our home. When the world starts changing, this rock will be standing here getting older and older. If this rock falls, it means no world. This rock will be called Winged Rock [Shiprock]. The different tribes should take care of this rock for always. Should go there and put turquoise away for the eagle. Sing for it and pray for it. If this is taken care of right, will last for many years. Otherwise—not long.

The white-necked reached in his feathers and pulled out a feather. Put it behind him. One was white tail for Sky White Tail, and one was yellow tail for Sky Yellow Tail. "This is your mind I am giving you," he said to both. "Hold the feather up and try to look through it. In there you will notice how many people there will be. You see heads. Those are the different tribes. At the top—blue eyes—white people. All these people are strong, but the strongest is at the top. All the tribes will come under the white people." He told Sky Yellow Tail to hold feather low and then up high. Then he should look through. Saw sheep, horses, cattle, everything which grown on earth. It's all there.

At this point the curer said that this was the end of one story and that another story started there but that he didn't dare tell that until after frost.

Discussion

The principal value of these materials is to provide documentation for investigation into the range of variation, an indispensable aspect of any scientific study of phenomena. Both of these episodes are, to be sure, coarse and fragmentary as compared to Newcomb's recording. They were obtained quite incidentally, and no effort was made to enlarge or supplement the stories by questioning. The first was spontaneously volunteered by the old man during an evening meal apropos of an inquiry of mine about some wild honey he had gathered. The second was proffered as supporting evidence when I had expressed scepticism as to Eagle Way being an independent and separate chant.

It is noteworthy that the only events of either account that enter into Newcomb's[2] complete chant legend are the subduings of stinging insects. Otherwise, the only resemblances are certain highly generalized ones of act and symbol that can be isolated from any body of Navaho mythic material. My informants were almost certainly much less learned in this specialty than Newcomb's. The first account, indeed, has a certain interest as representing that vulgarization of a legend known by a man of ceremonial learning but not a practitioner of the chant in question. We need material of this sort to compare with the full versions known by specialists. But, because the two episodes recorded by me contain so much not even alluded to in Newcomb's recording, are we justified in inferring that my informants are utterly ignorant on this topic or even charlatans? Not at all, I think. Jake I have known for many years, and his

2. The first episode shows general similarity in event sequences to a part of the Bead Way legend published by Reichard (1939, p. 32). On the connections between Bead Way and Eagle Way see (1938a) and (1940b). The correspondence of events in Reichard's Bead Way legend and in the Eagle Way episode as told by 2 should probably be regarded as further evidence for the association of Bead Way and Eagle Way. Dr. Wyman has made the following observation in a letter to me, and I present it as a useful suggestion that seems to me in accord with all data that we have at present: "My hunch is that Bead Way probably existed as a Holy Way chant at a time when the Eagle Trapping Rite was purely a Game Way ceremonial, and that the latter became a curing chant by accretion from Bead Way."

sincerity is beyond question. And "ignorance" would be a proper verdict only on the postulate that there is one and only one "correct" version of the Eagle Way chant legend. This would be absurd, although there has been not a little zealous bigotry on the part of ethnologists to defend supposedly orthodox forms of myths or ceremonies. Part of the trouble has undoubtedly been that investigators have identified emotionally with favorite informants who were held up as more learned or trustworthy and as knowing "*the* truth." At least with a tribe so large, so geographically dispersed, and with such heterogenous cultural origins as the Navaho, such a view is utterly indefensible. To return to the concrete matter at issue, it simply is a fact that two elderly, non-English-speaking Navaho ceremonial practitioners in the year 1937 gave as parts of a chant legend events that do not appear in another version of that chant legend recorded from another Indian at a different time and place. To us, as scientists, the question as to which is "right" or "wrong" is essentially meaningless. These data can claim our attention only as elements that may be used in inductions on participation in ceremonial knowledge, on distribution of myth elements, and on agreement and disagreement of Navahos on their mythology.

Sandpainting Ceremony Excerpt

SOCIOLOGICAL CONTEXT

P^3 was 11 (clan 18). She complained of being "sick all over," but probably had tuberculosis.[4] She died less than six months later. The ceremony was held in the hogan of her daughter (43) who acted as H_2. The daughter's husband (39) acted as H_1. S was bb (clan 22) from Two Wells. The only spectators were

3. Cf. 1940b, p. 17, f. 21. The abbreviations refer to participants in the ceremony as follows: P, patient; S, singer or curer; A, assistant; BH, bath helper: SH, sweat or emetic helper; H_1, H_2, H_3, etc., other helpers.

4. Newcomb (1940, p. 50) implies that the Eagle Way Chant was used only as an aid to success in hunting eagles. This may once have been true, but there is no doubt that at present it is carried out for curing.

my interpreter (ds) and myself (O). This excerpt had not been recommended by diagnosis. P had been ill for some time and had had a succession of treatments. She and her daughter and son-in-law had simply informally agreed to take advantage of the presence of S in this locality, to which he had been called by another family. There seemed to be no conviction on anyone's part that Eagle Way would be peculiarly efficacious for the ailments in question. The unstated premise appeared to be "Let's try everything we can."

NOTES ON EQUIPMENT USED

S's bundle included body-painting equipment, pouches containing various plant medicines, a whistle made of the femur of a jackrabbit killed by an eagle,[5] a gourd rattle of the same type as those used in Chiricahua Wind Way, a medicine cup of turtle shell, two prairie dog skins, and a beaver skin. Paints and plants had been obtained in the usual manner. The prairie dog skins were from animals trapped and skinned (apparently in no special way) by S. The beaver skin had been bought by S "from a white man in Farmington for five dollars." Other items of equipment had been purchased by S from fn, his maternal uncle and teacher. Sandpainting materials and equipment were, as commonly, provided by P's family.

SANDPAINTING CEREMONY

1. Sandpainting made, 10:20-12:30 a.m. by S and H_1 (paints had been ground by H_2). Pieces of corrugated paper from a carton were used as receptacles. Called "Eagles' nest." Represents two young eagles in nest in tree, surrounded by their food: to the north, a deer; to the south, a ground squirrel; to the west, a cottontail; to the east, a prairie dog. The parent eagles (large) stand guard to the east and west. Dimensions, about 2 by 7 ft.
2. Sandpainting set-up: none.

---

5. Cf. Kluckhohn and Wyman (1940b, p. 33). The context for all statements in this section is provided by this monograph, and serious students will find it necessary to make the appropriate comparisons there.

3. P entered (12:42). Meal sprinkling.

4. Chant lotion administered. By S to P. Song 1. Rattle used by ds. (Chant lotion has been placed on tail of east large eagle.)

5. Body painting.[6] By S only. Forehead solid white. Chin solid yellow. Ankles and wrists solid white. White dots up ventral center of legs. Then white dots up chest and down back. White cross between shoulders. Songs 2-8.

6. Prairie dog skin bound on P's right wrist. Beaver skin draped around her neck. Song 9. Whistle blown. Song 10.

7. P sits on sandpainting (center). Meander design drawn in black by S on top of white block on P's forehead and wrists. Songs 11-14.

8. Infusion specific (which had been placed on north wing of east large eagle) administered. By S to self, then to P with alternating thrust at sandpainting and administration four times. Short prayer.

9. Sand application. With second prairie dog skin. All sand-painting destroyed except west eagle.

10. Fumigation. Coal placed only for P. Song 15.

11. Eating mush. (Mush, in a Navaho cooking pot, had been placed between south wing and leg of west large eagle.) By all present. Songs 16-19.

12. P leaves sandpainting.

13. Sandpainting erasure. Song 20.

14. Sandpainting disposal. By H₂. Song 21.

15. P re-enters. S removes prairie dog and beaver skins from her. Songs 22-23.

Odd Bits of Unpublished Information on Eagle Way[7]

Eagle Way is often given first over a patient and then followed by Bead Way.

A gourd rattle is used in Eagle Way, but in Bead Way no rattle—only a basket drum.

6. According to gd, the entire legs should be painted white from the knee down, the arms white from the elbows down.

7. All obtained from gd.

There are four Eagle Way sandpaintings: Young Eagles in the Nest, Eagles Dressed in Snakes, and Eagle Trappings (two different sandpaintings).

Hastin Biyal Badani, who lives near Toadlena, still carries out the five-night form of Eagle Way.

8   CONCEPTIONS OF DEATH

AMONG THE SOUTHWESTERN

INDIANS

D URING THE LONG COURSE of human history individual men and women have probably thought, felt and done almost everything that was within the range permitted by anatomy, physiology, and the limits of external nature. An astonishing variety of these experiments in behavior were eventually institutionalized in those conventional designs for living that anthropologists term "culture patterns." If one considers the exuberant variousness of the solutions that different peoples have devised for perennial human problems, it is truly amazing that no known group has ever adopted the functionally simplest mode of disposing of its dead—merely abandoning corpses or disposing of them without a rite of any sort.

Even the Neanderthal race of the Old Stone Age seems to

1948d Reprinted by permission of the publishers from Clyde Kluckhohn, "Conceptions of Death among the Southwestern Indians" (Ingersoll Lecture on the Immortality of Man for the academic year 1947-1948), Divinity School Bulletin, Vol. 66, pp. 5-19.

have practiced regular interment: sometimes a flat stone protects the head; sometimes weapons are left in the grave; there are evidences that some have interpreted as those of funeral feasts; and bodies were often clearly arranged in a stylized position that presumably had symbolic significance. By the time of the Cro-Magnons ornaments were placed in graves, and the dead were occasionally imbedded in red ochre. In more recent times one can document a hundred—or a thousand—styles of burial or cremation or other types of disposal. There are bizarre rites of disinterment, scraping the flesh from the bones, and re-burying these or wearing or exhibiting some part of the skeleton. There is luxuriant variety in ritual style, but the vast uniformity of which I wish to remind you is that always and everywhere death and the dead are treated ritually. If one can look at this fact freshly and against the perspective of variation in most human institutions, its significance is challenging.

The challenge is the greater when one adds the fact that these rites are something more than an affectionate and cere-monial farewell. Historical records and the investigations of anthropologists demonstrate that the rituals of ethnologically known peoples are premised upon the assumption that death is not the end. Again, if one can consider the matter with fresh-ness and with scientific detachment, it is astonishing that Soviet Russia is the first major culture to proclaim the finality of physical death. Is the denial of the extinction of personality or soul simply a monumental proof of human egotism?

Clearly, the problem is more complicated than that. But the interpretation one makes of this empirical generalization will depend upon one's primitive postulates. The theologian is likely to see these data as evidence of an instinct divinely given to all humankind. Nor, given his premises, may one complain that this conclusion is illogical. The scientist, however, will seek first for a naturalistic explanation. He will attempt to explain this uniformity in terms of certain constants of the human situation and in terms of invariable properties of the human nervous system. Perhaps these two orientations are not as different as they may seem to us at first. The theologian's quest for the divine law and the scientist's quest for natural law may turn out to be somewhat different approaches to the same basic phenomena.

At any rate, the theologian and the scientist will agree that burial customs and beliefs concerning the afterlife may profitably be explored in the light of reason. This includes, of course, turning the light of reason upon processes that are essentially irrational or nonrational. The psychoanalysts may be right, at least in part, in insisting that mechanisms of projection and identification help us to understand the psychological dynamics of conceptions of immortality. Freud pointed to "the omnipotence of thought" as an all-prevailing human delusion. The fantasy becomes the thing. The wish to avoid being "swallowed up in the wide womb of uncreated night" is so powerful that it is projected as reality. On the other hand, one does not have to go so far as to plumb the unconscious to discover plausible reasons for the universal belief in afterlife. Tylor's theory has been condemned as intellectualistic; yet almost all primitives continue to cite the appearance of the dead in the dreams of the living as their rationale for assuming that personality outlasts the corruption of the body.

Whatever the ultimate causes of the conviction in an existence beyond the grave may be, it is certain that such doctrines and rituals have promoted the psychological adjustment of individuals and the integration and survival of societies. A funeral is a symbolic assertion that a person is important not only to his immediate relatives but to the whole group. The belief that the soul is not destroyed with the body usually implies a continuation of the individual's potency beyond the mortal life-span.[1] Indeed, the careful attention to ritual detail is less frequently envisaged as a triumphant affirmation of immortality than as a necessary instrument for protecting the living against the malignant powers of the dead. Rites are also a means of reintegrating the family and the larger group after the disruption caused by the loss of one of its members.

---

1. A somewhat different emphasis is found in Hindu and Buddhist thought, for, according to these views, even if the soul is reborn, it will be reborn as a different individual, even in some cases as a member of a different species. Some doctrines state that the greatest blessing is to continue to exist without taking individual form. Certain specialists assert that the soul-stuff that goes through reincarnations is not considered an individual soul but rather a part of the universal soul seeking release from any definite form or forms by attaining union with its source.

Some psychological correlates of intimations of immortality are less universal. Christians tend to think of the comforting prospect of being reunited with beloved comrades and of the compensation for misery in this life as "natural" appeals to the belief in an afterlife. Actually, these are somewhat special and unusual developments. Very few cultures picture the next world as a better one or as one in which the divine balance of justice is redressed. In many cases reunion is either not envisaged or is not presented in attractive terms. Even the threat of punishment after death is comparatively seldom used as a sanction to produce moral behavior on this earth. Finally, one can hardly consider immortality, in the strict sense, as a pan-human concept. Almost all peoples have conceived of some continuation, of something that was not extinguished with the last beat of the heart. But this is not invariably felt to be permanent. A gradual extinction is often portrayed, or a sudden annihilation after so many generations or other fixed period. When the soul is thought to be imperishable, personal immortality does not necessarily follow. The soul-stuff may be merged with that of others or in natural forces.

Death, what is done after death occurs, and conceptions of death—all of these topics can be and have been treated in a variety of ways. The famous physiologist Cannon (1942) showed how the fear of witchcraft could produce disfunction of the autonomic nervous system so that death, in fact, ensues. Polson, Brittain, and Marshall (1953) have provided a comparative treatise on the disposal of the dead. Hartmann (1952) fruitfully combines anthropological, linguistic, and philosophical viewpoints in considering the cult of the dead in Ireland. Some anthropologists and psychiatrists (Mauss, 1926; Aginsky, 1940; Wilbur, 1940) deal with the psychological aspects. I propose to take a paper by Boas (1922) as my model, but I shall restrict myself to the culture area I know best.

Many values and motivations that we are wont to think of as inevitably attached to the notion of immortality are in fact local in time and space. This emerges from careful consideration of any cultures that are apart from the Western and, specifically, the Judeo-Christian tradition. Those of the Navaho, Apache, and Pueblo Indians in the American Southwest will do as well as any. Much, though not all, of what may be said of these beliefs relating to the afterlife would apply to many other American Indian life-ways. I shall begin with the Navaho and give their beliefs the most extended treatment, because there I can speak from original field work. My remarks on the other groups will be hardly more than comparative comments.

Navaho

Let me first sketch a very general picture. The Navaho believe that life begins when wind enters the body through its orifices (particularly the ears) or when Changing Woman places a tiny bit of soul-substance in the infant's head just after birth. The question as to whether this soul existed before this is not raised. Most Navahos feel that a stillborn infant or a fetus lacks a soul. They say you can see the trail of the first death in the whorls of the fingertips.

Death is the end of all good things to the Navahos. They have no belief in a glorious immortality. Existence in the hereafter appears to be only a shadowy and uninviting thing. The after-world is a place like this earth, located to the north and below the earth's surface. It is approached by a trail down a hill or cliff, and there is a sandpile at the bottom. Deceased kinfolk, who look as they did when last seen alive, come to guide the dying to the afterworld during a journey that takes four days. At the entrance to the afterworld old guardians apply tests to see if death has really occurred.

Death and everything connected with it are horrible to The People. Even to look upon the bodies of dead animals, except those killed for food, is a peril. Dead humans are put away as soon as possible, and with such elaborate precautions that one of the greatest favors a white person can do for a Navaho is to undertake this abhorrent responsibility.

This intense and morbid avoidance of the dead and of everything connected with them rests upon the fear of ghosts. The other Earth Surface People who have fearful powers—witches—

are also very terrible, but they are, after all, living beings who can be controlled in some measure and, if necessary, killed. Ghosts are, as it were, the witches of the world of the dead, a shadowy impalpable world altogether beyond the control of the living.

Most of the dead may return as ghosts to plague the living. Only those who die of old age, the stillborn, and infants who do not live long enough to utter a cry or sound do not produce ghosts, and for them the four days of mourning after burial need not be observed, since they will not be injurious to the living. Otherwise, any dead person, no matter how friendly or affectionate his attitude while he was living, is a potential danger.

A ghost is the malignant part of a dead person. It returns to avenge some neglect or offense. If a corpse has not been buried properly, if some of his belongings that he wished interred with him have been held out, if not enough animals have been killed at his grave, or if the grave has been disturbed in any way, the ghost will return to the burial place or to his former dwelling.

Ghosts appear after dark or just before the death of some family member, in human form or as coyotes, owls, mice, whirl-winds, spots of fire, or indefinite dark objects. They are usually dark or black. They may change form or size before one's eyes or make recognizable sounds (as of familiar birds or animals) and noises of movement. Whistling in the dark is always evidence that a ghost is near. Since ghosts appear only at night, adult Navahos are afraid to go about in the dark alone, and all sorts of night shapes and sounds are fearful.

Ghosts may chase people, jump upon them, tug their clothes, or throw dirt upon them. Their actions not only are frightening in themselves but also are omens of disaster to come. When a Navaho thinks he has seen a ghost or when one has appeared in his dreams, he is sure that he or a relative will die unless the proper ceremonial treatment is successfully applied.

The Navahos always document their seeing of ghosts with actual sensory evidence: large or unusual tracks, a bit of owl feather in a strange place, a fire that is unaccounted for. Mission-aries and physicians sometimes speak as if the reports of ghosts were strictly comparable to the hallucinations and delusional experiences of the mentally unbalanced. Such a judgment overlooks the part played by cultural tradition (as opposed to the individual's "mentality") in interpreting the evidence of the senses.

As Hallowell has written (1938, p. 38):

> . . . psychologically, the actual order of reality in which human beings live is constituted in large measure by the traditional concepts and beliefs that are held. . . . Indians are able to point out plenty of tangible empirical evidence that supports the interpretation of the realities that their culture imposes upon their minds.

Night in the Navaho country is huge; in every direction there is silence, and strange forms and shadows sometimes give a start to those who have not been brought up to believe in ghosts. But if you *have* been reared on ghost lore, then you have a ready-made scheme for interpreting, for elaborating from an actual sensory experience. Almost all people believe what they find others believing—those others with whom they identify themselves. White men also believe many things on authority, not because they themselves have seen the evidence and worked out the theory from first principles themselves.

There is considerable inconsistency and indeed confusion among the statements present-day Navahos make about death and immortality. In part, this may be traced to direct and indirect influences of Christianity. In part, the disagreements relate to the fact that Navahos of different regions have had their main historical contacts with different tribes of other Indians. It is also true that Indians in general have not troubled to create systematic and completely congruent theologies that conform to the canons of Aristotelian logic. Navaho mythology contains the idea of an afterlife but discusses it only casually and fragmentarily.

Nevertheless, one finds virtual unanimity on a number of major issues. There is no sense whatever that life is a preparation for existence in the next world. Even the conception that there is a connection between the two modes of existence is a distinctly minor note. Perhaps one may cite the belief that the very young and innocent and those who die in respected old age need not be feared. However, the fact of the matter is that this belief is little honored in behavior. A few informants assert that witches and suicides go to a different place, but if this be a punishment, it is merely that of segregation. In any case, one suspects a borrowing of Christian doctrine. This suspicion attains practical certainty when it comes to the occasional statements one hears today that the evil dead go to a burning pit in the center of the earth. The aboriginal notion held out neither the hope of reward nor the fear of punishment in the life beyond.

Navaho thinking accords with the Greek epigram, "Death is evil; the Gods themselves have judged it so." Mythology pictures the Navaho supernaturals as fearing death. The mortality of human beings is sometimes rationalized in myth on the ground that otherwise the earth would become too crowded. But the solace of beneficent divine purpose is lacking. On the contrary, dying either is regarded as due to an experimental caprice of some divinity or is explained as the daily payment demanded by the Sun for carrying out his travel.

Death is evil, and the dead are feared. Every item in the funeral ritual is intended to prevent or cajole the deceased from returning to plague his relatives. The corpse's property is deposited with him, but this is no spontaneous gesture of affection nor a disinterested desire to promote well-being in the afterworld. Navaho lore teaches that any stinginess on the part of the living will bring swift and terrible retaliation.

It is significant that the living are most vulnerable to the ghosts of their own relatives. Indeed, if a ghost appears in or near a crowd, only the relatives will be sensitive to the apparition. There is little or no dread of the spirits of those long gone. Navaho thought is not clear whether this is because souls gradually cease to exist or because ghosts lack motivation to return from ghost-land after the relatives they have known in life have also disappeared from the surface of the earth.

This focus of anxiety upon the ghosts of known relatives is most plausibly explained by Opler's (1936) theory developed to understand similar belief and behavior among two Apache tribes. On the one hand, there is vehement mourning for the dead and, in most cases, genuine evidence of grief. On the other hand, there is exaggerated terror that the beloved relatives will return to take a living person back with them or at least bring severe "ghost sickness." Opler points out that physical survival demands the closest sort of cooperation in the family group. Feelings of antagonism and resentment must ordinarily be severely suppressed during life, for open conflict and competition would threaten the successful carrying out of subsistence activities. Yet the behavior of drunken Apaches and Navahos plainly evidences the intensity of submerged feelings of hostility toward some close relatives. Hence ghosts may be understood as projections of the largely unconscious hate and distrust that the living have felt toward dead members of the intimate family circle. Sentiments at death are best described as mixed. The positive side comes out in tears and the melancholy sense of loss. The negative side is expressed in fearful dreams and fantasies of ghost apparitions.

One of the reasons that Navaho conceptions of life after death are much less clearly formulated than other aspects of their religious beliefs is the reluctance to discuss anything connected with death or the dead. Only when some individual believes himself victimized by a ghost but feels a need to consult a diviner for more precise information as to which ghost is troubling him and what the diagnosis for ceremonial treatment is, does one hear unforced statements of Navaho theory.

Fear, however, is not the whole story. I have heard more than one Navaho utter the substance of Confucius' famous question, "We do not know life, how do we know death?" As the Navahos say, "These things are hidden from us." The Navahos accept the inevitability of dying, but in a religion that almost entirely lacks revelation and prophecy the afterlife is defined only by a few vague statements in the traditions of the people. Moreover, the whole of Navaho implicit philosophy maintains that it is this life that counts—partly on the ground that living here and now may be rich and satisfying, partly because such notions as there are of the next world portray it as a rather vague, misty, unexciting place. A very old man once explained his traveling around so much in this way: "I want to move around while I can. Soon I'll be dead and I won't be able to. I'll have to take a long rest."

A more positive note is sometimes struck in the statements of older Navaho intellectuals. It is said that for the living to be much concerned with death and the afterlife is both unwise and unhealthy. Indeed, Navaho religion considers such preoccupation to be symptomatic of psychic or organic illness, though the ordinary Navaho's interpretation would find the cause in the supernatural visitation of a ghost. Yet there is a deep current in Navaho thought that is congruent with Spinoza's proposition, "The free man thinks about nothing so little as about death, his wisdom consisting in the contemplation, not of death, but of life."

Navaho eschatology is almost entirely consistent in affirming that a "wind" or "breath" leaves the body at death for a spirit-land, although I have heard a few Navahos say something like this: "We used to believe that. Now we think when you die you stay dead." The spirit-land is most often located to the north (which is the fearsome direction to the Navaho). Sometimes it is placed to the west. It is usually said to be beneath the surface of this world and is often identified with the land from which the Holy People emerged in mythological times. Some accounts depict ghost-land as continually cloudy or shrouded in darkness; others describe it as a barren, desert place. Activity seems to be almost nonexistent according to some informants; other accounts suggest that dead Navahos farm, hunt, and carry out the other pursuits of terrestrial life, including ceremonials. A few informants consider that only the souls of animals and insects go below, while human souls have a home above ground. The dominant picture, though, is that of returning to an interior, dark place ("the dark earth"). The psychoanalyst will surely find here a standardized unconscious fantasy of return to the womb.

The Mohave Indians distinguish four soul-substances, but many Navahos speak of two. One of these appears to reside permanently in spirit-land. The other is variously described as lingering (at least for many years) about the grave or as moving back and forth between spirit-land and the homes of the living, often in the skin of a coyote, mouse, or owl. Some informants appear to distinguish between the fate of the good and evil incorporeal parts of the person. Only the evil leaves the spirit-land to return to the earth as a ghost. Some informants maintain that the good part of the soul goes to four different places, depending upon the time of day when a person dies. A few say that none of the good lives on after death.

There is conflicting lore with respect to the appearance of the dead. The dead leave their skins but are still portrayed as taking with them whatever they were dressed in. The gruesome aspect of the corpse itself is seldom mentioned. Ghosts are almost never seen in human form, although there are a few cases of apparition of skeletons. On the other hand, myths speak of spirits as combing their hair and painting their faces red. Those who have visited the netherworld in dream, coma, or unconsciousness readily recognize their relatives. In the opinion of Father Berard Haile, the best Navaho scholar, a spirit living without bodily form would be inconceivable to the Navaho. One myth affirms that women in the "dark place" will cease to have menstrual periods and to bear children.

The Navaho, then, do not yearn for immortality. They accept some form of continued existence as probable, but the prospect is more accepted than welcomed. It should be noted explicitly that Navaho dead are not thought of as joining their divinities. The divinities are in entirely separate places. Nor can the unacculturated Navaho regard the Christian belief in the resurrection of the body with anything but horror. This is almost certainly the reason that the two Ghost Dance movements that swept the western United States in the nineteenth century were rejected by the Navaho. As Hill says (1944, p. 525):

For the Navaho with his almost psychotic fear of death, the dead and all connected with them, no greater cataclysm than the return of the departed . . . could be envisioned. In short, the Navaho were frightened out of their wits for fear the tenets of the movement were true.

Lacking any sense that this life is a preparation for a more significant existence, the Navahos do not "solve" the problem of good and evil by their eschatological doctrine. Navaho morality is practical rather than categorical. Abstract moral standards are hardly necessary in a homogeneous, face-to-face society. Conceptions of heaven and hell are the logical counterparts in the afterworld of the philosophic abstractions of absolute good and absolute evil. "The Christian," as McNair (1948, p. 172) says in his doctoral thesis, "believing in these absolutes, is forced to posit them in an ideal world since they are not part of the world in which he lives." While the Navaho feels very keenly that life is *hard*, his outlook is quite foreign to that of "Life is real, life is earnest, and the grave is not the goal." To quote McNair (p. 175) again, "The Navaho has turned to witchcraft to explain the evils in his present world rather than to eschatological hopes of reward for himself and punishment for those who have caused his insecurity."

Apache

It is not surprising that there are many resemblances, down to small details, between the beliefs of the Navaho and those of the closely related Apache tribes. The most striking difference is that both the eastern and the western Apache speak of the netherland as a place of pleasure and plenty, free from pain, sorrow, and the necessity to work. Opler says that "the Mescalero conception of life after death is one of an underground paradise." One of his informants gave the following idyllic picture (1946, p. 460):

They say that when you die it is like falling off a high cliff. You fall and fall off into space and eventually you light easily on the floor of a beautiful valley. Here are many tipis, many people, all the friends you have known in your life, laughing, hunting, eating, having a good time. Life there is much like life here on earth, except that it is better. Everyone keeps his earthly appearance but there is more food and the women are more beautiful. The valley has many trees and is surrounded by high cliffs. The people who live there never die.

This is in sharp contrast to the typical Navaho view. I have never heard one Navaho suggest that the afterworld was a better place, and I have heard many emphatically state the contrary. There are two references in the literature to a pleasant afterlife, but both come from a region near the railroad where Christian influence is strong. Other differences are matters of detail. The Navahos usually relate that the guardians of the entrance to the land of the dead make new arrivals take one or both moccasins off and shake them for dirt to see whether or not they really are dead. The Jicarilla Apache variant of this test is that wild plums are offered; if they are eaten, the newcomer slides down into the underworld.

The White Mountain Apache believe that witches go to a special, unpleasant locality where they must continually work. The Jicarilla Apache hold that witches are segregated in a place made dangerous by poisonous plants and beasts of prey. The White Mountain Apache also specify separate locations for shamans of great power and for persons killed by water, lightning, or certain animals. These Apache also apparently fail to distinguish two aspects of the soul: they say simply that the "breath" goes to an abode in the north that is ruled by a Ghost Chief and from which any "breath" may return as a ghost.

Pueblo

There are numerous and important variations in belief and practice among the twenty-odd Pueblo Indian tribes. Nevertheless, without too much distortion, one may construct a generalized picture that accords with the Navaho-Apache at many points and differs interestingly at others. The Pueblos show a fear of the dead, though it appears to be appreciably less intense. There is a parallel to Navaho-Apache "ghost sickness." The dead are rather consistently described as carrying on the familiar patterns of Pueblo life. Funeral and other rites are utilized as techniques for keeping the individual dead from returning. The following formula, used in San Juan Pueblo, is typical enough:

Here is food for you. Do not be mean to people here. Do not come around. If you do come, do not let us hear you.

There are, however, some interesting differences. Among the Hopi, at least, there is belief in the reincarnation of dead children. People are not thought of as quite fully dead until four days after breathing has ceased; there are indications of this transitional stage in Navaho thought, but it is less clear-cut. The individual dead are less thought of as malevolent than as, in Robbins' happy phrase, "infected with a contagious disease." The dead very soon cease to exist as individuals.

The worlds of the living and of the dead are separated much less sharply. Corpses are put away with their kachina masks, their passports to the other world which they will wear there. One student of the Zuñi has remarked:

"Dead" isn't the way the Zuñis think of it—our word carries too much finality of separation. "Present but not seen" expresses the Zuñi feeling.

Some Pueblos seem to feel that the passage from one mode of existence to the other is never a natural phenomenon in the strict sense. Death is always due to witchcraft in the last analysis.

The dead, considered as a collectivity, are not feared but rather looked to as the source of rain and other blessings. They become divinities who are welcomed and in fact invoked back to the villages. In every Hopi ceremony the spirits of the dead are invoked—as kachina (divine beings) or as clouds or simply as the inhabitants of the underworld. Each earthly ceremony has its counterpart in the underworld but is carried out at the opposite time of the year. In the kiva, or sacred chamber, there is an opening to permit communication with the underworld.

However, the Hopi, like the Navaho, devote their thought to this life while it lasts. As Kennard (1937, p. 492) says:

Every individual has his own road to follow, his own will which he concentrates upon keeping happy, healthy, and arriving at old age. He, too, must live without mental conflict, worry, or trouble since these destroy his will and consequently lead to unhappiness, sickness, and death. A man who thinks of the dead or of the future life instead of being concerned with worldly activities is thereby bringing about his own death.

Robbins (1941, pp. 46-47) has well generalized the Pueblo attitude:

The Pueblo Indian's concern for the dead does not take him far in speculation about their condition. He is more interested in knowing what they have to do for him or to him. It is little wonder then that his last word is that his ancestors continue in death to do that which every good Pueblo tries to do in life—namely, to keep a healthy supply of rain falling upon the crops, for this alone insures the continuation of life. Whatever he says of the soul and its life after death, the reference is always to life on this side of the grave. Pueblo death beliefs make for the acceptance and neutralization of an instinctive fear which rises at the time of death. When the beliefs are well accepted and integrated, as they seem here to be, the fear itself tends not to appear and the calmer acceptance of an otherwise dangerous crisis becomes the customary pattern of behavior.

The Pueblo Indians, like the Navaho and Apache, stress the meaning of dreams of the dead. They too have their tales of visits to the afterworld in trance, particularly of those who are ill to the point of death. The Orpheus myth, in the strict sense, has been recorded for only Zuñi and Navaho, among all Southwestern tribes. This myth supplies an answer to the sceptic's question as to how humans come by knowledge of the afterworld and also explains why free communication between the two worlds is impossible. The minds of the Pueblo Indians are also confused concerning the fate of the soul after death. In Zuñi, for example, the general version is that the soul stays in Zuñi four days after death and then departs to the kachina village to the west or descends beneath lakes and springs. Others hold that at least some souls go to the place of emergence and those of certain priests to the four oceans of the world. The soul itself is not a very distinct entity; it is associated with the head and the heart but is most often called "breath-body."

The idea of future punishment by fire or transformation into insect or snake is occasionally heard among the Hopi. In the Rio Grande Pueblos punishment by flame, especially of witches, is almost standard—but probably derives from the friars. The notion of the afterlife as a place of reward never turns up (except as purely Christian doctrine) in the sayings of Pueblos or Apaches or Navahos.

Discussion

The constant features in the eschatology of all of these southwestern tribes are the fear of the dead (and the corollary that death is not the end), the concentration upon life as opposed to death, the relative lack of conscious rationalization to harmonize conflicting or contradictory conceptions, and the absence of any notion that the afterlife can reward good behavior on earth or that immortality is a goal. There is also a basic similarity in mythological framework (underworld, emergence place, four as ritual number, etc.), in spite of many variations in detail. The striking variables are the degree to which the next world is portrayed as more, less, or equally attractive when compared with life on this earth; the concept of punishment after death; and the idea of the dead as altogether dangerous or as (at least collectively) beneficent.

Every culture, as Max Weber showed, must provide orientations to such inescapable problems as death. The answers which the cultures of southwestern Indians give to this question may seem to imply the philosophy of Stevenson's phrase, "Take everything as it comes in a forlorn stupidity." I personally prefer Malinowski's verdict: "In short, religion here assures the victory of tradition and culture over the mere negative response of thwarted instinct."

9 *TWO NAVAHO CHILDREN*

OVER A FIVE-YEAR

PERIOD

THE PURPOSE OF THIS PAPER is to report materials that bear upon methodological issues in the study of primitive children. The two subjects have been followed since birth. Brief case histories up to 1942 have been published in *Children of the People* (1947a, pp. 195-200). The present report deals with the period between November, 1942, and September, 1947. It is restricted largely to problems arising out of personality tests administered during that period. First, however, personality profiles, based both on the tests and on the accumulated observation of the two children and their families by the writers and others, will be presented. These personality profiles obviously have an interpretative and, indeed, an impressionistic element.

1949g Reprinted by permission of the publishers from Clyde Kluckhohn and Janice C. Rosenzweig, "Two Navaho Children over a Five-year Period," *American Journal of Orthopsychiatry.*" Vol. 19, pp. 266-278.

Subjects

CARLOTTA

Carlotta, born in December, 1936, is a friendly, warm, winsome, and lively child. She has sparkling eyes and, like her father, an easy smile. Her face is unusually mobile. Within a few minutes she can look in turn coy, impish, angry, and sullen. Her gestures have the smoothness, the grace, and also the nonchalance typical of many Navahos. Her health is good. She is extremely spontaneous. At times she appears totally unaware of many elementary social restrictions, and her remarks and reactions are somewhat bolder and less inhibited than is expected from a Navaho girl of her age. She is rich in fantasy but not imaginative. When faced with new situations or material, she is not adaptive or creative. She is sensitive and reactive, unorganized in her thinking as well as in her emotions.

Carlotta has a will of her own and is on her way to standing up to her domineering mother rather than reacting to her in a passive way as she did formerly. Her interests are mostly limited to creature comforts and to sheep. She has not intellectual ambition, no drive toward the white world. She does like white people, however, for they mean to her a chance to be the center of attention, and they offer diversion from the monotony of her life. Carlotta is retarded in her intellectual and emotional development.[1] This is understandable on the combined bases of the isolation in which the family lives (an isolation unusual even for a Navaho family) and its heredity. She wants to make friends but has not been given a good chance to try herself out in this area. As she grows older, she is becoming more aware of standards and in some unusual situations feels her shortcomings.

Carlotta is the oldest of a family of four children: her next sibling is a boy of five; then follow a girl of three and a boy of nearly two. The family is located at the border of the Navaho group. Contacts are frequent with Mexicans and occasional with Anglos. Trips to relatives' homes or elsewhere are made rarely.

---

1. This and similar statements take Navaho children as the standard of comparison.

Carlotta has been herding sheep since she was four. At first this was unpleasant to her, but now it provides her with an escape from the domination of her mother, who has the firmness and authority of many Navaho mothers but lacks the warmth of most. It may be that the mother is re-enacting with her daughter what she herself suffered from her own harsh and tyrannical mother. Herding sheep also brings Carlotta the approval of her father and helps maintain a relationship with him which has always been exceptionally close. The family was always constituted of the two parents and the children only. As a result, Carlotta grew up without the benefit of the wide constellation of familial affections that is typical of Navaho extended families.

Carlotta is the only survivor of her mother's first five pregnancies; two children died before she was born, and two after. The girl who was her next sibling died after being bitten by red ants while out playing with Carlotta. During certain periods Carlotta was given more than the usual amount of care, affection, and protection by her parents; but this was traumatically withdrawn from her by her mother at least. She still enjoys being the center of attention, but rarely finds this opportunity at home now, since the parents' care is focused on the younger children. She welcomes the opportunity for attention when white observers come and has learned to play up to them. On these occasions she evidences resentment at her siblings, especially her chief rival, the next oldest brother. In the past five years she has noticeably matured and has gained security through her responsibilities toward her family: herding sheep, tending her siblings, and the routine chores that fall to the oldest daughter in a Navaho family.

The family is well thought of in the community but is not outstanding. The parents get on well together, and the family is a close unit. At times the father herds sheep for Mexicans, who commend him for his reliability. At other times he practices "hand-trembling" among the Navaho—that is, he is a diviner-diagnostician. The mother occasionally weaves and sells rugs, but the chief source of income is provided by the family herd, which, through good management, has steadily increased in recent years. They own goats as well as sheep and use milk in their diet. Their economic level in the past few years has risen from below average to about average.

Carlotta seems well on her way to making a satisfactory adjustment to the kind of life she will probably lead.

BILL

Bill, born in October, 1935, is bashful and sensitive, with an unusual need for warmth and affection but without the outgoingness and boldness to get them. He is kind, cooperative, willing, attentive to the well-being of others, and protective to those younger than he. He tends to hold his head down as if afraid to face the world and people but gains respect from his peers and is generally well liked. He is quiet but has spurts of activity and even aggressiveness. Bill is physically well developed for his age, a good-looking boy with regular features and a sad expression. His health is good, but his resistance to physical strain somewhat below normal. He is well poised, talks little except when perfectly safe and secure, but thinks a good deal. He seems to keep all his channels of expressive activity under strong control.

In school he is a slow, steady worker. He achieves best when left to his own pace and repeatedly reassured that he is doing well. He is self-critical and tends to be easily discouraged. He enjoys being with others but likes being alone, when he can daydream. Daydreaming is his chief outlet for creativity, since his imagination is so controlled. His intelligence is good, although his thinking is slow. His thought already indicates an integrated personality. Now that he is approaching adolescence, he is on his way to reaching emotional as well as intellectual integration.

Bill has attended school since 1943. For the first three years he attended the local Navaho school at Ramah; since 1946 he has been at the Albuquerque boarding school. School has been a major experience for him, hard at the start but beneficial after a while. It has certainly influenced his thinking and his social development considerably, but he is well rooted in the Navaho culture and so far seems to have been spared the often damaging results of a Navaho-white conflict. This is probably largely due to his family background, especially the strong influence of his maternal grandfather, who is a leading and respected singer in the community and sees to it that all his grandchildren know the values of the Navaho way.

Bill is the eighth of ten children. The family lives within easy range of the neighboring Mormon community. The immediate family is dominated by women. This was especially true when the oldest son was away in the army. The father, a relatively weak figure who came from another Navaho group, has gained respect locally but has not become a forceful figure. His wife is the stronger person by far. She is authoritative but kind, an affectionate mother. Bill, however, was deprived twice of her affection in favor of his two younger brothers. The mother's relationship to the last child is still extremely close. The parents are compatible. There is a constant going and coming of relatives of both parents. The family is above average in prestige and property. The mother's grandfather was the recognized leader of the Ramah Navaho; she herself is one of the best weavers in the area. Two older children in the family have gone to school several years. Now Bill and his next younger brother are going. The oldest brother, who went to school, was in the army for three years. On his return in 1945, he and his cousin were given charge of the local Navaho cooperative store located on the grounds of the school Bill was attending. With a weak father, an irresponsible next older brother, and an unusually attractive next younger brother, Bill finds his oldest brother a particularly important figure. Bill felt his absence in the army keenly and during this period was a somewhat neglected family member because of his age, his personality, and his position in the family structure.

Provided white people do not make him feel uncomfortable by attention of one kind or another, Bill has by now reached a matter-of-fact attitude toward them. Testing has been a painful experience for such a sensitive child. Bill will not be a leader, but he will be a useful and cooperative member of his group.

Interpretations of 1942 Rorschach

The records were interpreted by the tester and independently by another psychiatrist, a clinical psychologist, and an anthropologist. Only the tester and the anthropologist were familiar with Navaho culture. The tester alone knew the subjects. The agreements, disagreements, and independent points raised by the four interpreters are summarized in Tables I and II. A designates

TABLE I (Carlotta)

Interpreters

1. *Degree and mode of control*
   Some control at work . . . .   C D
   Control poor . . . . A B
   Beginning withdrawal . . . .   D
   Efforts to tone down reactions . . . .   D
   Evasion of necessity of doing something   C
   Avoidance   C

2. *Responsiveness of the subject's emotional energies*
   Strong responsiveness to external stimuli . . . . . A   D
   Uncontrolled response . . . . A B   D
   Spontaneous response . . . .   B C
   Inner life hardly expressed . . . . A   C
   Emotional development congenitally impeded . . .   B
   Impulsive response due to youth, marked femininity,
     or lack of mental discipline . . . . A
   Strong reactivity may take form of affection,
     aggression, diffuse discharge of emotions . . . .   D
   Lack of social technique or insight . . . .   D
   No aggressiveness, no hostility . . . .   B

3. *The subject's mental approach*
   Perseveration . . . . A B

4. *The subject's creative and imaginative capacities*
   Imagination poor . . . . A B C
   Imagination of the confabulatory,
     purely subjective type . . . .   B

5. *The subject's intellectual level
     and features of her thinking*
   Intelligence poor . . . . A B C
   Intellectual development congenitally impeded . . .   B
   Thinking poorly organized . . . . A B
   Erratic thinking of typical stickiness . . . . . .   B
   Thinking childish but normal   C

6. *An estimate of the subject's degree of security and insecurity*

	Interpreters
Anxiety	A B C D
Interest in birth process	A B C D
Preoccupation with birth process	B C D
Anxiety related to perseveration	A
Anxiety in birth process due to birth of a sibling or to awareness of role as a woman	C
Fear of being apprehended or eaten	C
Overconfidence of the simple-minded	B

7. *The subject's degree of maturity*

Very immature	A B

Prognosis

Good nature to be her most effective control	B
Anxiety to be resolved through exhaustion or early sexual satisfaction	B
Satisfactory adjustment within her informal society	A

TABLE II (Bill)

	Interpreters
1. *Degree and mode of control*	
Control actively at work	A B C D
Great constriction	A B C D
Withdrawal	A B C
Rejection	B
Overcritical attitude	B
Blocking and evasion	D
2. *Responsiveness of the subject's emotional energies*	
Feeling for emotional stimuli	A B C D
Inhibited response	C D
Aggression	B D
Total lack of cushioning	D
Accepts his inner impulses	A
Absence of free instinctual strivings	D
3. *The subject's mental approach*	
Critical attitude	B C
4. *The subject's creative and imaginative capacities*	
Imagination poor	A B C
Turn to fantasy possible	D

5. *The subject's intellectual level*
   and features of his thinking
   Intelligence good . . . . A B C
   Intelligence a little above average . . . . A   C
   Thinking impeded . . . . A B C

6. *An estimate of the subject's degree of security*
   and insecurity
   Marked free-floating anxiety . . . . A B C D
   Object-directed anxiety (social sphere) . . . . .   B C
   Anxiety suggestive of traumatic experiences,
        sexual fears, and guilt . . . .   B
   Sibling rivalry   C
   Awareness of conflict . . . . A B

7. *The subject's degree of maturity*
   Occasional signs of maturity . . . .   B C

Prognosis
   Satisfactory adjustment under favorable circumstances A B

the psychiatrist who took the record, B the second psychiatrist, C the clinical psychologist, and D the anthropologist.[2]

It is clear that there is a remarkable degree of agreement among the four interpretations, three of them done "blind." All four note the presence of anxiety in Carlotta's record and her preoccupation with the birth process. Three evaluate her intelligence as poor and speak of her uncontrolled responses. Each interpretation records Bill's obtrusion through active defense mechanisms, great constriction, free-floating anxiety, and feeling for emotional stimuli. In the two cases there is only a single instance of contradictory interpretation: B specifically states that there is no evidence of aggressiveness or hostility in the record of Carlotta; D, on the other hand, notes that strong reactivity may take the form of aggression. Other divergences take the form of variations in emphasis; for example, while all

---

2. The items mentioned under each of the main categories are mostly transcribed literally from the original interpretations. A few items, however, have been inferred from them. It is not an exhaustive list but brings out the main points. Table I is longer than Table II because it shows greater divergence, not because of any difference in the length of the interpretations.

rate Carlotta's intelligence as low, only B raises the question of "high moron." Mainly, divergence is expressed by what caught the attention of the various interpreters in the records. There is also evidence of some differences in basic orientation to personality theory.

Two Administrations of Certain Tests

A modified Thematic Apperception Test, the Stewart Emotional Response Test, and the Bavelas Moral Ideology Test were given to these two subjects in 1942. About ten months later they were repeated by different field workers. Scrutiny of the results was focused upon two main variables: the effect of continuous residence for some days with the family before testing and the administration of the tests directly in Navaho, without intervention of an interpreter.

Analysis is complicated by the time interval and by various uncontrollable situational factors. Full description of the details involved in weighing the evidence would take many pages. The following conclusions, however, seem to be justified by the facts.

1. Psychiatrists and psychologists should not anticipate that children in other cultures can be tested adequately on the basis of casual rapport established in a few hours or a day. At least as regards quantity, the familiarity between tester and child is crucial. For example, Bill's TAT record was more than three times as long when the tester had been living steadily in his family for about a week before the test was administered. The total number of words in the response to the other two tests was six times as great.

2. The role of participant-observer is far superior to that of tester.

3. The younger the subject is, and the more insecure, the greater the need to establish deep-going rapport.

4. Direct use of the native language on the part of the tester shows comparable differences. Carlotta's TAT record was five and a half times longer. Her performance was considerably

freer, more spontaneous, more natural. She gestured, asked herself questions, and corrected herself. Here the content of the responses also differed considerably, though this may have been influenced by familiarity as well as by the direct use of Navaho.

1946 Experiments

During a six-month period in 1946 the two subjects were put through a battery of projective experiments to bring out group attitudes and determine their place in the total personality configuration of the individual. Here, items of behavior will be drawn selectively from the total experimental record to build up a personality picture of each subject. Assertions will be followed by initials to indicate their main documentation: C (Clay: free clay modeling); D (Drawing: free and assigned crayon drawings); FP (Figure Plates: placement of figure plates representing three cultural groups); 5Do (Five Dolls: preferences among five differently colored dolls); DH (Doll House:[3] free play and responses to standardized scenarios); PE (Picture Experiment: response to pictured objects); Q (Questionnaire: self-identification and group knowledge); TQ (Test Questions: cross-check of other procedures; P (Photography: stills and movies taken during the first six experiments listed above). The experiments were conducted with forty-eight children—sixteen Navaho, sixteen Mormon, sixteen Spanish-American—all between the ages of seven and eleven. The experimental results have not been fully analyzed, so the comparative basis of the following judgments may require some revision in the future.

CARLOTTA

Two main currents seem to run through Carlotta's record:

1. Spontaneity and fantasy that give the superficial impression of a bright, alert, imaginative child (DH). This impression is

3. The doll houses were miniature replicas of the usual dwellings and furniture of the three groups in question.

reinforced by casual evidence of good observation (FL, PE) and sensitivity to her environment (5Do, DH).

2. Poor assimilation, poor observation, poor memory—in other words, evidence of her intellectual shortcomings.

She shows consistently throughout her record that she has difficulty in relating facts to concepts (FP, D, FL, PDO, DH, Q, TQ). Just as Bill's record is striking because it is so well integrated, Carlotta's is equally striking because it is so poorly integrated. Her thinking at times appears very disorganized: she dumped the dishes and furniture inside the hogan before arranging them (DH). One feels that there is no carry-over from one situation to the next within the same test (FP, PDO, DH, PE). At other times, however, she surprises one by the remarkable consistency and logic in the same test: for example, her consistent choice of preferred dolls, from lightest to medium, and of flags, from most like to least like the United States flag (seen on the white observer's car) (5Do, FL).

As for her creative capacities, she shows the same contradictory trends. She can dramatize beautifully, talking and acting freely when presented with a situation that is not too well structured (DH), but she is definitely limited in her creative abilities (D, C). At times she is able to let her fantasy run free to the extent of being quite original, but she is never creative enough to be called imaginative (DH). Her poor manual dexterity is a further handicap to free expression.

Her anxieties seem focused around an awareness of her intellectual shortcomings (FP, PDO, Q) and around food (DH). There may also be some death anxiety (PDO). When she feels faced with a very well-structured situation, she controls her anxieties through evasion, avoidance, and blocking. She frequently says, "It is too hard for me to guess, I can't guess what to say" (PDO, Q). She is well aware of sex differences (D) and shows a natural and free interest in sex (DH).

Her record contains many value judgments. These point to a strong awareness of superego forces (DH) but are not accompanied by a strain to meet standards (DH). There is evidence that she identified well with the Navaho girl-doll, and she shows a closer relationship to her father than to her mother (DH). The mother is the dominating figure even in sex (DH).

There is little group awareness in the record. She violated several Navaho patterns, putting the stove in the miniature hogan wherever she saw fit and ignoring incest taboos (DH). There are, however, hints that she is aware of being a Navaho, though not fully and consciously so (DH, PDO, PE). As for her awareness of other groups, she is still very confused (FP, PDO, Q, TQ, D, DH). She knows there are different groups, but she does not have clear-cut images of them. The isolation in which she has lived so far and her father's close past association with Mexicans certainly account in great part for her confused picture, but her poor perception and limited capacities perhaps account for the rest.

BILL

Bill's record, as compared with those of other Navaho children of his age, is characterized by a marked constriction in his responses, reinforced by tenseness in his general behavior. He gives a spontaneous response and elaborates on it only rarely (DH). He prefers to respond to questions, and his answers are usually very short (PDO, DH, Q). As for his general behavior, he tends to turn his body away from the experimenter and to make inhibited gestures (P, C, D, DH). The film shows him encircling the drawing board with his arm, his body turned away from the photographer and experimenter, a significant constricted position (P). In the free-drawing situation he chose to draw a fence, which may also be significant. Besides constriction, Bill's most usual modes of defense seem to include evasion, on the one hand, and meticulousness, on the other. His responses tend to be *either* evasive *or* meticulous; few of them fall in between, and those are usually of a definite constrictive character. He is evasive in the most uncomfortable situations for him (PD, DH, Q), such as when he is asked to answer questions about white people. He shows meticulousness in situations where he is somewhat more at ease (D, FL, DH). His perseverance, which appears strained, may well be another mode of defense (FP, C, D). He spent twenty-two minutes on a single clay model. This points to a tendency to shut himself out of a new situation that would require from him a new adjustment and some articulation. But, with this tendency, there is a sensitivity to noises around him. Perseveration, therefore, is not accompanied by concentration (FP, FL, DH, PDO).

There is evidence of anxiety, which seems to be for the most part confined to his social adjustment and channeled along specific lines. Any tense situation increases his anxiety rapidly and visibly; sometimes, although rarely, it climaxes in a fear reaction (DH, TQ). In the doll-house incident where the Navaho woman is visited at night by the Mexican man, Bill states that both the man and the woman are afraid (DH).

Aggression is present in the record. It is either indirect, in the form of passive resistance (D, C, PD, DH, Q), or covert—that is, not acted but only verbalized (DH). In these cases it is channeled along the lines sanctioned. There is little doubt that some of it is directed against the experimenter, who is identified with the white dolls.

Bill's intelligence is above average. His whole performance is consistent and shows a good integration of facts and experiences. He is observant and attentive to details (D, FP, 5Do, PDO, FL, DH) but also shows a certain variety within the limits of response he sets for himself (D, DH).

Bill's mind is orderly. His school experience may partly account for this, but his maturity and his attention to details stand out. He shows organization in his thinking (FP, PDO, DH). He puts things away before turning to a new situation (D, DH).

His knowledge is integrated in a broad frame of reference, as is evidenced by his clear concepts of Navahos, Zuñi, Mexicans, and whites. These concepts are solidly related to personal experiences, which he is able to account for and mention when he is carefully handled (D, FP, 5Do, PDO, DH).

His imagination appears to be limited (C, D, DH). He produced only one clay model, whereas the other children averaged six (his younger brother made five). He has only one free drawing and does not initiate situations in the doll house. But there are occasional signs of imagination (DH), again within the limited areas he sets himself.

His anxiety seems to center in the social sphere. Uneasiness and insecurity, manifested by the content of his response or by his behavioral reaction, are usually found when a social situation of some intensity is presented (FP, PDO, DH). In the doll-house situation he prefers to manipulate objects rather than dolls. He readjusts with care displaced furniture but leaves an individual doll where it has fallen (DH). It may also be of significance that he mentions lambs, calves, and little children in order of preference when asked specifically to name what he likes best in the world (TQ). There is evidence in his record that he tries to assert himself but that the world is for him full of older people who tend to overwhelm him (DH); it is tempting to relate this to his age, to his sibling situation, and possibly to his school experiences. He identifies with his father, and his sexual identification adjustment appears to be good (DH). There is, however, evidence of anxiety in the sexual sphere proper (DH).

He shows marked awareness of being a Navaho. He also expresses preference for his own group (5Do, PDO, DH, FP). He acts it and verbalizes it, choosing the doll whose skin color comes closest to that of the Navahos, placing the Navaho figure plates on the first line, and showing them consistently as the strongest and best when they are faced with Mexicans or whites. He also mentions that they are whiter than Zuñi or Mexicans (Q) and specifically says he likes them best of all. Together with these clear group concepts goes an awareness of social stratification (DH). The white man, accused of having stolen the Navaho's gun, denies it. The Navaho man is sure of it but, instead of insisting, goes home. With the Mexican who stole the Navaho man's money, a real argument takes place, and the Mexican man finally promises to return it shortly. Bill views the Mexican as more of an equal than the white man. There are signs that Bill is afraid of white people (DH).

1947 Rorschachs

In August, 1947, Bert Kaplan of the Harvard Psychological Clinic retested these two children. He gives the outstanding characteristics of the records as follows:

CARLOTTA

This girl is uncritical, easily satisfied with herself, and responds freely and directly to all kinds of external stimuli. Her response to emotional stimuli is impulsive and uninhibited, but also superficial. She is definitely on the extroverted side. There seems to be a paucity of inner life other than the sexual preoccupation.

Strong perseverative tendencies are present, which lead her to repeat certain responses like cloud, rock, and tree in almost every card. She seems to be preoccupied with only one problem in this record and works out this problem in almost the same way in every card. There seems to be an inability to shift to other problems or to other views of the same problem. This problem appears to concern the maturation of her sexual impulse to the point where the opposite sex has become the object. We infer this from the frequent perception, despite their apparent anxiety-provoking character, of phallic symbols. These symbols are only thinly disguised and do not seem to be avoided; they are given in eight out of ten cards. It is possible also to infer the presence of feelings of aggression toward the male. It is of interest that the anxiety does not serve to inhibit the sexual response. She cannot hold her basic expressiveness back, even though it causes pain. One might say that, with the exception of her evasiveness, she does not appear to have developed any defensive system.

Summary. Carlotta shows many signs of growth and increasing maturity since her last Rorschach five years ago, but in most respects the basic pattern is similar. Although the confabulatory thinking shown previously has disappeared, the vagueness and perseveratory tendencies remain. The preoccupation has changed from the birth process to the male sexual organs. This new sexual concern is anxiety-provoking but relatively uninhibited, and possibly calls forth aggressive and sadistic tendencies. Despite the precociousness of her sexual development, many features of this record are best explained by the hypothesis that she is functioning in a very immature and childish way.

BILL

The subject approaches the test in a shy, inhibited manner. His inner life is tightly constricted at the beginning of the test, and perseveration of a previous response is one of the first means used to cope with the demands of the test. The performance improves, however, as the test continues, and Bill responds more freely.

He uses as a defense against shading-provoked anxiety the method of going to tiny details in the blot. Within these tiny details he allows himself a certain amount of freedom and expression of the inner life. One could say that his previous mode has been to restrict sharply any self-expression, but that he has recently found a way of compromising between his inhibition and his natural spontaneity. He retreats into a world of tiny things where he does not feel overwhelmed, and there he achieves a certain amount of self-expression. The sharpness and ingenuity of these tiny details indicate that he has potential good intelligence, imaginativeness, and spontaneity, which, however, are not being realized except perhaps in daydreams.

He vacillates between giving strong animal figures, like the lion and the bear, and weak ones, like the mouse, rabbit, dog, and chipmunk. This is further evidence of the struggle taking place in him between identification with strong adult figures and also with weak, childish ones. This boy has made his first moves toward growing into adulthood. However, even the strong adult figures are passive. He is not yet bold enough to make his figures active, and although Bill is fundamentally passive, he may also be, through fear, inhibiting any active impulse.

Several nicely perceived "surface texture" responses show a strong emotional sensitivity. Although, on the whole, Bill is constricted, he does show in the one color response an ability to deal with emotional stimuli in a constructive way. Color is, however, not so important a stimulus for him as is shading, which is anxiety-provoking and is met by a retreat to the childhood world.

Summary. The general picture of constriction, especially regarding the expression of his own inner life, is tempered in Bill by two trends:

1. He expresses himself freely in minute details representing a childish fantasy type of response.

2. He expresses himself more freely and maturely after he has gained confidence and become habituated to the situation.

In the latter we see the possibility for growth—or, more precisely, the probability that growth has occurred. In the former we see inner resources that are always at his disposal even if they are used at the expense of his real life effectiveness. There are further signs of a conflict between adult and childhood identifications, though the two tendencies seem able to exist side by side without causing him too much trouble. Although it is likely that the adult identification will prevail, Bill will probably remain passive and inhibited, though possessing the ability to deal with most real-life situations. He will retain the capacity to express his inner life in some circumscribed area of activity that is divorced from the everyday concerns in his life. The constriction would seem much more serious if this record were not a considerable improvement over an even more constricted record of a few years ago.

Discussion

The picture obtained of these two personalities by different testers and interpreters using a variety of projective techniques is, on the whole, remarkably consistent. Much of the work was done independently. In no case did any tester or interpreter have full access to all the materials that have been assembled for the writing of this paper. At most, each student was familiar only with some fragment of the total data. The personality diagnoses made on the basis of projective tests also check well with the impressions of another set of field workers who used ordinary interview and observation methods. In short, the present paper constitutes a partial validation of projective tests in another culture, with the caution that significant results are peculiarly dependent upon the relationship between tester and subject.

The development of these two personalities over a five-year period corresponds in a general way to theoretical expectations; that is, the basic pattern persists in each case, but there are changes that may be traced to maturation processes, on the one hand, and to special situational determinants, on the other. Bill continues to be cautious, fussy about small details, and formal.

Carlotta remains impulsive, outgoing, and limited in intelligence. There is, however, evidence in each case for greater maturity and for some shift in the dynamic themes of the youngsters' problems. Carlotta has gained greater control. Her aggression toward her mother and her siblings is now more frequently acted out, less frequently expressed through blocking, withdrawal, or evasion. Her anxieties and preoccupations are now focused on different objects. Both subjects have throughout the period of study shown marked tendencies toward perseveration. Our total fund of information on Navaho personality indicates that here we are dealing with a culturally conditioned factor. Bill seems to be emerging from a somewhat dark phase of his life that was produced by his position in his family, the absence of the loved older brother, the somewhat unusual mother-father relationship, his own special need for affection, and probably the consequences of the latency period. The experience of going to school has influenced him significantly.

10 NAVAHO

MORALS

I SHALL BE CONCERNED almost exclusively with Navaho morals at about the turn of the present century. The contemporary picture, because of Christianity and other Western influences, is too complicated to discuss adequately in a brief essay. Since no adequate records on Navaho behavior of fifty or sixty years ago are available, this presentation will be limited to Navaho prescriptions and prohibitions, with a sketch of the underlying Navaho theory. Scattered observations in the literature published at that time do, of course, make plain the obvious fact that Navaho behavior often departed from the prescribed code.

A summary of Matthews (1899) may well serve as an introduction. Restoration must be made for theft, but the thief is not punished in any formal way. Theft, and, indeed, fraud, on the part of supernaturals is pictured approvingly and rewarded

1956c Reprinted by permission of the publishers from Clyde Kluckhohn, "Navaho Morals," in *Encyclopedia of Morals*, edited by Vergilius Ferm. New York, Philosophical Library, pp. 383-390.

by good fortune when directed against alien peoples. Incest is severely tabooed. The terrible crimes are, in fact, incest and witchcraft. Only witches and cannibals are guilty of incest. Adultery is disapproved, and a deviant woman is sometimes punished by a slight whipping; formerly the husband, with the consent of his erring wife's relatives, might amputate her nose or administer other mutilations. Truthfulness is not inculcated in Navaho myths, though evasion and prevarication should cease when a question has been repeated four times. Solemn promises are of a very sacred character. And Matthews records that he has not found Navahos in practice "less truthful than the average of our own race." The legends record benevolent and philanthropic actions on the part of gods and man alike. Hospitality, courtesy, and deference to age are enjoined. Good conduct is not supported by a doctrine of rewards and punishments in a future life. But a belief in the consequences of one's acts tends to reinforce the ethical code.

Subsequent research requires only some amplification and slight modification of these statements.

Prescriptions

Examining 335 statements from seventy-seven informants interviewed over a fifteen-year period, Hobson (1954) found the following recurrent positive themes related to wealth accumulation and socio-economic values: "make a good living," "have lots of property," "take care of things," "work hard and don't be lazy," "look after your family," and "help people out." Actually, these themes state or imply almost all that is central in Navaho ethics. Moreover, although Hobson considered slightly less than half of his sample as "conservative," all these injunctions were crucial in the Navaho code of the period before Western influence became maximal.

Security. Health and long life are primary Navaho goals, accentuated the more because there is no thought of happiness in or preparation for a future life. Industry and accumulation are means to these ends, both directly and indirectly in that the ceremonials required to ward off or cure illness demand a reserve of property. The four good things of life are often stated to be fire, maize, sheep, and horses. An old man used to tell vividly how his father would say (making an embracing gesture), "When you get something, hold on to it like that." A man who does not want to appear lazy must get up before his wife in the morning and make the fire. It is very damning for one Navaho to say of another, "He is too lazy even to tell a story." The Protestant virtue of care of possessions (though not the frequently paired one of cleanliness) is shared by the Navaho: destructiveness, waste, carelessness, and even clumsiness are disapproved of. Gambling is wrong "if you lose your mother's jewelry." Races, wrestling (for men), and other exercises are good "because they make you strong and not lazy." Games must not interfere with work. One must not even attend ceremonials too often lest this become a way of loafing. Knowledge, including ceremonial knowledge and sound judgment, are good because conducive to health and long life.

Decorum. Sobriety, self-control, and adherence to old custom are valued. Women are praised when they do not cry at desertion by their husbands or "too much" at the death of children. Display of anger, "bad talk" and quarrels should be avoided, particularly in front of those outside the immediate family. Drinking is wrong if it results in loss of superego control, if one "becomes wild and without sense." One should talk "pretty nice" to everyone. General courtesy and careful manners are enjoined. It is good to teach one's children to answer the questions of outsiders if the children know the answers. One should marry at the proper age and not marry again too soon after the death of a spouse. One should dress all of one's children (even those who may be defective) as well as one's means permit. One should carry out the ceremonials properly, not sloppily. The customary ways of life are to be respected as maintaining stability and regularity: many of the older people say today to their children something like, "I am not going to throw away the things that have come down to my people." It is good to do old things, "things that started with the Navaho." It is shameful for a Navaho family to lack a sweathouse: "Good people think about the sweathouse all the time." A ceremonialist will say to his approving audience: "This arrowhead is about three hundred years old. My old folks used to carry it." Or: "This is the earth the oldest people picked up from the top of the Holy Mountains. It is good."

One must also mind one's own business. One should give instructions or information only when asked. One should discipline one's own children, but it is bad to whip the children of others. Some informants hold indeed that, while one's own children must be taught to act responsibly and properly, they need not be given formal instructions in the old ways: "Just keep them yourself."

Reciprocity. One must look after one's parents in old age and otherwise repay them for what they have done for you. Reciprocal behavior among all relatives is the key ethic of interpersonal relations among the Navaho. Loyalty to one's family takes precedence over all other loyalties. The Navaho volunteered in large numbers for World War II, and both volunteers and draftees served well. But in occasional cases where a young man tried to evade service in response to the wishes of his mother, the Navaho community applauded.

But the principle "one good turn deserves another" is also given a wider application. Some of the Ramah Navaho refused attractive employment as United States Army scouts against Geronimo on the ground that the Chiricahua and Mescalero Apache had behaved kindly to them during the time of the Fort Sumner captivity.

Benevolence. The widest ethical generalization enunciated among the Navaho is perhaps "Behave to everybody as if they were your relatives." One often hears of injunctions to give food and money to unrelated poor people even when there is no realistic hope of repayment. If one has nothing else to give to the starving, one should feed them with one's sacred corn pollen. It is good not to interfere with those in economic distress when they trespass on one's range. Hospitality and other forms of generosity are widely praised.

In accord with the foregoing injunctions, such specific virtues as cooperation, personal independence and autonomy (so long as these do not transgress duty to relatives), general com-

172 CULTURE AND BEHAVIOR

petence, truthfulness and trustworthiness, obedience to parents, discretion, control over one's impulses (e.g., avoidance of theft and violence), and readiness to meet contingencies are valued. Courage is good. Bravery is good if it does not lapse into fool-hardiness. Pity is a worthwhile emotion—especially pity for loneliness or unusual distress. A sense of humor is a genuine virtue. Fluency in speech is prized. Fertility and having a good time are advocated.

Prohibitions

These, inevitably, will be largely the negatives of the above, but these negative formulations will add content to and clarify the positive injunctions. Hobson (1954) lists two negative themes: "Don't be too rich" and "Never get poor." These can be generalized under the "avoid excess" prohibition (see below), but further comments are in order. Anyone who is too prosperous is, by Navaho thinking, strongly suspect of failing in his obligations to his relatives and in general benevolence. A very poor person is by that very fact suspected of lacking industry and competence. Moreover, from the Navaho point of view, there are excellent practical reasons for avoiding the extremes. Riches provoke jealousy and antagonism. Both wealth and poverty are likely to arouse witchcraft gossip and the eventuality of the stringent sanctions that may be applied against those accused of witchcraft.

Father Berard Haile (1943) lists the negative commandments of the Navaho as follows:

1. One should not commit rape.

2. One should not steal.

3. One should not stealthily touch a sleeping woman.

4. One should not sex-jealously quarrel, because one's (pollen) bag becomes blood.

5. One should not say (or wish) that this person and his livestock shall die.

6. One should not laugh about men (and womenfolk) because the same (defect) may be one's punishment.

7. One should not commit adultery.
8. Man must not be killed.
9. Lies should not be told.

Most of these are the prohibitions necessary to orderly life in any group. There must be restrictions upon sex behavior, against crimes of violence, and against theft, lying, and vicious ridicule. The Navaho phrasing of the last-named is characteristic. It recalls other Navaho ethical clichés, such as: "Don't laugh at old people, because they might have a daughter or granddaughter you want to marry." The third prohibition refers to a distinctive Navaho sex crime (see Dyk, 1951). The fifth refers specifically to witchcraft. Only one general category of Navaho negative morality needs to be added.

Avoid Excess. Excess, even in approved behavior, is evil. Too much industry is bad because overwork leads to nocturnal emissions and other undesirable events. Food is good, but one should not eat too much. Wrestling in moderation is approved; engaging in it too often runs the risk of injury and death. Gambling is sometimes condemned altogether on the ground of waste, but, more often, it is only an addiction that, like any other form of excess, will lead to such consequences as blindness, "going crazy," "getting wild," "getting dizzy in the head." Sex in general is a good thing. The female and male sexual organs were created for enjoyment. But sexual promiscuity is strongly disapproved, partly, to be sure, on the grounds of interference with the stability of subsistence activities and social relations, but at least equally on the basis of the dangers of excess. There are special ceremonies to remove the inordinate passions of men and women. Occasional adultery is condemned no more strongly than laziness, poverty, or lapses from truth.

Other Points. Again there are, expectably, certain specific vices implicit in the more general categories. Stinginess, sneakiness, and meanness are bad. It is "mean," for instance, if a mother punishes her children overmuch for small things. One should not "talk rough" to others, nor should one cheat them. Stupidity and anger and irresponsibility are vices. Young men who marry rich girls only to squander their money are looked down upon. Drinking is bad when it leads to fighting, poverty, or destroying the dignity and efficacy of a ceremonial. One should avoid places and situations where fighting is likely to take place. Arrogance and "acting smart" are frowned upon. Unpleasantness, ugliness, and repulsiveness—anything contrary to the general harmony—are evil.

Perhaps a few words should be added on the negative aspects of the sex code.[1] While Navaho sex is generally lusty, there are "puritanical" notes too. There is generally some fear of the initial sex experience on the part of both boys and girls. Nakedness or any form of exposure is to be avoided lest "those around feel bad." Bestiality is condemned. The attitude toward adultery is complicated by the Navaho notion of property as well as by the "excess" theme and by the sense of danger and of affront to personal pride of the injured party. The Navaho code says, "Don't bother other people's property, including their women." On the other hand, sexual jealousy is a threat to other economic arrangements and to a wide circle of interpersonal relations. One hears statements of this sort: "You don't own it, and she can do what she likes with it as long as she does her work and looks after your children. You got yours." The Navaho notion could be generalized as: "Adultery is not bad in and of itself, but it is better for all concerned if you do not commit adultery." In the myths the supernaturals indulge themselves sexually without much comment. Only in adultery does friction or a moral tone enter into the text.

Navaho Ethical Theory

Reichard (1950, p. 124) says, "In Navaho life ethics is empirical rather than theoretical or theological . . . ." Haile (1943, pp. 83-84) notes that, while Navahos may speak of the mind of a culprit as "twisted" or "pink" or "full of meanness," a crime like murder or theft is "primarily a social crime, involving no personal guilt." Reichard (1950, p. 125) correctly observes:

The code tells a Navaho what he should or should not do, what the punishment is—not for the transgression, but for the correction of

1. See also 1948b.

error. . . . The nearest Navaho approach to the concept of sin is "being out of order, lacking control," a definition that involves rationalization, not salving a bad conscience; confession of error, not a feeling of guilt. . . .

In short, the Navaho conceives of nothing as good or bad in and of itself. Correct knowledge and following the rules emanating therefrom are good because they lead to long life and happiness. Morals are relative to situation and to consequences rather than absolute. Everything is judged in terms of its consequences. An old Navaho says, "I've obeyed my father, that's why I have gotten on so well." But the context of this interview indicates plainly that the Navaho does not attribute his success to the *virtue* of having obeyed his father, but rather to the ineluctable result of this event in a chain.

The clearest paradigm appears in the ceremonial lore. One does not benefit from placating or pleasing the supernaturals in the sense that they are then motivated to intervene in one's behalf. The supernaturals themselves are bound by the rules. Transgressions (and this does not mean solely willful violations but mere mistakes as well) bring penalties. As one myth says, "If you make any mistakes you will become blind and warped and crippled; your mouth will be twisted." To be sure, the consequences may under certain conditions be averted or mitigated by resorting to correct ceremonial procedures. Yet this is also an invoking of the lawful course of things. The Navaho is certainly a determinist, if not a mechanist. In the case of human beings the course of events is enormously complicated by the ceremonial order. Naive Navahos sometimes express surprise that dogs and other animals also get sick—presumably because animals are not under obligation to observe the ceremonial taboos. There is a generic Navaho term for crime or transgression (Haile, 1943, p. 86) that can best be translated "he took the chance"—that is, acted in the face of realizing that human life is mechanically governed by rules that have supernatural origin.

To say that Navaho morality is dominantly empirical, situational, and deterministic is not to assert that there is no explicit theory. Ladd (1957) rightly emphasizes that the Navaho moralist is a rationalist par excellence. Reasons are given for everything

—particularly, of course, by the more articulate Navahos. Death and sickness are rationalized on the ground that otherwise both people and animals would become so numerous that the earth could not accommodate them. Rationalism is evidenced in the basic Navaho premise that knowledge is power. Hence everything must be "talked over," and reasons must be found for everything that happens. Failing everything else, the Navaho will say, "That was the way the Holy People did it long ago," or, in effect, "That is just the nature of things." But acts rather than beliefs count. Behavior is judged—not verbal adherence to a theological or ethical code.

Nor does the Navaho invoke the supernaturals for moral guidance. To assume the attitude of supplication or of gratitude toward the divine is to devalue or humiliate the supernatural with whom the human being is to some degree identified (Reichard, 1944).

11   *PERSONALITY FORMATION*

AMONG THE NAVAHO

INDIANS

OR THE PAST ELEVEN YEARS a group of collaborators representing the fields of psychiatry, psychology, and anthropology have been studying the development of children among the Navaho Indians living near Ramah, New Mexico. The original sample consisted of twenty-four boys and twenty-four girls, selected to form as nearly as possible a cross section of the children in the community from the point of view of such factors as economic position, age of parents, birth order in the family, and the like. Nine of these children have died, and three have moved so far away as to make continued study impractical. However, eight replacements were added in the years 1938-1940. "Controls" have been achieved through investigations for special purposes of a sample of thirty-six children (by Dorothea Leighton, M.D., in 1942) and of another of sixteen children (by Janine Chappat, Ph.D., in 1944-

1946b Reprinted by permission of the publishers from Clyde Kluckhohn, "Personality Formation among the Navaho Indians," *Sociometry*, Vol. 9, pp. 128-132, edited by J. L. Moreno, M.D. Beacon, New York, Beacon House, Inc.

1946). These two groups were made up about equally of children from the longitudinal study and of other children from the same population. Also, during various years all the children in certain families have been observed by workers who were unaware which children were included in the long-term project.

Methods cannot be described in detail here. Basically, they have consisted in repeated short-sample observation of the natural historical type. We have constantly had our eye upon the need for an adequate quantitative basis for generalizations. Sociometric charting techniques have been utilized. Observation has been supplemented by interview of parents and other adults and of the children. We have also used intelligence tests, films, medical examinations, Rorschachs, various other projective techniques, and some simple experiments.

Data are extremely abundant and have been by no means thoroughly analyzed. It is to be emphasized that the tentative conclusions to be set forth are in some part impressionistic. They have been discussed with some of my coworkers, but I must assume responsibility for publishing them in provisional form at this time.

If one asks the question, Why are the typical personality manifestations among Navaho children of school age characteristically different from those typical of Hopi (Thompson and Joseph, 1944) or Papago (Joseph et al., 1949) children of the same ages in the same years? the following answer may be given in gross form with some confidence: because of

1. Culture (the contrasting patterns of child rearing and the differences in patterned ways of behaving characteristic of adults in these societies)

2. Situation (the "objective" problems which these peoples faced at the time the children were studied—to be sure, these problems were viewed and dealt with in culturally channeled manners)

3. Perhaps—genetic constitution (This is assumption, but it seems reasonable to postulate that some relevant genes are present in differing frequencies in these three populations.)

If one asks, How can fairly consistent differences in response patterns among the Navaho children of Ramah, Shiprock, and

Navaho Mountain (1947a) be explained? the order of importance of the variables would appear to be the following:

1. Situation (The pressures of non-Indians upon the Navahos of Ramah and Shiprock are of very different intensity from those upon the Navaho Mountain Navaho; on the other hand, the problems in wresting a living from the land faced by the people of Ramah and Navaho Mountain have more in common than has either with Shiprock.)

2. Culture (mainly as differentiated by varying degrees of acculturation—and consequent differences in patterns of child-rearing—in the three areas)

3. Possibly—genetic constitution (There are historical reasons for believing that these three Navaho groups cannot be considered random samples from one biologically homogeneous population; moreover, inbreeding has been characteristic of the first two groups for several generations.)

But if one turns to the question, How can the personality variations among forty-odd children who have been growing up in the same community at the same time best be understood? quite a different set of determinants predominate. It will be convenient to discuss these briefly under the headings of "constants" and "variables."

Constants. Although in a strictly literal sense no influence affecting the development of two or more different children can be regarded as precisely identical for different individuals, to a first approximation certain factors in the environment (in the widest sense) in which Ramah Navaho children have been maturing nevertheless appear to have about the same dimensions. They have all been exposed to approximately the same pressures from the climate, from topography, and from living in the same ecological area. They share a common group history, and they all identify themselves as "Navahos" in distinction from their English, Zuñi, and Spanish-speaking neighbors. The public health situation is about the same for all, though the relative geographical isolation of some families doubtless renders their children less likely to contract infectious diseases. In a broad sense, all the parents make use of or have access to the same technology. The greatest part of the culture can be regarded as a "constant"; there is certainly one generalized set of patterns for child-training and for male and female role behavior considered appropriate for individuals in various age groups.

Variables. Although there are observable differences in the degree of acculturation among families and in different parts of the Ramah area, in only one family does this seem to have gone far enough to produce identifiable personality differences in the children. As for individual biological inheritance, this must be presumed to be of importance. Nothing that is both specific and firmly established can be said at present.

In 1943 a school was opened for the Ramah Navaho for the first time. Some of the children in the study attend school; others do not. It is already clear that the school is leaving its mark upon its pupils—at least in certain superficial behavioral characteristics.

Other variables of demonstrable significance in personality formation are the economic situation and status position of each family. The latter is to some degree but not completely dependent upon the former. Economic level also, of course, influences nutritional standards, and hence energy level and general health.

But those variables which seem to have been most crucial in producing distinctive personality constellations in Ramah children are, for the most part, predictable neither from the group's culture nor from its situation. They can best be described (from the point of view of this system) as "historical accidents." In rough rank order they appear to be:

1. The idiosyncratic traits of parents and associates as these affect the carrying out of cultural patterns and social behavior generally,

2. Death of a sibling just older or just younger,

3. Loss of a mother,

4. The individual child's health history (dependent, presumably, both upon inherited constitution and upon health "accidents" of various sorts),

5. The child's birth order and the interval until birth of next child,

6. Frequency of child's interactions with others (depends upon size of biological family; whether marriage is monogamous or

polygamous; simple family or extended family; geographic location of family's dwelling),

7. Loss of a father (by death or divorce),

8. Age of one or both parents at time of child's birth.

It will be noted that most of these determinants fall within the category of "social" or "situational," rather than within that called "cultural." It would seem that culture is the factor of greatest importance in determining distinctive social stimulus value as between groups who possess contrasting life-ways and also, often, contrasting physical appearance. But it would also appear that social or situational factors are, along with genetic ones, of the utmost significance in creating those personal characteristics which distinguish one individual from another within a cultural group.

To some extent the characteristic personal adjustments that maturing human organisms acquire both through trial and error and through patterned learning are channeled and limited only by the presence or absence of other human beings in specified numbers, at particular points, and of specified age, sex, size, energy, and "intelligence." Human interactions that are subject only to the constraints supplied by the field of biological and physical forces can properly be designated as "situational." Of course, the concrete social (i.e., interactive) behavior observed among human beings must in most cases be assumed to be the combined product of biological and of cultural forces. Often, then, the situational-social and the cultural are inextricably intermingled in concrete acts. However, some situations are independent of pre-existing culture, and some social acts are not culturally patterned.

12 *A NAVAHO*

POLITICIAN

"HE DOESN'T COME to meetings any more. We shouldn't have as our tribal delegate a man who lives so far away. Only once in the last thirty years has he really lived among us. He stays up there at Willow Fence along with his wife's family and most of his own brothers and sisters."

"You are right. He doesn't come down here often enough. That is why our cooperative store is losing money now. Those two young boys, Eddie Mario and John Nez, who run it need advice and direction from an older man like our delegate. But he doesn't watch them closely enough."

1960f Reprinted by permission of the publishers from Clyde Kluckhohn, "A Navaho Politician," in *In the Company of Man: Twenty Portraits by Anthropologists*, edited by Joseph B. Casagrande. New York, Harper & Bros., pp. 439-465.

I am indebted to many collaborators in field work for the materials upon which this sketch is based. I owe a particular obligation to Drs. Alexander and Dorothea Leighton, who collected an extended autobiography from the subject. I thank Dr. Bert Kaplan for interpreting the Rorschach protocols of the subject and his wife. This chapter has benefited greatly from the criticisms and suggestions of Dr. Casagrande, the Drs. Leighton, and Dr. Kaplan. [*Author's note.*]

"Everyone knows he and his mother-in-law are bootleggers. They work with those Mexicans."

"Yes, and he himself gets drunk. He has had two car wrecks while drunk."

"He takes too much power to himself. He isn't supposed to preside at these meetings—that is the job of our chapter president, Jo Miguel. Little Schoolboy is supposed to represent us at the Council of our tribe. He can tell us about that, but he shouldn't be the head at these meetings."[1]

"No, you are wrong, my fellows. Little Schoolboy is the leader of the people here. He speaks best, and he knows the English language too. He works hard for the people. He respects the old ways, while the young man, Jim Chamiso, whom the missionary wants you to put in is going to destroy them."

"Exactly," whispered the local missionary to an official of the Bureau of Indian Affairs, "Bill Begay is the candidate of those men who still keep two wives."

"Well," the official replied, "it is true John Mucho has two wives, but you must admit he is smart and progressive. He is a young man and wide awake even if he does hold to some of the old customs."

The talk at this meeting in January, 1948, went on all day. Perhaps fifty adults—mainly men, but a few women—of the 600-odd Navahos in this local group had their say. Most of their speeches were long and involved, and those of the older men were delivered in the florid yet precise style of Navaho oratory. Often there was an hour of history, recollection of ancient days, and citation of experience and sayings of fathers or grandfathers, before the speaker came to the issues relevant to the decisions to be taken: Should Little Schoolboy be required to vacate his post as delegate? Should he be replaced by Jim Chamiso, a man in his early thirties who was a high-school graduate and a devout Christian? Should Eddie Mario and John Nez be forced

---

1. In the 1920's the Indian Service organized Navaho local groups into "chapters" who elected a president, vice-president, and secretary. Later, the Navaho Tribal Council was created, and each group elected a delegate. The existence of both a "president" and a "delegate" is still confusing to the Navahos, who were accustomed to a single "chief" or "headman" for each band. In most localities, as at Rimrock, the delegate ordinarily takes over the functions of the headmen of earlier days, but there are occasional attempts to reserve these for the "president."

to turn over the store to Charlie Blackbird, who was Christian and generally more "progressive"? The underlying issues, however, centered on a specific personality and then on a complex of more abstract problems. Was Little Schoolboy—known to whites as Bill Begay—of good enough character and sufficiently responsible in the performance of his duties to continue as delegate to the Navaho Tribal Council from the Rimrock band? The more general questions were those which have split tribes and tribelets of American Indians from the periods when they first felt intense pressure from European groups. Should they hold stubbornly to the old ways or should they join wholeheartedly with the whites in stamping them out? Or should they, perhaps, compromise? Should missionaries be welcomed, tolerated, or resisted? How much should they stand up to the government, passively resist it, or follow its lead—insofar as they could understand this?

It was true that Bill Begay was the favorite of the antimissionary, somewhat conservative faction. His program, however, was basically one of compromise. Respect for custom was to be combined with schooling for children, with support of the Navaho cooperative store, and with acceptance of all useful techniques and ideas introduced by government representatives or other whites so long as these did not deny any place whatever to Navaho religion and Navaho methods for curing the sick. Implicitly, Bill's position was: Of course, changes must come, but not so fast that we repudiate all the values of our ancestors and disrupt the stable fabric of our lives.

In Bill's own passionate defense of his record, he made or hinted at all of these points as well as replying to specific accusations (For example, "I've made the long, hard trip down here many times only to find that only a handful of you people showed up at the meeting."). Like other astute politicians, he appealed both to the economic interests of his audience and to their more diffuse sentiments. He spoke of his own situation: of his large family and more remote relatives dependent upon him, of the terrible mud on the roads that sometimes had prevented his getting to meetings, of the overpowering fatigue he felt when, as now, he had been speaking at length in Navaho and also translating the talks by himself and others into English for the benefit of government officials. He spoke of the conflict of religions:

There's lots of missionaries who hate the singers ["medicine men"] and the medicine used among us Navahos, but some of this medicine is pretty old. It carried down from our old people, and we are still taking care of that and the songs and the chants. All this stuff are from the old, way back, and we can't lay off that. We got to go by that and the missionary hasn't anything to do with that. He can't hate that.

He must leave us alone in the meetings, not to butt in or try to say something about the people. All he can do is to preach to our people. Not to baptize them, just to preach to them. If they want to come to church they can. If the children want to come, that's up to their parents.

Bill finished as follows:

I have worked hard for the people. I have been a leader of the people for seventeen years. First at Pine Valley, then at Willow Fence, and now here. Most men give out after a little while, but I have stuck to it.

The vote was ninety to twenty against Bill. Some adults present did not vote. Others claimed later that they thought they were voting only a censure upon Bill for not attending meetings rather than a demand that he vacate his office. Bill left for his home almost immediately after the vote, and an observer noted that he looked "like a drawn and shaking old man." Another observer said Bill looked "like a beaten puppy." It is further recorded that for two weeks thereafter he appeared "sick, tired, depressed." But then he developed a plan to defeat Jim Chamiso decisively and got busy. After the vote had been reported to the Navaho Central Agency at Window Rock, the Agency ruled it illegal to force a delegate to resign in this manner. However, it was suggested to Bill that he might wish to resign voluntarily because of the expression of lack of confidence. Bill did resign but spent several weeks campaigning with quiet vigor for the Rimrock chapter president, Jo Miguel, whom he persuaded to run for delegate against Jim Chamiso. Jo Miguel had two wives and was in every respect entirely satisfactory to the conservative faction. Others who had been mainly aligned with the progressives voted for Jo because they felt guilty about their earlier repudiation of Bill. Jim got only thirty-five votes to Jo's 109. Everyone regarded this outcome as a signal victory for Bill, and Jim was so disheartened that he promptly moved away from Rimrock to the land of his wife's family on the Reservation. Moreover, Bill obtained more than symbolic success. During the same period he maneuvered among Navahos and government officials in such a fashion that when Jo took over as tribal delegate Bill received a paying job as bus driver for the Navaho school in Rimrock and his wife the position of housekeeper at the school.

I was not a witness of these events of the winter and spring of 1948. I learned about them from letters and from reading the field notes of my associates who were on the ground. When I arrived at Rimrock that summer and went to visit Bill, I did not mention what had happened or allude to it obliquely. We carried on small talk for an hour, and only after I had said I must leave did Bill give me his account:

They have a new delegate here now. These people got all mixed up this spring. It was those relief checks that got them mixed up. They had quite a lot of money. And every week a whole load of food and clothing. John Mucho got some. So did Margarita Luciano and Mucho. [These three individuals all owned considerable livestock.] My wife and I didn't get any. That's why the store has done better. All those relief checks went to the cooperative store. That's what I told the people in the meeting—that the store would have done better even if John Nez and Eddie Mario had stayed there. But these young boys, Jim Chamiso and Charlie Blackbird, they claimed they were progressive and that's why the store did better. I think they knew this relief was coming—they had some understanding with Albuquerque.

Anyway they had a meeting this spring and elected a new delegate and chapter officers. But that didn't stand. I told them the delegate was Window Rock's business, and Window Rock said a delegate was elected for four years. Just Jim and Charlie and Walter Blackbird and Marcos wanted a change. The rest of the people didn't, but they got mixed up. At first John Nez and Eddie Mario and some of the other war veterans sided with Jim Chamiso until they found out what he was going to do to pollen[2] and the medicine men and all that. Jim made a speech over at the church. After that the people felt like someone feels when you come and hit them on the back of the head [gesturing excitedly], and they see stars. The people didn't like that at all. Jim Chamiso is a good man in many ways, but he wants to do away with the medicine men. We aren't ready for that yet. We don't understand all of the missionary's religion yet.

So Jim and Charlie Blackbird asked me if I would resign as delegate. I said, yes, I would resign if I could get some kind of steady government job. So they fixed it up with the Government that I get this job I have now.

Then we had another meeting. And I told the people how it was —that they had got mixed up and that Jim and Charlie were only working for some of the people. They just stuck with the missionary. And I had always tried to work for all the people. Sometimes traders and government people had tried to get me to work for them. But I never followed their track. I always stayed right in the middle. So I told the people now they mustn't split. They must stick together, just like we always had been doing. So they asked me to name a good man, since I was going to quit and take this government job. So I named Jo Miguel, and almost all of the people voted for him. He used to be with the missionary, but he isn't any more.

It is going to be down here just like it was on the Reservation —for a while a lot of people will go with the missionary, and then in a couple of years it will be all over. I spoke with the missionary at that meeting, and I told him how when he was living in Rimrock I helped him get this land down here so he could be right in the center of the people. But I didn't think he was going to try to force the people to take his ways. He shouldn't do that. I told him after all I had done for him I didn't like the way he was acting. When I finished he asked me to interpret. I said, "No, you have your own interpreter." He said: "Well, my interpreter can't always understand what you say. You use hard words." So then he said he didn't have anything against me, and that he wanted to be friends. Now every time I meet him he says that same thing to me.

Bill Begay is one of perhaps 85,000 Navaho Indians whose traditional country was in the present states of Arizona, New

---

2. Corn pollen is very important in Navaho religious symbolism and in the carrying out of rites.

Mexico, and Colorado in the area roughly defined by the San Juan River on the north, the Colorado on the west, the Gila on the south, and the Rio Grande on the east. Today about half of the tribe live on the Navaho Reservation, some fifteen million acres mainly in eastern Arizona and western New Mexico. Additional Navaho, of whom Bill is one, live on individually owned allotments or lands leased by the tribe or the United States government in areas adjacent to the Reservation. Some thousands now work all or most of the year as semi-itinerant railroad, mine, or agricultural laborers far from the Navaho country or have settled more permanently in cities as far away as Los Angeles and Chicago. There are Navahos living today in the remoter parts of the Reservation who have grown to maturity wholly within the self-contained orbit of Navaho culture. Others in the cities and on the fringes of the tribal land live largely in the white man's world. Bill's own experience has been overwhelmingly in a Navaho environment. He has seen some of the cities of New Mexico and Arizona and has worked two or three times as a migrant laborer in Utah, but, if one excludes the years he spent at school in Albuquerque, 99 per cent of his life has been spent within a fifty-mile radius of his birthplace.

He was born in 1892 or 1893, about twenty miles south of Gallup, New Mexico, the eighth and last of his mother's children. His mother died when he was eighteen months old. His father soon remarried, and three more children were born to the second wife. Bill, however, was not brought up by his father and stepmother but by other relatives. He was in school from 1901 until 1906, a time when schooling of even so short duration was a rarity for most Navaho youngsters. The Navaho name by which he is still known is "Little Schoolboy." In his late teens he went to work for the trader at Rimrock, and his time in the trading store appreciably increased the scanty knowledge of English he acquired at boarding school. His knowledge of written English can be judged by this letter he wrote me in 1937:

I will write you a letter today We are getting along alright here at Willow Fence country.
and I have think about the Hunting pipe which me and you

talk about the time you left us. I whish you let me know if
you still wanting the Two pipe yet. if you do we will send
them to you before Christmas.
Wife will send you something to.
I got everything here at home now all I have to do is to go
ahead and make Two pipe. these Two pipe wille be Navjo
hunting pipe. Whick was made back in old days.
let us know just as soon as you get this letter please
I will go some other place again after Christmas for work.

From yours friend
Bill Begay

In 1914 he married a daughter of a "chief" of the Willow
Fence band of Navaho, and a year or two later he married, as
a second wife, the younger sister of this woman. To anthropologists Bill has always insisted that he was never married to
these sisters at the same time, but his contemporaries—Navaho
and white—are unanimous to the contrary. His first wife gave
him two sons and a daughter; the second, one daughter. Both
of these wives died leaving infant children. About 1925 he married his present wife, Ellen, then a young woman of eighteen.
Her mother was Navaho, but her father was a white trader. She
and Bill have had seven daughters and three sons. Only one died
in infancy—a rare record among the Navaho. In 1952 Bill had
more than thirty living grandchildren, not an exceptionally large
number for the prolific Navaho.

Five feet, seven inches tall and weighing 156 pounds, Bill is
slightly taller and heavier than the average Navaho of his age
group in this region. Like many Navahos, he had pyorrhea, head
lice, and a few minor defects of the head and eyes, but a thorough
medical examination in 1948, when he was in his mid-fifties,
showed him in general good health and nutritional status. Today
he wears glasses continually and is as unhappy as a professor
when he misplaces them. Except for some excess of weight, his
body is well proportioned, and his gait and gestures have the
smooth and flowing quality that typifies Navaho movement.

In part, Bill's success in the field of power and politics must
be attributed to a control of English unusual in a Navaho of
his age and to the recognition by other Navahos that Bill understood whites and their ways, both skills deemed important in

coping with white deviousness. Yet others who had these qualifications have not entered the political game or have failed at
it. Bill likes people, loves to talk with everyone. He also likes
to have people feel dependent upon him. And—let it be said
candidly—he loves to manipulate people. Finally, his role as
"leader of the people" allows him escape from the family scene,
ruled firmly by his wife. These dispositions—even more than the
prestige and perquisites of office—have kept Bill in the political
arena. He not only is adroit in political behavior but is likewise
an accomplished orator. When I talked with him last during
the summer of 1958, the remark that he made to me with the
most feeling was that he had been invited to journey a considerable distance north to make a speech during an Enemy Way
rite: "These people way up there said they had heard I could
talk better than anyone near there."

As I think of Bill during the many years I have known him
intimately, his personality seems to me to embrace at least as
many obvious and blatant contradictions as in the case with the
rest of us. He is (as he himself says in English) a "leader of the
people." Yet he was terrified of his mother-in-law and is under
the thumb of his wife. He is the object alike of enormous trust
and mistrust from Navahos and others. I have never known a
Navaho of his age who was more deeply divided between the
Navaho and white worlds. When one comes to his home in
1958, one sees several substantial American-style buildings of
mill-processed lumber and cement. There is not even one hogan,
the traditional mud-domed Navaho dwelling of logs, in which
a Navaho rite can properly be carried out. There is no sweathouse. And yet Bill has always refused to become a Christian[3]
and has opposed missionaries under circumstances that he knew
were politically disadvantageous. He is proud of the fact that
he knows certain obsolescent rituals for hunting deer and antelope. He attends and participates in curing chants and other
ceremonials with great frequency. He is known to some as a
"progressive," as an accepter and introducer of American foods,
gadgets, and habits, but he publicly laments the decline of Navaho customs among the younger generations. He insists that

3. His third marriage took place in a Catholic church, but he has never
attended church services.

his English-speaking children speak some English to their children in the home, but he himself flaunts his classical (sometimes almost archaic) Navaho. His female grandchildren must learn to weave rugs in the old manner, though he comments loudly that this activity has become economically unrewarding. He himself was a Navaho silversmith for some years. He and his family own automobiles, farm machinery, and all manner of contemporary machine goods. Nevertheless, he treasures an ancient digging stick and a ceremonial fire-drill.

But I believe his most basic attitude is expressed clearly in this quotation:

I can never become white man. My skin is brown, not white; my eyes are black, not blue; my hair is black instead of some other color. I can never change that. I am an Indian, and I have to go by those things what were given us from way back. Those things are for us Indians. If I can change my skin and become white man, then I take the white man's religion. While I am Indian, I am not going to throw away all those things which have come down for our people.

My first meeting with Bill Begay in 1936 was hardly friendly. I had dropped into the hogan of the Son of Many Beads to check a few points on the Blessing Way rite of which he was a practitioner. In accord with the custom, I shook hands with the visitor, but he was less than cordial and proceeded immediately to ask the assembled company what business a white man had to pry into matters of Navaho religion. He reminded them that Jake Morgan, a leader from the Farmington area, was urging all Navahos to refuse to talk with whites except in necessary business transactions. This was a time of strong antiwhite feeling because of the government's stock-reduction program, increased pressure of various sorts from the Bureau of Indian Affairs under John Collier's administration, and the continuing impact of the depression. Although Jake Morgan was a Christian—and, indeed, an ordained Methodist minister—his movement had strong nativistic overtones, including some disposition to exclude whites from attendance at Navaho ceremonials and to become silent at inquiries about Navaho religion. But I had spent considerable time in the Rimrock country at various periods since 1923, long before I had any acquaintance with anthropology. My relation to the Navahos there had been established as a personal rather than a professional one, and this was the first time that my privilege to ask questions about—or, indeed, to participate in— rites had ever been questioned. I was hurt and shocked into silence.

The Son of Many Beads replied, however, with some asperity that he did not know much about Jake Morgan, did not like some of what he had heard, and in any case Morgan had no right to dictate what was or was not done at Rimrock. Moreover, he said, had Bill Begay been much around Rimrock in recent years, he would have known that I was a friend of the Navahos, addressed by many in kinship terms and considered almost as a Navaho; they would continue to discuss with me anything that I wished, just as they had found that I answered at suitable length all queries they put to me. I proceeded with my questions. Bill sat quietly at first. Then he interjected a remark that he was surprised I knew something about Navaho religion. Still later he joined warmly in an argument among the Navaho men on some technical points. We parted on moderately good terms.

The following summer I found that Bill Begay and his family had moved from their place at Willow Fence, eighteen miles south of Gallup, to some land adjacent to that of his wife's sister and her husband, thirty-odd miles southeast of the village of Rimrock. The late anthropologist Harry Tschopik was about to begin his field work on Navaho material culture and needed an interpreter. Bill Begay was at that time the only mature Navaho man in the Rimrock area who had a reasonably fluent, if ungrammatical, command of English. Because of my brush with him the previous year and because the local traders did not speak very well of his character, I hesitated about hiring him to work with Harry, but the two younger men who had adequate English lacked Bill's knowledge of the older Navaho culture. When I did invite him to become Harry's interpreter, he said he must consult his wife. They talked for an hour, and then Bill said he could start the following morning.

Bill worked hard and loyally for Harry that summer and the

next. Until 1954 there was not a year in which he did not serve
as interpreter for one or more field workers, mainly in the Rimrock and Willow Fence areas, but also in Chaco Canyon for
part of a summer. He worked for anthropologists, biologists,
psychiatrists, general physicians, psychologists, botanists, philosophers, and sociologists. Some of his employers were young and
raw graduate students. Some were experienced and sophisticated
men and women who had traveled and done research in many
parts of the world. Gradually, he became more a collaborator
in the investigations than a hired hand. He himself became committed to the minutiae of ethnography. He took the initiative
in writing me letters (without pay, though—as will be seen—
money was of constant importance to him) to say that he had
observed or heard something new or something contrary to what
he knew my associates or I accepted as fact. Increasingly, his
role toward me became that of "principal adviser and consultant
on the Rimrock Project." He acquired a good deal of the jargon
of the profession and frequently has made special trips to tell me
that I must admonish so and so "to keep Navaho customs" or to
warn me that "the tall young man's rapport is not good." He
firmly corrected all newcomers who failed to use the standard
English translations of certain Navaho technical terms that had
become established in anthropological usage.

Indeed, particularly in more recent years, his behavior toward
the young and inexperienced can only be characterized as domineering. He has laid down the law as to what they could and
could not do, insisted on setting his own days and hours of work,
brutally criticized their field techniques, and borrowed money
that he has not returned or worked out. From the youngsters
since 1946 I have heard more complaints about Bill than praise.
A composite of what they said would go something like this:

Oh, yes, he knows the people and their culture very well. And he
can give you a decent translation if he feels like it. But if you don't
check him closely he'll give you back three sentences after an informant has talked for half an hour. And he is so undependable. Five
times in the last two weeks he stood me up. He told me to come
pick him up at his place at a certain hour. When I got there, he
was away and his family gave me vague and conflicting stories as

to when he would be back. He talks you out of wages in advance or just begs a loan, and you can't trust his promises to make it up one way or another.

This picture is abundantly documented by the facts. There are certainly, however, elements of misunderstanding in the interpretation of Bill's character made by novices to Navaho culture. Many traits attributed to him are characteristic of Navahos in general and not of Bill as a unique personality. "Navaho time" is not equivalent to "American time." The "appointment" does not have the almost sacred character it has with us. As regards money, most Navahos are genuinely convinced that any white has access to an almost unlimited supply. Moreover, the average Navaho considers that one of the most delicate and pleasurable of games is fencing with a white for a gift, advance payment, or loan. With great finesse, the Navaho will "test the limits." An overly easy or generous response—taking into account the relationship of the two parties—is an occasion for biting jokes about the gullibility of the whites, a small triumph over the representative of a group that is, rightly enough, believed to have cheated and exploited the Navaho. Finally, the youngsters have underestimated the demands and complications of a Navaho's life that are different from those familiar to us but nonetheless real. Bill may receive a summons (unexpected when he made the "appointment") to assist in a curing rite for a relative or to attend to some political duty that has suddenly arisen. Or his wife might simply insist that he take her shopping in Gallup in his pick-up truck or to a ceremonial where she can gossip with relatives and do a bit of trading.

Nevertheless, the uninitiated graduate students are right in inferring that there is something in Bill's make-up that cannot be explained by differences in culture or by situational pressures. There is definitely a psychological dimension that includes a component of hostility toward whites. First, I would say that Bill derives some significant substitute gratifications from his whole role as interpreter or "research assistant." He enjoys directing operations and giving instructions. He has little outlet for these propensities at home, for his wife is not only shrewd and energetic but very strong and, not infrequently, hard. In

Navaho politics he can influence and direct as well as cajole. With younger field workers, however, he need no longer mask the iron hand. Moreover, I am certain that he finds a peculiar satisfaction in uttering commands and prohibitions to whites, in extracting unearned money from them, and in keeping their work at the mercy of his caprices.

Bill's attitude toward whites is—like that, I believe, of the majority of Navahos—deeply ambivalent. On the one hand, he respects their power and their skills and wishes to emulate them. All save two of his children have been to school, and the total number of years spent in school by them is considerably in excess of the average for Navahos of their age and geographical location. He ordinarily responds with sincere warmth to whites whom he judges courteous, understanding, and trustworthy. To their face, he usually behaves with deference, though especially to older persons whom he thinks have authority or position. On the other hand, a great deal of distrust and antagonism comes out. He continually repeats tales (true, partly true, and false) of dishonesty, greediness, arrogance, ignorance, or ridiculous acts on the part of whites. These stories are told more often, with more fervor, and with more embellishments when Bill's superego has been loosened by alcohol. Then, especially, he will also boast of getting the best of a white, sometimes by means that—according to his own standards—were not altogether ethical. His dreams reveal many incidents of overt aggression toward whites, and he repeats such dreams disingenuously, as if he were not at all implicated in the attitudes they imply. He talks with gusto and longing of the young days when whites were only beginning to be a real nuisance to the Navaho.

Bill Begay's autobiography, recorded by the Leightons, contains many episodes that describe, in effect, his rediscovery of Navaho culture after his return from school. He tells of attending a ceremonial performed over his sister's husband and of his surprise at learning this was conducted because his brother-in-law had been having frequent bad dreams:

I don't know what bad dreams means. After I came back from school I not trying to believe Navaho way, I believe American way.

I don't know any more Navaho way than before I went to school.
That man start to telling story about the dream.

A little later he was initially reluctant to have a rite performed
over himself:

We started from there early in the morning. This is to my other
sister where she is living we going. We got there in the afternoon,
late in the afternoon. That's where that little canyon, this side of
Rimrock. When we got there, my sister started to talk about the
sing. They want to put the sing over there by Many Beads, the
singer of Blessing Way. The reason they want to do that I was
away in school for. They say they said put that sing, I mean they should
have done it for me just after I came back from school. They want
the singer, that man, Moustache's father. They ask me, did I want
it? Told them I don't want it. [Bill laughs a little.] They keep asking
me till I say yeah. But I got no moccasins, they got to make moccasins for me first. First they just start to talk about it. After I say
all right, then there's some people around there, what living around
there. They come there and they put up new hogan. They sent
Joe back over here to this other place. Told the people down there
they was going to have a sing down there.

This "sing," Blessing Way, is considered by the Navahos a
prophylactic against danger. The Navahos say that Blessing
Way, which is the ceremonial held by the Divine People when
they created mankind and taught them skills and ritual, is the
cornerstone of their whole ceremonial system. Seldom does a
family go for six months without having Blessing Way sung at
least once in their hogan. Most Navaho rites have the ostensible
purpose of curing illness, but Blessing Way, as English-speaking
Navahos say, is "for good hope." It places the Navahos in tune
with the Divine People and so insures health, prosperity, and
general well-being. The rite is far less complicated than most
Navaho ceremonials. It has the dignity of great simplicity. There
are a few songs one night, a ritual bath in yucca suds with
prayers and songs the next day, and an all-night sing that night.
Cornmeal and pollen are prominently used throughout, and
drypaintings of these materials and pulverized flower blossoms
are prepared on buckskin spread upon the ground.

After his own ceremony, Bill learned from his father that the rite had been conducted because Bill had been exposed to the hazards of being among whites. At the same time the father, while disclaiming responsibility for Bill's being sent away to school, showed his own mixture of feelings by affirming that school is a good thing:

When I bring in the sheep that night, I asked my sister why did they had a sing for me. She told me ask my father. My father was still there, and I ask him about it. He says we didn't put you in school; your brother did, he says. And we all was so glad you got back over here without anything wrong with you. And Navaho, all the Navaho, they all do same thing whenever they sent the children to school. They do the same thing. They put up the Blessing. They all have to put up the Blessing sing for children. He says that's the way we Navaho work it with our children when our children goes to school. He told me that's about all I can tell you. There's some good reason for it, but that's too hard for you to understand. He told me some of the people says that school is very good for the children, and he thinks it's good too himself.

Perhaps his induction into ceremonies made Bill feel at home with his people again; perhaps he felt something inherently good in the ceremonies; possibly his father's hint that there was something deeper which Bill did not understand instigated him to apprentice himself to a ceremonial practitioner. At any rate, in his autobiography he relates with evident pride his learning and eventual mastery of the ritual ways of hunting. He is pleased to discover by himself some stones that are used in ceremonies. He exults in describing the minutiae of an unusual rite or in recounting the wisdom and sound moral exhortations of the old men. His satisfactions in finding good things in his own culture are plainly evidenced. Equally clear is his pleasure whenever in his experience a white (or, indeed, an Indian from another group) expresses interest in Navaho custom. Negatively, if it be true that one can understand people better from what they laugh at than from the gods they worship, Bill's *Schadenfreude* is most particularly directed against whites. Any act or belief that seems to him stupid or ignorant in a way in which a Navaho would hardly be stupid or ignorant brings forth a special laugh and a disdainful look reserved for such occasions. He loves—

as do most Navahos—to puzzle and pull the legs of whites. Once he spoke of an idiot as talking; when the anthropologist looked amazed, Bill went on with a broad smirk: "Sure she talks. The only thing is—no one can understand her."

His life story suggests that Bill would probably have returned to predominantly Navaho orientations had he not when still a young man gone to work for the trader at Rimrock. This man was intelligent and treated Bill with understanding and affection. Bill's affiliations were split again between the two worlds. This essential ambivalence emerges in the reproach he casts upon his older brother and two of his sisters for having earlier kept him from returning to school so that he could herd for them. Behaviorally, it comes out also in some happenings attendant upon his first marriage. Although the arrangements were made, Navaho style, by intermediaries from the two families, Bill took rather more initiative in the matter than was customary. And, on the trader's advice, he refused to agree to work for his prospective in-laws after the marriage. Both Bill's relatives and the girl's wanted a Navaho basket ceremony at the marriage, but Bill refused: he simply took his bride to live with him at the trading store and announced that henceforth he was going to work for whites. Nevertheless, he returned to live among his own people. While Bill, to my knowledge, has always spoken of this particular trader with warmth, he does in his autobiography repeat at length the remarks of other Navahos that when he left the trading store he did not get nearly as much money as he should have. There are as well other indications of his mixed feelings toward this man.

The same vacillation has marked our own relationship—and I think it fair to say that this trader and I have been the whites to whom Bill has been closest and whom he has most nearly accepted without reservation. For the most part Bill has shown himself devoted to me and more than faithful in his obligations. He has given me in the summer ritual information that should be divulged, if at all, only in the winter. He has worked—without extra pay—for more hours in a day than I was sometimes prepared to work. He has been very discreet with my confidences where a single offhand remark in a relaxed or drunken moment could have been exceedingly damaging to the work of my associates and myself. With great effort and skill at maneuver, and at considerable risk to his political fences, he obtained access for me to the secret rites of Enemy Way—the one aspect of Navaho ceremonialism from which whites are automatically excluded. He insisted, once over protest, that I attend and speak at Navaho political meetings deliberately called at times and places that were designed to prevent the presence of representatives of the Indian Service or other whites. Yet from time to time, in contexts not involving a failure on my part to respond to his requests or meet his expectations, he has turned on me. There have been a few outbursts of open and seemingly unprovoked anger. There have been more instances of moody or sulky withdrawal. There was one flagrant case of his taking advantage of me.

Over the years I had made small loans to Bill. Some other Navahos have never repaid such loans. Most of them have, however, made restitution—on occasion in cash after a long lapse of time during which the debt was never mentioned. Bill never paid back a loan in cash, but rather in work or in his wife's rugs, and always during the interval while the debt existed he would frequently make me aware that he had it in mind. Ten years ago he came to me with a plea for an advance that would enable him to buy supplies so that he and his family could sell hot dogs and pop at a "Squaw Dance" of Enemy Way. The sum was sizable enough so that I demurred, but his reminders of our friendship and his need and his categorical assurances that I would be repaid the very morning the three-day rite ended won me over. I presented myself promptly at dawn the final morning, because my personal funds happened to be low at the time and I needed to get most of the money back. He and his family had decamped two hours earlier, in spite of the fact that just before their departure customers swarm to such stands. I went immediately to his place and, not finding him there, then visited the hogans of relatives of both Bill and his wife. It was only a week before I had to return East, and repeated search and inquiry failed to locate Bill. By the time of my next trip to the Navaho country I had decided that Bill deserved a bonus if he felt that way, and I was curious as to what tack he would take. Neither he nor any member of his family has ever, however indirectly, alluded to the incident.

In part, I am sure that this behavior must be understood in the light of Bill's being unable to resist the exploitation of a white, although a friend.[4] But only in part. There were two other immediate instigations to his deception. There is no doubt in my mind that the money, both my loan and what he got from his sales, was urgently needed to buy clothes and meet other expenses in connection with sending five members of his family off to school within a few days. Secondly, I am sure (without proof) that Bill's wife, who has less conscience but more force than Bill, badgered him into this action.

If such an explanation of his deception is correct, his susceptibility to these two immediate instigations must be related to some dominant and recurrent features of Bill's personality. The distinctive features of that personality when I consider them against the perspective of other Navahos I have known, suggest the following generalizations:

1. His feelings toward whites are exceptionally mixed.

2. While he can be generous, he is more often grasping in money matters. (The Leightons have entered into their field notes a characteristic comment by Bill after a discussion of money: "That sounds good.")

3. He is generally skillful in interpersonal relations. Over and above possible material advantages, he takes intrinsic pleasure in having people listen to him, in arranging their affairs, in making them dependent upon him. And his skill shades over, in the opinion alike of Navaho and of white observers, into manipulation and calculated cunning. At the same time, one must remember the almost disinterested—as well as prideful—psychological reward he seems to get from reconciling a husband and wife or helping a family to get out of economic straits.

4. His own personality is a curious blend of assurance and almost frightened dependence, of responsibility and irresponsibility, of maturity and immaturity.

---

4. This interpretation is reinforced by a similar occurrence. Bill had for many years a white rancher as a neighbor. The two men were unusually friendly, and the rancher did many favors for Bill. Then a calf was stolen from the rancher, who tracked the thieves to Bill's place. Bill denied all knowledge, but it is virtually certain that the calf was taken by Bill's sons, with at least his tacit approval and possibly at his prompting.

It will be instructive to view these tendencies against the background of some crucial facts of the history of his early years and of the conditions he has faced as an adult. But first let us compare them with some Rorschach findings. In 1946 I administered the Rorschach test to Bill and his wife. These protocols were interpreted by a clinical psychologist, Dr. Bert Kaplan. Dr. Kaplan spent a summer testing subjects from four Southwestern cultures, including the Navaho. He met Bill Begay more than once. He has not, however, read Bill's life story or this chapter or discussed Bill's character with me.

Let us begin with a point with which I am in hearty agreement. Dr. Kaplan sees the total record as "typically Navaho," as ". . . in no sense deviant from the main framework of the Navaho way of life." When it comes to those idiosyncratic features that are—at least in their emphasis—specially characteristic of Bill, my experience likewise fully accords with Dr. Kaplan's interpretations when he writes of:

. . . freedom and spontaneity of self-expression and a proper appreciation of and sensitivity to the subtleties of the materials with which he is dealing. This ability is generally associated with strong ego forces and emotional maturity.

But the following interpretations are peculiarly congruent with the generalizations I have made above and with the biographical data which are to come:

a. Perhaps the most central theme in the protocol has to do with strength and masculinity. At least a half-dozen different responses involve these characteristics in association with bravery, vigorous action, overcoming difficulties through strength and endurance, withstanding challenges from a younger generation, maturity, adequacy as a provider of food, protectiveness toward the young, and acquisition of prestige and recognition. These qualities undoubtedly loom large in Bill's self picture and are, I believe, understood as aspects of his idea of strength, and assertion of these qualities in the responses should properly be regarded as a reaction to a basic uncertainty about possessing them. I am inclined to think, however, that, despite the fact that they are given quite freely and spontaneously, the responses do indicate a need to use energies to maintain this self concept and perhaps therefore a deep lying fear that they may not hold unless effort is made to maintain them.

b. A second theme involves the nurturance-succorance dimension. There is a definite preoccupation with the ideas of taking care of and being taken care of, which involves both infantile succorant attitudes and more mature nurturance and protective ones. Bill's identifications, in the balance, seem to be more with the mature protective figures than with the infantile ones. The image of himself as a provider of bounty is an important one, and he has apparently adapted a role complementary to the childhood one in which oral dependent attitudes predominated. Food and whatever it might symbolize remains important in Bill's personality economy, and one might speculate that he is still working through some residual problem of deprivation from his childhood. A related image involves the juxtaposition of very strong and aggressive figures with weak helpless ones.

c. Another recurring theme has to do with affiliative qualities in his social relationships. In at least two responses such relationships are given a pleasurable, spontaneous, "moving toward" quality. . . .

Because of his mother's early death, the number of his siblings, and his father's remarriage, Bill did not receive even the small inheritance with which many of his fellows of that day started. On his father's death, which occurred when Bill was already married, his sisters received some livestock, while Bill and his brothers got nothing. Since the day he came back from school, he was on his own economically, with only very minor assistance from relatives. His first two wives had expensive ceremonials in connection with their lingering, final illnesses. During a period of more than twenty years there was a new child almost every two years. Before the cycle of children from his third wife was complete, his daughter and two sons by his first wife were themselves married but continued to be to a large degree dependent upon Bill. His third wife was always demanding—of luxury items, of traveling about, and of aid to her relatives. In addition, Bill himself encouraged his own relatives to expect assistance from him. During most of his life he has been desperately poor, and during a number of periods he has barely been able to provide his family with a minimum diet. He has always been in debt, often to half a dozen trading stores and even more individuals, Navaho and white, at one time. His creditors pressed him so hard that he found it necessary to work out his debts a little here, then there. His wife's rugs and their few lambs and tiny crop of corn and beans would be zealously watched by traders and others so that they could be seized the very minute they were available. He ordinarily insisted on being paid in cash by anthropologists, for checks meant going to a trading store to cash them. Sometimes Bill had to avoid for years entering a particular settlement lest the trader catch him. A few dollars in cash not infrequently meant the difference between eating and not eating. In the literal sense, Bill and his family lived from hand to mouth until the last few years, when most of his children had become largely self-supporting or significant contributors to the family income and when he had a meager but assured income as delegate to the Tribal Council. He still works very hard at extra jobs he can get: hauling wood for Zuñi Indians or making arduous trips to a sacred lake to get salt he can sell at a profit to other Indians.

It is, I believe, this fierce and unceasing pressure that is primary in understanding certain aspects of his character that both Navahos and whites comment upon unfavorably. Let me sketch two relevant instances. About twenty years ago Bill married his second daughter to a senile man who had been a scout for the American Army against Geronimo. The difference in their ages was at least sixty years. Although traditional Navaho culture sanctioned a sizable or in fact a large age gap between spouses,[5] this was a bit too much, especially since it seemed clear that the couple did not live together as man and wife. In effect, the young girl was a kind of servant and companion to the old man. She prepared and served him his food and kept him clean—or fairly clean, by Navaho standards. Bill candidly rationalized the situation to me as follows:

I know people are talking. But he is a good old man and needs someone to look after him. We need the money—my daughter as much as the rest of us—what he gets from pension and from singing at

5. Not only did older men take young wives. It was also not uncommon for a widowed or divorced woman to marry a man ten to twenty years her junior.

the Gallup Ceremonial and from telling his stories. He won't live
very long and then my daughter can marry somebody else. My
wife and I will let her take her own pick next time.[6]

As a matter of fact, the daughter accepted the arrangement with
good nature most of the time and subsequently did marry
another man of about her own age.

Bill had a "cousin" who in the 1930's and early 1940's owned
one of the two largest herds of livestock in the Rimrock area.
In those days Bill was assiduous in his attentions to this man.
The slightest hint that his services would be welcome at lambing
or shearing time or advising in some problem with the government caused Bill to drop all other obligations and rush to his
"cousin." The latter, in turn, made liberal gifts to Bill from time
to time and guaranteed his accounts, now and then, at more than
one trading store. The gossip was that Bill hoped to become his
principal heir, for the old man had no son and no sister's sons
or sons-in-law whom he liked or trusted. Then the "cousin" fell
on evil days. He himself was no longer vigorous, and his shrewdness in Navaho ways no longer enabled him to cope successfully
with rapidly changing circumstances. Under these conditions
Bill, as everyone noted, ceased to be so readily available as helper
and counselor. It would not be factual to say that he "dropped"
the old man completely. He continued to be cordial and, in fact,
obsequious when they happened to meet. The malevolent attributed this show of attention to the circumstance that the
"cousin" still retained some influence that Bill wanted on his
side during political jockeyings. But, a year before he died, the
old man commented to me:

I used to think that my cousin was like the old Navahos. Relatives
didn't change toward each other when someone became rich or

6. To the Leightons Bill gave approximately the same account, but with
some additions and variations. He said the "marriage" was first suggested
by the local trader who wanted to continue to handle the ex-scout's
pension check. He claimed the decision was made by the girl and her stepmother, both of whom regretted it afterward because the old man drank
up most of his income. Bill admitted to the Leightons that he had been
criticized for "giving my daughter to that old man" and that the elders
were "chewing it over." He added he feared trouble from Indian Service
officials.

poor. He still talks to me the same way. But I can't depend upon
him as I could once. He makes me promises he does not keep. When
I send him word, he does not come.

The insecurity of Bill's early life was more than economic.
After his mother's death, he was shifted from one family of
relatives to another. Before his own marriage, he called seven
different places "home." Orphaned Navahos commonly experience one or two such shifts, but this is an unusual number. His
siblings were also scattered about. In his autobiography Bill recalls forgetting all about his sisters for a time, though later his
relations with at least two of them were exceptionally close. One
sister raised his oldest daughter, and his second daughter lived
with the same sister until Bill's third marriage. Bill quotes his
father himself as remarking, "After your mother's death I never
stayed very long at one place." And there is a matter-of-fact
yet still pathetic passage in which Bill describes meeting his
father among a group of adults shortly after he had come back
from school:

After I shake hands with these people there, one of them was my
father, but I didn't remember him. My father used to have a sister
there. That sister she is the one that's living there. But my father
is living way back over here with my brother.

Bill's relations with his present wife, Ellen, and her mother
attest to the validity of the Rorschach interpretation that Bill
is not altogether assured in his masculine strength. My feeling
is that he was drawn to Ellen because of her intelligence and
force, by a sense that she shared his ambitions and would be a
helpful economic partner, and possibly—unconsciously or half-
consciously—by the very fact that she was half-white. She was
already obese when I first saw her but must have been beautiful
when they were married. She has fine, brown hair with a low
wave, and her skin is a light color. In her own way, she is as
complicated and contradictory a person as is her husband. Her
Rorschach suggests some pathology, "an unspecified horror."
On the other hand, there is evidence of imagination, sophisticated perceptions, and intelligence. Her mind and her control

are good enough to repress and intellectualize whatever is profoundly troubling her.

The disturbance could well have had its origins in her infancy. In her autobiography she dwells on whippings and neglect from her mother. She says: "My mother was mean to me. My mother did not want to take care of me." Many Navaho women are shrewish, but there is universal agreement that Ellen's mother was an extreme case. After marrying a succession of Navahos, the mother became for some time the mistress of a white trader, Ellen's father. She called herself, "Mrs. Smith." Then she had still other Navaho husbands. The last one was liked and considered good by Ellen and Bill; they merely noted repeatedly his fear of his wife. The mother made a prostitute of one of her younger daughters and forced her to do away with an unwanted baby by exposing it. Ellen and Bill told many stories of her thieving, bootlegging, and conniving. Nor is this all. She was generally regarded as a powerful witch, and for this reason, as well as for her cunning and sharp tongue, she was feared by her own children and other relatives, by her sons-in-law, and by the community at large. "She hates everybody, and everybody hates her."

When Bill married Ellen, he went to live—as the Navaho pattern most often prescribes—where his wife and her mother were established. Navaho custom prohibits, under penalty of supernaturally caused blindness, any direct contact between mother-in-law and son-in-law. Ellen's mother announced her intention of treating Bill as a true son; therefore, she said, they would not observe the taboo. (It is significant for the positive polarity of Bill's feelings toward white behavior that he accepted the proposal.) But the old lady was not satisfied with the fashion in which Bill did her bidding. She determined to "run him off the place," as she had Ellen's first husband. Ellen, however, was loyal to her new husband and claimed the land was really hers rather than her mother's. The mother-in-law complained to the Indian Service authorities. Bill was jailed, and there was a long drawn-out quarrel, with Navaho elders, the Gallup sheriff and police, traders, and the Indian Service people all attempting to mediate or adjudicate.

Bill and Ellen at last won out, and Bill escaped—largely—from his mother-in-law. He continued to be terrified of her and on a few occasions to suffer from her machinations. He did not, to be sure, escape from his wife. She is steadier and less vacillating, or torn, as regards her purposes. Bill works hard but more episodically. Ellen loves to buy expensive things, yet she seldom squanders money. Her expenditures bear a far more consistent relation to her central and unchanging values—comfort, opportunity, and prestige for her family.

She exploited her stepchildren as much as she could. Over a long period she has made a drudge of Bill's second daughter. But to her own children she has been, by Navaho lights, an admirable mother. She demands their respect and can be harsh. But she has slaved and fought for every opportunity and advantage for them, tolerating Bill's political and ceremonial activities only to the extent that she felt they served her primary ends for her family. Bill gratefully recognized this quality and saw that she was a rock of tougher, more abiding and unyielding quality than he. In the families of older Navahos the wife is almost always consulted by the husband on important decisions; Bill, though, is timid about taking even minor steps without Ellen's assent. Up to a point he accepts and, in fact, enjoys his dependence upon Ellen. Theirs has been, as these things go, a happy partnership. It has certainly been a firm one; and Navaho marriage is typically fragile. I have heard Ellen and Bill argue with heat. I have heard angry words. Even one of Ellen's own children once said of her: "She is mad all the time, day and night. I hate her." And Bill added in desperation: "She always gets mad. That's what's the matter all the time." On those rare occasions when Bill got angry enough to express aggression toward his wife, he would actually stand up to her; once, for example, when he was injured in an accident, she kept nagging him to go to the hospital, but he stubbornly refused.

The surprising thing is that never once, either in my own observation or according to rumor, has there been the slightest intimation of a dissolution of the marriage. Still more amazing—the exceedingly active network of Navaho gossip has never accused Bill of infidelity.[7] And yet there is a wistfulness in some

---

7. The single hint in our files of notes came from a Mormon woman who knew little about Bill.

of Bill's utterances about his wife. His unending praise of her
intelligence, energy, and dependability does not altogether mask
a resentment at his surrender of male autonomy. There is an
apparent compulsive aspect to his activities in those spheres of
behavior where he can, to some degree, assert his autonomy—
rituals and politics. His self-assumed role as "provider of bounty"
I see also as, among other things, a masculine protest.

It may be meaningful that Bill is a specialist in the hunting
rituals. These, along with some of the war rites, are the only
ones that exclude women completely and also demand sizable
periods of sexual abstinence before the ritual begins and after
it has been concluded. Women are, of course, patients in the
curing ceremonials, and they attend these exactly as do men.
After the menopause, women may even become chanters. But
the hunting rituals are defined as exclusively masculine business.
Women may not so much as hear most of the songs and prayers,
let alone witness the ritual acts.

Navaho women are by no means excluded from political
activity: older women occasionally speak in meetings; in recent
years a few women have been elected as chapter officers, and
one has been elected to the Tribal Council. But politics remains
overwhelmingly a male sphere, and Ellen, who is in many respects conservative, intervenes in Bill's political affairs on one
pretext only—that he is neglecting his duties to his family.
Politics for him is thus an area of autonomy comparable to his
ritual life. It may be added, however, that his political behavior
has exhibited more guile than force. He did not, as did Jim
Chamiso, condemn or accuse his enemies in public. He lacks
the masculine authoritarian quality that characterized Jim as a
political leader. Jim was all too ready to make decisions at the
top. Bill allowed each person to have his say and then was
evasive or reluctant or dilatory in bringing matters to a head.

This relative indecisiveness, this unsureness of himself, is also
of a piece with his disposition to flee the field when stress
mounts. It would seem that when his inner tensions become
unbearable, Bill's typical response is to escape by leaving the
stressful situation or by failing to appear where he is expected.
This, I think, is behind his absenteeism from political meetings
and sometimes behind his failure to meet his promises to anthro-

pologists and others. To "leave the field" is a frequent Navaho response when the pressures accumulate, but this response is accentuated in Bill.

I have spoken little of Bill's sly but seldom unkind sense of humor. I have said nothing, directly, of his manifest affection and supportive attitude to his children, nor of his warmth and charm in many of his dealings with nonrelatives. The Leightons will later give us a more complete and more accurate portrait.

I leave Bill now with the most recent news I have had of him— making a speech in the Navaho Tribal Council on December 9, 1958, in which he complained of the encroachments of whites on the lands of the Indians he represents and also asked for a clearer definition of the area covered by his constituency. The motives of economic pressure and of mixed feelings toward whites are still prominent. (These he shares with most Navahos, but Bill's case shows characteristic stresses.) The politician and the schemer are also probably behind this speech. And I have no doubt that some of his neighbors are complaining that he irresponsibly failed to attend one or more sessions of the Council or that he neglected to bring up a matter that he had promised to raise. In the account of his speech I also imagine Bill happy in acting as an alert man who can operate successfully without the counsel or intervention of his wife, taking pleasure in his skill with words, in his prestige, in his capacity to move other men to action. Yes, in this final posture, I see my old friend, "Little Schoolboy," with great clarity.

13 RECENT STUDIES
OF THE "NATIONAL CHARACTER"
OF GREAT RUSSIANS

B Y "NATIONAL CHARACTER" I mean those modalities
of behavior and of view of the world and experience
in it that are found or claimed to be characteristic of
a specified national or ethnic population at a particular period
in time. In this instance I shall not be talking about "all Russians" or all the citizens of the U.S.S.R., but rather only about
recent inhabitants of Great Russia, speakers of the Russian
language proper. It is on Great Russians that the richest
materials exist. I shall avoid methodological and theoretical discussion as much as possible. I must inevitably sketch some
central facts concerning data utilized and basic viewpoints and
methods. Otherwise, for purposes of this paper, I shall assume
that, while there are certainly methodological and theoretical
issues of great urgency, the over-all "initial character" approach

1955g Reprinted by permission of the publishers from Clyde Kluckhohn,
"Recent Studies of the 'National Character' of Great Russians,"
Human Development Bulletin, papers presented at the Sixth Annual
Symposium, February 5, 1955, Chicago, pp. 39-60.
1955h "Politics, History, and Psychology," *World Politics*, 8:112-123.

is a tenable one and that problems of sampling and other aspects of method have been sufficiently met to warrant taking some findings seriously. It is my impression that the blaze of controversy over conceptual and procedural questions has too much deflected our gaze from the empirical substance that has gradually emerged in the shadows not highlighted by the fires of dispute. I want primarily to summarize what seem the most interesting generalizations thus far made by behavioral scientists who have studied Great Russians.

The first statement I know by a social scientist on Russian "national character" is Sapir's (1924, pp. 407-409). Though based upon reading and experience rather than upon systematic research, it still seems to me so penetrating and so fundamental as regards the traditional Russian character as to be worth quoting at length:

. . . the tendency of the Russian to see and think of human beings not as representatives of types, not as creatures that appear eternally clothed in the garments of civilization, but as stark human beings existing primarily in and for themselves, only secondarily for the sake of civilization. . . . The one thing that the Russians can take seriously is elemental humanity, and elemental humanity, in his view of the world, obtrudes itself at every step. . . . For his environment, including in that term all the machinery of civilization, the Russian has generally not a little contempt. The subordination of the depths of personality to an institution is not readily swallowed by him as a necessary price for the blessings of civilization. We can follow out this sweeping humanity, this almost impertinent prodding of the real self that lies swathed in civilization, in numberless forms. In personal relations we may note the curious readiness of the Russian to ignore all the institutional barriers which separate man from man; on its weaker side, this involves at times a personal irresponsibility that harbors no insincerity. The renunciation of Tolstoi was no isolated phenomenon, it was a symbol of the deep-seated Russian indifference to institutionalism, to the accreted values of civilization. In a spiritual sense, it is easy for the Russian to overthrow any embodiment of the spirit of institutionalism; his real loyalties are elsewhere. The Russian preoccupation with elemental humanity is naturally most in evidence in the realm of art, where self-expression has freest rein. In the pages of Tolstoi, Dostoyevski, Turgenev, Gorki, and Chekhov personality runs riot in its morbid moments of

play with crime, in its depressions and apathies, in its generous en-
thusiasms and idealisms. So many of the figures in Russian literature
look out upon life with a puzzled and incredulous gaze. "This thing
that you call civilization—is that all there is to life?" we hear them
ask a hundred times. In music, too, the Russian spirit delights to
unmask itself, to revel in the cries and gestures of man as man. . . .
It is hard to think of the main current of Russian art as anywhere
infected by the dry rot of formalism; we expect some human flash
or cry to escape from behind the bars.

There have been many subsequent speculative essays on
"Russian personality" and its changes during the Communist
period. Some of them have contained fragmentary observations
not without interest (e.g., Steinberg, 1929). A few studies have
had some philosophic and historical depth (e.g., Lieb, 1945;
Tomasic, 1953). But here attention will be concentrated upon
a small number of empirical studies carried out by Americans
during the past decade.

Columbia University and
American Museum of Natural History Studies

This multidisciplinary group, organized originally by Ruth Benedict but directed during most of its course by Margaret Mead,
utilized literary, historical, and other published materials; personal documents and folklore; films and photographs; and some
interviews (mainly with individuals who had been away from
the U.S.S.R. for some years). The essential assumption was that
one is dealing "with a system which can be delineated by a
small number of very highly specified samples." Mead (1952,
pp. 9 ff.) spells out the detailed implications of this assumption
in a fashion that deserves careful attention:

The anthropological use of informants is closer to the historian's
use of *documents* than it is to the sociologist's use of respondents or
the social psychologist's use of experimental *subjects*. Each informant
is evaluated individually against a wide knowledge (on the part of

the interviewer) of the culture of the informant, the social structure of which the informant is a part, and the particular subject about which the informant is being interviewed. Here the anthropological interviewer's skill parallels that which an historian, trained in a particular period, brings to the interpretation of the reliability and significance of a new document from the period in which he is a specialist. So, for example, it is possible to judge whether Informant Kom–3 is basing a statement about the Komsomol mainly on reports on–or experience of–a particular congress; to check statements from an informant in Rostov against a knowledge of movements and counter-movements of the Russian and German armies through Rostov in World War II; to judge whether the vocabulary used by an elderly informant is congruent with the particular educational claims which he puts forward. Furthermore, each interview or series of interviews with a single informant is studied as a whole; different statements are viewed contextually, in the sequence within which they occurred, and in connection with the affect displayed by the informant (using here the methods of interview valuation developed within clinical psychology, psychiatry and psychiatric social work. Statements of opinion are placed within this depth context and are treated not as matters of fact, but as parts of a total response; so in this method there is no use for percentage statements, such as, "Twenty per cent of the informants said they never read the front page of *Pravda*," or "Fifteen per cent claimed that the ritual creation of Stakhanovites was necessary," which would not be any more meaningful than the statement, "Of the surviving documents on the early history of New England, fifteen per cent said that Providence was good." Interviews are cross-compared for pattern and within the pattern apparently contrary factual statements are fitted together, such as: "I never read the papers because it was all just what the regime wanted you to think," and "I read the papers very carefully to give me a clue to what was going to happen next, to be prepared." Both are statements about the informant's belief in the amount of control exercised over the press. The contrasting statements about reading and not reading can in turn be related to the position, age, and personality of the two informants and to statements by other informants. From such study, significant relationships between status –or type of involvement within the system–and dependence upon clues from the press, may or may not emerge. If systematic interviewing of carefully selected groups within the Soviet Union were possible, the contrast between those who do and those who do not report reading the press could be investigated, and perhaps systematic relationships to age or sex or echelon or type of activity could be found. But we still would not know how this was related to whether people actually did or did not read the press; quite separate methods would be necessary to determine this. But, as with the use of available historical documents on a period which is past, the reports of informants—whose availability has been determined, not by some ideal sampling process, but by a series of historical accidents often arbitrarily rather than systematically related to each other—cannot be used to make statistical statements. Nor is the number of informants or the number of interviews with single informants of very much importance—subtracting any given informant or any given interview from the total would produce a change, not by diminishing the reliability or validity of the whole group, but by impoverishing in a specific way the fullness of the pattern which can be derived from the whole. . . .[1]

COMMENT

Although Soviet intellectuals strenuously deprecate American culture and personality studies, nothing could be more certain than that Soviet leaders in fact believe that personalities can be shaped more or less according to specifications by employing carefully chosen techniques of socialization, education, environmental control, and indoctrination (cf. Bauer, 1952). Many of the utterances and acts of the leadership also strongly suggest that the Soviet elite hold a view of the traditional Russian national character similar in many respects to that of Western social scientists.

In my selective summary of conclusions and hypotheses I shall for the most part give preference to those that seem to have at least some support from more than one publication of this project and/or from other sources:

1. There is a sizable gap between the modal personality type advocated by the Soviet leadership (and attained to varying degrees by many of the elite) and that most characteristic of Great Russians in general.

2. The people are warmly human, tremendously dependent

---

1. Numerous publications along similar lines have appeared; cf. Erikson (1950, ch. X), Gorer and Rickman (1949), Mead (1951, 1954), Mead and Métraux (1953).

upon secure social affiliations, labile, nonrational, strong but undisciplined, and needing to submit to authority.

3. The counteractive Bolshevik ideal demands stern, ascetic, vigilant, incorruptible, and obedient personalities who will not be deflected from the aims of the Party and the State by family or personal ties and affections. Instrumental rationality must prevail. At any given point in history there is only one "truth" that describes a particular situation. But since those who are not for the Party line of the moment without reservations must be presumed to be altogether disloyal, and since every individual (alike from the people and the elite) must be assumed to harbor some forbidden attitudes, any person is capable of complete betrayal. In spite of the theory of the remorseless working out of the "laws of historical materialism," the leadership operates in practice upon the premise of intensely personal causation. When something goes wrong, some individual must be at fault. Genuine guilt is less important than preservation of the principle that the pattern of personal responsibility be preserved by punishment rationalized with standard clichés. This is in accord with the general tendency of the elite to build "as complete a semblance as possible of the world as they wish to see it."

4. The regime's program of educating the masses toward independent and conscious action that is highly goal-directed, self-stimulated, and self-sustained is contradicted by the varied pressures constantly applied, producing apathy or cynical indifference among the people and the so-called inner emigration among frustrated or disgruntled elite. Conflicts of conscience beset some of the recruits to leadership.

5. The attitude of the people remains, on the whole, that strong external authority is both hateful and essential.

Let us now turn to some points that are interesting but perhaps less solidly established. In his luminous chapter Erikson (1950) makes much of "vasomotor excess" in a people both "isolated and effusive." "It is as if each individual were strangely imprisoned in himself as in a restraining box of strangled emotions." Erikson sees the Bolshevik movement as "delayed Eastern Protestantism" that tolerates no sectarianism, trying to liberate "swaddled souls" from "apathy, lethargy, and serfdom." The people must escape from the mother image, "the manic identification of earth and woman," from "the imagery of an ancient agricultural revolution," from their weakness in enduring what enslaves them. The Bolsheviks explain and excuse their imparting further suffering by the fact that suffering is part of the human condition. "To leave the ruins of men and systems behind seems a job which does not call for any expenditure of emotion." Discipline rather than atonement is central. Parents, sacrifice, and ego restriction are unimportant compared to exclusion from a creditable part in the historical process. Leaders can wait patiently, but eventually they must act, must "grasp life," must at all costs avoid "sinking back into dependence" or "regressing to the traditional morality and the ancient folkways of the people."

In two fragmentary but highly suggestive working papers in Mead and Métraux (1953), Leopold Haimson makes notes on thinking in the traditional culture (reversibility; lack of specificity, consistency, and completeness; readiness to equate whole and a part or the outside and inside of an object) and sketches the Russian style of playing chess. This latter, he hints, may constitute a small paradigm of the elite's ideal of "conscious activity" that should be a central characteristic of the "new Soviet man." The Soviet chess masters, according to Haimson, study carefully the opponents' favorite style of play and predilections. They try to seize and maintain the psychological and material initiative, gaining advantages on position and tempo and committing their adversaries to static and passive defense. When the other player has an initial advantage, they "direct the game into tense and complex positions, introducing new and relatively untested variations." They strive to hold to positions that are familiar to and psychologically suitable to themselves and unfamiliar to and psychologically inappropriate for their opponents. Soviet players are adept at developing relatively short-range combinations.[2] Now some of this has an oddly

---

2. An Air Force officer (he prefers to remain anonymous) who is a skilled chess player made an independent study of sixty games in which the six ranking Soviet chess players participated. Although he started with extreme scepticism about Haimson's delineation of Soviet chess style, he concluded that Haimson's description was validated in all major respects. From other investigations he found evidence that Soviet leaders apply

familiar ring when one thinks of the Soviet style of political maneuver. It is perfectly true, as Haimson freely admits, that chess as a game played internationally is influenced by new modes of play developed in various countries. Nevertheless, he makes a good case for there being some distinctive elements in the Soviet style. Anthropologists and others can think of many parallels. For example, Australian cricket playing has its own special flavor, though the "test matches" bring together teams from many countries in the British Commonwealth.

One can hardly speak of the work of the Mead group without paying one's respects to the most controversial of its members —namely, Geoffrey Gorer (1949). That he is guilty of loose statements, unwarranted assumptions, dubious analogies, and factual errors is unarguable. I agree with most of Goldman's (1950) criticisms. And it cannot be emphasized too strongly that the reader hardly ever knows where he stands on evidential grounds. Gorer speaks of "three or four hundred interviews" but never makes it clear how many of these were with Russians, how many with men and women of specified ages; whether given generalizations represent a consensus of informants or a particular category of individuals; etc. On the other hand, I believe that one must take Gorer's work seriously in the face of all these methodological deficiencies. He seems in many significant respects to have been right in spite of inadequate evidence, perhaps in some cases to have been right for the wrong reasons. Dicks (1952, pp. 157-158), in whose clinical judgment on this matter I have the most trust, writes:

For the earliest level, only Geoffrey Gorer has, so far, evolved a coherent hypothesis. His critics have done the very thing he warned them against; mistaken the paradigm for the theory. Nothing in my observation has contradicted his views.

Even on the "swaddling hypothesis" Erikson, another sensitive clinician, speaks of "smoldering vasomotor madness." True,

---

"chess-type" thinking to international problems, and that therefore analogies between international conflict situations and chess situations "will be generally instructive." The officer, however, remarks finally, "Correlation between the Soviet style of operating on the international scene is high but may be misleading." Agreed!

Erikson was influenced by Gorer (and perhaps vice versa). In any case, I agree with Mead (1954) that much of the furor over swaddling was misplaced (though Gorer is at fault for placing his qualifications mainly in brief footnotes). I do not agree that data on the frequency of swaddling by time period and social class are irrelevant. To my knowledge, the first information on this point that is not impressionistic or inferential, consists in figures gathered by the Harvard Project which will appear later in this paper. On the general theoretical issue Mead's most recent (1954, pp. 398, 401-402) formulation is:

Stated concretely, the Russian institution of a strong leader, whether called Czar or Stalin, is not to be attributed to swaddling. But the forms of the acceptance of such a leader are grounded in the way children are reared to be members of Russian culture. . . .
   From an analysis of the way Russians swaddle infants, it is possible to build a model of Russian character formation which enables us to relate what we know about human behavior and what we know about Russian culture in such a way that Russian behavior becomes more understandable.

Much of Gorer's argument in his main text still seems reducible (though he does not use these words) to an oversimple formula for "Russian character": "If I accept constrainment, I get milk (i.e., food and general support)."

Three "Political" Studies

Here it seems appropriate to review three recent books (Almond, 1954; Leites, 1953; Leites and Bernaut, 1954) that ask political questions of materials that are largely historical in nature, using methods, such as content analysis, that derive from the behavioral sciences and theory that is dominantly psychological. Leites, at least, was directly influenced by the Margaret Mead group.
   H. A. Murray has said that there are three classes of information about every personality:

1. What the individual knows about himself and is willing under certain circumstances to reveal
2. What he knows but will endeavor to conceal
3. What he does not realize about himself that is nevertheless true

What holds for personalities also holds for political systems and those who develop and run them. And the salient characteristic of these books is that all are most deeply concerned to demonstrate features of certain aspects of Communism that the Communists either hide from the public gaze or of which they themselves are almost completely unconscious. These authors use documents (and, in the case of Almond, interviews) as projective materials.

No careful reader can fail to agree that the inquiries were searching and impressive even if the conclusions are not completely persuasive on every point. Indeed, if an outsider may be permitted this observation, it would seem clear that these volumes strongly indicate the relevance of a requirement for some technical study of psychology by all, or most, professional students of government. The whole content of political science is, obviously, not psychological even in an oblique sense. There are historical, philosophic, economic, and organizational aspects where psychological competence is at most peripheral. Yet the study of government remains inescapably the study of political acts and the products of these acts (constitutions, treaties, and the like).

All human behavior has a psychological dimension, and this dimension can be comprehended only very imperfectly and superficially by "common sense." This is even more so the case with the totalitarian governments in Asia and Europe, where the sense that is "common" rests, increasingly, upon premises quite distinct from those that are taken for granted in the Western democracies. Technical skill is also of peculiar importance where governments intentionally and skillfully and with full power restrict the dissemination of information to a degree unparalleled in many centuries. One can, as ordinary Russians say, learn by experience and shrewdness to "read between the lines" of official communications. But this is intensely difficult and time-consuming to do unsystematically and without benefit of prolonged residence within the Communist orbit. Contemporary psychology and psychiatry are, admittedly, still in rudimentary phases of their development. There is substantial controversy within these professions, but there are also today more substantial ranges of agreement on many fundamental and unobvious points than most laymen realize. These books attest the illumination of a political order that may be obtained from the restrained use of, even, psychoanalytic doctrine.

A Study of Bolshevism (Leites, 1953) is so packed with empirical content and subtle (occasionally elusive) interpretations that any attempt at outlining its central arguments and its new contributions is doomed in advance to, at best, very incomplete success. The book is so completely organic that selection will necessarily be more than ordinarily invidious. On pp. 27-63 ("Prologue: The Politburo and the West") and in a brief Epilogue ("From Lenin to Malenkov"), Dr. Leites provides in effect his own summary insofar as practical politics are concerned. No serious student, however, will make the mistake of stopping with these pages. The body of the volume and—even for the nonspecialist on Soviet affairs—the notes at the end require reading and rereading.

The essential method of the book is what Woodbridge and others have called "exposition of texts." A typical pattern is that the author states one of his own propositions formulating the Communist operational code and then offers a quotation from Gogol or Mayakovsky or some other literary figure, followed by texts from Lenin and Stalin in chronological order. The extensive excerpts from Russian literature are justified on the ground that only in this way can one "find a clear and vivid description of the feelings and the moral sentiments which are opposed by, or continued in, Bolshevik belief." It is a technique for revealing "some of the unexpressed content of Bolshevism." Leites says explicitly that he believes "there has been a significant measure of continuity in Bolshevism from 1903 to 1952." It is also clear that he feels some of the continuities—or patterned reactive discontinuities—go back into nineteenth-century revolutionary and radical thought in Russia. The specifically Russian features of contemporary Soviet Marxism can be understood only in these terms. These views fit extremely well with the thesis developed by the British psychiatrist Henry Dicks (1952).

The four substantive parts of the book codify Bolshevik theory on goals, operations, techniques, and situations. Communist conceptions of ontology, epistemology, and logic are dealt with in detail and with great analytic power. The sources used are widely various in date, authorship, and type. There are official documents, private letters, and other papers; radio talks; scientific and technical articles. Leites is of course fully aware that there are contradictions in Communist theory both through time and at particular points in time. He tries to concentrate on what appears central and persistent and traces change and development with great skill. Some representative chapter titles and subheadings will give a notion of scope:

Chapter V. The Control of Feelings

    Varieties of Control over Feelings
    The Danger of Intrusion of Feelings into the Line
    The Danger of Sensitivity
    The Danger of Excitement
    The Danger of Emotional Incontinence

Chapter XIX. Retreat

    The Expectation of Setbacks
    Facing Setbacks
    The Danger of Distress about Setbacks
    Retreat to Avoid Annihilation
    Retreat to Avoid Futile Loss
    The Legitimacy of Retreat
    From Retreat to Advance
    The Danger of a Vicious Circle of Retreats

We might also take as a brief summary example the interesting sections on the time-orientation of the Communist elite. The orientation looks to the past but emphasizes the future. It is the Party's past that is meaningful; there is an aversion to any other past. Even the Party's past can be dangerous to contemplate, because this might interfere with manipulations of things present and to come. Even the present is a means only.

Very ingenious is the tracing out of the psychological origins of some modal reactions of the Bolshevik elite—from bad manners to the compulsive need for certainty. These are largely seen as reaction formations to some patterns and situations attributed to the earlier intelligentsia. The special role played by the intellectual in the family and by intellectuals within Russian society is given careful attention. The demand for unequivocal certainty is related to the ineffectualness in action of the Tsarist intelligentsia coupled with their opportunity to think things out down to the last split hair. Leites suggests that cruelty stems from a revolt against the sentimentality and compassion of famous nineteenth-century literary figures. Rather similar, though much more technically psychoanalytic, arguments are developed by Erikson (1950) in his chapter on "The Legend of Maxim Gorky's Youth." In fact, these portions of Leites' book strike one who has worked extensively in the so-called culture and personality field as representative exercises of this currently (or recently?) fashionable approach.

Leites, however, goes out of his way to assert with emphasis that he does not make any affirmations about "Russian national character." Perhaps not in the strict sense, for he seldom talks about Russians in general or even Great Russians as a total population. He is dealing constantly with elite groups: the intelligentsia of two centuries and the recent Party leadership. We can strike out the adjective "national," but he is surely dealing with the thought and emotional modalities characteristic of certain defined segments of a people. Looking back at an earlier article by Leites (1948), one sees that he tends to restrict "culture and personality" to efforts to associate *childhood* training and experience with patterns of the adult culture. Nevertheless, in this same well-known article one sees the germs of many, though admittedly not all, of the kinds of analysis distinctive of these two books published five and six years later. In the broad, nonliteral sense, this is first and foremost a "national character" study—and easily the best thus far of those based on documents. In particular, such passages in *A Study of Bolshevism* as that on pp. 314-341 seem to me classical "national character" statements. And, with some variant shadings, they accord well with the analysis of Dicks already cited and with the results of the Project on the Soviet Social System of the Russian Research

Center. Since these latter are based primarily on interviews and psychological tests, while Leites worked entirely with published materials, the degree of agreement is heartening.

Many of Leites' central findings are already familiar from the writings of American scholars such as Kennan, Fainsod, and Mosely. Tactics and short-range strategy change, sometimes with bewildering rapidity. Final goals endure. A genuine and lasting "settlement with Capitalist powers" is "inconceivable" to present and recent leadership. One must push (often rudely) to the limit but know when to stop, avoiding adventures that would risk the continued existence of the regime and retreating before unquestionably superior force. There are no neutrals. Internally, passivity must constantly be changed into instrumental activity. All of these points could be matched in the work of one or more of the leading Western students. The difference in Leites is that all of these and many other features are integrated into a coherent whole with psychological and structural underpinnings. Leites may be—very probably is—too "coherent."

Nevertheless, his theory and various parts of it are, in ways that he notes, testable. They will receive a severe test during the next few years. Here there appears to be a small discrepancy between *A Study of Bolshevism* and *Ritual of Liquidation* (Leites and Bernaut, 1954). The former seems to assume consistently a steady continuity of Bolshevism, at least so far as some "unchanging cores" of Communist thinking are concerned (e.g., the central question, "Who will destroy Whom?"). Yet the latter book in its final sentence hints that Bolshevism (not the name but the doctrine) may be utterly dead.

Perhaps I have made insufficiently explicit my views as to wherein lies the distinctive nature of Leites' approach. It is perfectly true that the critical use of texts has been standard procedure in classical political science and history. It is likewise true that this is far from the first book on politics to make use of psychoanalytic theory. What is unique in Leites, in my opinion, is the following combination:

1. A juxtaposition of literary, personal, organizational, and "state" papers in a theoretically designed way

2. An orderly selection of quotations in terms of stated

limitation of sources and in terms of a complex (*partly* psychological) conceptual scheme of which the author was consciously aware and which he makes largely overt to his readers

3. Consistent and balanced attention to manifest and latent elements in the documents and to both change and continuity

In short, while there are familiar parallels with every feature of Leites' method (except possibly his ingenuity in bringing together variegated texts), this particular unification of features is an innovation. And the comprehensiveness of his scheme and his own consciousness of his assumptions are, to assert the very least, unusual. A learned, experienced, and wise writer of an article in, say, *Foreign Affairs* may draw upon as wide a range of sources—page for page—but the selection will ordinarily be more "intuitive," less rigorously within the framework of a testable theory.

Leites has written a limited but not a modest book. Given its plan, it is difficult to think of studies more "thorough" than this. Only intense preoccupation with the data over years made such a volume possible. He provides developmental models of both "the enemy within" and "the enemy without." One may question the selection of categories and the reliance upon psychoanalytic analogies (Leninism to Stalinism appears almost as a clinical case of "regression"), and one may regret the paucity of behavioral data—though these were largely unavailable, and it would take another very long book to bring Leites and the materials of the Columbia and Harvard projects together. The study is more genetic perhaps than dynamic, even if Leites himself conceived this as an investigation of the "state of soul" of a politically important group in all of its historical-dynamic interrelations. Yet, when all these and other possible qualifications and reservations are made, *A Study of Bolshevism* remains, in my opinion, a work of gigantic stature that is likely to *faire école* in politics and the other behavioral sciences for many years to come. Its detailed significance is almost impossible to exhaust, and the over-all picture of Communist mentality as somewhat like paranoia (precision of sorts imposed upon a distortion of reality) stays with one. Subsequent events may prove Leites wrong in major particulars. But scholarship learns as much from grand failures as from grand successes. There is nothing petty about the architecture of this book. It is written on the scale of grandeur.

Ritual of Liquidation (Leites and Bernaut, 1954) is more microscopic. It is also less well pulled together. There is no summary or set of conclusions. Only in a few places (e.g., pp. 73 ff. and 337 ff.) is there much approach to generalization or integration. The analysis of *A Study of Bolshevism* continually and perceptibly underlies this later volume. The method ("exposition of texts") and the psychoanalytically oriented viewpoint are also very much the same. The exact place that a quotation appears "expresses a point of analysis." Even more than in Leites' study, some of the most intriguing excerpts (especially literary) are relegated to the more than 100 pages of notes at the end.

This is a dissection of the motivations for the behavior of the defendants in the Moscow trials, especially those of August, 1936, January, 1937, and March, 1938. The major motivations of the Stalinists in carrying out these trials are only sketched. Leites and Bernaut emphasize their conviction that, except for a few small splinter groups, the "deviationists" shared with Stalin the belief that "the only sacred object in the world" is the Bolshevik Party. Those on trial felt too that the Party must have "firmness" and "solder," must be "steely," "strongly built," and "hewn from one block." They accepted the dogma that the Party leadership had unlimited freedom in deciding what roles should be played by any member. Therefore, "The defendant's compliance during the trial had the double purpose of giving to the Party what was its due and of reuniting him with the Party, abolishing an intolerable isolation." Most of the defendants still identified with Lenin's statement that Marxian philosophy is and must be "cast from a single piece of steel." Any in-between position is by definition "internally inconsistent or otherwise invalid."

Many of these materials show a most arresting similarity to words and behavior related to witchcraft in nonliterate societies. The witch is likewise the person who finds himself intolerably isolated from his group. By confession, he too can achieve reunion, if only a temporary one. There is that identification with the attacker (cf. p. 97) that is so frequent a phenomenon in witchcraft lore. Projection and pseudo-projection (cf. pp. 337-342) are probably the two dominant psychological mechanisms in witchcraft fear, accusation, and practice. There is even a specific reminiscence of an image current all over the world about witches from Paleolithic times on, that of object intrusion and purification by extraction. Zinoviev is said to have remarked, "I am telling you all that I think, and thereby I am extracting from my body the last splinter of the crimes that are being unfolded." The very word "splinter" is precisely the right one in the witchcraft context! Finally, the Moscow defendants are in the same position as witches because they have violated the really ultimate and untouchable values of the culture. They have threatened Party unity and defied discipline. "Primitive" witches are those who commit incest or murder their near relatives, most often their siblings.

The more theoretical sections are largely expansions of, or further documentations upon, topics treated in *A Study of Bolshevism*. There is a psychologically acute and exceedingly illuminating set of "hypotheses about a type of Russian family." The parallels to the trials and the motivations of both sides are a bit strained at points, yet convincing in a general way. There is a brief section on "veiled language" that adds to the "unexpressed content" theme of the earlier book. "The Image of Betrayal: 1949-54" takes up Slansky, Hostov, Tito, and others as a case history, as it were, for pp. 234-237 of *A Study of Bolshevism;* this is "the enemy within." The penetration of the enemy into the Party leadership is an expected event. Indeed, the Stalinist expectation is that through long periods of time "they may form the majority of entire leadership groups of Communist parties rather than being isolated cases."

This is a very able, concentrated study. On the psychological side it is not likely to be surpassed for many years. For fuller minutiae on historical and narrowly political points we shall have to await the publications of Ruth Fischer and others who have been investigating the source materials on the trials over a long period.

The Appeals of Communism (Almond, 1954) is based upon interviews with sixty-four American, fifty British, fifty-six French, and fifty-one Italian former Communists; biographical data on the present members of the Central Committees of the Communist parties of France, Italy, and the United States; and thirty-five psychoanalytic case histories of American Communists. There is a linkage with Leites' work both in the interdisciplinary and specifically psychological approach and also in the fact that Leites' earlier book, *The Operational Code of the Politburo* (1951) and personal contact with Leites influenced some aspects of Almond's investigation, particularly the conception of "the Party militant."

Professor Almond is modest and cautious on the methods and research materials utilized by himself and his collaborators. He faces openly and realistically almost every possible objection on the sampling process and research design generally. If anything, his own reservations are stated overdarkly. For, as he himself remarks, "When a large body of individual findings cohere in a meaningful system, another kind of test of validity is satisfied." Moreover, some of the findings have been confirmed by independent public-opinion surveys in France and Italy.

Part I reports on some very astute content analysis of Communist media in various countries. The biographical studies and the literature of social psychology dealing with radicalism are also drawn upon. Historical sampling of Marxist theory makes quantitatively evident the gradually decreasing attention given to "the ultimate stage" ("withering away of the state," and the like). The structure of Communist communication involves various levels and processes of preparation and formal training, esoteric versus exoteric communication, and integral association and integral antagonism. There are some arresting and instructive contrasts between content and style in editorials in the Cominform periodical and in the *Daily Worker*. For the most part, the first ninety-six pages confirm, supplement, and raise rather minor qualifications on issues that Leites treated independently in somewhat different language, using another (and, in the purist sense, less "scientific") method. The nationality angles and some close scrutinies of Communist semantics are new and welcome. Almond concludes that "This sharp break between the inner and popular representations of political reality provides a clue to the main vulnerability of the Communist movement."

Part II takes the reader more immediately into the key queries of the book: What different types of party members are there? How do these categories relate to the actual processes of assimilation into and defection from Communism? What are the attractions and repulsions of the Party for people of certain temperaments, experiences, and social positions? The second and third of these questions are treated empirically and at length in Parts III and IV.

The militance and aggressiveness of the Party seems to have been an outstanding attraction. Sheer doctrine counted much more with early recruits than with those who joined in the post-Popular Front period. The defectors were fully aware of the Party model of impersonality and rationality, but they did not experience the emotional atmosphere of the Party in this way. Rather, they report internal espionage, fear, and distrust. Especially in more recent years, it was the activism, the sense that "something was getting done," that pulled. In many instances joiners seem to have been importantly influenced by the "wave of the future" premise. To this reviewer one of the mildly astonishing findings is the extent to which people became Communists with only the vaguest notions of the Party's ostensible goals—let alone its theory. As Almond points out, however, this does not mean that all or many of the converts were just "innocent dupes of the Party."

The appeal of the Party has varied substantially from place to place, group to group, and time to time. Almond says, "We must talk of types of appeals, to various types of persons, in different kinds of situations." Economic considerations, social disorganization and personal social isolation, the "secular religion" appeal, private psychological susceptibility, and strictly institutional political factors are all shown to have a place. But a pat formula is impossible. The largest proportion of joiners from urban-industrial areas came from middle- and low-income groupings but not from poverty-stricken homes. The relatively small percentage who reported high-income backgrounds were primarily intellectuals and professionals. Occupation and education ordinarily correlate with social origin, though there are national differences here. The evidence is not conclusive, but it does not appear likely that this sample was characterized by downward social mobility. A large number of the respondents had either withdrawn from religion or had actively rejected it before joining the Party.

There were many persons who had strong and compulsive needs to attack authority. "The American and British respondents in particular included a large proportion of emotionally maladjusted individuals who were seeking to solve their emotional problems by attacking society." This tendency for the total sample is indicated by the fact that only 25 per cent began to engage in radical activity after the age of twenty-three. Revolt against the immediate family does not bulk prominently, however. The largest single group of respondents possessed a left-wing family background. Fifty-four per cent first joined a front organization. More than twice as many of the middle-class ex-Communists manifested neurotic tendencies as compared with the working-class group. A somewhat higher proportion of the later recruits exhibited neurotic problems.

To an anthropologist some of the national differences are fascinating. Of those joining in the United States 70 per cent are classified as motivated by self-oriented interests, with all three other countries falling under 40 per cent. Group-related interests fall from 54 per cent in France to 26 per cent in England. The French Party seems to have the largest core of fully indoctrinated and dedicated militants. The Italian Party, while numerically large, may be one of the least well integrated and indoctrinated. The British include a very small number of persons who had studied Communist doctrine at the time of joining. The British Party stands out for lack of stress upon hatred of the "enemy." A sizable part of the leadership and membership of the American Party is of foreign birth or parentage, but total membership has never been high. Almond concedes soundness "in the most general sense" to Philip Selznick's hypothesis concerning the erosion on an unprecedented scale of older primary and community ties and loyalties in the United States. Yet he criticizes Selznick's sociological determinism and his underestimation of human capacity to create new and satisfying bonds rather quickly. Surely the facts are on Almond's side. Selznick's theory to the contrary notwithstanding, this country has proven only minutely vulnerable to Communist subversion.

The problem of adjustment for former Party members appears more grave in France and Italy than in the United States and England. "In general, the 'moderateness' of the British party as well as of British policy toward the party reflects a general society confident of its solidarity, ready to tolerate deviance because it is basically secure." The Communism of Western Europe is less "stomach" Communism than "heart" Communism, "since what is involved in most cases is not so much hunger, as feelings of rejection and neglect." Almond sums up by saying that "while Communism in the United States and England may be viewed as an aberration, in France and Italy it takes on the proportion of a sub-culture."

The final chapter abandons somewhat the austere detachment of the first twelve chapters: "The history of Communism may be told in terms of the degeneration of its political ethics. . . . This is not the first occasion in history in which a movement purporting to seek the highest humane ends has in fact achieved their obverse." These sentences are less detached, but they still correspond to objectively demonstrable fact. Some of the policy implications of the research results are spelled out sensibly but eloquently. One of the most obvious but also most useful of these is the urgent need to reject Communist mythology as veridical: the United States cannot afford to behave as if Communism in all countries and all Communists were in fact (as opposed to the façade) unisolable portions of a world-wide monolithic unity.

The Appeals of Communism is both solidly and brilliantly executed. To be sure, further research involving larger samples (and perhaps samples differently selected) is needed. There are numerous small pedantries that could be raised. For instance, do "middle class" and "working class" represent a fine enough breakdown? Considering the size of the four national samples, I suspect that a finer sieve would have been inappropriate in this investigation. On major issues of method and interpretation I simply have no criticism of any substance, other than that the book tells us *more* about the reasons for and the difficulties of defection from Communism than about its appeals. Some reviewers have complained that this book told us nothing about "real" (i.e., U.S.S.R.) Communists. In the first place, apart from the beginning doctrinal section, the book does not pretend to do that. In the second place, I would like to note that, on the basis of my participation in the Russian Research Center study of some thousands of nonreturners and defectors from the Soviet Union, I believe much of what is said here holds for this group also. There are, of course, the inevitable national differences and the differences, probably increasing, between those who have lived their whole lives under Communism and those who have experienced a free society. But many of the psychological and situational theses apply, in my judgment, even across these barriers.

These books all attest to the growth—and perhaps even early maturity—of a study of politics that ranges itself among the various behavioral science specialties. This approach considers political boundaries of hallowed academic tradition. I think that when the history of behavioral science is written in fifty or a hundred years, these three volumes will all have an honorable place.

Russian Research Center: Project on
the Soviet Social System[3]

With another recent study I am more intimately familiar. My colleagues, however, must not be held responsible for what I say. I have ventured to select from their unpublished documents, to modify in some instances, and to combine. My own connection with this project was largely administrative and advisory. At best, I have the fairly comprehensive overview of the educated dilettante.

One of the various pilot studies of this project has been reported (Dicks, 1952). Dr. Dicks lived eighteen years in Russia and speaks Russian as he does English. He had previously had intensive and highly successful experience doing work of this sort with German prisoners of war when he served as a psychiatrist attached to British intelligence. In the Russian case

3. See 1951o and 1954s. For a general account of the project, see 1956a, *How the Soviet System Works*.

he had only twenty-nine subjects, but all of them had left the
Soviet orbit in the years after 1947, and the interviews lasted
between fifteen and eighteen hours. Only five of the subjects
were over forty-five or over. Dicks' central theses appear in the
following quotations (pp. 136-137, 142; 168-169; 169-170):

One of the dominant and persistent conflicts in Russian society (both
pre-Soviet and especially recent Soviet) is that between the ancient
Russian *oral* character structure typical in many ways for the
culture, and an *anal-compulsive* ("puritan") pattern characterizing
the *élite*. Further, this same conflict operates to a marked extent
within members of the *élite* itself, under the pull of its own recent
emergence from the traditional pattern, and of its identification with
the norm-models demanded by an originally "Western" type of
industrial and administrative social development . . . it would not
be amiss to apply to the analysis of Soviet *élite* behaviour the categories and concepts subsumed under the term of "the authoritarian
character."

. . . the outstanding trait of the Russian personality is its contradic-
toriness—its ambivalence . . . Russian behaviour oscillates in large
swings in relation to self, to primary love object, authority figures,
and outgroups. I think of the quality of these swings in terms of
the oral character: at one end the "omnivorousness," the lusty greed,
the tendency to rush at things and to "swallow them whole," the
need for quick and full gratification, the spells of manic omnipotence
feeling and optimistic belief in unlimited achievement, the over-
flowing vitality, spontaneity, and anarchic demand for abolition of
all bounds and limitations. At the other end, the melancholy, dreary
apathy, frugality, closeness and suspicion, the anxious and sullen sub-
missiveness, moral masochism and grudging idealization of a strong
and arbitrary authority which is thought of as the only safeguard
against the excesses of the Russian nature. In this mood we find the
capacity for subtle introspection and ruminative self-doubt and self-
torment. Outward servility and secret mulish obstinacy co-exist, as
if one could bend the knee to Caesar in outward conformity and yet
inwardly remain wholly on the side of God, before whom all men
are equally small and fallible. The Russian can feel that he is no good,
yet also superior to all the rest of mankind. Whether in his bac-
chanalian mood or in his depression, he always needs direct, spontaneous, heart-to-heart contact and communication, and respects
that need in others. He is intolerant of hauteur, formalism, and bureau-
cratic protocol and hierarchy, preferring the direct, informal, face-

to-face handling of problems, and spontaneous improvisation in tackling difficulties. Elaborate hierarchy troubles him, as does any kind of rigidly and uniformly controlled activity.

. . . this behaviour is in great contrast to that expected of and by the *élite.* . . . Charisma attaches . . . to those who can demonstrate their mastery over oral gratification needs.

. . . The surrender of passivity and oral spontaneity in favor of leader-like abstinence requires defense mechanisms. . . .

. . . *manic denial*—shown by the stress on unlimited achievement, on restless organizing ability and on tempo; by the great importance they attach to technology, machines, and other "assurances of mastery" over nature and internal threats. Manic denial could also be responsible for the contemptuous avoidance of and, one might almost say, taboo on depressive moods, pessimism, doubt, sentimentality—all the "minor key" sides of Russian personality. There must be no guilt and no bad objects which cannot be "controlled."

. . . *persecutory anxiety*—on the one hand there is the pressure to project the tormenting bad object into foreign aggressors—capitalists and imperialists. On the other hand there is an identification with the aggressors manifested in the persecution of "Id" qualities within "the people" as projections of the Self; the scenting of revolt, ill-will or opposition in everyone's motivations; the anxious and organized analysis of these motivations amounting to a paranoid interpretation of minimal misdemeanors as deliberate; the intoleration of sloth, "bourgeois" individualism or easy-goingness, and the progressive petrification of an ideological orthodoxy in the world of beliefs, including the same kind of condemnation of subjective art which the Nazis once labeled *"Kulturbolschewismus."*

The materials used in our later work were:

1. Extended life-history interviews and Sentence Completion Tests from 330 subjects,

2. Intensive clinical interviews, projective questions, Rorschach Tests, two TAT Tests, Episode Tests with fifty-five subjects.

All of these are interpreted in the light of the information coming from a much larger population that gave us more than 10,000 written questionnaires, 1,200 short answer items, and about fifty manuscripts written by escapees on their personal observations and experiences within the U.S.S.R. Finally, a group of interviews and psychological tests was done on a group of Americans matched for age, sex, and occupation with 100 of the Soviet emigrés. In general, the findings from this much larger body of data square well with Dicks' interpretations. The major discrepancies would appear to be:

1. We did not discover the Russian people to be psychologically driven to be submissive. They do desire supportive and nurturant superiors. (We also found little evidence to support Erikson's "masochistic identification with authority.")

2. We did not find the outstanding aggressiveness reported by Dicks, even though our sample was weighted toward the young Soviet male from the middle elite.

3. Our Russian data when compared with our American do not give clear-cut evidence for the "oral" emphasis in the traditional character structure of Great Russians.

In addition, the findings of the main project add many details of interest and put some flesh on the bones skillfully x-rayed by Dicks. I shall draw primarily on a synthesis recently completed in manuscript by our two senior clinicians, Drs. Eugenia Hanfmann and Helen Beier (1954), although many others also had a significant part in the analysis of these data.

The "modal national pattern" to be delineated is found in its extreme "primary" form among workers and peasants, is attenuated among those upwardly mobile, and almost disappears at the top of the social hierarchy. "Modal" subjects showed a great need for intensive face-to-face relationships and derived deep satisfactions from them. They "welcomed others into their lives" but were not tensely anxious about the opinions of others or compulsive about clinging to relationships once established. They see others in immense concreteness yet make their judgments less on the basis of the behavior of others than on their conception of the basic qualities and attitudes of their friends and acquaintances. They value people in terms of what they are rather than in terms of what they have done. They are unthreatened by mutual dependence, whether in the family or in the peer group.

These Russians are expressive and emotionally alive. They exhibit fewer defense mechanisms than do Americans of comparable age and occupational position. The issue between isolation and conformity is less pronounced than among Americans. Russians, as might be expected, do show greater fear of external authority. In general, they express fear, depression, and despair more frequently and openly than Americans. "They viewed the ambiguous situations presented in the tests in terms of danger and threat on the one hand, of privation and loss on the other." They accept the need for impulse control but are nevertheless rather prone to excessive indulgence. They are, however, seldom punitive toward themselves or others for giving way to impulses. They are less persevering than Americans and more accepting of the passive sides of their nature.

While a little puritanical about verbal discussion of sex, the Russians exhibited little conflict in this area and showed less confusion about their sex identification than did the Americans. Aggressive content emphasized the material realm: robbing, stealing, depriving. Among the Americans "aggression appeared more often diffuse or displaced onto trivial external annoyances. The Russians more often focused it on inimical and depriving people and situations." Defenses of the Russians were not only less prominent but also less stabilized; they were supplemented by the utilization of the sympathy and support of others for the expression and management of disturbing emotions.

Some other Russian-American points are worth summary. American stress upon autonomy, social approval, and personal achievement appears little in the Russian protocols. Russians demand and expect moral responses (loyalty, respect, sincerity) from their group. Americans care more about just being liked. Neither the Russian nor the American groups reveal marked needs for dominance or aggression—two trends often emphasized in previous "national character" studies. Americans are more optimistic, former Soviet citizens more pessimistic. In spite of the passion of the Russians for close social interaction, they exhibit considerable mistrust of others. They ask, "Is he wearing a mask?" or "Where does he really stand with respect to me?" But the dilemma is much more "outside" in the relationship rather than within the self. Americans, on the other hand, exhibit more acute self-awareness, self-examination, and doubt of their own inner motivations.

Americans are appreciably more worried about their failures

in achievement, lapses in approved etiquette, and inability to meet social obligations. Russians are shamed most deeply by dishonesty, betrayal, and disloyalty. Americans are less aware of other individuals as unique entities as opposed to performers of familiar roles. The Russians value identification with and participation in the larger collectivity more than Americans. At the same time, they are less timid about expressing their individuality within the group. Yet they are extremely sensitive to public humiliation, to impersonal treatment by superiors, to what appears to them as violation of the dignity of the unique personality. In approaching new interpersonal situations Russians characteristically take a very large view initially, and then make a very detailed and specific analysis, which usually takes an individualized and unstereotyped form. Russians and Americans both love material things, especially gadgets. The desire for "mastery" is stronger in Americans than in nonelite Russians, but Russians of all kinds often manifest great bursts of activity. Nonelite Russians are less likely to project their own hostile impulses on to others. They see mothers as nurturant and supporting and their fathers as arbitrary and demanding more markedly than do Americans. Americans exhibit more inner conflict as to the dilemma of "rebelling or submitting."

The elite group are notably less expressive emotionally, less socially committed, much more strongly characterized by defense structures, and less unequivocal in their sex identifications. They are more capable of unconditional obedience, ruthlessness, and disciplined and orderly behavior. They are more persistent in goal trends. They are more prepared to shoulder responsibility for socially unacceptable actions. Hanfmann and Beier suggest that the marked discontinuity between the top layer and the rest of the population indicates a strong selective factor "beyond those coincident to advanced education and training."

Among the elite Raymond Bauer (1953, Beier and Bauer, 1955) has distinguished three personality types—idealist, conformist, and careerist—corresponding to three dominant motivation clusters. The "idealist" has, as a youth, interiorized the more utopian values of theoretical Communism. However, he tends to make increasingly his own interpretations of how these ideals should be implemented and hence becomes disillusioned with the regime or rationalizes his conflicts over loyalty. The more intelligent and genuine of this type become concerned with the violation of their psychological selves through compromises with the regime. Those who finally turn consciously against the status quo usually withdraw into the "inner emigration." This type appears to be becoming more and more rare among adults in the Soviet Union.

The person motivated primarily by a need for psychological security (the "conformist") finds this by submerging his identity in Communism and by giving complete obedience to the strong system and its leader. Both "idealists" and "conformists" have an external aspect of devotion and dedication. The "conformist," however, is more rigidly correct in his behavior and never swims against the current of the times. He is seldom able to let his doubts become conscious unless the leaders with whom he has personally identified fall or he loses faith in the strength of the system. He then becomes directionless or apolitical or suffers mental collapse.

The type more and more prominent among the younger elite is the cynical "careerist." He pursues his own immediate self-interest—material gains, personal recognition, leisure, recreation —within the established system of rewards and controls, but he is really apolitical in his approach. He makes the appropriate political noises when necessary and conforms where this is necessary to his objectives. These ambitious men appear to be more correct in their behavior than the members of the Presidium, but this conformity is instrumental. Actually, he is neither loyal nor disloyal to the system. He is intensely loyal to himself, using his intelligence and energy to advance and to protect such position as he has gained.

Swaddling

In view of the controversies among "experts" as to swaddling practices in Great Russia within the last two generations, it seems worth while to report upon perhaps the only systematic

body of data available in the West. Of 172 Great Russian respondents interviewed on their life histories, only three (all
young) professed unfamiliarity with the practice, while another
four or five refused in effect to discuss the subject. A majority
of the subjects manifested some tension or uncomfortableness
in this part of the interview. They laughed or smiled nervously
or expressed irritation by verbal or other behavior. Often this
took the form of an explicit rejection of the Gorer hypothesis,
of which a considerable number had heard, though usually in
vulgarized or distorted form. The theory as such received no
support from any of our interviewees, though some appeared
to agree with the empirical generalizations on which it is based.
Usually the theory was termed inadequate, "stupid," or "ridiculous." Some said plainly that questions of this sort "hurt one's
feeling of self-respect" or that "This question implies that Russians are wild animals."

On many points our subjects were in rough agreement. In
the Pre-Soviet period swaddling was "compulsory" or "obli-
gatory" in almost all sectors of the society. During the past
generation it has gradually become less frequent. It is much
more common in rural areas, and in urban areas in recent times
it is seldom practiced except among families of workers and the
"uneducated." Swaddling is "old-fashioned," "primitive," and
"not cultured," though a few of our informants (including two
individuals under thirty) defended the custom:

The child could kill itself.

The baby is straighter and stronger if swaddled.

. . . just like sticks. It's good that way. He is firm and supported and
can't hurt himself.

The medical profession has opposed swaddling for some time,
our interviewees affirmed. The attitude of the government was
generally agreed to be unfavorable, though the dates of an
official pronouncement were variously given as between 1924
and 1936 and there were accounts of instruction in swaddling
in government nurseries as late as immediately before World
War II.

There was clear consensus on cultural rationalizations for swaddling. About half of the interviewees stated that swaddling was "to keep the child from harming himself." The most frequent specific instance was to prevent the infant from scratching his face or his eyes. Prevention of thumb or finger sucking was mentioned only a few times. Some informants spoke of protection when the child had to be left alone in a room. Others said their families had believed that swaddling was an insurance against colds. Straight limbs and avoidance of spinal curvature were frequently stated as being prominent in folk belief. The same may be said for swaddling as an aid to the child's sleeping long, "quietly," "peacefully." Such grounds were often connected with a more practical justification. Busy parents were less disturbed if the child was swaddled; they had more peace and could do their work better. At least one subject said that this factor entered into the practice in government nurseries. If there was only one nurse for ten or more children, there were practical reasons why the children had to be swaddled.

Some of the reasons invoked by those who rejected swaddling were interesting:

Why should I torture my children? I was educated.
We should all be free and grow up normally.
Doctors say it isn't healthy.
It is really a terrible thing to torture babies with swaddling.
I did not swaddle my child so that he would not be tortured and would develop.
But I probably was not swaddled because my father loved me very much.

The wide variation in reports of swaddling customs may plausibly be interpreted as reflecting wide variation in actual practice. The modal figure for the duration of swaddling was three to five months, but a number of informants extended the period to a year and one to a year and a half. Some said that after three or four months "the bones are stronger," and hence the child needs to be swaddled less if at all. Others insisted that full swaddling occurred only when the child was taken out of doors in cold weather. Some stated that hands and/or feet were left free "after the child could sit up" or "after eight months."

Apparently "tight" and "loose" swaddling were rather consistently contrasted, and different families and regions were said to follow varying patterns. Our informants, however, disagreed among themselves as to whether the two Russian terms ordinarily applied to swaddling could be differentiated according to the "tight" and "loose" categories. There was likewise disagreement as to the extent to which standard practice required the pinioning of the arms: some insisted that this was usual throughout the swaddling period, others that it was true only at night or during the earlier months. A few reported that their mothers freed the arms of those children who did not show a tendency to scratch their faces or suck their thumbs. The richness of detail on the materials used, the actual techniques of binding and cleanliness, and other ethnographic data would demand a small monograph for adequate presentation.

Ninety-six Great Russians said that they themselves had been swaddled. Only two of these were born before 1895; thirty-five were swaddled during the Soviet period. Of these latter, all except ten came from rural backgrounds. Five were reared in large cities and five in small cities. Of informants who had themselves been swaddled, twelve reported that their children had also been swaddled. However, of the individuals so reporting, all except four were born before 1900 and only one was born in the Soviet epoch. In one instance the swaddling of the second generation was attributed to the grandmother rather than the parents. Eight individuals in the group who had been swaddled specifically stated that their children had not been. Twenty-six Great Russians said they themselves had not been swaddled; of these, only seven had definitely rural backgrounds. Twenty-two individuals explicitly professed ignorance as to whether they had been swaddled or not, but in a number of these instances there are grounds for suspecting that in fact they had been. The context of the interview often indicates that the subject was reluctant to admit the fact to an American. In another case the respondent gave the information that his own child had been swaddled: "If you don't, their legs will be crooked or their arms will be crooked." The remainder of the 172 Great Russians either evaded this question or made equivocal statements.

Discussion

The findings on Great Russians by behavioral scientists thus far are all points of departure, not points of arrival. And yet on some issues it is possible to make with considerable confidence statements about the relatively enduring and salient personality characteristics of the contemporary Great Russian population. Different observers and analysts, using different methods and data, are in excellent agreement among themselves—and, indeed, with the Russians. The results obtained by the use of a variety of psychological instruments are also in some respects remarkably congruent. For example, the Russians, when compared with Americans and other groups, stand out for their passion for affiliation, for their sense of belongingness, and for their warmth and expressiveness in human relations. All students likewise agree on a strong need for dependence, for—to quote Dicks—"a positive drive for loving protection and security . . . care and affection." There is, however, disagreement as to the extent to which dependence and submission blend. Similarly, the consensus as to the contrast between the modal personality of people and elite does not extend to an acceptance of Dicks' typology of "oral" versus "anal-compulsive." Compare the historical "explanation" advanced by Tomasic (1953): the elite are nomad Eurasian warriors; the peace-loving peasants and workers are the old Slavs. The reality of some contrasts between people and elite is irrefutable, but no theory, either psychological or historical, thus far set forth is entirely satisfying. It is clear, however, that social changes and aspects of general social situation under the Soviets (as well as historical tradition and child-rearing practices) have had their perceptible consequences in modal personality.

A national character drama is now being played out in the U.S.S.R. The plot centers on the following themes:

1. Warm, expressive expansiveness versus formality, control, and orderliness

2. Personal loyalty, sincerity and responsiveness versus distrust and conspiratorial mentality

3. Strong identification with the face-to-face groups of which

the individual is a member versus a single tolerated loyalty
(upward to people not known personally)

4. Being versus doing, or dependent passivity versus ceaseless
instrumental "conscious activity"

This spectacle cannot fail to engage us as scientists as well as
from the point of view of the potential consequences of various
outcomes for the future lives of ourselves and our children. This
is an experiment on the grand scale. Can a small minority, under
the spell of a fierce and intolerant ideology, remold a people in
a direction quite contrary to the most fundamental propensities
of their traditional national character? If so, how soon and after
how much destructive activity at home and abroad? While we
must not evade the fact that there are some traits in the contemporary character structure of the Russian *people* that tend
to make for support of the present dictatorship, personally I
think Riesman (1952, p. 168) is on the right track when he
writes:

. . . many of the defenses I have discussed are little better than
forms of paralysis which, by their presence, evidence the resistance
men put up against seemingly implacable destinies. I would prefer
to see men fighting back through paralysis than succumbing through
active incorporation of the enemy. But this is hardly an optimum way
to live one's life, and we cannot be—even apart from the danger to
ourselves—unmoved by the plight of those now living and dying
under Communist regimes. All we can do while we seek ways to
bring those regimes down without war is to find our way to a more
robust view of man's potentialities, not only for evil, about which
we have heard and learned so much, not only for heroism, about
which we have also learned, but also for sheer unheroic cussed
resistance to totalitarian efforts to make a new man of him.

Dicks (1952, p. 174) is really saying somewhat the same thing
when he writes:

. . . the Soviet system works chiefly because of the obstinate persistence of unofficial, un-Communist, but uncommonly Russian patterns
of "backsliding" into fraternal, affectionate, and easy-going human
relations; because of the capacity of the Russians to tolerate and
cope with bad objects in virtue of the undoubted deep optimsim

created by the good though fitful nurturance they experience as infants, and because any developing society gives some scope for constructiveness and the kind of achievement which raises morale.

These valid points must not, however, be interpreted in too optimistic a fashion. The situation is not static, and there is evidence that larger and larger segments of the young people are moving closer and closer to the type of personality advocated and planned for by the regime.

14 STUDYING
THE ACQUISITION
OF CULTURE

ITH A VERY FEW notable (and mainly recent) exceptions, anthropologists have failed to give systematic attention to the problem of how specific bits of culture are transmitted from individual to individual within particular societies. Such factual material as is available in the published literature is almost wholly anecdotal in character. Such general statements as have been made tend to be grossly impressionistic. A total conceptual scheme for attacking the question may be said to be nonexistent. Freud (e.g., 1933, pp. 90-91), it is true, has given us (in his discussion of the role of the superego in culture change) conceptual tools that seem to be generally congruent with the crude and broad empirical generalization we are at present in a position to make. But I would point out, first, that the mechanisms which he postulates apply primarily to the acquisition of value systems and

1939e Reprinted by permission of the publishers from Clyde Kluckhohn, "Theoretical Bases for an Empirical Method of Studying the Acquisition of Culture by Individuals," *Man*, Vol. 39, pp. 98-103.

affective attitudes toward the formal cultural structure and, secondly, that his concepts need testing upon quantities of particular data gathered in widely differing societies.

In short, I feel it is fair to say that at the moment both the substantive[1] and the theoretical aspects of socialization and culturization[2] (if I may coin an admittedly horrid word) acutely need investigation. It is not merely that culturization is a subject of great interest and importance in itself. Until we have learned something about it in a detailed and comparative way, the premises basic to our discussions of culture change and development (to select the most obvious but by no means the only relevant topic in general anthropology) can have, at best, only the justification of highly imperfect inductions.

What sorts of field material will best satisfy this need? Clearly, we can not be satisfied with information that goes no further than describing in neutral tones positive acquisitions of skills and of overt standardized behaviors generally. Data must have the affect dimension and bear upon the emotional structure of the transmission of culture. In my opinion, life-history documents that have the amplitude of detail of Dyk's *Son of Old Man Hat* (1938) will prove invaluable supplements to other sorts of data. However, the length of time, quality of informant, and other conditions prerequisite to securing such life histories

---

1. Fortes (1938) has given us admirable empirical material. This work—as well as Firth's excellent contribution (1936, pp. 147 ff.), to which Fortes calls attention—I had not seen until after this paper had been written, but I find myself in general agreement with Fortes' and Firth's delimitation of the theory of the problem, except that I differ sharply (as will later be elaborated) with the following statement (Fortes, p. 8): "For most problems of social anthropology variations are of minor importance as compared with the 'typical,' and an all-round knowledge of a culture is sufficient check of typicality." At very least, it would seem to me that such a statement is unjustified at present in default of concrete testing of this postulate.

2. To a large extent I mean by "culturization" what social psychologists and sociologists have meant by "socialization." Undoubtedly socializing a young human animal consists mainly in conditioning him (in so far as possible) to the responses expected of him in a particular cultural or subcultural framework. But I think that the new word might have some little utility in directing attention explicitly and directly to this phase of the process.

probably mean, as a practical matter, that we cannot hope to
have a very great number of such documents until the number
of persons doing field research is materially greater. Nevertheless, I should like to state emphatically my conviction that the
system of observations that I shall suggest must continually be
revised in terms of such insights as we get from careful
inductive analysis of life-history materials.

In the course of extended investigation of the Navahos living
in the Ramah region my coworkers and I have developed a
method that could be used somewhat more generally by the
field worker who is not able to devote the whole or major portion of his energy to obtaining life histories but who can,
perhaps, look forward to repeated visits to the same people. It
hardly appears worthwhile to elaborate here the more technical
aspects of the method, for these would vary widely in detail
from field situation to field situation. There are, however, two
postulates upon which its validity must rest, and, since these
are of more or less universal application, it seems important to
bring them into the realm of conscious and explicit discussion:

1. Even in relatively homogeneous nonliterate societies there
are differences in the behavior of individuals that cannot be
fully explained in terms of age, sex, and the other factors upon
which sociological status and role depend.

2. Range of variation (in ideology, in practice, in the divergence between these two) is sufficiently significant to make
consideration of the sampling process vital.

Both of these premises merit extended discussion, but I must
dismiss the first briefly. I should like, first of all, to suggest that
it is not necessary, for our purposes here, to beg the question
as to whether such variations rest upon inherited differences of
genetic constitution, upon various accidents of the conditioning
process,[3] or upon combinations of both of these and perhaps
other classes of factors. It is essential only to grant that such

3. I am thinking of the following kind of possibility: An individual, A,
who is approximately the equivalent of another individual, B, in so far as
age, sex, status, etc., are concerned might (under defined conditions) behave differently from B because, let us say, there had been a marked age
difference between his parents, whereas the father and mother of B were
of about the same age.

differences do exist and that they are worth investigating. It follows (as in the case of Professor Boas' studies of the physical growth of children) that it will not be sufficient simply to sample a community with regard to age, sex, status, and the like; it will be necessary to follow the same children over a period of years. I concede the practical utility of the presumption that what was observed to be true of the acquisition of an aspect of culture by one individual in defined sociological circumstances would hold for a different individual in similar circumstances. I only urge testing the chance that an appreciable margin of error enters in, which could be eliminated by having the same observer or observers follow the same individuals over a relatively long period.

The second postulate seems to me so critical and so scandalously neglected in the work of most anthropologists that I should like to discuss it a greater length. To begin again with a negative consideration, this premise does not imply that the observed incidences of any given class of behaviors would, if plotted, approximate the form of the so-called normal curve, nor, indeed, of any particular curve known to statistics at present. It is premised merely that (even in numerically small and remarkably consistent and coherent societies) responses to the same situation are not identical; there are variances and covariances, and these and their frequency distributions must be taken into account.

Heretofore we have been too often content with purely formalized descriptions that give, in effect, simply the ideology of the culture—perhaps as conceived by a very few informants. The meaningful question of "goodness of fit" between theory and practice has almost entirely been passed over. Girls in a particular tribe are expected at a certain age to learn from their biological mothers such and such technological skills. It is very interesting and very important to know this, but we can hardly hope to get a satisfactory intellectual grasp of the behaviors in question unless we also have concrete data indicating what proportion of the actual individuals in the tribe in question follow out more or less the letter of the ideal pattern, what proportion deviate somewhat (and in what directions), and what proportion disregard the ideal patterns almost entirely. We have too many statements of the form "The Navaho learn this (or that) from their fathers (or their mothers)." Now such sweeping generalizations have little scientific meaning unless we are given controls, unless we are given some indication of how many concrete observations formed the basis for such statements of uniformities. Clearly, if such statements are to be used by comparative sociologists making inductions as to very general regularities in human behavior, a distinction must be made between general statements based on the word of one informant out of a population of fifty, one informant out of a population of 1,000, twenty informants out of a population of 400, and the like. Similarly, general statements based on observation of one relevant incident are surely of a different order from those based on observation of 100 incidents. And there remains the whole question of differentiating between generalizations based upon statement, generalizations based upon observation, and generalizations based upon both statement and observation. Almost never in ethnographic monographs does the author consistently give the reader control information of this sort. We have been insufficiently tough-minded in accepting "general knowledge of the culture" as a substitute.

Now in the case of someone who, like Malinowski, has lived long in the society and who speaks the language we are, in the greater number of cases, probably not unwarranted in taking his word (or implicit suggestion) that a given incident is typical or atypical. And yet—in terms of what we know and suspect as to the intrusion of the "personality" of the field worker into the selection of his data and the crystallization of his dominant impressions—would we not be justified in demanding—even from this brilliant field observer—some dispassionately factual controls of this sort? Malinowski (1932, p. xlviii) himself remarks that "The competent and experienced ethnographer . . . will easily see from the data presented throughout this book where the documentation is thin and where it is full."

But isn't this entirely too rough and ready a sort of test for even a would-be science? Malinowski normally documents his "context of situation" in almost every particular. This is admirable, but I sometimes suspect that this sureness of documentation (together with a general impression of firm mastery of his data

that he manages to convey to almost every reader) makes Malinowski a trifle more convincing than a really cold-blooded
scrutiny of his work would warrant. A distinguished anthropologist has been heard to remark: "When you read *The
Argonauts* you felt that the kula is everything in the Trobriands,
when you read *Sex and Repression* or *The Sexual Life of Savages* you decided it was really sex that counted. Now—with
Coral Islands and Their Magic you have to conclude that, after
all, neither sex nor the kula are really central—it is magic." Now
no one (and certainly not the anthropologist whom I have
quoted) would maintain that these remarks constitute a fair and
balanced verdict on Malinowski's work. But there is, nevertheless, a certain grain of truth that bears on what we are talking
about. Until Malinowski gives a synthesis in which he shows us
—in a steadily maintained perspective—how these various elements of action that have formed the central motifs of his various
books are interrelated one with another, how and where one
"interest" prevails over or is subordinate to another, in some of
us a nasty suspicion will pop up from time to time that Malinowski's conceptual scheme is rather far from a neutral, uniform
set of operations consistently applied to various assemblages of
discrete data.

It would be quite improper to call Malinowski's approach
anecdotal. Would it, however, be very far from the truth if we
described his method as that of the well-documented anecdote
set firmly in a ramified context? There is surely a tinge of the
anecdotal so long as an ethnographer gives us no check upon
his statement or implication that a behavior or a patterned set
of responses is or is not typical—in the sense that type is "a
measure of central tendency in a range of material."

It is from such a theoretical background that the method I
propose to outline in a schematic way was developed—after a
good deal of preliminary fumbling. The method has two sepa-
rable aspects. The first consists merely in extended and systematic
analyses of the relationships between teacher and learner in the
various activities where the learning process is recognized as
such. From exactly whom did every ceremonial practitioner
learn each portion of his ceremonial knowledge? Who taught

every weaver, every silversmith, every potter, every basket-maker, and the like? What uniformities of kinship or sociological or other patterned relationship emerge from sifting the data bearing on each case? Figures might, to be sure, be very misleading unless adequacy of sample were demonstrated. My procedure, for the moment at least, is to rule out the problem of sampling here by gathering every (or virtually every) relevant datum in the society being studied.

The second aspect of the method is slightly more complex. There are about 500 individuals in the community in question, and of the 150-odd children putatively under sixteen years of age I selected twenty-four boys and twenty-four girls, divided equally between the following six age groups: newly born infants, children under a year of age, children over one year but unweaned, weaned children under five years of age, children between five years of age and pubescence, and adolescents. Adopted children and stepchildren are included. In making the selection, care was taken to insure that the various sublocal groups and four economic strata were represented in approximately equal numbers.

These forty-eight children have represented a kind of focus of interest during successive seasons of field work but not a project demanding exclusive attention. In fact, I feel that in the long run the material is likely to be more satisfactory because it was obtained (for the most part) incidentally. While we have made an effort to gather certain information about each child rather systematically, my coworkers and I have not preoccupied ourselves in so concentrated a fashion as to risk the danger of forcing our data (if only by unconscious selection) into a Procrustean bed of preconceived notions. Rather, this work has been kind of field knitting, as it were—a set of tasks to which we could turn in otherwise idle moments while visiting certain families. For any ethnographer or group of ethnographers to say that they record "everything" in the field is, of course, a monstrous self-delusion. If truly everything observable were noted down, the writing of field notes would take as long as the carrying out of all the actions. At best, the conception of recording everything about everything is a counsel of perfection. One can, however, record nearly everything (so far as one's unconscious blind spots will allow!) bearing on certain selected universes of behavior. One such for us is the doings and sayings of these children—and of adults directly interacting with these children.

To date four observers (one a woman) have participated in the investigation. Of these, two (who have spent nineteen weeks in the field) did not have the list of specific children but were asked to take particular pains to record the actions and speech of all children. It is felt that these data afford a measure of control over those more pointedly gathered. We make a point (in the course of attaining other objectives) of spending a somewhat disproportionate amount of time with the families involved. We also have opportunities for seeing the children at various ceremonial and other gatherings. On every occasion when we have the opportunity to observe the child directly[4] we endeavor to write down everything that we see and hear with particular reference to the interaction of the child with older individuals. We also get interview material (both active and passive) from the children when they are old enough to talk. This we supplement with opinions of the children collected from the adults who are with them most. Our effort, I repeat, is to record everything seen and heard, but, because at most this can be but a trifling sample of the child's total behavior, and also because we are convinced that even under the most favorable conditions an observer will not record everything that he actually sees or hears or feels, we have prepared rather extensive lists of topics that we believed to be of rather crucial importance. We do not regard these as complete by any means, but we feel that if we keep them (as a minimum) tenaciously in consciousness, we shall be likely to miss less. The sheer printing of the lists would occupy a number of pages, but some excerpts (printed just as

4. Although the bulk of our field work is necessarily done during the months of June, July, August, and September, I have been among this group of Navaho at least once during every month of the year, and before the study is completed I shall systematically observe these children during nonsummer months. It would therefore seem possible to make most of the corrections necessary for distortions consequent upon the fact that most of the data have been gathered during a particular season of the year.

they occur on the memoranda we take into the field) will suggest the scope and kind of behavior we are trying to cover:

Has the child remained with the biological mother? Was it suckled by others than the biological mother, and, if so, by whom, under what circumstances, for how long, etc.? How many "mothers" in the classificatory sense were present in the extended family during what age periods? Detailed observations on interaction with these. Has the child had stepfathers, and, if so, how many, at what ages, etc.? Has the mother been without a husband at any period? Observations of suckling behavior in infants—does the mother appear to find pleasure therefrom? Is the infant suckled, day or night, whenever it cries? Does the infant ever manifest aggression with respect to nipple or breast? Sample records of how many hours and minutes out of twenty-four the mother is actually in direct physical contact with the infant? For how many minutes is the mother out of sight? Proportion of time spent by the infant in being nursed, being fondled, sleeping, and the like. Particular attention to groupings of children with one another and with adults in regard to birth order, sex, siblings, other sociological relationships. Actual instances of discipline (and praise and blame generally) by whom? Under what conditions? Are there threats of punishment? By whom? Carried out? Statements by children as to favorites among adults and among other children—to what extent are others consciously taken as models? Concord with observed behaviors. Expressions of rivalry in children? Evidence of competitive and aggressive behavior. Full accounts of somewhat formalized teaching of children. What is kept secret from children of various ages? Are male and female children weaned at about the same period, other things being equal? Is there any evidence that male children find the weaning process more traumatic than female children (or vice versa)? After a child is weaned— any attempt to touch or caress the mother's breast? Other evidences of symbolization of the breast? Instances of parents (or other elders) competing for the child's attention? How and when is physical modesty taught? After weaning, what persons actually give the child food? To what differing extent do the various children seem to experience satisfaction or frustration in activities common to all? Evidences of leadership. Sharing of food and of property. With what elders is conversation carried on at different ages, for what duration, and on what topics? Amount of work demanded of children and degree of responsibility involved. Does a distinction seem to be made in the rewards for accomplishment by individual initiative and by cooperative effort? Cases of play being regulated by adults. Behavior of adults with reference to quarrelling, bullying, and the like on the part of children.

Already we have embarrassingly copious notes on these and many other topics (including, of course, the more obvious ones, such as date at which walking, talking, sphincter control, and the like began; thumb sucking, nail biting, and other minor aberrations). It will be seen that many of these foci of observation will tend toward providing highly detailed documentation on the extension of behavior patterns toward wider and wider circles of individuals. It is also patent that many converge on two crucial questions: Is there evidence that various external stimuli are associated with primary biological impulses? What are the chief foci round which the rudimentary sentiments of the child appear to form? A preliminary analysis of the material indicates certain rather striking and hitherto unrecognized patterns in the development of Navaho children and in the transmission of culture in both its structural and affective aspects. Numbers of instances are such that (for the most part) analysis is simple, though tedious, for it proceeds largely by simple induction and by the method of agreement and difference.

In conclusion, let me restate in another and more general way the theoretical bases for this method. If we are to deal with any problem (such as that of the acquisition of culture by individuals) in a way that is reducible to actual human behaviors, generalizations must be given a quantitative basis. In respect to any particular class of behavior, the range of variation, the frequency distributions, and something comparable to the "standard deviation"[5] must be indicated—even though in many cases the data can provide only the roughest of first approximations to these categories. It can no longer be regarded as adequate for a field worker to assure us that a specified response is "typical." Does he mean to define typical in terms of operations comparable to those by which the statistician defines "mode" or

5. "Standard deviation" suggests only the kind of problem involved— there is no implication here of "normal" distribution.

to those by which the statistician defines "median" or one of the several "means"? How rich or how meager are the numerical bases for types so construed?

To say that an attempt must be made to give generalizations a quantitative basis is not to suggest that ethnographies should consist solely of horrendous masses of figures. It seems to me legitimate and desirable that the field worker should give us his impressions at various stages of his work, that he should by any means at his command attempt to communicate to us the "feel" of the culture as he got it. We must demand, however, that "impressions," "hunches," and the like be labeled as such. We must know clearly upon what more or less objective ground we stand at every point in the presentation. This means, indeed, that some studies in social anthropology will make less racy reading than in the recent past. Social anthropologists have been a little too ready to skim the intellectual cream. At least some social anthropologists must devote rather more attention to seeing how much of nutriment can be obtained from rigorous separation of the skim milk of field observations. Some of us must, I think, be content to work more patiently and less spectacularly on smaller canvases that we rework for many seasons. To reverse a point made by Lasswell, I suggest that anthropology must supplement its *extensive* excursions with more *intensive* penetrations.

15 THE LIMITATIONS

OF ADAPTATION AND ADJUSTMENT

AS CONCEPTS FOR UNDERSTANDING

CULTURAL BEHAVIOR

SINCE ABOUT 1920 the most fashionable major current in anthropological theory has been that commonly labeled "functionalism." The ideological derivation of functionalism is ordinarily traced from Durkheim and his associates and followers of the Année Sociologique group, with an almost complete (though partially implicit) statement of the theoretical position appearing in Mauss's famous *Essai sur le don* (1923-1924). However, most of the questions raised by the English anthropologists who made a slogan of "functionalism," Radcliffe-Brown and Malinowski, had been dealt with earlier by Boas and some of his pupils, though they did not advertize this approach as a conceptual platform. Malinowski and Radcliffe-Brown made the theory explicit and, to a degree, systematic, and they popularized it in the English-speaking world. Their own views are not identical, and their empirical studies differ im-

1949b Reprinted by permission of the publishers from Clyde Kluckhohn, "The Limitations of Adaptation and Adjustment as Concepts for Understanding Cultural Behavior," in *Adaptation*, edited by John Romano. Ithaca, Cornell University Press, pp. 99-113.

portantly in emphasis, but, on the whole, their discourse proceeds from the same basic premises.

There is no doubt that the functionalist movement made significant contributions to the development of anthropology. Malinowski and his pupils dramatically documented the reticulate nature of cultures, the fact that cultural organization as well as cultural content must be described, and the intricate interdependence of the various aspects of a culture ("The canoe has also its sociology," and so forth). Radcliffe-Brown and those influenced by him explored intensively one area of these interdependences—namely, that between social groups—more intensively than had ever been done before.

By 1935 the functionalist approach had made its impression upon even the movement's most professedly hostile critics. Many anthropologists, both in the English-speaking world and out of it, had absorbed many of the main ideas, though remaining outside the "school" of either Malinowski or Radcliffe-Brown. Thurnwald had developed what Lowie has termed "tempered functionalism." The *Struktur-Lehre* of Kraus was hardly more than an amalgam of Malinowski and Radcliffe-Brown with a coloring of German philosophy. Benedict's *Patterns of Culture* (1934) marked a genuinely new development, for, as Boas pointed out, she was concerned more with the discovery of fundamental attitudes than with the functional relations of every cultural item; nevertheless, many of her postulates are substantially identical with those of the functionalists.

Some theoretical refinements have been introduced. The sociologist Robert Merton suggested a distinction between "manifest" and "latent" function, and another sociologist, Kingsley Davis, an essentially similar one between "purposed" and "nonpurposed" function. One can easily point to cultural forms that lack manifest function. For example, a cowboy will spend an hour catching a horse, which he then rides for a distance considerably shorter than he covered on foot while catching the animal. Taken literally and superficially, this act (and the subcultural pattern of which it is a manifestation) seems distinctly nonfunctional. It does have no manifest function, but more than one latent function may be pointed out. The cowboy escapes the ridicule to which he would be exposed if another cowboy saw him walking on any other mission than that of catching a horse. He also preserves his own sense of self-respect and of the fitness of things. Of course, the basic relation between cowboy and horse that is symbolized in this pattern is functional (i.e., has survival value).

All apparently nonfunctional elements in cultures, all so-called cultural dysteleologies, have been regarded as having latent functions of a similar order. The at present mechanically useless buttons on the sleeve of a European coat are said to subserve the function of preserving the familiar, of maintaining a tradition. People are, in general, more comfortable if they feel a continuity of behavior, if they believe themselves to be following out the orthodox and socially approved forms of behavior. Experience, much of which is actually unpredictable, is given the simulacrum of safety to our minds by making some aspects of it truly expectable because they conform to the past. Saying "five houses" when "five house" would be sufficient at the level of manifest function has also been interpreted as fulfilling the latent function of bolstering the individual's security through adherence to a familiar and established tradition.

Another attempted improvement was my own responsibility. The psychologist O. H. Mowrer introduced me to an attractive distinction between adaptation and adjustment. In our chapter on "Dynamic Theory of Personality" in *Personality and the Behavior Disorders* (1944c) we spelled this out as follows:[1]

The view that living organisms make movements when stimulated and that this is the end of the matter is definitely *not* a functional theory of behavior. Physical machines and other inanimate objects may be said to "respond" to forces which impinge upon them, but it is only living organisms which possess in any high degree what may be called the capacity for *self-regulation*. There are, however, two important schools of thought as to how this is achieved. Under the sway of Darwinian biology, many writers of the last century conceived of the behavior of all living organisms as being determined primarily by instincts. These were defined as genetically inherited patterns of behavior which were relatively fixed as far as the lifetime of a given individual was concerned but which were capable of changing from

---

1. From O. H. Mowrer and Clyde Kluckhohn, "Dynamic Theory of Personality," in *Personality and the Behavior Disorders*, edited by J. McV. Hunt. Copyright 1944, The Ronald Press Company, New York.

generation to generation through the mechanism of natural selection ("survival of the fittest"), or *adaptation*. More recently, writers have stressed the importance of *habits*, which are defined as ways of behaving which have been acquired by the individual through the course of his life history. It is true, of course, that heredity, in both the genetic and the cultural sense, is a potent force in determining what a given individual's life experiences will be and thereby greatly influences the kinds of habits that are developed; but the habits that come as a result of both the genetic and the cultural determinants must be equally understood in terms of learning.

Learning theory represents an attempt to explain the genesis and nature of habits, and in order to make this theory adequate to its task the concept of *adjustment* (reward, satisfaction, gratification) has come into prominence. According to the instinct theory, behavior functions, or is functional, if it keeps the individual alive, healthy, and reproducing; according to learning theory, behavior functions, or is functional, if it leads to the elimination of the stimulation, or tension, which caused it. Failure to distinguish between adaptation (which develops and changes inherited ways of behaving) and adjustment (which develops and changes habits) has been the cause of endless confusion. Living organisms are so constructed that adjustive acts are, in the overwhelming majority of cases, also adaptive. Thus, eating food when hungry ordinarily functions both to satisfy the hunger and to keep the organism alive. However, an animal *may* eat palatable but poisonous food, in which event its behavior is adjustive but not adaptive. Although the concept of adaptation is useful in explaining instincts and also culture in the most general sense, it is only by adopting the adjustive conception of individual behavior that psychoanalysis, anthropology, and learning theory have made their greatest advances as separate sciences and present the favorable possibility which they do for systematic unification.

In its simplest, most basic form, adjustment implies that living organisms tend to go into action and to remain in action until the source of their activity is removed. The proposition that "the behavior of all living organism is functional" thus comes to mean merely that their behavior tends to result in the elimination of the stimulation, or irritation, which produces it.

At about the same time, I based an attempt at interpretation of Navaho witchcraft on a modified functionalism that utilized these two categories of adaptation and adjustment. My basic postulate was that no cultural forms survive unless they constitute responses that are adjustive or adaptive, in some sense, for the members of the society or for the society considered as a perduring unit. I used "adaptive" as a purely descriptive term referring to the fact that certain types of behavior result in survival (for the individual or for the group). "Adjustive" referred to those responses that removed the motivation stimulating the individual. Thus, suicide, for example, is adjustive but not adaptive. I then tried to show how the corpus of Navaho witchcraft belief and practice constituted a storehouse of culturally defined adaptive and adjustive responses—given the Navaho situation, Navaho history, Navaho social structure, the Navaho socialization process, and so forth.

My analysis, however, was basically a functional one. I would suggest merely that the phrase "adaptive and adjustive responses" is a means for avoiding the ambiguities that have inhered in "functional," since that word has diverse connotations from physiology, mathematics, and other disciplines. Moreover, the concept of "adjustive response" perhaps directs attention to the contributions that this aspect of Navaho culture makes to the preservation of the equilibrium of individuals. Anthropological functionalism has too often been so interested in formulating the relations between the abstracted parts of the social structure that there has been a tendency to lose sight of the concrete human organisms. The motivations and rewards felt by persons have been lost sight of in the preoccupation with the significance of a culture pattern for the total social system. In this framework the operations by which the functions of a culture pattern are defined consist in showing how the fulfillment of the pattern promotes the solidarity or survival of the society and/or the gratifications of its component members.

Nevertheless, these are at best refinements that accept the underlying presuppositions of functionalism. Nor has the basic theory been seriously challenged by anthropologists—except to the extent that Lowie and others have pointed out that the short-time cross section used by the functionalists may result in "explaining" in situational terms what can only be understood in the light of the accidents of history. The main controversy between the "historicalists" and the "functionalists" in print, however, has been centered on the rather sterile question of whether the primary task of anthropology was to reconstruct the history of nonliterate societies or to discover how societies and cultures work. This dispute is now largely ended, with all parties agreeing that the two approaches are not mutually exclusive alternatives but rather necessary supplements of one another. Other criticisms of the functionalist position are simply to the effect that function is overstressed at the expense of form, that functionalists sometimes overstrain to show the interdependence of the features of a culture, and the like.

In brief, in spite of arguments on some issues, certain basic postulates about human nature and human psychology tend to be uncritically accepted. Nor is this limited to anthropology. Elements of the same conceptual scheme underlie need psychology, psychoanalysis, and learning theory. All of these disciplines reflect to greater or lesser degree the mechanism derived from classical physics, the Darwinian stress on the struggle for survival, the hedonism basic to nineteenth-century economics, British empiricism, and the stress on irrational or unconscious factors that Freud, Bergson, Pareto, and others introduced early in this century. Mowrer and I have maintained that anthropology, psychiatry, clinical psychology, and learning theory all tend to accept the following postulates:

1. Human behavior is functional.
2. Behavior always involves conflict or ambivalence.
3. Behavior can be understood only in relation to the field or context in which it occurs.
4. Behavior tends toward a state of maximal integration or internal consistency (homeostasis).

As Witmer (1939, p. 98) has observed, "The light which psychoanalysis shed on individual behavior by its insistence that there was meaning and purpose in the most incoherent talk of a psychotic is the same that functional anthropology brought to the study of group behavior."

Theories based on these premises have markedly increased our ability to understand human behavior and have even led to a limited capacity to predict in certain areas. But I must confess to an increasing dissatisfaction with them as they stand. They pay too little attention to the long- or short-term cost of "functioning" institutions. They are certainly incomplete, and I believe there are important elements of distortion in them. They do not enable us to deal with some outstanding problems, and they take no account of large masses of evidence that do not square with them, though admittedly this evidence is particularly intractable to the techniques and methods at the disposal of contemporary science. They emphasize out of all proportion the push of the total situation, neglecting the pull of ideas and of ideals. They constitute in fact a valuation in terms of survival and of adjustment, despite the common judgment of humanity that the "best-adjusted" individuals often tend to be empty automatons.

The stress upon adjustment to the environmental pressures leads to the relief-from-tension formula as the primary or the sole explanation of motivation. To say, as Murray and I have recently (1953a, p. 36) said, "that it is not a tensionless state . . . which is generally most satisfying to a healthy organism, but the *process* of reducing tension" helps only a little. We were forced to distinguish between "end pleasures" and "mode pleasures" to bring the more spontaneous and expressive forms of behavior under the tent of our formula at all. The frequently observed phenomenon that individuals actually seek tension, novelty, and thrills can only be handled by logical squiggling. Our notion of goal and climax may be culture-bound. In some cultures satisfaction appears to inhere in the perduring situation itself.

In the cultural field, it is when one comes to the all-important problem of culture change that one sees the inadequacy of the functional approach. Functionalism is adequate to strictly structural questions but not to those of process. Functional studies in anthropology have been synchronic, not diachronic. Once the time variable is introduced and one tries to account for the origin of new cultural forms or the elaboration of old ones in certain directions and not others, the concepts of adaptation and adjustment do not suffice. Even at the flat-time level the functionalist must strainfully invoke the idea of latent function and of indirect adjustive value to explain why days and even weeks are spent in polishing the nonbusiness faces of axes. Prestige symbols, yes. But why axes—in cultures where stone axes have had no manifest function for hundreds of years?

Functionalist anthropology has attempted to explain cultural phenomena in terms of drives and needs. I have spoken of needs earlier, and they are real enough—they are simply not the whole story. That the patterns of all cultures do crystallize around foci provided by certain biological imperatives and by certain other inevitables of the human situation, no one would question. But the different ways in which various cultures have provided their standardized answers to the same fundamental problems cannot always be illuminated by showing that they are appropriate responses to the special character of each particular environment. The matter is clearly more complicated than this, especially when we think of value systems. Here one can perhaps see the varieties of human temperament obfuscating the neat schemata of the functionalists. One of the principal difficulties with the functionalist premises, incidentally, is that they take insufficient account of the propensity toward variation in the biological stuff of human nature—and hence in human behavior. The anthropological functionalists still tend to think in a mechanistic and Darwinian fashion: given a biological species of generalized properties and a specified stimulus situation, the functionally appropriate responses will gradually become standardized as cultural patterns and may continue even after the situation has changed in accord with the principle of latent function. Up to a point this is certainly true: neither a society nor an individual will survive unless behavior makes a certain minimum of sense in terms of environmental demands. But the theory is true *only* up to a point. One of the "laws" which the earlier functionalists advanced was that those animals and plants in a people's habitat which have economic value become invested with symbolic significance. This is probably a valid statistical generalization, but after it was advanced as the "explanation" of totemism, such totems as flies, sting rays, sparrow hawks, bile, and anal sores were discovered in Australia. One clan alone was reported by Sharp to have 227 distinct totems. Radcliffe-Brown and others had to do some awkward squirming.

How is one to account for the enormously diverse conceptions of time found in the cultures of the world? The ancient Egyptians were pioneers in astronomical and calendrical investigations. This makes good functional sense, for Egyptian agriculture was tied to the periodicities in the inundations of the Nile. Why, then, is the dominant theme in Egyptian thought—as we have recently been assured by Frankfort (1948)—the conviction that the universe is static and that only the changeless is ultimately significant? Did the Judaic conception of sin originate in the Near East because this had unusual survival or adjustive value under the circumstances of life in this area? This seems unlikely. Rather, conceptions of time and of the good life were surely determined in part by the accidents of history, including the genius and temperament of individuals who happened to be born at a crucial period and to key positions in the social structure. Societies make what, for want of a more accurate word, we may call "choices." Such decisions are of special importance when a new culture is being created or when an old one has become relatively loose and malleable under extreme stress. But with societies, as with individuals, any crucial choice is to greater or lesser degree a determiner of later ones. Once a society starts down one road, the paths that would have opened up on another route that was physically available will seldom be traversed, and if they should be, the territory will be reacted to, not freshly, but in a fashion colored and shaped by the experience upon the first road. The principle of "limitation of possibilities" is operative.

Individuals and peoples never, after birth, react simply to a stimulus situation. Between the organism and the environment there is always interposed an intervening variable, unseen but powerful. This is the total apperceptive mass that defines and limits the perception of the stimulus situation. Except in reflexive behavior or under conditions of extreme physiological stress, human beings react not to environmental press but to this press as interpreted by apperception. Thanks to the work of McCulloch and Pitts and others, we now know something of the neurological basis of this apperceptive mass.

The functionalist assumption that culture is solely the result of response to physiological drives and needs as modified by acquired drives reduces culture change to the tautology of "culture begets or determines culture." The systemic quality of each may tend to give all cultures the property of immanence or orthogenesis. Some culture change may well be predetermined once fundamental organization has been assumed. Much more, however, culture change seems to be due to the ceaseless feedback between factors or idiosyncratic and universal human motivation, on the one hand, and factors of universal and special situation, on the other. For dealing with such systems of organized complexity we lack, as Weaver (1948) has pointed out, conceptual instruments.

Nevertheless, this much seems clear. We must not continue so glibly to posit needs on the basis of observed habits. We must take account of the possibility that some functional necessities of societies are referable primarily to the collectivity rather than to the biologically derived needs of the component individuals. We require a way of thinking that takes account of the pull of expectancies as well as the push of tensions, that recognizes that growth and creativity come as much or more from instability as from stability, and that emphasizes culturally created values as well as the immediately observable external environment. As Lee (1948, p. 394) has noted, "Culture is not . . . 'a response to the total needs of a society' but rather a system which stems from and expresses something had, the basic values of the society." All cultures create problems for individuals as well as solve them. Only in part is culture an adaptive and adjustive instrument.

16 ETHICAL RELATIVITY:

SIC ET NON

FROM THE ANTHROPOLOGICAL STANDPOINT, ethical relativity is a special case of a wider category, cultural relativity. This category applies to cognition, epistemology, and the like as much as to the realm of value. The work of some of the linguistic anthropologists—notably, of B. L. Whorf—has suggested that "concepts of reality" are relative to language and other accidents of the historical process. Whorf held that all observers cannot arrive at the same picture of the universe unless their linguistic backgrounds can "in some way be calibrated." The sociology of knowledge is another particular form of cultural relativity. As with linguistic relativity, the sociology of knowledge makes for distrust of all questions in the form, "Is this proposition valid?" It turns attention rather to the question, "How did it happen that such views developed?" The approach of cultural relativity in general stresses the uniqueness

1955b Reprinted by permission of the publishers from Clyde Kluckhohn, "Ethical Relativity: *Sic et Non*," *Journal of Philosophy*, Vol. 52, pp. 663-677.

in the human record and tends to neglect the recurrences. It often implicitly denies that "history repeats itself." It will be useful to refer more than once to the general concept of cultural relativity, but let us now turn directly to ethical relativity.

Professor Edel (1955, p. 30) says, "Indeterminacy—the fact of no definite answers available or achievable—seems to be the heart of the relativist position in ethical theory." Professor Brandt (1954, pp. 11, 87 ff.) takes substantially the same position when he remarks that " a necessary condition for the tenability of ethical relativism" is to hold in principle that two people may assert "contradictory ethical views without either being mistaken." The thesis of this paper will be that recent developments in the behavioral sciences have tended to narrow the areas of indeterminacy while still affirming the necessity of ethical relativity in certain contexts.

Few anthropologists would today defend without important qualification Ruth Benedict's famous statement (1934, p. 278): ". . . the coexisting and equally valid patterns of life which mankind has carved for itself from the raw materials of existence." In part, I think we must admit, the abandonment of the doctrine of untrammeled cultural relativity is a reaction to the observation of social consequences. If one follows out literally and logically the implications of Benedict's words, one is compelled to accept any cultural pattern as vindicated by its cultural status: slavery, cannibalism, Naziism, or Communism may not be congenial to Christians or to contemporary Western societies, but moral criticism of the cultural patterns of other people is precluded. Emotionally and practically, this extreme position is hardly tolerable—even for scholars—in the contemporary world.

But, actually, the trend of strictly scientific inquiry had shifted before there was general awareness of the more immediate implications of extreme relativism. During the nineteenth century anthropologists had tended to stress the unity of mankind and the diversity of the inanimate environment. At about the turn of the century, however, this emphasis came largely to be reversed. This was due in considerable part to Franz Boas. He stated explicitly that anthropology was interested in historically created diversities, leaving to psychology the exploration of common human nature. For at least a generation American anthropology (and, to a considerable degree, anthropology in the world in general) concentrated its attention upon the differences between peoples, neglecting the similarities. Recently the balance has been righted somewhat. This occurred, no doubt, under the influence of factors of the sort studied by sociologists of knowledge. This is not, however, the whole story. Also significant was the breakdown of the isolation of anthropology from psychology and sociology. Since the present anthropological stance on relativity can be grasped only in the light of the interdisciplinary thinking that has flourished of late, I shall briefly review some of the most relevant facts and theories of psychology and sociology. I shall turn then to a more extended consideration of the field where I can speak with greater competence.

The Psychological Contribution

During the phase of the predominance of radical behaviorism most American psychologists eschewed the realm of values and everything immediately pertinent to ethics. By 1935, however, E. L. Thorndike gave his presidential address to the American Association for the Advancement of Science on values. In 1945 even Clark Hull published a paper on values. And over the past fifteen years Allport, Ames, Cantril, Frenkel-Brunswik, Hastorf, Maslow, and Woodruff—to name only a few—have discussed at considerable length the implications of psychological findings about human nature to values and specifically to ethics.

To summarize quickly this considerable literature is impossible. I shall therefore limit myself to some representative points from the writings of academic and of medical psychologists. Maslow (1954, pp. 77, 81) for example, writes:

Once granted reliable knowledge of what man *can* be under "certain-conditions-which-we-have-learned-to-call-good," and granted that he is happy, serene, self-accepting, unguilty, and at peace with himself only when he is fulfilling himself and becoming what he can be, then it is possible and reasonable to speak about good and right and bad and wrong and desirable and undesirable. . . . The key concepts in the newer dynamic psychology are spontaneity, release, naturalness, self-acceptance, impulse-awareness, gratification. They *used* to be control, inhibition, discipline, training, shaping, on the principle that the depths of human nature were dangerous, evil, predatory, and ravenous.

Frenkel-Brunswik (1954, p. 470) likewise asserts the significance of social science for valuation:

. . . individuals and cultures do, on the whole, not differ widely with respect to what are considered the ultimate ethical goals, so that the arbitrariness in preferences is more a matter of means . . . the knowledge accumulated in the social sciences may help us to make a choice between alternative value systems. In renouncing any metaphysical or absolute position, we do not need to go to the other extreme of utter relativism. Although the social scientist, as a scientist, cannot make the ultimate choice for mankind, his function is to throw as much light as possible on the implications involved in existing value systems, and to make explicit all the ramifications inherent in the options.

Brandt (1954) uses psychological theory (and especially the theorems of utility and of reward) to explain Hopi ethical norms. Asch (1952, pp. 375-378) presents a particularly cogent discussion:

The insufficiencies of an absolutist psychological theory of ethical judgments are obvious. It has no means for dealing with cultural diversity (or, for that matter, with intra-individual diversity). On the other hand, although the observations to which relativism refers have greatly widened the horizon of the social sciences, the psychological interpretation they have received poses equally serious difficulties . . . required-ness is not a property that belongs to an action irrespective of its setting and relations. Every judgment of the value of an act takes into account the particular circumstances under which it occurs. There follows the important consequence that the *same* act may be evaluated as right because it is fitting under one set of conditions and as wrong because it violates the requirements of another set of conditions. . . . The essential proposition of ethical relativism states that one can connect to the identical situation different and even opposed valuations . . . the fact of cultural differences cannot be automatically converted into an argument for a relativism of values. . . . Cultural differences are compatible with identity in values.

The Gestalt notions of "intrinsic requiredness" or "intrinsic appropriateness" have also been considered in detail by many other psychologists. On many grounds it can be argued that universal human nature has implications for ethics. I think, for example, that Pascal was right in insisting that it is the nature of man to believe and to love. There is something in the Stoic aphorism "No man is so like unto himself as he is like to all."

The medical psychologists have likewise turned their attention increasingly to some of the problems of ethics and of universal psychological processes. Hartmann, Kris, and Loewenstein (1951, p. 11) consider man's psychic equipment to be "relatively independent of environmental conditions in the same sense as physiological processes are." On the other hand, they warn anthropologists against inferring from observed behavior to underlying motivations, since similar impulses find different expressions in varying environments.

Again, I must stop with a few examples, but I do wish to call attention to some efforts by British psychoanalysts. Money-Kyrle (1944, p. 111) maintains that there are "three fundamental subjective principles of primary morality" and that:

The basis of morality is therefore neither *a priori* and universal as the metaphysicians claimed, nor empirical and relative as critical philosophers and anthropologists maintain, but empirical and universal in the sense that it is a quality, like binocular vision or an articulated thumb, which is found to be common to all mankind.

Flugel (1945) sketches a "psychology of moral progress"; from egocentricity to sociality; from autism to realism, moral inhibition to spontaneous "goodness, aggression to tolerance and love, fear to security, heteronomy to autonomy, and oretic (moral) judgment to cognitive (psychological) judgment. Dicks (1950, p. 8) refers with approval to Money-Kyrle's concept of "natural morality" and adds:

In simplest, proto-mental ways the rudiments of love rooted in the social-biological dependence on protective, nourishing objects, are clearly present and capable of flowering and maturation in human beings.

Contemporary psychologists and psychiatrists differ, of course, in their views on many of the issues with which we are here concerned. Yet there appears to be a growing trend toward agreement on two fundamentals:

1. Psychological fact and theory must be taken into account in dealing with ethical problems.

2. There are pan-human universals as regards needs and capacities that shape, or could at least, rightly shape, the broad outlines of a morality that transcends cultural difference.

The Sociological Contribution

The sociologists have similarly been placing greater emphasis upon the universals. Kolb (1953, p. 187) writes:

The basic field conditions for the emergence of the human psyche have been relatively the same since man has been man: society, culture, symbolic interaction, and the potentialities of the biological organism interacting in the basic process of socialization. All social psychologists recognize these universal conditions and processes. Yet, impressed by the facts of social and cultural differences among societies, they have failed to inquire into the qualities of the universal emergent: human nature. . . . Surely it is probable that psychic systems the world over have certain identical basic structures and functions organized around universal psychic needs.

The methodological arguments advanced against universal psychic needs attest only to the difficulty of determining their nature, not to their absence.

In American sociology at least as far back as Cooley there has been a current of stress upon universals that cut across all cultures. The fact that every human being, irrespective of culture, has had the experience of intimate association with "the primary group" upon which he was emotionally and otherwise dependent has been held to lead to the so-called universal sentiments: love, jealousy, respect, need for respect, and the like. All moralities, if not built upon these sentiments, must at least take account of them. This total conception, although arising from a different perspective, comes to about the same conclusions as the psycho-analytic view. The universal sentiments leading to a "natural morality" have a biological basis, but the resultant is sociological rather than biological.

Parsons and Shils (1951, p. 171), in rejecting radical relativism, point to functional interdependences and to the limitations of possibilities:

The exhaustive character of the classification of pattern variables has far-reaching implications for the analysis of systems of moral standards; it provides a determinate range of variability and it allows only a num-ber of combinations of alternatives which—on this level of generality at least—is sufficiently small to permit analysis with the resources we possess at present. There has been a tendency, under the impact of insight into the wider range of differences among cultures, to think, implicitly at least, of a limitlessly pluralistic value-universe. In its ex-treme form, the proponents of this view have even asserted that every moral standard is necessarily unique. There is much aesthetic sensibility underlying and justifying this contention, but it is neither convincing logically nor fruitful scientifically. If carried to its logical conclusions, it denies the possibility of systematic analysis of cultural values. In fact, of course, all patterns of moral standards are interdependent with all the other factors which operate in the determination of action.

Once again, although the language used and the data cited are different, there is marked congruence between certain recent sociological and psychoanalytic views. Roheim (1950) argues the limitation of possibilities in the light of the facts that human in-fants invariably are dependent, have two parents of opposite sex, face the emotional problems of being in competition with their siblings for the attention of these parents, and possess basically similar neurological mechanisms for defenses and other-wise dealing with their dilemmas. He (along with Rank, Abraham, Marie Bonaparte, and other psychoanalysts) mobilize evidence for psychic universals in myths and other culture forms. Roheim maintains that in addition to demonstrable universals there are many other "potential universals." Erich Fromm takes the same general line in many recent writings.

The Anthropological Contribution

Ethical relativity with specifically cultural emphasis long ante-dates anthropology as such. One may instance Xenophanes, Boethius, and others. Strictly anthropological formulations in fully explicit form are, for all practical purposes, the work of this century. In spite of its title, "L'Antropolgia in servigio della scienza morale," published by Rosmini-Serbati in 1838, is solely "philosophical" as opposed to "ethnographic" anthropology.

Edel (1955) begins his consideration of the contemporary status of "cultural relativity" with a subhead, "The Vagueness of the Concept." Certainly it has been employed, by anthropologists and by others, in importantly different senses. Hartung (1954, p. 118) defines it along the lines of Benedict: "Cultural relativity . . . asserts that any set of customs and institutions, or way of life, is as valid as any other." But he leaves out what any anthropologist holding the relativity position would immediately add: "for a group living under certain circumstances and having had a particular history." Hartung's statement, as it stands, comes close to the popular vulgarization of the doctrine, which suggests, for instance, that if premarital promiscuity is approved in a certain tribe this gives "validity" to such practices among any people. Actually, Hartung (p. 122) himself says, ". . . I could just as logically adopt the conventions of any other culture I chanced to learn about. . . ." No anthropologist would subscribe to this interpretation of cultural relativity. Quite the reverse, in-deed, for the doctrine of cultural relativity demands, precisely, that one look within rather than without.

Macbeath (1952, p. 356), I believe, expresses the central and dominant anthropological view when he writes, ". . . the simplest self-contained unit of conduct, which can justify or render intel-ligible a final moral judgment, is a way of life as a whole, or at least a very substantial part of such a way of life." To be sure, there are anthropological embroideries. Some anthropologists have stressed, and probably overstressed, the inherent dignity in each humanly created custom. Others have underlined the "functional" interconnections between ethical standards and the specific nature of the economy (e.g., Goldschmidt, 1951) or environmental situation. A few have implicitly, and perhaps explicitly, advocated cultural relativity on the romantically tinged ground that the sheer variety of standards, including moral standards, added enormously to the richness and piquancy of the world. In some cases relativity is used to bolster a special kind of ethical absolutism (cf. Edel, 1955, p. 209).

No anthropologist, however, doubts that the theory of ethical relativity is in some sense forced by the facts and meaningful. There is an exuberant variation in ethical codes, and surely a satisfactory interpretation of morality must be able to account for the moral judgments found in all cultures. Where anthropologists are not in full agreement is the extent to which this variation is basic or comparatively superficial. Is ethical *intent* very similar if not identical the world over? Are variations largely related to means rather than ends? Are means and some of the more proximate ends determined by historical accident and local circumstance? Is the whole picture needlessly confused by the local symbolisms for expressing ultimate goals and enforcing ultimate standards that are universal or near-universal?

UNIVERSALS

From the anthropological viewpoint, the question as to whether there are ethical universals is a part of a larger question: Are there universals or near-universals of any sort that cut across cultural boundaries? There is good agreement that there are—in some form or other. In the 1911 edition of *The Mind of Primitive Man* Boas called Chapter VI "The Universality of Culture Traits." In the 1938 edition (p. 195) he wrote:

The dynamic forces that mould social life are the same now as those that moulded life thousands of years ago. We can follow the intellectual and emotional drives that actuate man at present and that shape his actions and thoughts.

While Boas held, as do most psychologists and psychiatrists, that the needs of men and their "thought processes" are essentially the same throughout the world in time and space and hence give rise to similar cultural forms such as values, Wissler was almost the only one of his associates or students who devoted empirical attention to this question: in *Man and Culture* (1923) he wrote a chapter on "The Universal Culture Pattern" in which he showed that the "ground plan" of all cultures is very similar. More recently, Murdock (1945), Kluckhohn (1953b), and Trimborn (1949) have examined these issues both conceptually and empirically. And White (e.g., 1943), Childe (e.g., 1951), and Steward (e.g., 1949) have looked specifically at environmental, technological, and economic "determination" of cultural similarities.

That music, graphic arts, dancing, parallels in linguistic structure, standards of personal excellence, kinship terminology, and such categories as age grading and many other formal similarities exist in all known cultures no one questions. Nor, on the other hand, does anyone dispute that such resemblances as approach universality are broad likenesses rather than concrete identities. Argument centers on three questions:

1. How numerous are these similiarities?

2. Are they simply "empty frames" that do not enable us to escape from the impasse of complete cultural relativity?

3. Are they cultural or subcultural or the "conditions for culture"?

On the first question not much can be said at present beyond the fact that not enough research has been done to give more than an impressionistic answer.

The next two questions can be considered together. Professor Kroeber (1949, p. 188) writes:

. . . such more or less recurrent near-regularities of form or process as have to date been formulated for culture are actually mainly subcultural in nature. They are limits set to culture by physical or organic factors. The so-called "cultural constants" of family, religion, war, communication, and the like appear to be biopsychological frames variably filled with cultural content. . . .

Since cultures include organization as well as content, I myself would include these "frames" as part of culture. They are incorporated—admittedly with variable content in detail—into ways of life and socially transmitted as part of the total tradition. In any case, whether these phenomena are cultural or subcultural is, for purposes of the present paper, an academic haggle.[1]

What is significant is that such categories remove cultures from the status of completely isolated monads and make some valid comparisons possible. While scientific analysis commonly unites what the lay mind distinguishes and separates what common sense groups together, these broad similarities at very least provide a starting point for valid comparison. Here I stand with Lévi-Strauss (1945, pp. 525-526) in his reply to some earlier strictures of Kroeber's upon "fake universals":

> Indeed, if behind such broad categories as Sacrifice, or Gifts, or Suicide, there are not at least some characters which are common to all forms—among, of course, many others which are different—, and if this does not allow the use of those categories as starting points for the analysis, then sociology may as well abandon every pretention to become scientific, and the sociologist must be resigned to pile up descriptions of individual groups, without any hope that the pile shall ever become of any use, except, perhaps, to cultural history.... When Durkheim studies division of labor, it is in order to reach such abstract, hidden categories as "organic solidarity" and "mechanical solidarity"; when he analyzes suicide, he formulates the notion of integration of individual to the group; when Mauss undertakes a comparison between the different types of gifts, it is to discover, behind the more diversified types, the fundamental idea of reciprocity; when he follows the transformation of the psychological conceptions of the "Ego," it is in order to establish a relation between social forms and the concept of personality. These categories may be good or bad; they may prove useful or be wrongly chosen but.... They do not resemble the categories of "long," "flat," or "round," but rather such categories as "dilation," "undulation," or "viscosity," of which the physicist has precisely made his study.

Linton (1952, p. 646) is squarely in the main stream of contemporary anthropological opinion when he says, "Behind the seemingly endless diversity of culture patterns there is a fundamental uniformity."

---

1. I would accept as valid a contrast between certain constant "factors" in human life (e.g., the unconscious) that are not "built into" cultures and the empirically discovered *cultural* similarities or uniformities.

ETHICAL UNIVERSALS

The first point to note is the universality of moral standards in general. Morality is as genuine a human universal as is language. All cultures have moral systems—that is, standards for conduct that go beyond temporary circumstances or special situations and standards that are not infrequently obeyed in the face of conflicting personal needs of the moment. To the philosopher and social scientist this generalization may appear too commonplace to require comment. But the universality may not strike the general zoologist as so obvious. Not only is *human* social life inevitably a moral life in theory and to a large extent in practice, but ethical principles are the fundament of most of the rest of the culture. Fortes (1949, p. 346) remarks:

Every social system presupposes such basic moral axioms . . . these axioms are rooted in the direct experience of the inevitability of interdependence between men in society. . . . The focal field of kinship is also the focal field of moral experience.

Every culture has a concept of murder, distinguishing this from execution, killing in war, and other "justifiable homicides." The notions of incest and other regulations upon sexual behavior, of prohibitions upon untruth under defined circumstances, of restitution and reciprocity, of mutual obligations between parents and children—these and many other moral concepts are altogether universal.[2] The philosopher Feibleman (1955, p. 106) goes a bit further than most anthropologists would in saying: ". . . the context of ethical values as of other values, changes constantly; but the values have a striking similarity and even, we strongly suspect, an identity." Anthropologists are more comfortable with a treatment like Linton's (1954), which emphasizes that the likenesses are primarily conceptual and that variation rages rampant as to details of prescribed behavior, instrumentalities, and sanctions. This is important, as is also the fact that universality as such is not transmutable into a categorical

---

2. A dramatic, if bizarre, example of "similiarity in intent" is the Eskimo practice of killing parents who are too weak or otherwise incapable of surviving Arctic rigors. The killing remains a manifestation of "filial piety."

imperative. Pascal's suggestion that moral canons exist in spite of such empirical universals may be correct in certain instances.

Universality may be due, or largely due, to diffusion or other historical accident. Universality may reflect the general moral immaturity of the human species; that is, present agreements may in some instances indicate no more than that human cultures have thus far evolved only to a roughly similar moral stage. Near-universality in other cases may indicate only that there are many "sick societies." Nor does the fact that the simple but basic wants of all men are similar lead us inevitably to sweetness and light; it has made and can continue to make for bitter struggles for scarce goods. Similarly, as everyone knows, some of the worst wars in history have been fought not over "final" goals but rather over "means." Nevertheless, the universalities in wants and the universals and near-universals in moral concepts do generate two fairly cheerful propositions:

1. The similarities in human needs and human response-potentialities across cultures do at any rate greatly heighten the possibilities of cross-cultural communication once these core likenesses have been somewhat disentangled from their cultural wrappings.

2. While we must not glibly equate universals with absolutes, the existence of a universal certainly raises this question: If, in spite of biological variation and historical and enviromental diversities, we find these congruences, is there not a presumptive likelihood that these moral principles somehow correspond to inevitabilities, given the nature of the human organism and of the human situation? They may at any rate lead us to "conditional absolutes" or "moving absolutes," not in the metaphysical but in the empirical sense.

However, the task of finding and vindicating either specific rules or more abstract principles as having genuine universality of application is more difficult than the empiricists have been willing to recognize. Verbal acceptance of the value of "truth" does not always imply motivational acceptance. The emotivists and linguistic pluralists have taught us much about the noncognitive aspects of valuational terms. They have also directed our attention to the variations in meaning of such terms in a particular context or a particular type of context. To attempt to reduce value judgments entirely to value-free facts is to commit the naturalistic fallacy. Neither, on the other hand, is one justified in taking the emotional satisfaction of the individual—in a direct and simple way—or the individual's information (as opposed to the actual state of affairs) as criteria of the validity of ethical judgments.

Nevertheless, both the cognitive maps of individuals and of groups and scientific depictions of situations and their outcomes are relevant to the assessment of universality or near-universality of ethical rules and principles. Such rules and principles may—if only at present in a very rough and ready way—be vindicated or justified by human experience. Philosophers despair at reaching a watertight theory of induction and deduction. And yet the working principles of induction and deduction are vindicated by the inescapable need to think consistently and predict with some accuracy.

Discussion

Two kinds of ethical universals or near-universals have been documented by behavioral science:

1. Rules approving or forbidding specific kinds of acts (e.g., truth-telling and incest)

2. General principles or standards of evaluation which make for the stability and continuity of groups and for maximizing the satisfactions experienced by individuals

The second kind of universal is always at a higher level of generality or abstractness than the first. Presumably, indeed, the specific rules follow, in intent, upon the principles. If there are premises prescribing what should be done in general, there are consequences as to what ought or ought not to be done in particular.

In both cases the escape from relativity is only a proximate one. The maxim "incest should be avoided" is not contradicted by another judgment that can claim equal validity. But the proscription is universal and "the same" only speaking very broadly.

The stringency with which all universal rules apply and the precise circumstances under which they apply vary from culture to culture and within a single culture over time. The universal principles also have their cultural weightings and shapings. Any formulation that is to be genuinely pan-human must be carefully qualified; thus, one must say something like this: "The preservation of the life of *in-group* members *under most circumstances* is always and everywhere an ethical value." The Jains, however, have made the preservation of *all* life a supreme value. This is a special case of the universal value. In its extremity it is culturally relative. The universal principles are also relative to the motivational, affective, and intellectual make-up of man as a species. Man wants to live and to enjoy living. These are "givens"—at least as statistical generalizations. These existential facts are basic to many values, both universal and culturally distinct. But even the universal ethical principles are relative to the psychological and cognitive facts which are prior to evaluation.

The relativity, in turn, is only a partial aspect. I agree with Wein (1950, p. 123): *"weder Relativismus noch Absolutismus."* The repeated recurrences of certain rules and principles suggest that they correspond to persistent human needs as these operate in situations that have elements of constancy. Psychology, psychiatry, sociology, and anthropology in different ways and on somewhat different evidence converge in attesting to similar human needs and psychic mechanisms. What are ostensibly methodological arguments against the existence of universal psychic needs usually boil down to correct statements as to the difficulties of determining their nature—exactly what they are. I have yet to encounter a psychologist or psychiatrist who denied categorically that there are some needs and processes that may properly be attributed to mankind as a whole. It has often been noted that, while culturally patterned behavior varies in accord with each distinct historically created tradition, responses to new and unfamiliar situations for which there are no cultural patterns may be fundamentally similar across cultures.

Asch (1952, p. 374) maintains that a full-bodied theory of *human* psychology is not congruent with radical cultural relativity. A psychological basis for cultural relativity must be found in simplified and mechanistic behaviorism. "Drive" and "reward" are adequate polar categories for rats and other animals that do not have symbolic systems. Asch thinks it "highly questionable whether they apply without modification to social action."

Similar needs and psychic processes, plus the rough regularities in the human situation regardless of culture, give rise to widespread moral principles that are very much alike in concept—in "intent." These considerations make the position of radical cultural relativity untenable. Indeed, relativity when pressed to its logical limits soon reaches absurdity. If one is to evaluate an act or a moral judgment *entirely* with reference to its unique context, it is inescapable that no two contexts are literally identical. Abstract moral principles then become impossible. And yet all cultures possess ethical principles of some generality, and the behavior of participants is influenced by them.

Human beings generalize as well as particularize. The human parade has many floats, but when one strips off the cultural symbolism, some of the ethical standards represented are akin. Zuñi culture prizes restraint; Kwakiutl culture encourages exhibitionism on the part of the individual. These are contrasting values, but in adhering to them the Zuñi and the Kwakiutl show their allegiance to a universal value; the prizing of the distinctive norms of one's culture. And thus, continually, the relative and the universal are intermingled. What Macbeath calls the "operative ideals" of each culture must be considered in the light of time, place, total situation, and sheer taste or preference. This does not mean that in every case variations may be dismissed with a shrug and, "It's just a matter of taste." An accent upon "self-effacement," as opposed to one upon "exhibitionism," may conceivably be evaluated in terms of canons of universal applicability. But it certainly does mean that some specificities of moral rules are relative to particular contexts. "Relativity" often designates "complexity." The details of an ethical code may expectably vary between societies according to their histories and present circumstances.

The indeterminancy contingent upon limited but valid cultural relativity may well diminish as science spreads through the whole world. If there is any "pan" movement in the world today, sweeping behind both "curtains" and into the "uncommitted third," it is science. And, as Hocking has remarked, if there is to be a common science in the world there will also arise, to some extent, a common conscience. Even then, however, *both* within and between cultures moral behavior in specific instances and in all its details must be judged within a wide context *but with reference to principles which are not altogether relative.* This combines what Perry and Rice have called virtuous relativism and virtuous absolutism, though I much prefer "virtuous relativity," because the word "relativism" seems to imply the utter incommensurability of the entities. Each culture must allow for the differentiation of individuals, tolerating and indeed supporting psychological minorities as long as this pluralism does not violate universal morality. As Macbeath says (1952, p. 17):

> If, then the principle of moral judgment is the same everywhere, any account of it which is to be satisfactory must show that it is consistent with this diversity of moral judgments, that indeed the different moral judgments are really expressions of the same principle having regard to the different conditions and beliefs and cultures of those who pass them.

Meanwhile, are there any criteria which can aid us to choose between varying forms of the same moral principles, between those principles that are in fact different, and between contrasting hierarchies of principles? I believe there are, while granting fully that each remains to be worked out more adequately. First, I am attracted by Northrop's idea that the primitive concepts and primitive postulates of moral systems must be concordant with natural science knowledge. This is no naive "social Darwinism" that identifies the "is" with the "ought," attempting to derive ethics directly from science. Rather, this view correctly insists that in the world of real experience there is never a complete divorce between cognitive and existential propositions, that in the chains of feeling and reasoning that actually occur these two categories link in interdependence. Therefore, a morality based upon a theory that human nature is innately evil or innately good ought to check its primary existential premise against the observations the child psychologist makes of newborn infants, their tendencies and propensities. Just as there are some "psychic necessities" that are to a large degree autonomous and comparatively independent of each specific culture, so also it is possible in principle to check the logical and cognitive underpinnings of ethics against facts that are independent of culture. I have cautiously chosen a restricted application of Northrop's general thesis on natural science. I believe, however, that different cosmological standpoints are relevant to moral systems, though the relation may be both more vague and more complicated than Northrop has argued.

Second, although confessing to some scepticism as to whether this is not Kant's categorical imperative in thin anthropological disguise, I think there is something worth careful consideration in Macbeath's theorem (1952, p. 436):

Any way of life whose general structure or scale of value does not admit of being extended to mankind as a whole, without denying the common humanity of some men and their right to be treated as persons, must be regarded as unsatisfactory; and the more remodelling it needs to make this extension possible, the more unsatisfactory it is.

This I would provisionally accept, provided it not be taken to apply to those "secondary" moral categories that correspond to "taste" and to the determinations produced by unique history and situation. However, not all culturally created values are of equal validity.

Finally, I subscribe—at least as an eventuality—to Anatol Rapoport's (1950, pp. 232-233) thesis that "objective relativism" can lead to the development of truly explicit and truly universal moral canons:

... it is incorrect to say that the scientific outlook is simply a by-product of a particular culture. It is rather the essence of a culture which has not yet been established—a culture-studying culture. Ironically, the anthropologists who often are most emphatic in stating that no non-cultural standards of evaluation exist are among the most active builders of this new culture-studying culture, whose standards transcend those of the cultures which the anthropologists study and thus give them an opportunity to emancipate themselves from the limitations of the local standards. . . .

The moral attitudes contained in the scientific outlook have a different genesis from those contained in ordinary "unconscious" cultures.

They are a result of a "freer choice," because they involve a deeper insight into the consequences of the choice.

"Objective relativity" will increasingly be a corrective to the ethnocentrism of all cultures, loosening their rigidities, but it does not necessarily—or logically—lead to nihilism. What is right for Hindus in 1955 may not be precisely the same as what is right for Americans in 1955, but it will be of the same *kind*—which is only a rephrasing of Plato's argument in *The Republic*. Relativity has an indispensable place in judging acts in all their concreteness but must be balanced by universality as regards the broad issues of principle, especially those at a higher level of generality. Some values are invariant. Certain of these we know already. Others will be discovered by a combination of further empirical research and sound analysis. "Residual indeterminacy" will thereby be decreased. Radical relativity exaggerated the significance of outward form and of the historically determined accidentals in human cultures. While the specific manifestations of human nature vary between cultures and between individuals in the same culture, human nature is universal. All value systems have to make some of the same concessions to the natural world of which human nature is a part. Some needs and motives are so deep and so generic that they are beyond the reach of argument: pan-human morality expresses and supports them. Hence there must be respect alike for individual and cultural differences and for the more embracing needs and norms that must be commonly met. Principles as well as contexts must be taken into account.

Man is capable of satisfying his biologically and culturally derived needs in a variety of ways. But this relativity of proximate means does not imply that some goals are not salient for mankind in general. Nor should tolerance of a variety of means suggest any rejection of a passionate and uncompromising affirmation of pan-human ends. And these ends may change through time in important particulars. As Steward (1953, p. 314) says: "Evolutionism is distinguished from relativism by the fact that the former attributes qualitative dictinctiveness to successive stages, regardless of the particular tradition, whereas the latter attributes it to the particular tradition rather than to the developmental stage."

I believe that further progress on this difficult question of ethical relativity will be achieved by a combination of hardheaded empirical research with a theoretical analysis that begs as few metaphysical questions as possible. The "oughts" in all cultures (and the sanctions attached thereto) are observable and formulable in "is" terms. The existence of empirical universals or near-universals should be known as fully as possible. Each exception to a general rule poses a specific problem, but a problem of a somewhat different order. The traits of a zoological species are not the less objective or in a sense "universal" because of the occasional birth of "sports" or monstrosities.

The present position is that neither extreme relativism nor extreme absolutism is tenable as a guiding hypothesis for further empirical inquiry. The contribution of behavioral scientists has made essential the use of the concepts of both universality and of relativity in the investigation of human acts in their cross-cultural dimension. Much remains to be done. Especially we require operational techniques for controlling differences of meaning among apparently similar values and for validating similarities when the phenomena appear quite various to the eye of the naive observer. And the sheer demonstration of empirical universals does not, of course, settle any question of absolutes or right or wrong. It is a significant step and would seem to place the burden of proof upon those who would deprecate such values. But, in the main, such proof of universals will merely pose further questions. We must move from description to the testing of hypotheses, from positions to defend to searching for facts that will verify or reject a position. Both extremes have had their chance to speculate, to reason, and to speak out. The proper formulation of the elements of truth in these two extremes, forged in the teeth of the stubborn and irreducible facts now available, will require the cooperation of philosophers and behavioral scientists to the end of carefully pointed empirical investigations that may gradually settle the issues.

Present knowledge may be briefly summarized as follows:

In the realm of human psychology, social life, and culture there are similarities as well as differences. We must indeed recognize similarities within differences. There are many sets of coordinates. There are cross-cultural regularities both in the processes of

cultural development and in basic functional relationships between isolable cultural features, synchronic and diachronic.
There are some cultural universals in content; there are a greater
number of conceptual equivalents. Other regularities occur under
similar conditions without being universal.

While there are some ethical cognates between cultures, much
value pluralism is found in the cultural world. Some of the variance may be attributable to ignorance or to mischance. Some remainder of the variance must be accepted as suitable to the
different backgrounds and contemporary situations of the groups
in question. Some moral judgments are relative to the ways of
life of different peoples. Nevertheless, there are some rules and
some principles that all human groups take seriously. The simple
but fundamental things that people want the world over are
pretty much the same, and they have learned from repeated and
similar experiences that certain aspirations and regulations are
more compatible with optimal fulfillment of these wants than
others. Ethical universals are the product of universal human
nature, which is based, in turn, upon a common biology, psychology, and generalized situation. Finally, this "human condition" includes the circumstance that men perceive, observe,
and reason. Ethical conceptions are related to what people believe
to be "the facts" about the world in which they live. And truly
scientific knowledge provides some, though not complete,
criteria against which to decide whether a given rule or principle
is more sound and defensible than another. While values are not
"in nature" in the sense that mass and energy are, one can nevertheless agree with G. E. Moore, that, although "good" is not
a natural property, it does depend upon the natural properties of
that which is said to be good. Moreover, whatever view is taken
of the applicability of the *findings* of science to the critique of
values, the *activity* of science surely carries value-commitment
(Bronowski, 1959; Anatol Rapoport, 1950). The realm of science
points to the realm of values, and vice versa. One cannot derive
values from scientifically established facts, but these facts can be
meaningful in validating ethical norms.

17 EDUCATION, VALUES, AND ANTHROPOLOGICAL RELATIVITY

T HE MATTER OF VALUES is certainly the prime intellectual issue of the present day. The practical implications of this problem also are of the most intense importance. Our cohesiveness and strength as a people depend upon the achievement of greater clarity and force in making explicit among ourselves and to the outside world what we conceive to be good, what we hold to be right or wrong in private acts, our official duties, and the responsibilities of our nation in its dealings with other nations. We cannot hope to discharge satisfactorily either to ourselves or to other peoples the leadership that history has forced upon us at this time unless we act upon reasoned and clearly stated standards of evaluation. Finally, all talk of an eventual peaceful and orderly world is but pious cant or senti-

1952b Reprinted by permission of the publishers from Clyde Kluckhohn, "Universal Values and Anthropological Relativism," in *Modern Education and Human Values*. Pittsburgh, University of Pittsburgh Press, pp. 87-112.

mental fantasy unless there are, in fact, some simple but powerful beliefs to which all men hold, some codes or canons that have or can obtain universal acceptance.

The challenge to the educator, and specifically to the American educator, scarcely requires elaboration. From primitive tribes to Egypt, China, Greece, and the Christian world in its flower, the task of education has been first and foremost that of transmitting, expounding, and in some cases refining the great values of each culture. The teaching of information and of skills, until recently, has been essentially little more than a means to the more ultimate end. Today, among us, the picture is startlingly different. Except in religious institutions of learning, most teachers shy away from any direct consideration of values.

The public-school teacher must tread warily, for the citizens and parents to whom he or she is ultimately responsible hold different religious faiths and varying political convictions. The only safe course is to stick to "factual" information—and perhaps to refrain from calling attention to portions of this. To the law of the land, to be sure, we are all officially committed. It is true that the Constitution, the Gettysburg Address, and a few other utterances of our most famous leaders still embody some of our deepest values. These can be taught both properly and safely. They are taught—but sometimes with considerable vagueness. On the other hand, parents, teachers, and pupils all have an uncomfortable awareness of widely varying degrees of explicitness, a sense that we are in the midst of a period of vast changes and that hence the gap between our codified laws and our actual values is often tremendous.

Some classics of English and American literature are relatively "safe," but I hardly need remind you of recent public controversies about which literary masterpieces may or may not be taught in public schools. The same kind of attitude applies to strictly aesthetic values, for various sorts of "modern" painting and music are held to have moral and even political implications. So the cautious teacher of the humanities in institutions deriving their support from taxation does not feel he has a free hand, quite apart from those values ordinarily considered ethical or religious. The scientifically trained instructor has been indoctrinated with the cliché that "Science has nothing to do with values." So he says, "Here are the facts so far as we know them" and lets it go at that.

The net result is what Sibley (1946, p. 80) has described: ". . . each subdivision of knowledge is cultivated as if it were independent of the whole of culture and hence as if it were ethically neutral, not subject to evaluation in terms of any transcendent standards of value." Yet citizens and educators alike are all too confused to be able to follow Sibley's recipe (p. 72): ". . . the colleges must undertake to lead the American mob out of the mire by helping it see what it is semiconsciously striving for, by focusing its attention on ultimate goals and values rather than on the details of the passing moment."

Why are Americans so inarticulate about what they believe to be right for themselves and for all human beings? In part, there is the problem of communication, immensely difficult in this contemporary world even within the borders of a single nation, let alone internationally. There are those who have stated a national creed and attempted a world creed. Sometimes these utterances have been loud, and some indeed have been forceful, but none thus far has been at once comprehensive and broadly persuasive. All have failed to capture the implicit agreements that exist among most Americans and, I am convinced as an anthropologist, those very general understandings which bind all creatures of our species together.

There is confusion because there is doubt or lack of agreement as to what are valid reasons for belief in values by men of the mid-twentieth century. Over the whole of recorded history until our times one finds, broadly speaking, three types of convictions as to the basis and sanction of values: divine revelation or command, tradition and custom, and human intelligence. These are, to be sure, abstract polarities. Probably no culture has relied completely upon one to the complete exclusion of the other two. The king or priest has more often than not served almost equally as the vice-regent of the divine order and as the interpreter and enforcer of hallowed precedent. But there is a difference between the theocratic value system of the age of Innocent III and Roman morality, which was just what the etymology of the word implies—adherence to the mores or sanctified customs. The Greek philosophers and Confucius gave the world its first systematic conceptions of how human beings might derive their values in other than an authoritarian manner and with the possibility for change and growth.

For contemporary man, even within a single country like the United States, no one of these is clear-cut. Precedent, or "the accumulated wisdom of the ages," is considered inadequate under the special conditions of life today. There is rivalry between various sets of rules that claim to be based upon supernatural authority. Increased knowledge of the processes of the physical and biological worlds has engendered widespread skepticism of all doctrines based on authority and revelation rather than upon scientific investigation.

Nor is there agreement as to the procedures by which human intelligence could resolve these issues, if only for the time being. Since the time of Kant it has been a firm tenet of our intellectual folklore that values are outside the realm of science. As W. H. Auden has said:

> . . . parting
> All that we feel from all that we perceive,
> Desire from Data.

Values do not consist in "desires" but rather in the desirable—that is, what we not only want but feel that it is right and proper to want for ourselves and for others. Values precisely are abstract standards that transcend the impulses of the moment and ephemeral situations. Nevertheless, the poet is right in principle. Much of our confusion arises from the artificial separation of "feeling" and "fact," of what should be and what is.

More specifically, the reasonable grounds for adherence to values pretending to universality have been challenged by the movement toward relativism in the intellectual history of the past 100 years. This movement has had many facets. The psychoanalysts—at least in the vulgarized form in which their teachings have reached the wider educated public—have seemed to be debunking "conscience." They have appeared to argue that a "strong conscience" was by no means an unmitigated good; that, on the contrary, a harsh and tyrannous superego led to persecution, demagoguery, and, eventually war.

The Marxists have preached a still more threatening form of the relativism of values. Engels wrote: "We maintain that all moral theories are the products in the last analyisis of the economic stage which society has reached at that particular epoch." In other words, values are simply rationalizations of the status quo, instruments of a class that wants to hold its power.

The logical positivists have appeared—again to the nonspecialist audience—to deny all meaning to propositions about value. Wittgenstein is said to have remarked: "Values. A terrible business. You can at best stammer when you talk about them." Carnap has observed (though in a technical, cognitive sense) that the commandment "do not kill" does not assert anything and cannot be proved or disproved and that the statement "killing is evil" is merely a paraphrase of the meaningless commandment.

Next, the core of moral agreements tended to vanish in proportion as the belief in the individual's freedom to choose was weakened by philosophic determinism and scientific evidence of "conditioning," of the rooting of character structure in early infancy, and the like. One does not exhort a star to observe the moral law nor blame a meteor that has crashed into the earth. To the extent that the behavior of everything, organic and inorganic, conforms to ineluctable laws of nature, values seem at best to be verbal rationalizations after the facts.

Finally, anthropologists have made their contribution to the deflation of all notions of universal value, and this is what I particularly want to talk about at present. The doctrine of cultural relativity, in its earlier form, denied general truth to any set of values. In Ruth Benedict's classic phrasing, all cultures are "coexisting and equally valid patterns of life which mankind has created for itself from the raw materials of existence." This rampant form of anthropological relativism claimed, though in a less limited form than the Marxists, that all standards and values were relative to the culture from which they derived. I shall try to show you that this extreme view is not substantiated by the very facts of anthropological research.

But first let me make two points for perspective. The controversy over relativism is nothing completely new under the sun. In at least seven of his dialogues Plato examined critically the relativism of the Sophists. Especially in the *Theatetus* he showed the superficiality of Protagoras' anticipation of the untrammeled variety of anthropological relativity: "Man is the measure of all things—of those that are that they are, of those that are not that they are not." Second, most of the writers and thinkers whom the judgment of humanity has called "great" have come to the conclusions that men are influenced in their behavior by transcendental standards and that these standards are by no means completely culture-bound but have elements of universality.

So far as the force of values in human life is concerned, no more striking literary testimony can be produced than from three French writers of this century. On the whole, Paris more than any other single center has been the intellectual capital of the Western world throughout modern times. France has also been the country where the "moral decay" and moral confusion of the last generation have been most glaringly evident. Proust we tend to think of as the diseasedly sensitive diagnostician of the vagaries of individual deviation within a sick society. And yet he writes:

Everything happens in our lives as though we had entered upon them with a burden of obligations contracted in an anterior existence; there is nothing in our earthly condition to make us feel that we are under an obligation to be good, to be morally sensitive [être délicats] even to be polite; nor, to the artist, to begin over again twenty times a passage which will probably be admired only when his body has been devoured by worms. . . . All these obligations, which have no sanction in our present life, seem to belong to a different world, a world entirely different from this one, a world whence we come when we are born on earth, perhaps to return there and live once more under the rule of the unknown laws which we have obeyed here because we carried their principles within ourselves, without knowing who decreed that they should be; those laws to which every deep intellectual labour draws us nearer, and which are invisible only—and not always!—to fools.

Sartre has proclaimed, "God does not exist . . . all the implications of this must be made explicit." Nevertheless, the anarchist who is the hero of Sartre's short story, "The Wall," refuses to save his own life by the simple expedient of betraying his friend, though he is puzzled by the "absurdity" and "obstinacy" of the inner compulsion that regulates his action. The persistent theme in the writings of Camus is the new variety of man who is freed of illusions and aware only of "factness"—as the German existentialists call it. However, in "Letters to a German Friend" (1945) Camus shows that Frenchmen at considerable risk to themselves banded into resistance groups against the Nazis in spite of their intellectual uncertainties as to the moral justification for such a course.

With the conclusion, albeit somewhat reluctant, of these literary figures that the empirical observation of human behavior compels a recognition of the role of norms the anthropologist is of course in complete agreement. Human life is—and has to be —a moral life precisely because it is a social life, and in the case of the human species cooperation and other necessities of social life are not taken care of automatically by instincts as with the social insects. Perhaps the outstanding induction which a natural historian would make from studying carefully this particular kind of animal would be: man is an evaluating animal; he talks and argues continually about values and shows by his behavior that values really count in what he does or refrains from doing.

But can any values be conceived, if not as basically absolute, as at least universal? Or are all values inherently relative and conformable? Are they merely fluctuations around the means of common denominators or, as the Communists claim, sheer functions or reflections of the reality adaptations of technology and economics? Is the search for panhuman values really a disguised attempt to impose "a monotonous standardization of human experiences" (along the lines, of course, of our own private or our own cultural values)—and one doomed to failure by the inherent inertia of each monadic culture? William Empson (1955, p. 83) puts this problem into a fine sonnet:[1]

> Not wrongly moved by this dismaying scene
> The thinkers like the nations getting caught
> Joined in the organising that they fought
> To scorch all earth of all but one machine.

---

1. From *Collected Poems of William Empson,* copyright 1935, 1940, 1949, by William Empson. Reprinted by permission of Harcourt, Brace & World, Inc.

It can be swung, is what these hopers mean,
    For all the loony hooters can be bought
    On the small ball. It can then all be taught
And reconverted to be kind and clean.

A more heartening fact about the cultures of man
    Is their appalling stubbornness. The sea
    Is always calm three fathoms down. The gigan-

-tic anthropological circus riotously
    Holds open all its booths. The pygmy plan
    Is one note each and the tune goes out free.

To me it is clear that the answer to these questions must be given not in an "either-or" but in a "both-and" form. Certainly, some values are relative to specific cultures. The values underlying the use of the cradleboard and other aspects of the child-care practices of the Navaho Indians make sense in terms of the total circumstances of Navaho life but are not fully applicable under the conditions of Indonesian life or contemporary American life. There are many values that are a question of taste, and the fact that the taste of other peoples does not coincide with our own does not make them stupid or ignorant or evil.

Moreover, in a world society each group can and must learn from other cultures, can and must familiarize itself with divergent value systems even when it prefers, in the last analysis, to hold in the main to its own traditional norms. Hence, the "Great Books" of Mr. Hutchins are a gigantic piece of cultural impudence. The Harvard report on General Education, published in 1945, is in many respects a wise and, indeed, a noble document; yet not one word is said of the need of the educated citizen to know something of the great religions of Asia nor of the aesthetic values of non-European languages. Africa remains the completely dark continent in spite of Benin bronzes and Bushmen paintings. The significant values of human culture are taken as limited to the Mediterranean Basin, Europe, and America. A peaceful revolution must dethrone such parochialism.

The inescapable fact of cultural relativity does not justify the conclusion that cultures are in *all* respects utterly disparate and hence strictly incomparable entities. There is a generalized framework that underlies the more apparent and striking facts of cultural relativity. All cultures constitute so many somewhat distinct answers to essentially the same questions posed by human biology and by the generalities of the human situation. Every society's patterns for living must provide approved and sanctioned ways for dealing with such universal circumstances as the existence of two sexes; the helplessness of infants; the need for satisfaction of the elementary biological requirements such as food, warmth, and sex; and the presence of individuals of different ages and of different physical and other capacities. The basic similarities in human biology the world over are vastly more massive than the variations. Equally, there are certain necessities in social life for this kind of animal, regardless of where or in what culture that life is carried on. Cooperation to obtain subsistence and for other ends requires a certain minimum of reciprocal behavior, of a standard system of communication, and, indeed, of mutually accepted values. The facts of human biology and of human gregariousness supply, therefore, certain invariant points of reference from which cross-cultural comparison can start without begging questions that are themselves at issue. The broad outline of the ground plan of all cultures is and has to be about the same, because men always and everywhere are faced with certain unavoidable problems that arise out of the situation "given" by nature. Since most of the patterns of all cultures crystallize around the same foci, there are significant respects in which each culture is not wholly isolated, self-contained, and disparate, but rather related to and comparable with all other cultures.

Nor is the similarity between cultures limited to the sheer forms of the universal culture pattern. There are at least some broad resemblances in content and specifically in value content. Considering the exuberant variation of cultures in most respects, the circumstance that in some particulars almost identical values prevail throughout mankind is most arresting. No culture tolerates indiscriminate lying, stealing, or violence within the ingroup. The essential universality of the incest taboo is well known. No culture places a value upon suffering as an end in itself—as a means to the ends of the society (punishment, discipline, etc.), yes; as a means to the ends of the individual (purification, mystical exaltation, etc.), yes; but of and for itself, never. We know of no culture in either space or time, including the Soviet Russian, where the official ideology denies an afterlife, where the fact of death is not ceremonialized. Yet the more superficial conception of cultural relativity would suggest that at least one culture would have adopted the simple expedient of disposing of corpses in the same way most people do dispose of dead animals —that is, simply throwing the body out far enough from habitations so that the odor would not be troubling. When one first looks rather carefully at the astonishing variety of cultural detail over the world, one is tempted to conclude that human individuals have tried almost everything that is physically possible, and that nearly every individual habit has somewhere at some time been institutionalized in at least one culture. To a considerable degree this is a valid generalization—but not completely. In spite of loose talk (based upon an uncritical acceptance of an immature theory of cultural relativity) to the effect that the symptoms of mental disorder are completely relative to culture, the fact of the matter is that all cultures define as abnormal individuals who are permanently inaccessible to communication or who consistently fail to maintain some degree of control over their impulse life. Social life is impossible without communication, without some measure of order: the behavior of any "normal" individual must be predictable—within a certain range—by his fellows and interpretable by them.

To look freshly at values of the order just discussed is very difficult because they are commonplaces. And yet it is precisely because they are *common*places that they are interesting and important. Their vast theoretical significance rests in the fact that, despite all the influences that predispose toward cultural variation (biological variability, differences in physical environments, and the processes of history), all of the very many different cultures known to us have converged upon these universals. It is perfectly true (and for certain types of inquiry important) that the value "thou shalt not kill thy fellow tribesman" is not concretely identical either in its cognitive or in its affective aspects for a Navaho, an Ashanti, and a Chukchee. Nevertheless, the central conception is the same, and there is understanding between representatives of different cultures as to the general intent of the prohibition. A Navaho would be profoundly shocked if he were to discover that there were no sanctions against in-group murder among the Ashanti.

The fact that a value is a universal does not, of course, make it necessarily an absolute. It is possible that changed circumstances in the human situation may lead to the gradual disappearance of some of the present universals. However, the mere existence of universals after so many millenia of culture history and in such diverse environments suggests that they correspond to something extremely deep in man's nature and/or are necessary conditions to social life.

When one moves from universals to virtual universals to values that are merely quite widespread, one would be on most shaky ground to infer "rightness" or "wrongness," "better" or "worse," from relative incidence. A value may have a very wide distribution in the world at a particular time simply because of such historical accidents as the political and economic power of one nation at that time. Nations diffuse their culture into the areas their power reaches. Nevertheless, this does not mean one must take all cultural values except universals as of necessarily equal validity. Slavery or cannibalism may have a place in certain cultures that is not evident to the ethnocentric Christian. Yet, even if these culture patterns play an important part in the smooth functioning of these societies, they are still subject to a judgment that is both moral and scientific. This judgment is not simply a projection of values, local in time and space, that are associated with Western culture. Rather, it rests upon a *consensus gentium* and the best scientific evidence as to the nature of raw human nature—that is, the human nature that all cultures mold and channel but never entirely remake. To say that certain aspects of Naziism were morally wrong—even for Germans—is not parochial arrogance; it is—or can be—an assertion based both upon cross-cultural evidence as to universalities in human needs, potentialities, and fulfillments and upon natural scientific knowledge with which the basic assumptions of any philosophy must be congruent.

Any science must be adequate to explain both the similarities and the differences in the phenomena with which it deals. Recent anthropology has focused its attention preponderantly upon the differences. They are there; they are very real and very important. Cultural relativity has been completely established, and there must be no attempt to explain it away or to deprecate its importance because it is inconvenient, hard to take, or hard to live with. Some values are almost purely cultural and draw their significance only from the matrix of that culture. Even the universal values have their special phrasings and emphases in accord with each distinct culture. And when a culture pattern such as slavery is derogated on the ground that it transgresses one of the more universal norms that in some sense and degree transcend cultural differences, one must still examine it not within a putatively absolutistic frame but in the light of cultural relativity.

At the same time one must never forget that cultural differences, real and important though they are, are still so many variations on themes supplied by raw human nature. The common understandings between men of different cultures are very broad, very general, and very easily obscured by language and many other observable symbols. True universals or near-universals are apparently few in number. But they seem to be as deep-going as they are rare. Anthropology's facts attest that the phrase "a common humanity" is in no sense meaningless. This is also important.

The one thing that we surely have to thank the Communists for is forcing us to take stock of our own position. On the whole, the record of the past ten years shows that our Western democracy has one of its essential strengths still: that, at least in time of crisis, people—the majority of the people—will do some rethinking.

The mistakes that we make on the international scene and have made in the past decade and more are primarily political mistakes. This is in part because the ideas that our leaders do have are largely *ad hoc* ideas—some of them, in my judgment, excellent (the Marshall Plan, for example)—that do not add up to a long-term positive policy.

One of the broadest and the surest generalizations that anthropology can make about human beings is that no society is healthy or creative or strong unless that society has a set of common values that give meaning and purpose to group life, that can be symbolically expressed, that fit with the situation of the time as well as being linked to the historic past, and that do not outrage men's reason and at the same time appeal to their emotions.

We at present largely lack such a creed that is appropriate to the times in which we live and to the tremendous economic and social changes that have taken place in our own country.

There is surely one thing in this whole picture that is, I trust, a comparatively temporary phenomenon—namely, the kind of disillusionment and cynicism that followed after the Wilsonian period. It became fashionable, and to some extent still is, not to talk about these things, so that one avoided discussion of our larger and more abstract values.

You remember from *Alice in Wonderland* the question, "Cheshire Puss, would you tell me please, which way I ought to go from here?" and the answer, "That depends a great deal on where you want to get to." I think our greatest weakness today is that we seem to know only where we do not want to go. We repudiate the brutal tyrannies of the police state, and we are not particularly eager to follow in detail the program of British Socialism, but even the famous Four Freedoms are mainly negative. At best, on the positive side, we can say that we want to preserve certain things: we want to keep our high standards of living, our educational opportunities, and our rights to choose our own occupation, to move freely about in our community, to speak our opinions on political and other questions, and to attempt without interference from the state to influence others.

But we no longer seem to be explicitly creative and forward-looking in the realm of ideology and our national values. This is unfortunate, because perhaps the greatest strength of the democratic tradition has been its capacity for growth, its insistence that there were no pat formulas that gave all the answers for all men in all times and in all situations.

One experience left a deep impression on me when I was in Japan after the war. The Japanese, particularly some of the Japanese intellectuals, were shocked by the fact that few of us could utter even a coherent sentence or two about our national values beyond a vague reference to the Declaration of Independence or something of that sort. Japanese after Japanese said to me in substance, "Why, I even asked a Colonel in your Army, and he couldn't tell me what Americans believed as a nation and what the long-term objectives of American policy were."

The present struggle is, in the last analysis, an ideological combat. The great power of the Communists outside Russia and the satellite states is a system of ideas that has pretensions to explain and to unify the economic, social, and political aspects of the contemporary world. In countries like France and Italy a large proportion, the rank and file, of the Communist Party are idealists in a sense in which, historically, Americans have been idealists; that is, they think that they have in the Party an answer to the meaningless chaos and confusion that they have seen, and they are powerfully drawn and powerfully motivated by the comprehensiveness and the explicitness of its scheme.

The fact that Communist ideology is itself terribly dated and scientifically unacceptable does not make it less threatening to the democracies as a Messianic secular religion unless and until we can oppose to it a formulation that is equally impressive, equally coherent internally, but more soundly founded upon the facts of external and human nature.

I am firmly convinced that there are some things that the vast majority of us do believe in and that do not, in any sense (as Europeans and Asiatics often interpret), constitute a crass materialism. But, unfortunately, these beliefs that bind us together remain largely implicit.

What can we do about it? I think we need to gather together in small and large groups, local and state and national, as did our forefathers in the late eighteenth and early nineteenth centuries, in order to be able to say explicitly what America is and, even more, what we want her to become. This is not a question of an official—that is, a governmental ideology that, down to the last crossing of the t and dotting of the i binds all of us. It is rather what the Americans of the Revolutionary and post-Revolutionary period created outside the government by collaborative effort in local groups at first and then between the states, something that would enable the United States to speak once more in the international realm with a clear philosophy so that the voice of America would no longer be muffled and confused.

I think we may lose the Cold War—and a possible hot war, if we continue to fight with the technology of 1962, which we do very well, but with the ideas of 1862. I should like to conclude with some wise words of Professor Oliver Reiser (1951) of the University of Pittsburgh, from his address to the American Association for the Advancement of Science in December, 1951:

The failure of civilization is in part the failure of communication—not only the breakdown of already established symbolism *within* ethnic groups, but the failure to establish new symbolic bridges *between* separate groups around the world. . . . To point this out is not to present an argument for a monotonous standardization of human experiences [either for individuals or for social groups]. Evidently the best solution is a middle-of-the-road policy: within a common framework of the psychological and social uniformities necessary to a coming world federation, each ethnic group should be free to enjoy its own customs, myths, traditions, [language], art-forms, and other forms of symbolic expression. Regional groups would be permitted to act out their social heredity—the mimesis of cultural symbolisms—provided there is toleration of similar cultural deviations of other peoples from the norms of a world community. Thus the world would in time become a self-integrating multiplicity of the culture-patterns [that are] indigenous to disparate areas of the earth's surface.

18 GROUP TENSIONS:

ANALYSIS

OF A CASE HISTORY

Introduction

BECAUSE OF A PREFERENCE for dealing with data with which I have first-hand and long-continued familiarity, and because I am convinced that social science (except perhaps in a few matters such as public-opinion polling), is not yet equipped to deal with other than very small canvases in anything approaching a rigorous manner, I shall approach the more general problems of group tensions in the context of a case history. Tensions among the Navahos and in their relationships with their non-Navaho neighbors have been acute during the past decade. Much experience and observation suggest that the strategic factors in social pathology (like those

1945c Reprinted by permission of the publishers from Clyde Kluckhohn, "Group Tensions: Analysis of a Case History," in *Approaches to National Unity*, edited by Lyman Bryson, Louis Finkelstein, and Robert M. MacIver. New York, Harper & Bros., pp. 222-231.

in the disease of individual organisms) emerge most clearly at critical phases. The scene is small enough to be sketched with a relative minimum of distortion in a brief space and yet not so tiny nor so comparatively uncomplicated as to be simply irrelevant to issues within the total American society.

The contemporary facts have been substantially sampled by a number of different investigators of different professional training and of varying personal backgrounds and present situations. On most points of description (though not of interpretation or "cure") agreement prevails among the vast majority of students of contemporary Navaho life. The historical facts for the period between 1870 and 1930 must be regarded as only fairly well established. Nevertheless, some aspects of this less well-known period will be introduced, for the dangers of diagnosing a human situation from the perspective of a too limited time dimension are well established.

I shall preface the "case" by a condensed conceptual scheme, making explicit the central assumptions upon which the argument for the relevance of the analysis of the case to a general theory of group tensions would rest:

1. In spite of the significant differences in cultural tradition, population genetics, and social situation that have been observed among human groups, there are still both biological and social processes that are universally human.

2. Almost every instance of antagonisms between biologically and/or culturally differentiated units is based upon one or more "realistic" conflicts of interest *and* upon "unrealistic" dislike. (For example, the mutual distrust between British and American businessmen over postwar control of oil and of air or sea traffic is "realistic"—given the culturally defined high valuation of "economic" success and of nationalism. But the irritation of many Americans at the "affectation" of "the British accent" and the annoyance many English people feel at the "brash vulgarity" of American manners are "unrealistic.")

3. Tensions that center around "realistic" conflicts of interest are often insoluble except at the price of severe deprivations to the members of one group or of a mutually unsatisfactory compromise that perhaps engenders a greater total amount of discontent than does a resolution that satisfies one interest. In

such cases the eventual outcome within the frustrated group is often either (a) a compensatory movement bringing greater social solidarity and generating hostility directed toward the frustrating society or (b) a gradual shifting of group goals in other directions or gradual alteration of the goals themselves. (Other possible outcomes need not concern us here: extinction of the frustrated group or absorption of one group into the other.)

4. Where "prejudices" are most commonly rationalized on "unrealistic" grounds and where hostilities are manifested with great frequency over trivial matters, the situation may ordinarily be described in one of two ways or a combination of the two. Either an impasse has been reached over "realistic" conflicts or aggression displaced from other sources is being channeled into group tensions (or there is a mixture—in varying proportions—of these two situations).

5. In every human society there appears to exist a varying amount of "free-floating aggression." This is thought to be mainly the product of the restraints put upon all immature human organisms during the socialization process *and* of the deprivations and frustrations incident to adult social life in all societies. People are blocked from doing what they want to do or from attaining what their culture has encouraged them to expect. Historical events interfere with customary means of activity. Or people become tense simply because they do not know what to do.

"Free-floating aggression" also derives from the anxieties current in a society. Anxieties, in turn, are both "realistic" and "unrealistic." The latter are those which arise from the special picture of the world furnished by the culture or are generated by "accidents" of individual experience. Every culture also provides means for the catharsis of anxieties through personal observances of "superstitious self-protection" and through social rituals. In times when insecurities are heightened, new cults are usually developed and old rites often gain a renewed hold upon the people. However, there ordinarily remains a residuum of "free-floating anxiety" that is not dissipated by the totality of available releases, some part of which becomes an increment to the magnitude of "free-floating aggression."

In some societies this "free-floating aggression" has been mainly drained off by periodic (or almost continual) wars. Some cultures, at certain periods, seem to have been able to channel much of it into socially creative channels (literature and the arts, public works, invention, geographical exploration, and the like). In most societies, most of the time, the greater part of this energy is diffused into various streams: the small angry outbursts of daily living, constructive activities, occasional wars. But history shows that at epochs in the careers of most nations much of this aggressive energy has been, for longer or shorter periods, concentrated against segmental or distributive minorities within the society.

6. It is primarily from the angle of the "unrealistic" tensions and displaced aggressions that we may hope to find a case history like that of the Navaho instructive. Where conflicts have "realistic" bases, the historical moment is critical—and unique. The precise circumstances of the "realistic" situation will not repeat themselves, and so we must not expect to discover many trends, nor any uniformities. But the human body as a psychological reacting instrument is being constantly reproduced with variations that are important for individual lives and creativity but minor so far as mass trends in reaction are concerned. In the uniformities of human neurological equipment and in the universality of the great dramas of human life (birth, dependency, death) may be found the conditions for universal sociopsychological processes. The *forms* vary culturally. The circumstances under which the expression of aggression is tolerated; the classes of persons or things toward which hostility is channeled; the symbols that evoke (or express) aggression— these are functions of the designs for living shared by distinctive groups. But the processes are the same. Failure to obtain satisfaction occurs under outward circumstances that vary. But inwardly *something* happens. If enough individuals are disappointed in their needs, hopes, or expectations enough of the time, if feelings of insecurity for the person or for the group are hypertrophied enough, *something* happens on a social scale. This may not be an increase in the total quantum of "free-floating aggression." The dominant response may be withdrawal or mass melancholia or increased addiction to narcotics. If the

principal result *is* heightening of hostilities in individuals, we cannot now predict with full confidence the circumstances under which the aggression is most likely to be focused within the family or the larger face-to-face circle, or turned toward outside scapegoats. But dissection of cases and cross-cultural comparisons are likely to reveal some common denominators in superficially divergent phenomena. We should be able to learn much about the circumstances (cultural, social, "economic," etc.) under which mass movements are most likely to take the form of self-blame and self-punishment (with hypochondria tending to be general) or to take the form of more neutral withdrawal or to seek scapegoats within or without society. Moreover, if details are not too easily surrendered for high abstractions, we should gain a healthy respect for the complexities of such phenomena and humility about our capacities for devising remedies.

As the seemingly outstanding features of the Navaho case are set forth, I shall draw some general references that I shall try to link to the foregoing general theoretical framework. "Theorems" will draw attention to those processual uniformities which have been stated above in the belief that they are already established and that the Navaho material therefore merely validates them anew. "Working hypotheses" will be those additional processes (or refinements of "theorems") which I am confident could be supported by much data from other societies but which hardly yet fall into the class of "theorems." "Tentative hypotheses" will be those inferences as to regularities which seem no more than leads for further investigation and testing.

The Case of the Navaho Indians

When the defeated Navahos, who had been held captive at Fort Sumner for four years, returned to their Reservation in 1868, the most widespread reaction seems to have been that of confusion. A note of despair is also prominent. But hostility toward whites seems to have been restricted to a small and not very influential minority. This is attested by contemporary government report and by recent interviews with old Navahos who were young adults in 1870.

WORKING HYPOTHESIS 1: *The immediate response of a conquered people is not necessarily hostility toward their conquerors.* (Cf. the dominant trend in German public opinion immediately after the 1918 Armistice and the persistently positive reactions of large and important groups to the United States and Britain for many years after 1918.)[1]

By 1875 most of the Navaho tribe were well on the way toward economic prosperity, and the period between 1875 and 1890 was a time of relative affluence. This same epoch, however, was marked by sharply heightened agitation over witchcraft, by several mass executions and numerous isolated killings of "witches."

THEOREM 1: *A people forced to make readjustments are likely to display increased hostile energy in some direction, even when their "objective" situation is more favorable than in the status-quo-ante period. This prediction is particularly indicated when the people have been deprived of habitual outlets for aggression.* (The Navahos were, after 1868, suddenly prevented from engaging in warfare, which had been their almost constant pursuit for at least 100 years. There is some evidence that personality types who had organized raids and reprisals prior to 1864 found the practice of witchcraft congenial after 1868.)

WORKING HYPOTHESIS 2: *The destructive aggression, which seems always to appear in social reconstruction after a major trauma, breaks out only after an interval.* Increased practice of witchcraft and the explosion against witches were not remarked at Fort Sumner or immediately after the return—any more than Fascism took over immediately after Caporetto (and Italian disappointments in the Treaty of Versailles) or Hitler immediately after the Armistice. There seems to be a period when a people are too crushed for any particular response to become frequent, when the general state is that of many varying trial-and-error efforts toward a new equilibrium or re-establishment of the old one.

---

1. Today one could add the post-1945 Japanese and Germans.

The decade from 1932 to 1942 was also an epoch of magnified tensions. These had important "realistic" bases. By 1930 Navaho economy had become sufficiently dependent upon the national economic structure that the disappearance of markets and the fall of prices hit the tribe very hard. The impact of the general economic crisis created an even more "unrealistically" disturbed environment among the Navahos than in American society as a whole, for most Americans had at least clichés about "business cycles" and the vulgarizations of various economic theories to give a semblance of orderliness and rationality to the events, and some, at least, were inspirited by the activities of the New Deal. To Navahos the whole thing was bewildering in the way the caprices of supernatural forces are bewildering. To many their loss in power to exchange or to purchase appeared as either a phase in the planful exploitation by whites or as a type of motiveless malignity. Navaho difficulties were also complicated by the fact that their population had tripled between 1870 and 1930. Their lands were crowded, and the resources of those lands had been savagely depleted by the combined effects of overgrazing and the recurrence of a natural erosion cycle. The personal insecurity manifested by most Navahos during the thirties was founded, in part, upon altogether justified worries as to how they were to escape starvation.

By 1930, also, there were large numbers of Navahos who were at home in neither the old Navaho world nor the non-Indian American world. Contradictory sets of values and techniques, absorbed in the early years at home and in later years at school or while working for whites, had produced a "lost generation." Bilinguality made this generation the most articulate medium for the dealings of the whole tribe with all classes of whites (government officials and teachers, missionaries, ranchers, merchants in the neighboring towns).

In 1933 a vigorous new administration of Indian Affairs began one of the most rapid and all-embracing restructurings of the whole life of a people that has ever been attempted. Unfortunately, the critical character of the actual situation and the temporary availability of large government funds necessitated a haste prejudicial to balanced planning and to adequate communication between Washington and Indian Service representatives on the Reservation and between these latter and the Navahos. The whole subsistence basis of Navaho society was altered with a speed which upset and antagonized many of the Indians. Similarly, many of the old-time local Indian Service personnel (whom Washington did not find time or the means to recondition, and who were not, at the start, impregnated with the wisdom that, on the whole, prevailed in the top policy-making group) were apathetic or became covertly hostile to the innovations and carried out active and passive sabotage.

WORKING HYPOTHESIS 3: *If reconstruction is to be minimally productive of aggression, the education of actual field adminis-trators and adequate, fluid, two-way communication from the top administrative group through all channels to the administered are as important as rationally ripe plans for the end results.*

The struggle between the expanding Navaho population and the growing numbers of white stockmen over lands on the border of the Reservation is very real. So also is the Navaho sense that, whereas in time past "Washington" contented itself with forbidding war, restraining their wanderings, and a few interferences with native customs, now "Washington" has the smallest threads of the texture of their livelihood in its hands. To all the "realistic" sources of anxiety and insecurity there have, of course, been added many derived "unrealistic" fears. Some of these arise out of Navaho conceptions of supernatural dangers. Others are the product of interactions between differ-ing Navaho and European-American basic assumptions and categories. In both the literal and the figurative senses the two groups "don't speak the same language." There are tremendous and harmful misunderstandings on both sides, which, for the Navahos, add to their confusion and generalized uneasiness. In this psychological climate *all* acts of *all* whites tend to be inter-preted as potentially threatening.

The negative and positive cultural freedoms that the John Collier administration has granted and encouraged are but little appreciated or indeed realized by the tribe. Even the benign intentions of the Office of Indian Affairs and the protection that has been provided against predatory local political interests are repudiated by a large proportion of the Indians. In an atmosphere of distrust, *part* of which is well founded upon observation of the unscrupulousness of *some* traders, the ambivalences and inconsistencies of *some* missionaries, the exploiting advantages that *most* whites in the surrounding territories take of their privileged position, and the discriminations that almost all whites (including members of the Indian Service) make against Indians, the Navahos generalize from the incompetency and dishonesty of *some* past agents and superintendents and from the political expediency (and worse) that often—between 1870 and 1928—characterized the Washington office.

There can be no doubt that the more highly placed personnel of the Indian Service in recent years have had benevolent intentions toward the Navaho. That mistakes, and serious ones, have been made, this group would be the first to admit. That, however, their policies were altruistically envisioned seems to me beyond argument. And yet the dominant image the Indians have formed of these officials has been that of suspicion and—during at least the earlier period when the program of reducing the numbers of sheep and horses was being enforced—that of active enmity. It was curious to notice how when this administration drilled wells, built hospitals, and carried out other indubitably advantageous and constructive achievements for which responsible Navaho leaders had long been clamoring, there was no chorus of unqualified approval. Dissent over locations was uttered, grumblings waxed over who was and was not employed in the public works, and rumors spread that all women would be *forced* to have their babies in the hospitals and that "medicine men" would be compelled to give up their practices.

WORKING HYPOTHESIS 4: *A people reacts to an imposed program in terms of the logic of their sentiments. If insecurity prevails and if some central sentiments are offended, uncritical, nonrational, and irrational generalizations are endemic. Even those projects which the administered group had but a little earlier themselves demanded will be resentfully repudiated. The most technologically correct and necessary programs can wholly or partially founder.*

Some statements already made have perhaps suggested that the Navahos lump together all "whites," except in so far as they make occupational differentiations (government representatives, missionaries, traders, etc.). Most whites certainly divide the scene into Indian and non-Indian portions, and, at a broad level, this is probably true increasingly for Navahos as well. But many niceties of the tensions that Navahos feel and express will escape valid analysis unless one realizes the more refined categorizations that they still usually make of their neighbors. In many contexts they classify all Pueblo Indians by a single word, which means "town dwellers." The feeling-tone is an intricate mixture of the old contempt (for Pueblos as poor fighters and as a trifle effete generally) and fearful respect (for Pueblos as skillful magicians and as sophisticates in rational techniques), together with "realistic" hostility in those cases (Hopi, Zuñi, etc.) where there are disputes over land rights. Paiutes, Utes, Havasupais, and Walapais are usually spoken of (and sometimes treated) with a slight superciliousness tinged with mockery. More adequate generalizations about the relationships of Navahos with their Indian neighbors would enter into many complications, but one interesting fact for present purposes is the growth during recent years of a sense of solidarity with all other Indians—in spite of historical particularism and animosities.

TENTATIVE HYPOTHESIS 1: *Minority groups of different cultural and physical heritage will tend to pool their defensive energies against a common oppressor when the threat reaches a certain pitch of intensity.* (Cf. the interest which Jewish leaders have shown recently in the political and other rights of Negroes.)

Navahos almost invariably make a distinction between "Americans" and "Mexicans" (most of whom are the descendants of Spanish colonials whose settlement of New Mexico long antedated the founding of the present Mexican nation). The differentiation made by Navahos has an historical foundation but also reflects present-day variations in behavior. The relationships between Indians and Spanish-Americans in towns like Gallup, Grants, and Flagstaff show many instructive nuances. On the one hand, there are many subtle recognitions of the fact that both are "depressed groups." A common front is implied in frequently reiterated verbalizations and expressed in action as well. For example, Spanish-Americans will not only sell Indians liquor for profit but will also obtain it for them as a favor. They will shelter drunken Indians and otherwise protect them against "Anglo" law. It is exceptional for Indians to receive hospitality in white homes in the towns, but many Indian and Spanish-American families maintain a connection of reciprocal "guest-friendship." Thus far our "tentative hypothesis" above is validated. On the other hand, gangs of adolescent or young adult Spanish-Americans often waylay, beat up, and rob Indians (especially intoxicated ones) by night, in a mode they would not dare employ against Anglo-Americans. Bitter and bloody knife fights occur between small groups of Indians and Spanish-Americans.

While in many contexts Navahos lump all Anglos together, they ordinarily refer to Mormons and not infrequently (fairly consistently in some areas) to Texans by distinct words. The complete story behind this differentiation of terminology would be interesting but long. My point here is that the Navaho respond, if inchoately, to the cultural distinctiveness and hierarchically varying status positions of groups within the larger non-Indian society.

TENTATIVE HYPOTHESIS 2: *"Pecking order" phenomena may be manifested when a frustrated group reacts to a frustrating group that is hierarchically segmented.*

Most Indian Service administrators have had an overly simple, overly schematic, cognitive map of the attitudes Navahos have toward other groups in the region. Resident administrators have been aware of active or latent hostilities among the Navaho and other tribes. But they have seldom realized, on the one hand, that cross-tribal solidarity has developed in some situations and, on the other, that the Navaho have perceived the segmentation of Anglo society and, on occasion, played off one segment against another. An articulate Navaho, giving a picture of group tensions in his locality, depicts complicated alignments and antagonisms within the framework of a multifold division that does not correspond to the Indian versus non-Indian or Indian, Spanish-American, and Anglo of the modal administrator. The discrepant maps have sometimes led to failure of communication, ineffective administration, and rise of tension.

TENTATIVE HYPOTHESIS 3: *Predictive diagnosis requires that*

*feuds and schisms be seen within the schemas of all the groups
involved, not merely from the viewpoint of the dominant group
or of a supposedly "objective" position.*

The next point is possibly too banal to mention, but it is
part of the story. An appreciable number of the field personnel
of the Collier administration had joined to their generally
"liberal" stance certain rudiments of anthropological knowledge.
They understood—or thought they did—the principle of cultural
relativity. Hence they talked sincerely, if sometimes loudly,
about the rights of the tribe to its own customs, about their
respect for Navaho religion, and the like. In contrast to this
verbal behavior, however, only a few exceptional individuals
made other than rare, awkward, and purely symbolic attempts
to participate in Navaho life outside the Agency or governmental
setting. I know of literally two who learned any of the Navaho
language beyond a few conventional phrases. If one may
intellectualize in our (rather than their) terms a representative
Navaho reaction, it would be, I think, somewhat like this:

Yes, it is true that these new people tolerate our customs more than the
old-time Government employees or the Protestant missionaries. But
they still stand apart. They live their own lives in their own way, and
they do not really invite us to join in that way. In fact, they seem to
want to keep us different.

For some minority groups an implicit pressure from the
dominant group to keep the minority permanently distinctive
is even less tolerable than other kinds of discrimination. The
Navaho sensed this pressure in some administrative policies as
well as in the daily behavior of government personnel. Let me
give only one instance. The "idealists" of the Collier group were
determined that the Navaho should have "the best" or "the most
advanced" in educational procedures. Educational practices in
the rural and small-town schools of New Mexico and Arizona
seemed to them "backward." Methods were therefore imported
from "progressive" schools in the East and Middle West. Many
Navahos, understandably, reacted to this as yet another device
to enforce their differentiation from their neighbors. When I

once attempted to defend government policy, a wise old Navaho replied:

Maybe you are right. Maybe these are better ways of teaching. I don't care. I want my grandchildren taught as Anglo and Spanish-American children around here are being taught. My grandchildren are going to live here and not in New York City. They have got to learn the ways of the other people around here. That is what counts.

In brief, "enlightened" plans can run afoul of the stubborn realities of immediate situation and of neglect of the universal bases of good human relations. To a government official who vehemently protests his admiration for Navaho chants, a Navaho prefers a trader or a missionary who is openly contemptuous of his religion but who nevertheless speaks his language, eats his food, and visits his hogan in friendly fashion. In spite of alley fights and some tendency to cheating, Navahos feel more linked to Spanish-Americans who share the underprivileged status of a minority group than to civil servants who will participate with Navahos only "on business." The Spanish-American with whom experiences have been shared is likely to be given more fundamental trust than the official who talks grandly of abstract goals and who makes comparisons that are meaningless to a Navaho. While the history of relations between Mormons and Navahos is too complex to dismiss in a few sentences, there is one issue that is directly pertinent here. The Book of Mormon teaches that American Indians derive from the Lost Tribes of Israel. Not always, but rather frequently, this teaching is conveyed to the Navaho as a Mormon conviction that Indians have a genuine part, and a worthy part, in the total world. And this is contrasted, however inarticulately, with the feeling that the Indian Service says: "You have your ways, and we respect them. But they are —and will remain—outside the world that we image."

TENTATIVE HYPOTHESIS 4: *Detached intellectual understanding is not a substitute for intensive face-to-face experience that is shared, particularly when "understanding" tends toward perpetuation of differentiation.*

Different sets of Navahos (depending, partly, upon age, schooling, and location of residence as this affects frequency and intensity of non-Navaho contacts) have shown different major responses to the insecurities, deprivations, and frustrations of the immediate past. The same Navahos, of course, manifest different responses on different occasions, but most age, age-sex, areal, and other groups tend eventually to settle down to one or more preferred reaction patterns. Some focus their energies upon trying to be as like whites as possible. Some find relief in becoming followers of vocal Navaho leaders. Others dissipate much hostility in factional quarrels or scatter their aggression in family fights, in fantasies about witchcraft or in attacking "witches," or in vocal and other indirect hostilities toward whites, or they turn their aggression inward, with resultant fits of depression. The culturally patterned releases in humor and in "joking relationships" with certain relatives continue to play some part. The central response of certain individuals is flight —either actual physical withdrawal or the escape of narcotics, alcohol, and sex. Still others turn principally to intensified participation in rites of the native religion and to new cults. Partial solutions are achieved by a few individuals through rigid compartmentalization of their lives and feelings and by various rationalizations. The greatest contrast to the picture of the 1875-1890 period is the much more exuberant variety of the solutions tried by distinguishable sectors of the population. Presumably this correlates with the greater pressures, "realistic" and "unrealistic," experienced by the contemporary society. The solutions are not only more varied. They have a much more general tendency toward the pathological. As Rosensweig (1944, p. 384) says:

Just as the body in its resistance to infectious disease adopts non-disruptive protective reactions as long as possible but eventually resorts to defense reactions which, as symptoms of the illness, seriously interfere with the patient's normal behavior; so when psychological constancy cannot be achieved in more adequate ways, less adequate ones are inevitably adopted.

THEOREM 2: *Press of insecurity and frustration produces sociopathic manifestations. These may be aggressive (toward groups or individuals external to the society, toward groups or individuals within the society, toward the self), or they may take the form of "unrealistic" adaptations or "realistic" or "unrealistic" withdrawals of various types or of mystic experiences.*

TENTATIVE HYPOTHESIS 5: *The variety of alternative responses is—at least up to an undetermined point—directly proportional to the degree of tension existent. In an atmosphere of insecurity variable behavior is more frequent. Thus tension may be productive of social change.*

Let us now consider some of the main types of response in a little detail. Those who set themselves to follow the white man's trail find themselves—as have representatives of other minority groups—in an (rationally) odd dilemma. While as youngsters they are rewarded by schoolteachers and others for behaving like whites, as adults they are punished for having acquired skills that make them competitors of their white contemporaries. The more intelligent ones had, by early maturity, realized that their "education" would bring them into conflict with or isolation from their own unschooled relatives. But the experience of being "turned on" by their white mentors comes as a painful surprise. They find they are seldom received on terms of social equality, even by those whose standard of living, dress, and manners they have succeeded in copying. They learn that they must expect to work for a salary lower than that a white person of comparable training and experience receives. They overhear remarks by the same categories of whites who had goaded them to give up "those ignorant Indian ways":

You can never trust these school boys.

Give me a "long hair" every time. They may be dumb, but they're honest and they work hard.

Educated Indians are neither fish nor fowl. They give me the creeps.

Rejected by the white world they have made so many emotional sacrifices to enter, some attempt a bitter retreat to the Navaho world. Others, in sour disillusionment, abandon all moral codes. Still others achieve a working (but flat and empty) adjustment.

WORKING HYPOTHESIS 5: *Transitional generations must be warned that they will get punishments as well as rewards for learning the ways of a superordinate group. This superordinate group must also cushion the transition if they do not wish to assume the responsibility for added hostile or shiftless or amoral individuals.*

The only times when Navahos have followed leaders of other than strictly local influence seem to have been the confused and war-filled period between about 1800 and 1868; the 1875-1890 epoch, and the post-1930 decade. Some, at least, of the recent leaders have approached the type of the demagogue. However, before we draw too sweeping a conclusion from these facts, we must glance at the contrasts in the history of the Pueblo Indians. They have been exposed to pressures that parallel, in many respects, those upon the Navahos. But among them the sense of belonging to a group with a distinctive culture has largely replaced the need for relying on a leader. Although internal frictions have been severe and almost constant, the Pueblos have been much more tenacious of their culture, much more resistant to mass turnings toward non-Indian designs for living. The strategic factor here may be a difference in the patterns of child training. The Navaho analogue of "conscience" appears to be formed rather after the fashion of the Judaeo-Christian tradition —by introjection of the parental (or grandparental) superego. This seems to provide a psychological background favorable to the rise and success of demagogues. On the other hand, would-be demagogues appear to be unsuccessful among those whose socialization has followed the lines of, say, the Hopi.

TENTATIVE HYPOTHESIS 6: *Critical times favor the rise of strong leadership in some psychological climates, but in others the tendency is toward the intensification of resistances to culture change.*

Late years have seen some development of factionalism among the Navahos, both at tribal level (antigovernment and pro-government) and in local groups. But this tendency has a different character than among the Pueblos. Navaho factionalism is weaker, less steady, less clearly bipolar. Factionalism seems to be an inherent propensity of Pueblo social organization. The personal composition of factions is constantly shifting; the ostensible issues of cleavage change with the times, but factions (and usually only two main ones) go on forever. An unusual disposition toward division seems characteristic of many American Indian societies. One may guess that the degree of factionalism that develops under stress is primarily a function of social structure. And note that social structure is in part culturally determined and in part socially determined. For instance, the cultural pattern among the western Pueblos—that a town consists of clans that have never fully surrendered their autonomy to any central organization—undoubtedly favors factional alignments. But this is not all of the story. The social facts of the contrasting numbers of interacting individuals among Navahos and Pueblos, of the limitation upon possible face-to-face contacts in the Navaho tribe, play their part in conditioning the differing Navaho and Pueblo manifestations of factionalism. There is always, of course, a connection between numbers, isolation, and the suppression of in-group aggression.

TENTATIVE HYPOTHESIS 7: *Increased tensions make for factionalism, but the extent is a function of existent social structure and of the self-limiting tendency inherent in trends toward presenting a solid front against the aggrandizement of a larger or more powerful external society.*

Nativistic religious cults have arisen among the Navahos since about 1920, but they have become much more numerous and prominent since 1930. Some (notably *peyote* rites) are mainly passive and inward-turning; others provide a setting for displays of antiwhite sentiments and attempts by supernatural means (the only safe ones!) to destroy the powers of the whites. There have also occurred markedly more frequent performances of the old ceremonials. These seem to subserve the functions of alleviating anxieties of individuals and of reintegration for the society; that is, heightened ceremonialism is both adaptive and expressive (adjustive in a special sense). Carrying out one of the ancient rites constitutes a powerful symbolic assertion of the values of Navaho culture. This is more comparable to a main feature of Pueblo resiliency. (It is notable that no Pueblo "liberal" or "progressive" faction has ever advocated giving up the old rituals. Their programs have always called for retention of the native religion along with some concessions to white culture in technological and "educational" directions.) The Pueblos have tended to take over various white *means* in order to resist

more effectively the adoption of white *goals*. It would be valuable to know for certain whether ceremonial participation waxed
noticeably among the Navahos between 1875 and 1890. Careful
interviewing among elder Navahos has failed to dislocate any
evidence that it did. My hunch is that whites were so few in
the Navaho country at that period that Navaho culture hardly
seemed threatened. The old equilibrium was able to re-establish
itself, with comparatively small modifications, within a decade
after Fort Sumner. Lately, the basic equilibrium has been continually tottering.

The fact that the native religion provides many socially
approved outlets for the neurotic tendencies engendered by
contemporary pressures is important. "Social aberrations" (witchcraft phenomena, nativistic cults, etc.) occur on a fairly wide
scale, but individual neuroticism is rarer than one would anticipate under present conditions. When the hold of the old
beliefs and practices upon the populace weakens markedly, one
may anticipate—if other circumstances remain at all comparable
—that neurotics will become much more numerous.

THEOREM 3: *Religious activities are heightened in difficult
times.*

TENTATIVE HYPOTHESIS 8: *New cults (or—in "civilized"
societies—new "secular religions") centered on hostility or withdrawal are sociopathic manifestations. Revivals of ancient
religions are apt to be last-ditch defense against radical culture
change.*

The recent increase among the Navahos in fantasies, gossip,
and overtly aggressive behaviors arising out of beliefs in witchcraft is partly consequent upon progressive dissolution of the
native culture, with its sanctions for checking these forms of
social disruption. (The position of the Indian Service is, for
obvious reasons, a difficult one in regard to "witchcraft." The
"law and order" division can hardly hope to substitute effectively for the aboriginal social organization in controlling most
activities based upon a belief that our culture says is false.)
Distances, bad roads, insufficient numbers of police, and problems
in fixing responsibility likewise hamper the efforts of the Indian
Service to curb mounting crimes of violence within families and
between neighbors. This pathology may also be laid partially
at the door of weakening Navaho sanctions. But both these and

witchcraft aggressions must be connected, too, with the incapac-
ities of Navahos for directing their hostilities toward those (the
whites) against whom a large proportion of aggression should
"realistically" be expressed. The lesson of defeat in war and of
Fort Sumner took strong hold upon the Navaho imagination.
Although there have been a few outbreaks since, and there
threatened to be serious and widespread ones in the thirties,
Navaho experience in small incidents has reinforced what had
been learned by 1868: whites are *very* strong, and it is dangerous
to behave aggressively toward them except verbally or by the
sabotage of noncooperation.

WORKING HYPOTHESIS 6: *Aggression release within a society
is—other things being at all equal—inversely proportional to
outlets for external aggression.*

Study of a large sample of cases indicates that schooled (including mission-schooled) Navahos are as afraid of witchcraft as
nonschooled ones. What the schooled Navahos primarily learn
is to conceal—under most circumstances—from whites that they
continue to share these beliefs and fears. Indeed, there is some
warrant for saying that those Navahos who are acculturated to
the extent of abandoning belief and practice (entirely or for the
most part) in the "good" side of their religion are *more* preoccupied with witchcraft than unacculturated Navahos. The
sole Navahos who seem, as a group, to approach complete eman-
cipation from these anxieties are those who, *from earliest infancy,*
were brought up by whites or in Navaho households that were
insulated from Navaho culture.

WORKING HYPOTHESIS 7: *Rational instruction of school-age
children can modify but cannot overcome earlier absorption of
basic emotional attitudes.*

TENTATIVE HYPOTHESIS 9: *While "intellectual truth" may in
the long run (over a number of generations?) prevail against
"irrationalities," such as belief in witches (or "race prejudice"?),
if the situational determinants are not too unfavorable, we are
deluding ourselves if we think a quick victory can be won by
any such means. On the contrary, the first result may often be
the destruction of the more positive and stabilizing aspects of a
corpus of beliefs and increased "regression" to malignant and
destructive conceptions.*

In the very general sense of scapegoats, "witches" have probably played some part in all social structures since the Old Stone Age. They may be either a minority within the society or an external group. In contemporary America, for instance, we have the "reds," the "niggers," the "capitalists," the "New Dealers," the "Japs," and many others. It may be too much to say that all societies *must* necessarily have their "witches"—that is, persons whom it is proper (according to the standards of one's own group) to fear and hate and, under defined circumstances, to behave aggressively toward. Some social systems are much more efficient than others in directing hostility into oblique or socially nondisruptive channels. But there is no doubt that witchcraft belief is one of Navaho culture's principal present answers to the problem that every society faces: what to do about satisfying hate so as still to keep the core of the society solid. Among other things, witchcraft is the Navaho's substitute for our own "race prejudice." The Navahos blame their troubles upon "witches" instead of upon "Jews" or "wops." Instead of selecting its scapegoats by the color of their skins or by their separate religious tradition, Navaho culture selects certain individuals who are supposed to work evil by secret supernatural techniques.

WORKING HYPOTHESIS 8: *In attacking many specific phenomena of social pathology, one is attacking "symptoms"—not "causes." The result, if successful at all, will be merely to shift the currents of hostility—not to eliminate them. An attack upon "causes" must consist (a) in ameliorating basic situations that are productive of "realistic" worries and hostilities and (b) in devising improved techniques of child socialization and of subsequent interpersonal relations so that the total amount of "free floating aggression" is decreased.*

Admitting the personal misery and the social disruption involved—the net contribution of witchcraft beliefs and practices, under all the other existent circumstances of the Navaho people is favorable in identifiable respects to the maintenance of the equilibrium of individuals and the survival of the social system. Does this mean defense of the proposition that "witchcraft is a good thing"? Not at all. The assertion is only that the manifest and latent "functions" are in the direction of *present* stability. Whether preserving this uneasy stability is worth the cost is another matter entirely. But societies and cultures, like organisms and other ongoing systems, are prone to proliferate structures that are adjustive and adaptive from the point of view of maintaining a semblance of the status quo but highly pathological from the standpoint of eventual development of patterns that will make possible life more rich and more fulfilling for larger numbers.

TENTATIVE HYPOTHESIS 10: *While too rapid social change can be needlessly destructive, while the value of a balance between "persistence of aggregates" and the "instinct for new combinations" is freely admitted, men of good will must scrutinize with unusual care all social habits which have the function of stabilization—most especially those that smack of supernaturalism. Is the longer-run effect that of perpetuation of values that are no longer appropriate to humanity's actual situation, including man's knowledge of the external world and of himself?*

The writer is keenly aware of the incompleteness of the foregoing presentation as regards data, justification of concepts and of reasoning, and relevant topics not touched upon at all. But he hopes others will consider the treatment as he does—as having no pretensions to scientific "proof" but as setting forth (for whatever stimulation or suggestiveness may be afforded) some of the wider inferences that have occurred to one student after years of preoccupation with a relatively small body of data and after long reflection upon the broad implications of these data.

Discussion

One final conclusion suggests itself. At least twenty variables of some significance have been mentioned, and others have surely been omitted. It has perhaps been possible to make some approximately correct diagnoses as to the contribution of certain variables to the total picture, but let up suppose that not one but a half dozen of these were appreciably altered within a brief space of time. Who could do more than speculate as to the consequences in other aspects of the system? We can predict that every feature would present a different facies, for the theorem of the interdependence of variables in a social system is perhaps the surest induction of the sciences of man. This is something, but the recipe for action we must draw from it seems that of caution, of modest expectations as to what can be accomplished by "planning," of humility as to what may be validly predicted with present instruments for observation and conceptualization, and of preference for *vis medicatrix naturae* in many social situations.

Indications are not lacking that an appreciable number of social scientists, exhilarated by newly discovered skills and possibly a trifle intoxicated by the fact that for the first time men of affairs are seeking their advice on a fairly extended scale, are encouraging hopes that their science is not mature enough to fulfill. To restrain social scientists from irresponsible pronouncements, the profession may need to develop sanctions comparable to those that law and medicine have developed to control irresponsibility, charlatanism, and malpractice.

In larger perspective the Navaho case only confirms the tough-minded and closely argued warnings as to the limitations of planning set forth in Chester I. Barnard's (1944) luminous paper in last year's Symposium of this Conference. This does not mean that social science has not attained *any* practical utility. It is one thing to be able to make some useful predictions as to what is likely to happen—and by thus foreseeing to be able to prepare somewhat for contingencies that might otherwise have been succeeded by utter chaos. But it is quite another thing to *interfere*, willfully to introduce new complications into an already tortuous social maze. More attention to individuals and less (proportionately) to over-all social planning may be advisable. One of the wise things which Niebuhr says in *The Nature and Destiny of Man* (1941-1943) is that the contemporary world overestimates the powers of the "collective will" and underestimates those of the individual will. At least when it comes to large canvases, the social scientist would still do well to abide by what has proved a helpful rule in many medical cases: "Do nothing. Sit tight. Watch. Prepare for probable developments but do not interfere with natural forces making for recuperation until you are sure that action will be helpful, or, as an absolute minimum, do no harm."

19 MID-CENTURY MANNERS

AND MORALS

IT IS ALL TOO EASY to be wrong about the United States. Its apparent uniformities mask infinite variations, and there are, one suspects, implicit highest common factors underlying some of its most obvious diversities. The discovery of America by social scientists is far from complete. Existing studies, valuable and stimulating though they are, represent hardly more than occasional soundings made by explorers drifting around a vast sea of ignorance in a rowboat. We have a far firmer picture of the manners and morals of the Eskimo or of the Ashanti than we have of our own. We must still turn largely to the professional wise men in our midst, to poets and novelists, and to the impressionistic accounts of foreign observers.

Yet trial must be made. One fact of considerable interest is the birth rate, especially the differential birth rate of various groups in the United States. The Bureau of the Census has revealed that in 1947 the replacement index of women with one

1950a Reprinted by permission of the publishers from Clyde Kluckhohn, "Midcentury Manners and Morals," in *Twentieth Century Unlimited*, edited by Bruce Bliven. New York, J. B. Lippincott, pp. 303-315.

to three years of college had climbed to 1,070, as against 672 in 1940. The trend during the last ten years toward larger families among the college-educated population is confirmed by the Indianapolis study. This probably reflects a value change as well as economic prosperity and the psychology of war and postwar times. However, women of all levels of educational attainment have participated in the increase in fertility between 1940 and 1947. The replacement index of women who had less than five years of school went from 1,382 to 1,776. Though the increase is proportionately greater by advancing educational levels, there was in 1947 still a consistent inverse relationship between fertility and amount of education. If economic conditions worsen, it may be the educated classes who are familiar with and have a rational attitude toward contraceptive techniques whose birth rates will again drop disproportionately. Under favorable economic conditions the educated groups now practice birth control only to the extent that is dictated by considerations of health, spacing of children, and attainment of desired family size, for the arrival of children soon after marriage is no longer taken as evidence of lack of knowledge of contraception.

Something should be said of the most talked of social document of the postwar period, the first Kinsey report. In view of all the published commentary, it is not necessary to discuss many aspects of Kinsey's data and methods, but there is one aspect which has received insufficient attention outside professional social science journals. This is the extent to which the sex behavior of American males is class-typed. This finding is independently confirmed in August Hollingshead's *Elmtown's Youth* (1949) and shown to extend to many other kinds of social behavior. The same trend is evidenced in a survey of attitudes toward the atomic bomb. The upper middle class is far more concerned over the implications of the bomb than is the lower lower class and appreciably more so than even the lower middle class. In part, this can be explained as a function of educational levels. Also involved, however, are differential stakes in a stable social structure and differing senses of power over the environment.

In short, the Kinsey report, along with many other recent studies, suggests that our society is in some respects less fluid than it was and that a somewhat different kind of heterogeneity is developing. The patterns of physical growth and maturation and the system of formal education in the public schools are roughly the same for middle- and lower-class children; yet they grow up in different worlds from a psychological and socio-logical point of view. One must not exaggerate the influence of "class" or decrease in social and economic mobility. It should not be forgotten that W. Lloyd Warner and his associates have had a propensity for studying the more static communities. Perhaps one should avoid the word "class," with its misleading European connotations, and speak of "status groups," since membership in Warner's six classes is so highly correlated with occupational position and educational level. But Kinsey's find-ings confirm the view that, to some extent, one must think about present and future social behavior in America in class terms.

To me, however, the significance of Kinsey's work for the understanding of the contemporary scene does not rest primarily in any of its facts, important as these are to science. I do not think that these data prove a dangerous growth of immorality, concomitant upon a weakening of religious faith. There is doubtless some connection between these two factors, but my hunch is that a number of Roman Catholic commentators have hit the nail on the head by saying, in substance, "We knew this all along." Certainly Perry Miller has demonstrated that all types of deviation from the approved sex code occurred even under the severe Puritan regime. The viewing with alarm has probably about as mythological a foundation as Herbert Goldhamer and Andrew W. Marshall have recently (1949) shown the hue and cry over the supposed increase in psychoses during the last two generations to have.

In my opinion, the foremost significance of Kinsey's work as an indicator of long-term trends consists precisely in its being done at all, in its generous support and publication. The truly astonishing fact is that this research was backed by the highly respectable Rockefeller Foundation and carried out in a western state university. This is of a piece with the public airing of American military strategy in October, 1949. This could not have happened in any other major contemporary nation, and the atti-tudes that made it possible are at once the strength and the weakness of these United States. In the second place, the Kinsey report is of a piece with the national polling organizations and the other gigantic efforts made by Americans to hold up a mirror to themselves. No other people has been so curious about itself, nor so willing to subject itself to scientific analysis, nor so avid to read even the most sneering and superficial criticisms of outsiders.

Still strong is John Dewey's "faith that if given a chance men living together on this Continent will grow and be able to generate the knowledge and vision required to guide collective action." The Kinsey studies testify to the continued vitality of a childlike trust in knowledge, particularly scientific knowledge, as an instrument for individual and social improvement. Nor, after this war, has there been that revolt against the loss of innocence which was the "flaming youth" movement of the early twenties. F. Scott Fitzgerald is popular again, but as a serious writer, not as the apostle of a new Jazz Age. College teachers uniformly have been impressed by the maturity and earnestness of their students of the past five years. Nurtured amid failing banks and the WPA as well as seasoned in the war, these young men and women are not easily fooled or romantically disillusioned. Though perceptibly more conscious of problems of personal security than was the pre-depression generation, their eyes remain, in good American fashion, upon the potential rather than the actual society.

Of course the G.I. bill itself is proof that the United States really believes its creed of equal opportunity, experiment, and education as a magic means of tapping the reservoirs of ability in economically underprivileged groups. This, together with measures recommended by the President's Commission on Higher Education, may have the effect of creating within ten or fifteen years what Seymour Harris (1948) calls a "B.A. and Ph.D. proletariat." If present trends continue, in fifty years one-third of all American adults will be college graduates and half will have at least a junior-college education. Openings in professional and managerial occupations can hardly increase in the same proportion, so the expectations of many would be disappointed. Nevertheless, the relevant point here is that, however unpleasant the actual economic prospect may be, and whatever the hard realities of increasing class stratification, the United States is for the moment tenaciously committed to the historical American creed.

It could, to be sure, be argued that the G.I. bill and proposed legislation for federal aid to education are also evidences for a somewhat new theme in American culture, that of the "Welfare State." There is surely something to this interpretation. But the power of the old sentiments must not be underestimated. What impressed an Oxford debating team on a recent tour of fifty-nine American colleges was that our students regarded private enterprise not just as an economic method but as a way of life:

A citizen either believes in it or he does not, and if he does not he does not believe in America. . . . During many a debate one felt that, if America went to war, it would be for Private Enterprise against Collectivism rather than for Western civilization against Eastern tyranny.

As Daniel Aaron has pointed out, the real protagonists in Ayn Rand's *The Fountainhead* are individualism versus collectivism. This book sold 350,000 copies between 1943 and 1946. Since it is not especially remarkable for plot, literary style, or sex appeal, its success may presumably be traced in large part to its striking home to the core of sentiments. The hero affirms that the United States ("the noblest country in the history of man") was not based "on selfless service, sacrifice, renunciation, or any precept of altruism. It was based on a man's right to the pursuit of happiness . . . a private, personal, selfish motive."

The reception of Miss Rand's novel could plausibly be interpreted as a confirmation of Henry James' fears over "the rising triumph of the superficial and the apotheosis of the raw." There are, and have been, strong currents of this sort in American life: romantic, anarchic individualism; deification of selfishness; and feverish visions of power and sex. Yet it is noteworthy that Miss Rand tells her readers that she wants most to set forth a *morality* of individualism.

Except for one large and various small minorities, most Americans are less and less influenced by institutionalized religion. But this does not mean that they are correspondingly indifferent to problems of standards and of values. On the contrary, perhaps the most impressive of contemporary social and intellectual movements is the increasing concern with such matters. The other day I picked up at random eleven journals, some general and some professional, from the tables of a club. Each had at least one article with a title like the following: "A Scientific Basis for Ethics," "How Can an International Morality be Created?" and "National Interest and Moral Principles in Foreign Policy." There is an almost compulsive quality about the present American need for explicitness and definition of private and national norms for conduct. There is increasing dissatisfaction with rules that pretend to supernatural authority and increasing recognition of the inadequacy of those that are merely hallowed by custom.

Even those who worship the idol of the solitary, ruthless titan seem to feel that egoism requires a moralistic justification. And American men and women who never enter a church except to participate in a rite of passage agree that common values are urgently necessary to a healthy society. They realize that the magnetism of Communism—at least outside the Soviet Union and its satellites—is that of a secular religion. To confused and frightened human beings of the twentieth century a "new synthesis"—a systematic, explicit, and emotionally toned system of values—speaks as strongly as the promised land of economic security. In accord with the logic of our American sentiments and, in part, on the basis of our more earthy experiences, the overwhelming majority of Americans reject Communism. But they long for a creed less partisan, less vague, and less anachronistic than that of most of their own political oratory.

Certainly the United States needs a good five-cent ideology far more than it needs a good five-cent cigar. In a wise and eloquent article (1949, pp. 530-531, 539), Robinson has written:

Our principal weakness today is not economic or military but ideological—not a matter of goods or guns, but of ideas. This is our chief weakness abroad, precisely because it is our chief weakness at home. It is not piecemeal answers that inspire men in "their finest hour"; it is a total conception of the good life. . . . In this situation, there is urgent need for philosophic reconstruction and renewal. . . . If this renewal can be brought about, our people will feel a new strength and a new sense of purpose and direction. This country can have again, in Europe, an even greater moral influence than it had a century and a half ago;

perhaps it can even extend that influence to Asia and Africa, where
Communism ought not to be the only accessible philosophy of change,
in societies that have got to be remade.

   This felt need for a positive, clearly defined national faith is
matched by gropings at a more personal level. At the end of
1946 Gordon Allport questioned 500 college men and women on
their attitudes toward religion. He reports (1948) that a bare
quarter were essentially orthodox in their adherence to such
items of Christian doctrine as the Incarnation and personal
immortality. More than half did not regard the system of faith
in which they were reared as adequate to their present needs.
On the other hand, only one in ten among women and two in
ten among men declared that they had no need for religion. A
majority of the war veterans among the group stated that the
war made them "more interested in the problems religion seeks
to solve." The prominence of religious books in the best-seller
lists of the last few years is also eloquent testimony.

   To a considerable extent this interest in religion and even in
churches must be understood in terms of one of the most serious
dilemmas of social life in the United States, that of social participation and of social identity. The individual does not have the
support of a primitive clan nor that of a European parish. The
American family, if not in a state of disorganization, is in the
throes of transition to a new form of organization—and this gives
little comfort to participants. The American takes part in a
range of compartmentalized and segmentalized social roles that
he rightly feels do not mesh into a harmonious unity. He is torn
by conflicts between obligations and interests involving those
with whom he works, his neighborhood, and the various associations he has joined. He often cannot vote or otherwise influence
the course of events in the locality where most of his working
hours are spent. Much of his interaction with others is impersonal
an even anonymous. When the butcher does not have to stop to
look at the meat and cut it but merely reaches for a package already prepared, there is not even an occasion for an interchange
of remarks on the weather. Interest groups like labor unions
have not grown to sufficient maturity to be satisfying functional
equivalents for the church. Shifting sexual attachments do not

provide for many a real answer to the American's hypertrophied desire for acceptance as a genuine person, for love and understanding.

One crucial dimension to the problem of social participation is that of women. Treatment of American women by American men and by the society as a whole is ambivalent, to say the least. Women are increasingly trained for skilled and professional careers but expected to assume household responsibilities for which they get a minimum of training. With smaller families and labor-saving devices in the home, the mother whose children are already in school all day has time on her hands. She is encouraged by advertisements to continue the glamorous role of courtship days, but her success-driven husband is seldom up to playing his part. He abdicates to her the total family participation in "culture," but she has sense enough to realize that he and the society generally treat this role with half-concealed amusement or contempt or regard it as a nice but peripheral luxury of middle-class life. Up to a point, this problem is being solved by increased entry into the occupational structure: about twenty-six out of every 100 workers today are women, as against fifteen in 1880; 5 per cent of doctors, dentists, and architects are now women. The part-time career for women who have finished child-bearing and whose children are of school age is a constructive solution for many. But discrimination against married women teachers and women in the professions exists, and a radical change in the attitudes and expectations of husbands must occur before this particular dilemma of participation is solved.

It all comes back to the matter of values, which is surely the most urgent question of the day. Unless some progress can be made along this line, we are crippled both internally and abroad. The Horatio Alger economic and achievement values that still have an important place in our formal and informal educational procedures undoubtedly embody a distinctively American view of the world, and few of us would want to see the convictions that effort counts and that something can be done disappear from the American scene. Yet we need a new set of success values that is better geared to economic and political realities. No social order is secure in which a high proportion of adults feels cheated of goals that they had been taught as youths were rightfully attainable by everyone who worked hard and intelligently. The disillusioned are the manpower reserve of demagogues and of all apostles of irrational social movements. The gap between the preached level of aspiration and that which is attainable on a mass level must be narrowed.

At least until our technology is revolutionized by atomic energy, unskilled workers are necessary. Immigration no longer supplies a constant flow of new manual laborers and domestic servants whose children can become skilled workers and *their* children white-collar professionals. To some extent a needed revision in our prestige categories is already occurring. There is evidence that the members of the highly paid trades are increasingly regarded as more "successful" than those in the lower white-collar jobs.

The main problem, however, is that of bringing to consciousness and communicability some of the underlying elements in our value system which, historically, have counterbalanced the tensely competitive pressures toward social mobility. From the outside these have had too little visibility in contrast to our "materialism" and "go-getter" philosophy. This is the real meaning of the expressions heard so often in the mouths of sincere but despairing American officials in Germany and Japan: "They don't really understand us. I guess you just can't talk about American democracy. I guess it just has to be lived and felt."

Certainly foreigners have found it far easier to discover the more superficial aspects of our way of life, and all except a few of the greatest, such as de Toqueville, have characterized us in these terms. Immigrants quickly absorb the external features of American life but are still emotionally conditioned to, for example, dependence on authority. Foreign nations also react primarily to the external in our ethos because we do not explain and synthesize our deeper values, except in a superficial way.

We do have values that are not bound up in materialism and the success system, but, under normal circumstances, we are ludicrously inarticulate about them. Battle-fatigue cases under psychotherapy were given "truth serum" so that they would feel free to talk uninhibitedly about their emotional difficulties. They not only did this but, to the surprise of the psychiatrists, set forth, eloquently and vehemently, their conception of the American creed. The experience of the last fifteen years indicates on the whole, I believe, that when educated people in the United States are hit by forces that require rethinking, they do rethink.

The conflict and competition between Christian sects has weakened the authority of all. Increased knowledge of the processes of the physical and biological worlds has engendered widespread scepticism of all doctrines based on authority and revelation rather than upon scientific investigation. The existence of contrasting value systems is now apparent to many citizens rather than to a handful of philosophers and anthropologists. Nor can contemporary man so easily dismiss these discrepancies as the aberrations of "ignorant savages" or the benighted ways of heathen who have never had the benefit of instruction in the one true Gospel. Thoughtful Christians have begun to question the underlying values of a civilization whose material achievements are unparalleled but which also produced the holocausts of Hiroshima and Nagasaki. As General Omar Bradley has remarked, "Ours is a world of nuclear giants and ethical infants." Confused moderns have come to look with new respect and even with longing at the apparent order and serenity of some of the simpler societies. As Elton Mayo has phrased it, "We have the goods, but they have the morale."

The most dramatic of all current conflicts in value systems is, of course, that between those of the United States and of the Soviet Union. Our age is hostile to nuances, and many European and Asiatic peoples do not like the choice between what seems to them the purposeless materialism and moral chaos of American culture and the equally or more abhorrent culture patterns of a brutal police state.

The crisis is intensified by the sheer rapidity of change. As Paul Valéry (1948, p. 143-144) has said:

Instead of playing an honest game of cards with destiny as in the past ... we find ourselves from now on in the position of a player who is shocked to discover that his partner's hand contains cards he has never seen before, and that the rules of the game are changed at every throw.

Yet people are loath to abandon accustomed values. In all the great cultural traditions values have been important precisely because they were stable, because people half-consciously or unconsciously felt they could rely on their values as representing the distilled essence of human experience. However, as Whitehead (1933, p. 117) has pointed out:

The whole of this tradition is warped by the vicious assumption that each generation will substantially live amid the conditions governing the lives of its fathers and will transmit those conditions to mould with equal force the lives of its children. We are living in the first period of human history for which this assumption is false.

Belief in God as revealer, judge, and punisher has unquestionably weakened in the whole Western world. An increasing number of men and women reluctantly accept death as annihilation, however much they may continue their formal participation in the Christian church as an institution. For millions and millions these powerful sanctions for conformance to established values have lost their effective force. The result is personal and social disorganization, individual unhappiness and human misery on a vast scale, with irrational political movements that both symbolize and add to these disasters.

People can, and many do, beat a frightened retreat to older orthodoxies. They can bear chaos as best they are able and wait for the miracle of a new religion to occur—this is what most of the prophets of doom seem to be telling us to do. Or they can at least try to use the scientific approach in this as in other realms of human behavior. Dewey has warned us that "a culture which permits science to destroy traditional values but which distrusts its power to create new ones, is destroying itself."

To me at least it is therefore apparent that science, and especially social science, must "put up or shut up" on this problem. Social science may as well resign itself to shallow descriptivism unless it can create the logical categories and the empirical methods and techniques necessary to deal with valuating behavior. Otherwise, explanation and prediction will be impossible, except at the levels of reflexive behavior, reactions under conditions of extreme physiological stress, and sheer statistical conformance to cultural pattern. For human beings do not respond to stimuli, or to stimulus situations, as machines respond to the pressing of a lever. It is never simply a question of a human organism and his environment (including other people). There is always a third factor, an intervening variable, which is unseen but ever present. This is the total apperceptive mass that each of us develops both as a result of our strictly personal experiences and by virtue of our participation in a specific society and in particular subgroups of that society. Thanks to the work of Warren S. McCulloch, Walter Pitts, and others, today we even know a good deal about the neurological basis of this apperceptive mass.

If human beings had shown themselves able to accept existence on a level like that of the other animals, I should be more willing to dismiss the problem of value with James Joyce's "I fear those big words that make us so unhappy." But it seems to be in human nature to crave an integrated and coherent system of values and to insist that it is part of man's experience as a creature of the world of nature that real values exist and can be discovered. Even the writings of the French existentialists document again and again the fact that the most disoriented human beings sense the significance of standards that go beyond mere physical survival. It is a fact of observation, part of the natural history of man, that the human being is so constituted that he needs not only personal goals but also goals that identify him both with particular groups and with humanity generally and that give a place in a large context to his purely personal goals.

The two most vast empirical generalizations that can be made about Homo sapiens are that he is a symbol-using animal and an evaluating animal. These generalizations are intimately related and they transcend all cultural differences. Always and every-where men say: "This is good and that is bad," "This is better and that is worse," "This is to be sought and that avoided," and "This is preferable to that." Such evaluation is not restricted to what is deemed beneficial or injurious in terms of survival and adjustment. All cultures have had their categorical imperatives that went beyond existence and pleasure. This fact is an astonishing one, if one can look at it all freshly, but one need not invoke the supernatural to explain it. Human life is a moral life because it is a social life.

Equally incorrect is the view that "science has nothing to do with values" and the moral nihilism inherent in the psychoanalytic, Marxian, and older anthropological standpoint. There is an alternative between dogmatism and anarchy. Ethical relativism correctly saw the diversity of actual moral codes among different peoples and quite rightly pointed to the scientific and logical flaws in metaphysical and theological ethics, but it quite wrongly concluded that there were no pan-human values and that no code was worth defending.

20 INDIAN AMERICANS

IN A WHITE MAN'S

WORLD

A "CULTURE" in the technical anthropological sense, is the distinctive, total way in which a group of human beings habitually live together. Each culture is a special pattern of selections.

The great variety of customs from which selection can be made permits many possible combinations, with differing points of emphasis. The way a culture is "put together" as a whole is just as important as its specific constituent customs taken singly. One can never understand an alien way of life by making a mere inventory of details, although this may be useful as a first step in the process.

The last 100 years have seen more attempts at purposeful culture change on a vaster scale than ever before in history. Many of these have been noble in intent: Christian missions, idealistic efforts on the part of laymen to introduce Western

1955d Reprinted by permission of the publishers from Clyde Kluckhohn, "Indian Americans in a White Man's World: a Study of Indian American Values and Culture Change," *Advance* (Congregational Christian Journal), Vol. 147, pp. 13-15.

medicine, technology, and standards of living in other parts of the world. Other gigantic schemes for planned culture change cannot be characterized as noble, even in intent: Fascism, Naziism, and Communism. In all cases, however, no matter what the motive, some of the results have been regrettable from almost any point of view.

Well-informed people have now come to realize that, in part at least, these unforeseen and unintended consequences have come about through failure to comprehend the cultures that were being made to change. One cannot start with a clean slate—ever —so far as other than newborn human beings are concerned. One may not like what he finds already there, but he has to take account of it nevertheless.

There are sound and practical reasons for "respecting the native culture." This does not involve a sentimental or romantic exaggeration of its virtues. It does not imply a moral acceptance of its character. The first argument for such permissiveness is based on the elementary scientific principle that one never tries to alter any system of any sort until he can discern and then describe it.

A second reason for this permissive approach is found in the "wholeness" of cultures. If those who intervene to change a culture in some of its particular aspects do not comprehend the dynamic interrelation of all its parts, they may breed confusion so disastrous as to offset every beneficent change they have tried to bring about.

In all cultures men are constantly talking and arguing about what is true and good, what is better and worse, what is right and wrong. While no individuals and no tribes or nations unqualifiedly live up to their own abstract standards that transcend all times and situations and human impulses, there is abundant evidence to support the assertion that values not only count as ultimate goals in human life but directly influence human conduct and everyday existence.

Anthropologists are recognizing more and more that if the formative basis of culture is selectivity, the essence of that patterned selectivity resides in the value structure and there alone. Values are in effect more rather than less powerful because ordinary people under ordinary circumstances are not in the habit of verbalizing them either articulately or adequately. For if one but observes with a modicum of care how consistent people are on the whole in their "choice" behavior, he will see how clearly there stand out in these choices from day to day the central pervasive strands that bind a culture together in its own unique fashion and manner.

This is especially true under conditions of stress and at the extremes of social or individual tension. If, for example, one knows what people will die for or in what order they will sacrifice their values and possessions, he knows the essence of their cultural allegiance.

These observations apply to the Indian Americans with particular force. Indian Americans are a proud people who resent any derogation, whether direct or indirect, of their ancient life-ways. They respond with trust and warmth, on the other hand—although perhaps only gradually and circumspectly because of suspicions built up over many years—to those who show a genuine interest in their cultures. Nor need such interest indicate acceptance. It does help, however, if the visiting outsider thinks and acts upon the assumption—which can be accepted as a factually reasonable one—that there must be something "good" as well as "interesting" in every culture.

Most Indian American groups require ample time for a steady but sympathetically guided process of transition. I do not in the least agree with what I call "the zoological park philosophy for Indian Americans": that which would keep them shut up on reservations "with all their quaint customs" and "preserve" their cultures at all cost. This is not only rank and immorally romantic sentimentality; it is also an obvious impossibility.

The matter of timing, I repeat, is crucial. These so-called aborigines must not be pushed too fast toward Christianity, nor toward "education," nor toward improved public health practices, nor toward anything else of any sort. A forced pace may indeed bring quick results, but the ultimate cost is tremendous.

Of course, they should know how to read and write the English language. Yet if this is made too important a goal *per se*, an objective to be attained at the price of a violent break with everything in the past, the result is bound to be disruptive, since the needful continuity of life and its relationships will have been destroyed.

Indian Americans frequently acquire our technology (including our verbiage) without having either absorbed or even become aware of our values, which put certain curbs upon our love of gadgets, our "materialism." Their own cultures having been largely demolished, however, they do not integrate themselves with ours save on the most mechanistic levels. They gain from us only the externals, the "objective" parts of our culture, without its total fabric. Hence, in effect, they have for a time at least no culture at all. And a people without a culture is in the same desperately isolated straits as an individual who has lost his memory.

While such generalizations apply to the Indian Americans as a whole, there are cultural differences within the total group of which account needs to be taken. There are many Indian American cultures more or less similar to each other. Each of these has a value system of its own, partly quite distinctive and unique, partly a repetition and a rephrasing of value judgments that are either humanly universal or are at any rate characteristically Indian American.

An instance of this cultural phenomenon may help to clarify the discussion. Most Indian Americans rebel, whether consciously or unconsciously, at the white man's "individualism," though they themselves have had their own kind of "individualism." Their culture made room for considerable autonomy so far as each personality was concerned. Yet the individual carried on his existence within an extensive network of formalized personal relationships that reached out beyond the biological family into the framework of his community or tribe. Herein lay his psychological security, for he could express and fulfill himself with confidence in this particular setting. That is why life in the wider society or in the artificially created environment of school or mission has been so disrupting and demoralizing to Indian Americans. Outside their limited but natural orbit, they are quite literally "lost."

Besides the cultural variations among these people, especially in the realm of values, there are almost as many different situations and conditions as there are tribes. One group may be relatively prosperous while another lives in chronic destitution. Yet another may be experiencing radical economic changes for the first time within tribal memory. This tribe has felt a comparatively gentle pressure from the whites, but that one has been exploited, betrayed, despoiled—and is bitterly aware of it.

Because of all these variegations, both cultural and economic, and because of conditions brought about by policies in the past, the missionary or educator or physician or government employee who works among Indian Americans today has an extraordinarily sensitive reconnaissance to make, a very demanding calculus to perform. He must inquire into cultural attitudes and practices, into both the ancient and the prevailing value structures, into the present situation and into historical backgrounds. He has but few general rules to guide him and some specific cautions to save him from serious mistakes. The task requires intelligence, knowledge, industry, and dedication.

Let me conclude with a "case history" from the Indian people whom I best know and love—the Navahos. The account will be necessarily brief; yet, by focusing upon a single tribe, it may be possible to make what has been discussed in general terms appear considerably more graphic.

Personal and social disorganization is presently rampant among the Navaho people. This is due partly to certain concrete facts. The Navaho country is heavily overpopulated and the range is overgrazed. Few Navahos have the occupational skills to compete with white people.

But that is not the worst of it. Navaho culture is becoming an ugly patchwork of meaningless and unrelated pieces, whereas it was once a finely patterned mosaic. This is due primarily and chiefly to the disintegrative power of alien ideas and values. The Navahos recognize and respect the strength of the dominant American culture. Many of them agree unreservedly that their tribe's only hope of salvation rests in mastering the language and way of life of the larger society.

Yet when the qualities and traits of another culture are learned superficially and are picked up piecemeal, while the underlying concepts and values of that culture remain unabsorbed, the learners feel uncomfortable. They sense the lack of fitness in their relationships, they feel that they do not belong, and they miss that moral support that is needed if they are to have a real part in any American life-way. Being introduced, for instance, to the external side of the white man's individualism without being shown and taught the inner checks and balances that accompany it, the Navahos are plunged into confusion.

The substitution of individually paid labor for collectively organized reciprocal services is not in itself a thing to be deplored. But unless there is a commensurate growth of individual responsibility to replace the lost sense of collective interdependence, the entire structure of cultural values is distorted, emotional maladjustments ensue, and personal relationships are increasingly demoralized. A widespread resort to escape mechanisms, especially to alcohol, is symptomatic of the resulting social friction and moral decay. For when human groups with different cultures and social structures and with value systems that differ in important respects are out of internal sympathy with each other, everything goes to pieces. The linkage is so fundamental that when a social organization can no longer hold itself together, morality disintegrates at the same time.

The influence of white American ideas and values is, of course, not entirely a matter of choice on the part of the Navahos themselves. They are torn willy-nilly between their own former standards and those that are urged if not actually thrust upon them by teachers, missionaries, and others from outside their tribes. Some of these outsiders have conscientiously endeavored to take account of individual Navaho customs and even of the external patterns of Navaho culture. But when, as too often has happened, no account of underlying values has been taken, the outcome is pronounced deplorable by Navahos and whites alike.

An appreciable number of Navahos are so confused by the conflict between the precepts of their elders and the teachings of their white preceptors that they tend to set aside the whole problem of morality (in the widest sense) as either meaningless or insoluble. Their only guide to behavior, for longer or shorter periods in their lives, is that of pure expediency in meeting the exigencies of each immediate situation. With the loss of predictability in social behavior and of dependability in personal relations, the breakdown of satisfactory social life is well along its

way, while the absence of generally accepted values among individual members of the tribe leads to moral chaos. This applies
equally to the Navahos and to other Indian Americans.

Orderly and creative group life prevails only so long as an
overwhelming majority of individuals find enough satisfaction
in socially approved goals and in culturally acceptable means for
their attainment to make up for the constraints that group life
imposes upon uninhibited response to impulse.

There is much in every way of life that to an outsider appears
more or less chaotic. But if the behavior patterns on the whole
make sense to the participants in the light of their own values,
an adequate measure of stability is guaranteed. Disorder and
amorality take over only when the participants begin to feel
that the ends and means of their culture are no longer unified
in an authoritative value system.

Certain major Navaho value premises are essentially incom-
patible with certain major value premises of our American
culture. If those who propose to alter Navaho culture were
more clearly aware of and could make more explicit to the
Navaho exactly what these basic divergencies really are and what
they actually entail, the transition would at all events be eased. It
may be, however, that in the long run a resolution of the difficulty might better be sought by reference to a scale of cultural
value assumptions that transcends the present level of both
cultures—one that, from the broadly human standpoint, is both
more ultimate and more nearly universal. To see that peoples all
over the world, speaking different languages (in both the literal
and figurative sense), actually have and are aware of the selfsame
needs and that they value the same fundamental objects and objectives, is to prove that one has seen beneath the superficial
cultural veneer into the very heart of the human problem.

21 THE FIELD

OF HIGHER EDUCATION

IN THE SOUTHWEST

THERE ARE PERHAPS two outstanding national traditions of university education in the modern world. The German tradition has looked mainly to the enrichment of the student's mind with information and to the accumulation of published knowledge. The English has tended to regard study in a university as the final step in that formuation of the character that is the primary end of the whole British educational system: the universities of Cambridge and Oxford were training schools for incorruptible public servants whose minds, if not too well informed, were balanced and disciplined. American practice has had regard for both of these conceptions of higher education. Such universities as Johns Hopkins and Columbia have followed, on the whole, the German pattern, which was also the model for almost all graduate study in the United States. The liberal-college ideal, on the other hand, has its roots in the English tradition. Princeton under Wilson and Amherst under

1937 Reprinted by permission of the publishers from Clyde Kluckhohn, "The Field of Higher Education in the Southwest," *New Mexico Quarterly*, Vol. 7, pp. 23-30.

Meiklejohn exalted college education as the preparation for a rich life that would be of value to society. Either of these conceptions, pushed too far, has results that would be almost universally regarded as undesirable. We are all aware of the absurdities to which the Ph.D. system sometimes lends its name and countenance. At its worst, the English method promotes an unthinking, inflexible preservation of the existing order of society. André Maurois makes an Englishman say, "Nous n'allons pas au collège pour nous instruire mais pour nous imprégner des préjugés de notre classe sans lesquels nous serons dangereux et malheurex."

But I think we might all agree that any system of higher education would ideally have regard for some elements at least of both these conceptions of education. Hence it will be convenient to discuss the field of higher education in the Southwest with reference to these two categories. Most of what I say will be directly relevant to the University of New Mexico, for that is the educational institution with which I am familiar, but most of it will also, I think, be applicable, with adjustments, to other colleges and universities in the region.

As to research and training for research, any realistic discussion must start from the premise that the universities and colleges of the Southwest will be obliged to operate on relatively restricted budgets. The revenues from taxation are small indeed compared to the areas involved, and there is small prospect that they could be measurably increased for some time to come. Nor will many of the sons and daughters of the citizens of these states be able to pay more than very moderate tuition fees. Therefore, any attempt to take the great state universities of California, Michigan, or Wisconsin as models to be imitated slavishly foredooms the higher educational institutions of the Southwest to inferiority. The University of New Mexico, for example, will never (at least during the next generation) be able to provide the expensive facilities for research in *all* branches of physical and biological science that the more thickly populated, wealthier states have supplied. Adequate provision for all the staples of the undergraduate general grocery must be made (and to a very considerable extent already has been). Likewise, the states of the Southwest must eventually, I think, establish and maintain at a decent standard the basic professional schools: law, medicine, dentistry. But it must be recognized at the outset that the fancy intellectual foods of that academic delicatessen, the graduate school, can be supplied only in very limited quantities if the quality of the product is to be assured. Emulation of the graduate schools of the large state universities can only result in emasculation of the whole program of graduate training and research.

If, however, available resources are concentrated upon the exploitation of the advantages that sheer geographical location gives certain fields of study, the outlook is infinitely more promising. Let the higher educational institutions of the Southwestern states be content to build up the greater number of departments of instruction only to the point needed for proper undergraduate instruction and for such graduate instruction leading to the master's degree as is called for by the needs of the teachers of the state. They will then (and only then, I feel sure) be able to develop some few departments that will have real distinction as agencies for the advance of knowledge. In four fields the situation of the University of New Mexico gives it some possibilities that cannot be matched outside the Southwest. These, if I may be so presumptuous as to list them, are anthropology, Southwestern history, Spanish language and literature, and bilingual education. There are three additional fields that, it would seem to me, have certain possibilities that may be equaled but are seldom excelled elsewhere: art, plant and animal ecology, and geology. Naturally, there are other more specific opportunities. For instance, any aspect of the natural resources or environment of New Mexico can be studied more efficiently and with less expense by someone living in New Mexico than by someone teaching nine months a year in New York City. But I think, primarily, of more general problems.

Let me illustrate in the concrete from one discipline, and perhaps I may be pardoned if I choose my own. I do not mean simply that New Mexico is a better place than Wisconsin to study Southwestern archaeology. That I take to be self-evident. Rather, I am driving at the fact that New Mexico is ideally located for a unified attack upon the central problems of human behavior from an anthropological point of view and with anthropological techniques. There are coherent nonliterate cultures that are still

going concerns. But these are not merely splendid islands in a
sea of ignorance. There is historical documentation for many of
them for nearly 400 years. The material cultures of the societies
from which they developed remain for study. The bones of the
makers of these artifacts can be measured and observed, blood
types can sometimes be determined, and the conclusions compared and contrasted with our knowledge of the human biology
of the modern populations. Thanks to the tree-ring method, a
comparatively full and exact record of the environmental vicissitudes through which these cultures passed is being built up. The
clash of cultures and the effects of different ethnic groups upon
one another can be observed in fullest detail; the opportunities
for the investigation of this highly important cultural process are
magnificent. And so data on the archaeology, biological anthropology, social anthropology, climatology, and acculturation of
Southwestern cultures are all available. Seldom has the anthropologist had so full a record over so long a time. In many anthropological investigations the historical variable is unknowable,
and the environmental is most often unknowable in such time
depth. In many archaeological studies we never hope to obtain
any knowledge of the dynamics of societies highly similar to
those responsible for the technological products remaining.

To be sure, this highly favorable concentration of circumstances, this approximation to the laboratory controls of other
sciences, can be exploited by research organizations outside the
Southwest. But the situation can be utilized with least expense,
with least difficulty, and very possibly with greatest prospect
of success by an institution in the area whose investigators are
fully familiar with all manner of local conditions and who can
study the living cultures at all seasons of the year. In any case,
I wish more particularly to draw attention to the educational
potentialities of the set-up. A student at Columbia or at Harvard
may well study anthropology for a number of years before he
ever sees or talks to a member of a nonliterate culture. His
knowledge is vicarious and not experiential and has all the unsatisfactory qualities of such knowledge. At New Mexico I used
to take my classes before breakfast to Isleta Pueblo to see
ceremonies, and, whatever other limitations they may have had,
my better students were quite free from the naïveté and crudity

of belief about the behavior and thought of nonliterates that is almost characteristic of many students of anthropology in eastern universities. The point is that New Mexico is a natural laboratory for the study of man such as no amount of money could produce. The relative sparseness of population, slowness of acculturation, and comparative stability of physical environment tend to prevent the investigator and student from morassing themselves in the bog of subjectivism that is the peril of hideously complicated interrelationships.

And so I maintain that, in so far as higher education in the Southwest is going to contribute significantly to the general stream of scholarship, it must do so through the medium of educational institutions that are frankly "regional" in their outlook and policy, that valiantly eschew every endeavor to make them conform to a more general pattern of which they could, in any case, only become fourth-rate imitations. To a considerable extent, I am, of course, only describing what has already been either attained or contemplated at the University of New Mexico.

If Southwestern universities are not only to contribute to productive scholarship but also to form character and aid their students to better living, they must indeed embody the distinctive features and vitality of the Southwest. In respect of the second as well as of the first motivation of higher education, these colleges and universities must unashamedly make themselves regional universities. Another reason why the Southwest is a paradise to the anthropologist is that there one finds four great cultural traditions (the Pueblo Indian, the Spanish-American, the pioneer Anglo-American, and the contemporary Anglo-American) still in vigor, still quickening daily experience by contrast. Now I am not one of those who advocates, in Mr. Ferguson's phrase, "crawling back into the womb of the cultural past." The full integrity of the first three cultures has gone, and it is idle to try to revivify them. But I am concerned that certain elements in each should become incorporated into the emergent composite Southwestern culture. Nor should one forget the Navaho and the Apache.

It is one thing to accept certain trends in the culture in which one lives. It is quite another, I feel, to submit supinely to every ripple of the cultural wave. The "Americanization"—or, more pointedly, the standardization—of culture in the Southwest is, to a degree, inevitable. Granted. But need it become altogether an extension of that gray amphictyony of manners, beliefs, and material culture that stretches (with some interruptions and enlivenments) from Ohio to Colorado? The relative sameness of those regions may be ascribed in part to the circumstance that they were settled by people who had a certain homogeneity of tradition, and that the cultures already existent in these areas were insufficiently developed to produce much cross-fertilization (with attendant "hybrid vigor"). But the astonishing tenacity of Pueblo Indian culture and the partially successful resistance of Spanish-American life to the ruthless onslaught of "middle-westernism" suggest that these upstanding cultures have values that merit intensive study on the part of anyone who is to live in the region to which they are highly specialized adaptations.

As a kind of more radical regionalism in higher education than has yet been applied, I should like to suggest that no person should be permitted to take a degree from the University of New Mexico who has not mastered the elements, at least, of the Spanish language and acquired some knowledge of the Indian cultures of the Southwest. In the choice of new members of the faculty (for whatever department), I submit that, other things being equal, preference should be given to applicants familiar with Spanish. Similarly, present members of the faculty should be encouraged and assisted to study Spanish. Finally, I should like to see some of the larger courses in the University offered in English and in Spanish in alternate years. This would be advantageous both to students whose first language was Spanish and to Anglo students who wished real practice in the use of Spanish. Certainly, in all candor, it seems to me inexcusable that at present teachers are allowed to go out from the College of Education into communities primarily Spanish-speaking without a knowledge of even the rudiments of Spanish. In such ways the University of New Mexico could gradually acquire that truly bilingual character that is appropriate alike to its historical and social heritage and to its present-day function in the state. Nor, in view of the history of the province of Quebec, can such a view be condemned as impracticable sentimentalism.

Many other concrete proposals to this general end could be formulated, but I have already passed beyond the ten minutes in which souls can be saved. In sum, I affirm that higher education in the Southwest will best subserve both its principal functions in proportion as it becomes regionally differentiated. Thus will higher education best reveal what the region and its cultures have to teach humanity. Thus, also, by preserving and institutionalizing one of the few composite American cultures that is rooted deep in the buried past of this continent's peculiar story, will higher education in the Southwest enable young men and women of the Southwest to form their characters under the influence of a tradition that has continuity, harmony, and integrity (rare qualities in the modern world). And, of course, the two ends are ideally but one. The nuclear aim is to liberate the mind so that it can perceive unobvious connections between things. Where better than in the stirring natural environment of the Southwest (which warns the thinking man against the specious and spurs him away from the merely acceptant attitude) can—if the total situation be envisaged both realistically and imaginatively—the scholar and the student seek the range of the human spirit and its limits. May the higher educational institutions in the Southwest lead the way in forsaking the frustrating educational haplology of the modern world, rededicating themselves to the enduring quest of all true scholars and true students, described so long ago by Lucretius:

> Ergo vivida vis animi pervicit et extra
> Processit longe flammantia moenia mundi
> Atque omne immensum peragravit mente animoque,
> Udne refert nobis victor quid possit oriri,
> Quid nequeat.

22 SOME NOTES

ON NAVAHO DREAMS

W HEN I BEGAN SERIOUS field work among the
Navaho and Pueblo Indians, my position on
psychoanalysis was a mixed one. I had been
analyzed and was thoroughly convinced that Freudian psychology
was the only dynamic depth psychology of much importance.
I had also been influenced by the writings of psychoanalysis on
anthropological matters. On the other hand, I tended to believe
that psychoanalysis was strongly culture-bound. I was persuaded,
for example, that Malinowski's interpretation of the Oedipal
situation in the Trobriands was substantially correct.

I still believe that some of the cautions uttered by Boas and
others on the possible extravagances of interpretations in terms
of universal symbolism, completely or largely divorced from
minute examination of cultural context, are sound. But the facts

1951c Reprinted by permission of the publishers from Clyde Kluckhohn
and William Morgan, "Some Notes on Navaho Dreams," in *Psychoanalysis and Culture,* edited by G. B. Wilbur and Warner Muensterberger. New York, International Universities Press, pp. 120-131.

uncovered in my own field work and that of my collaborators have forced me to the conclusion that Freud and other psycho-analysts have depicted with astonishing correctness many central themes in motivational life that are universal. The styles of expression of these themes and much of the manifest content are culturally determined, but the underlying psychologic drama transcends cultural difference.

This should not be too surprising—except to an anthropologist overindoctrinated with the theory of cultural relativity—for many of the inescapable givens of human life are also universal. Human anatomy and human physiology are, in the large, about the same the world over. There are two sexes with palpably visible differences in external genitalia and secondary sexual characteristics. All human infants, regardless of culture, know the psychological experience of helplessness and dependency. Situations making for competition for the affection of one or both parents, for sibling rivalry, can be to some extent channeled this way or that way by a culture, but they cannot be eliminated, given the universality of family life. The trouble has been—because of a series of accidents of intellectual and political history—that the anthropologist for two generations has been obsessed with the differences among peoples, neglecting the equally real similarities upon which the "universal culture pattern" as well as the psychological uniformities are clearly built.

Having made this general "confession of faith," I wish to proceed to some concrete material. After the termination of my analysis in Vienna, I taught for two years at the University of New Mexico. During this period I worked at intervals with some Navaho families living about twenty miles from Gallup, New Mexico, not far from the Santa Fe railroad. The individuals in question had previously been informants of Dr. William Morgan, with whom I had had extensive contacts. His widow, Mrs. Christiana Morgan, a psychologist like her husband, has kindly made available to me his unpublished field notes, and I have combined his data with my own. Both of us worked on dreams, among other things, and since both of us were psychoanalytically oriented, we endeavored to obtain associations. The anthropological field method was essentially that of participant observation: we lived with and among these people on a friendly basis;

we took trips with them and participated in many aspects of their life in an informal way, more often than not taking notes in their presence. I had known most of them for some years prior to my anthropological training, so that the relationship was predominantly personal rather than that of ethnologist-informant. Most of the group were rather highly acculturated and English-speaking. I used some Navaho with them, but most of the data obtained by both Dr. Morgan and myself came directly in English.

The materials presented come from a larger body of materials (dreams, brief life histories, folklore, observational details) on a family of five persons. The mother (Jennie) was close to thirty years of age and had attended a Mission school (she had been converted to Christianity by a mystical experience). She had a tyrannical superego, expressed a great deal of hostility, and was even more cruel to animals than most Navahos and very jealous of her husband. Her eldest daughter (Rose) was the child of her first husband, a Navaho; Rose at this time was ten and eleven years old and in the fourth and fifth grades at a nearby Mission school. The second daughter (Mamie) was the child of Jennie's second husband, a Paiute Indian; she was seven and eight during this period and also in the Mission school. The third child (Junior) was the son of Jennie's current husband (Bob) and was five and six. Bob was two years younger than his wife, tall and handsome, a persistent and successful seducer. He drank a great deal, being usually sullen and stubborn then, in contrast to his usual good humor. He appeared far less anxious than his wife, less often annoyed with the three children; he participated enthusiastically in Navaho ceremonials (which his wife theoretically rejected) and enjoyed the simplest joke.

I. Jennie

The first fairly systematic interviews with Jennie consisted in an attempt to get her life story and discussions of child-training practices and bits of folklore. For the most part she talked as she wove. She was pleasant but reserved at first. Gradually she spoke more freely and with fewer intervals of silence. Eventually she began to volunteer material and seemed to tell some of her stories with genuine zest. Dream material came from the eighth and succeeding interviews.

She grew up near Flagstaff. Her father died when she was a small child. She attended a day school near her home, and then went to school in California for six years. She met her first husband there, returned to the Reservation with him, deserted him for her Paiute husband, and left him after about a year for Bob, her present husband. Her second child (a daughter) by her first husband died after she had married Bob. She almost never laughed, refused to associate with other women, and expressed open hatred of Bob's relatives.

DREAM 1

After my little girl died, I dreamed I was sleeping and a little girl just like her came into the hogan and she wore earrings, but my little girl didn't have earrings and she came over to me and she knew me and she was good to me and I had a noise like an automobile in my head. [Did you have a headache too?] No. And this little girl was kind to me. She didn't speak to me and she only laid her head on my head. And then there was that noise in my head and I tried to speak to her but I couldn't. Then after a while the little girl walked out and went away.

Associations. The Navahos, they don't have a story about heaven and they are afraid of dead people, but I don't believe that. I went to see my little girl when she was dead and I wasn't afraid. I believe she is still alive and is happy where there is no misery like here, and someday we will all live together again. Well, I think there is someone who puts these ideas into everyone's head so they won't worry. Someone sends those ideas so they will know the dead people are living again. I thought that way when I hear those songs like "Nearer My God to Thee." [You believe your little girl is alive since you heard that singing?] Yes, I think they live and sing like that.

Once I dreamed we were in that hogan and there were some bullets lying close to the wall on the south side of the hogan and the children built a fire too near them and they began shooting. We were outside and we could hear the bullets in the air, and we ran a long ways off and we came to a house like the trader's and the bricks were broken by the bullets, and we ran away inside and as far through it as we could go.

[Was Bob there?] No.

[Were those Bob's bullets?] Yes, they were his.

Interpretation. The most plausible latent meaning, partially confirmed by material to be presented shortly, is that her relationship to her children by her earlier marriage is threatened by Bob, specifically Bob's phallus (bullets). Jennie had internalized Christian norms with respect to the sanctity of marriage and family life. In these terms she evidenced guilt on many occasions over her living with three men in succession (the last two without benefit of clergy). There was some friction with her husband over the children by her earlier marriages. On this occasion she jumped spontaneously and rapidly from the theme of reunion with her dead child to the story of the bullets. "We" —in the next to last sentence of the associations—presumably (from context) means the dreamer and her children; they are fleeing from Bob (his bullet-phallus): a good and wanted relationship is menaced.

One could also, of course, make something of that part of the content of the dream that is wish fulfillment (return of the dead child to life). This would, however, repeat only what is familiar in psychoanalytic literature on animistic beliefs, the omnipotence of thought, and the like.

Various comments on manifest content as it relates to Navaho culture and to the culture-conflict situation in which Jennie was placed might be made of this and succeeding dreams, but my emphasis here is deliberately upon the psychoanalytic aspect. I shall only note that the reference to "a noise like an automobile in my head" would lead a careful investigator to a whole corpus of Navaho belief about warning noises. This—and later points that there is not space to bring out—confirm Róheim's (1947, p. 89) claim that dream materials will "reveal ethnological data that might otherwise escape notice."

DREAM 2

And one time I dreamed we were sleeping. And it was last spring when I was sick. And I dreamed something black and round came toward our hogan. And it came into the hogan and sat on my chest and it was heavy and I couldn't breathe and I tried to scream but I couldn't and then I woke up.

Associations. The Navahos have that kind of dream and they think it is an evil spirit. I don't know what it looked like; it wasn't like a person. [Did you have a sing?] No. I never had a sing. I don't have those. [You had one once to protect yourself, didn't you?] No, that wasn't a sing. We only took some medicine. Maybe I had one when I was a little girl. I don't know. Bob's sister wants me to have a sing for my sore eyes, but I don't believe those things.

Interpretation. This dream was told immediately after the associations to Dream 1. It is probably significant that Bob is (through his sister) more or less explicitly repudiated. (Jennie was living with and near her husband's people in a culture that favors matrilocal residence; she was in almost constant conflict with his family). The primary latent content of Dream 2 would appear to be resentment of intercourse, fear of intercourse, or guilt over intercourse. In other words, the deeper meaning is very similar to that of Dream 1. There is also, perhaps, a suggestion of the psychology of a helpless frustrated child.

DREAM 3

I used to have a dream lots of times and I thought I was walking in a garden and there were lots of beautiful flowers and there were roses as high as that gas tank. And there were lots of squash and melons and fruits. And I went everywhere looking for the very best flowers and ripest melons.

Associations. [Did you find them or did you look and look?] I picked some. And sometimes I dreamed we were on a train and we went by beautiful blue mountains and when we came home we remembered those hills and mountains. Once I dreamed I was walking along in a valley and there was lots of corn and flowers and I came to my aunt's hogan.

Interpretation. In part, the pattern of this dream is the converse of Dream 1. There the child comes to the mother (dreamer). Here the child (dreamer) goes to the mother ("aunt"="mother" according to Navaho kinship terminology).

This dream reflects again a stressing of the mother-child relationship. But there is other symbolism here. The flowers and melons may be equated with phallus and testes (note the height of the roses). The picking of the flowers may represent castration or hostility activity on the part of the dreamer—which fits well with her actual behavior. It may even be that the dreamer is here in a masculine role, with the walk into the valley equaling insertion. Does an unconscious homosexual attachment to the mother ("aunt") link up with the negative attitudes toward intercourse with her husband suggested for Dreams 1 and 2?

II. Rose (Older Daughter)

This child was in the Mission school and much influenced by Christianity.

DREAM 1

Something with red eyes of fire came into the hogan last night. We were all in a summer hogan. Some boy threw a ball at this thing and it ran into the hogan. I was frightened and they woke me up.

Associations. All I could see were its red eyes of fire, and I didn't know whether it was a man or an animal. It pulled the covers off everyone. Then I woke up.

Interpretation. In general pattern this resembles Dream 2 of the mother. "Something with red eyes of fire" and "something black and round" are both culturally defined as ghosts. These are both typical Navaho anxiety dreams. Presumably we have the superego or guilt component manifesting itself.

DREAM 2

Bob [stepfather] had been to the store and brought me some candy. It was just before supper and he would not let me eat it. He said "get me a basin of water." I did and went outside. As I was coming back in, he did not see me and threw the dirty water over me. I laughed and so did he.

Associations. He [stepfather] is always joking and teasing me. But yesterday he scolded me about something.

Interpretation. The day residue of this dream is probably the conflict with the stepfather over discipline. Although Bob interfered little with his stepchildren, they resented his disciplining them at all. The latent content of the dream is surely that of intercourse with the stepfather (water equaling the seminal fluid). Candy may represent the gift which a Navaho man ordinarily makes in payment for sexual favors. Since this dream was told immediately after Dream 1, it may be conjectured that the ghost who pulls the covers off people and threatens in the hogan at night is also the disguised stepfather.

DREAM 3

We were living in a section house, and next door was a white family. And the screen door was open, and I went in and climbed into the cupboard, and my mother came in and rolled under the bed. My little brother got into the bedclothes, and my sister Mamie ran from the back of the house, and a bear came in the door. Bob was behind the door, and there was a strap hanging there. He took it and hit the bear on the nose and the bear ran out.

Associations. The white people caught the bear and put it back in its cage.

[Have you ever seen a bear?] No, but I have seen pictures.

I wanted to go to the cage and the bear almost bit me. Then I woke up.

Interpretation. There seems a clear preoccupation with the primal scene: dreamer entering into cupboard; small brother into bedclothes; mother rolling under bed; aggression of father and bear. Less clear to me is the relation of stepfather and bear. Is the bear simply a reduplication of the father? Or is he a lover of the mother, threatening such stability as the family has? Or does the bear represent the bad father who wants to sleep with the mother, while Bob in the dream is the kind parent who brings

candy to his little stepdaughter? (This dream was told immediately after Dream 2.) Is the bear who almost bites Rose the
threatened punishment for her unconscious fantasies of sexual
union with her stepfather? Do the whites who put the bear
back in the cage stand for the missionaries who forbid (or protect
from) intercourse with a stepfather—which is a permitted and
fairly frequent pattern in aboriginal Navaho culture?

This much seems certain: there are primal scene and Oedipal
elements in this dream.

DREAM 4

I sold a white rug for ninety-five cents and bought flour and baking
powder and lots of things and some candy. I went home to give candy
to Mamie [younger sister], and it wasn't there. I must have dropped
it and a Mexican boy took it. I sent Mamie after it, and she said the
Mexican boy had it. She was going to buy some with her pennies. I
have her twenty-five cents. She bought mixed candies, and she put
them in a big cup of water. Then she threw them away and cried. She
was little and didn't know about candy and she wanted them.

Associations. The Mexican boy was like Junior [younger brother].
Junior picked up the candy, and his mother told him not to eat them.
He ate a lot and then he took a piece of meat and all his front teeth
stuck in it. He was going to put his teeth back, but he didn't want his
mother to know because she would know he had eaten the candy. He
was crying.

Interpretation. There is a great deal of content here. The
dominant latent theme is that of sibling rivalry, though there
seems to be an element of identification with the mother also
(caring for younger children, applying mother's standards to
them, etc.). This note of identification with the mother recurs
in many of Rose's dreams not published here. The ambivalence
expressed toward the sister is less strong—presumably because
of a secondary identification with her. The younger brother is
castrated, and the castration is phrased in *vagina dentata* terms
(well known in Navaho mythology). Note that in the associations Rose says first that the Mexican boy was "like" her brother.

In the next sentence she immediately and spontaneously dropped the analogy and spoke directly of her brother by name.

In a number of other dreams strong hostility to Junior (often with castration symbolism) is expressed, followed by restitution. One example will serve:

A giant man bigger than Bob came to the store and he bought a big watermelon and gave it to Junior and he took it over there on a hill and he made a hole in it and he ate all the watermelon and he made it into a house and he made chairs and tables and he worked all day. And then Bob came home and he went up to see it and he rolled down the hill and it rolled way over there and onto the roof of a freight train and it was carried to Gallup and there it fell off and broke into pieces. Junior couldn't find his house, and he cried and then the giant man came back from Gallup and gave Junior a muskmelon.

Another dream involving her younger brother appears to be a brother-sister incest dream.

III. Mamie (Younger Daughter)

DREAM 1

I was at a summer hogan. A wolf came up. I grabbed his ear and stretched out his neck a long ways. I threw him on the ground, and he was dead.

Associations. The neighbors have a white dog that looks like a white wolf. One time I dreamed about that dog too. Another girl and me walked up into the woods and sat under a tree. That white dog came up after us. I ran home and I was scared and then I woke up.

Interpretation. This looks like an Oedipal theme, with the dream told in the associations being somewhat the converse of Dream 1. "Stretching out his neck a long ways" may be interpreted as an unconscious fantasy of playing with the father's erect penis. There is conceivably an implication of penis envy. The father is killed in the end.

DREAM 2

I dreamed there was a little boy [gesture indicating about eight inches high] and he had shoes on as long as that [about four feet]. He could hardly step. And there was a big man, and he had the biggest feet in the world but his shoes were too small. I said to the little boy "let me try on your shoes." Then I took them away from him.

Associations. One time I was at our hogan and it rained. I went out with Bob's shoes which were too big for me and I had to cross a mud puddle, and my shoes fell off and stuck in the mud and I didn't know what to do. My stockings were all muddy.

Interpretation. If shoes equal penis here, this is in part a penis-envy dream. It is possibly also a fantasy on the difference in size of the penes of her stepfather and younger brother. "Then I took them away from him" may mean castration of the younger brother.

DREAM 3

One time I dreamed there was a mean elephant. And a little boy came and the mean elephant took his nose and lifted the little boy up and the little boy cried, and the elephant was scared and let the little boy go. Then the little boy ran home and told his mother and she came and scolded the elephant and after that he was good and they didn't tie him any more.

Associations. [Did you ever see an elephant?] Yes, Junior and I saw one in Gallup, and he was tied to a weed.

[Did that hold him?] Yes, he didn't try to get away.

In that dream I thought the elephant said "If you come again I'll swallow you." And the little boy said, "I won't. You're too mean."

Interpretation. The elephant is the father and his trunk ("nose") the father's penis. Father denies the son sexuality, but mother scolds father (Oedipal motive). Dreamer has oral-sadistic attitudes toward her brother and fantasies of oral incorporation on her father's part. One general meaning of the dream is: If the nurturant mother did not protect her children against the sexual father, they would be hurt or destroyed.

SOME NOTES ON NAVAHO DREAMS   361

IV. Junior

DREAM 1

I was playing with my sister [actually "cousin"—a girl of eight]. She died. They dug a round hole for her like the kind they use for baking a big corn cake, and they put the girl into the hole, and they built a fire on top of her. I walked away with my father and a white sheep dog came after him, and my father ran near the hole. A ghost came out and chased him.

Associations. I think the ghost was like a man, but I am not sure. My father yelled "I am not dead yet." Then the ghost fell down on the ground, and my father came and stepped on it.

Interpretation. Ambivalence to the father is the keynote of this dream. The father triumphs, however, in the end. Death wishes for the sisters are also indicated. The dog is perhaps Junior himself. The significance of the ghost is not clear, unless it is also the sister who is finally destroyed by the father (resolution of sibling rivalry).

DREAM 2

We were in our hogan, and a wolf came and he had long teeth and he frightened us and Mamie ran to the bed, and I ran outside where my mother was and I hid behind her and she scared away the wolf.

Associations. Yesterday I was playing in a deep arroyo. And above it my father was building on the adobe house. And I built some steps up the arroyo so I could climb out. The white dog and puppies came down into the arroyo. I got scared and couldn't find the steps. So I ran home.

Interpretation. The dream itself is Oedipal. The general pattern is already familiar from dreams of the other children: "Father threatens children. Mother protects us." Wolf in the dream and dog in the associations seem to be equated. The long teeth may represent the penis, but they also recall the *vagina dentata* motif. Crawling out of the deep arroyo represents birth, and the whole of this part of the association suggests speculation about the father's part in the birth process.

362   CULTURE AND BEHAVIOR

V. Bob (Father)

Bob was willing to talk at length about ceremonials, witches, and local gossip, but he professed to dream seldom and never to remember his dreams. This is probably connected with the fact that he had never been sick and had a very low anxiety level for a Navaho. Only two dreams were obtained from him, and both had occurred some years previously. (More than thirty dreams each were told by his wife and two older children.) He could not or would not produce any associations.

DREAM 1

My brother ["cousin"] and I went off about 112 miles to a camp to cut wood. We slept together. My mother ["aunt"] was very sick, and one night I dreamed she died and everyone cried and she was buried. It was just like it really happened. That was a very bad dream and I was scared. But I couldn't do anything because I did not have my bag of corn pollen. My cousin got up early but at lunch I said I had a terrible dream and he said he had too and I said tell me yours, and it was just the same as mine. That was the worst dream I ever had.

Commentary. Perhaps an unconscious death wish toward his classificatory mother is represented—with consequent anxiety. She was the mother of the "brother" with whom he was traveling. Bob's mentioning explicitly "we slept together" is rather unusual in Navaho parlance and seems particularly irrelevant here. One may wildly speculate that there were feelings of unconscious homosexuality and that the dream results from guilt punishment.

DREAM 2

When I was at school I dreamed we were riding in a truck to play baseball, and we went down a very steep hill. We got down all right but when we came home the truck couldn't get up that hill and it began sliding downward, and boy it sure went fast and at the bottom was a deep arroyo and it threw me off and when I woke up I was lying on the floor. I was sure scared.

Commentary. This is another anxiety dream—perhaps reflecting fear of the vagina? Driving downhill is ordinarily taken as a coitus symbol.

Discussion

The collection published here is small but representative. These dreams could easily be lost in the total body of Navaho dreams known to me. They are typical in their emphasis upon anxiety, in the absence of overt references to sexual experiences, and in many other ways.

No attempt has been made to exhaust their psychological significance, and the cultural aspect has barely been alluded to. The intent has been only to document the universality of certain emotional problems and the universality of certain symbolic ways of reacting to them. It has been demonstrated that with little straining psychoanalytic concepts such as the Oedipus complex and sibling rivalry give a meaning to these verbal symbols that is not otherwise apparent and that is reinforced rather than contradicted by the situational and cultural data.

The anthropological utility of the study of dreams is, of course, not limited to the investigation of depth psychology. Comparative studies are fruitful for elucidation of explicit and implicit culture and for formulating and testing hypotheses about modal personality (cf. 1945a, pp. 105-106).

REFERENCES

Aginsky, B. W. (1940), "The Socio-psychological Significance of Death among the Pomo Indians," *American Imago*, June, pp. 1-11.

Albert, Ethel (1956), "The Classification of Values: a Method and Illustration," *American Anthropologist*, 58:221-248.

Allport, Gordon W., James M. Gillespie, and Jacqueline Young (1948), "The Religion of the Post-war College Student," *Journal of Psychology*, 25:3-33.

Almond, Gabriel (1954), *The Appeals of Communism*. Princeton: Princeton University Press.

Asch, Solomon (1952), *Social Psychology*. New York: Prentice-Hall, Inc.

Baldwin, Gordon C. (1939), "The Material Culture of Kinishba," *American Antiquity*, 4:314-328.

Barnard, Chester I. (1944), "On Planning for World Government," in *Approaches to World Peace*, ed. by Lyman Bryson, Louis Finkelstein, and Robert M. MacIver. New York: Harper & Brothers, pp. 825-859.

Bauer, Raymond A. (1952), "The Development of Attitudes towards the Society Regime. Selected Case Histories." Unpublished report. Cambridge: Russian Research Center.

―――― (1953), "The Psychology of the Soviet Middle Elite," in *Personality in Nature, Society, and Culture*, ed. by Clyde Kluckhohn, Henry A. Murray, and David Schneider. New York: Alfred A. Knopf, Inc., pp. 633-650.

Beier, Helen, and Raymond A. Bauer (1955), "Oleg: A Member of the Soviet 'Golden Youth,'" *Journal of Abnormal and Social Psychology,* 51:139-145.

Benedict, Ruth (1934), *Patterns of Culture.* Boston: Houghton Mifflin Company.

Boas, Franz (1922), "Religion and the Future Life," ed. by E. Hershey Sneath. New York: Fleming H. Revell Co., pp. 9-26. Reprinted as "The Idea of Future Life among Primitive Tribes," in *Race, Language, and Culture,* New York: The Macmillan Company, 1940, pp. 596-607.

———— (1938), *The Mind of Primitive Man,* revised edition. New York: The Macmillan Company (first edition, 1911).

Brandt, Richard (1954), *Hopi Ethics: A Theoretical Analysis.* Chicago: University of Chicago Press.

Bronowski, Jacob (1959), "The Values of Science," in *New Knowledge of Human Values,* ed. by A. Maslow. New York: Harper & Brothers, pp. 52-64.

Camus, Albert (1945), *Lettres à un ami allemand.* Paris: Gallimard. (Reprinted as "Letters to a German Friend," trans. Justin O'Brien, in *Resistance, Rebellion, and Death.* New York: Alfred A. Knopf, Inc., 1961.)

Cannon, Walter B. (1942), "'Voodoo' Death," *American Anthropologist,* 44:169-181.

Childe, V. Gordon (1951), *Social Evolution.* London and New York: Henry Schuman.

Colton, Harold S. (1939), "Prehistoric Culture Units and Their Relationships in Northern Arizona," Bulletin 17. Flagstaff: Museum of Northern Arizona.

Curtiss, W. E. (1905), "Education and Morals among the Navajos and Pueblos," *American Antiquarian and Oriental Journal,* 27:259-264.

Dicks, Henry V. (1950), "In Search of Our Proper Ethic," *British Journal of Medicinal Psychology,* 23:1-14.

———— (1952), "Observations on Contemporary Russian Behavior," *Human Relations,* 5:111-175.

Dutton, Bertha P. (1938), *Leyit Kin, a Small House Ruin, Chaco Canyon, New Mexico.* Bulletin 333, Monograph Series, Vol. 1, No. 6. Albuquerque: University of New Mexico.

Dyk, Walter (1938), *Son of Old Man Hat: a Navaho Autobiography.* New York: Harcourt, Brace and Company, Inc.

———— (1951), "Notes and Illustrations of Navaho Sex Behavior," in *Psychoanalysis and Culture,* ed. by G. Wilbur and W. Muensterberger. New York: International Universities Press, pp. 108-120.

Edel, Abraham (1955), *Ethical Judgment.* Glencoe: The Free Press.

Empson, William (1955), *Collected Poems.* London: Chatto and Windus. New York: Harcourt, Brace, and Company, Inc.

Erikson, Erik H. (1950), *Childhood and Society*. New York: W. W. Norton & Company (especially Chap. 10, "The Legend of Maxim Gorky's Youth").

Feibleman, James (1955), "Introduction to an Objective, Empirical Ethics," *Ethics*, 55:102-115.

Firth, Raymond (1936), *We, the Tikopia: a Sociological Study of Kinship in Primitive Polynesia*. London: George Allen & Unwin, Ltd.

Flugel, J. C. (1945), *Man, Morals, and Society: a Psychoanalytic Study*. New York: International Universities Press.

Ford, C. S. (1942), "Culture and Human Behavior," *Scientific Monthly*, 55:546-557.

Fortes, Meyer (1938), *Social and Psychological Aspects of Education in Taleland*. Supplement to *Africa*, Vol. XI, No. 4, London.

—— (1949), *The Web of Kinship among the Tallensi*. London and New York: Oxford University Press.

Frank, Lawrence K. (1939), "Cultural Coercion and Individual Distortion," *Psychiatry*, 2:11-27.

—— (1943), "Man's Multidimensional Environment," *Scientific Monthly*, 56:344-357.

Frankfort, H. H. (1948), *Ancient Egyptian Religion*. New York: Columbia University Press.

Frenkel-Brunswik, Else (1954), "Social Research and the Problem of Values: a Reply," *Journal of Abnormal and Social Psychology*, 49:466-471.

Freud, Sigmund (1933), *New Introductory Lectures on Psychoanalysis*, New York: W. W. Norton & Company.

Goldhamer, Herbert, and Andrew W. Marshall (1949), "The Frequency of Mental Disease: Long Term Trends and Present Status," Report R-157. Santa Monica: RAND Corporation.

Goldman, Irving (1950), "Psychiatric Interpretations of Russian History," *American Slavic and East European Review*, 9:151-161.

Goldschmidt, Walter (1951), "Ethics and the Structure of Society," *American Anthropologist*, 53:506-524.

Goodwin, Grenville (1938), "The White Mountain Apache Religion," *American Anthropologist*, 40:24-37.

Gorer, Geoffrey, and J. Rickman (1949), *The People of Great Russia*. London: Cresset Press.

Haile, Father Berard (1938), *Origin Legend of the Navaho Enemy Way*. Yale University Publications in Anthropology, 17. New Haven: Yale University Press.

—— (1943), "Soul Concepts of the Navaho," *Annali Lateranensi*, 7:59-94.

Haimson, Leopold (1953), "Russian 'Visual Thinking'" and "The Soviet Style of Chess," in *The Study of Culture at a Distance*, ed. by M. Mead and R. Metraux. Chicago: University of Chicago Press, pp. 246-248, 426-431.

Hallowell, A. I. (1938), "Fear and Anxiety as Cultural and Individual Variables in a Primitive Society," *Journal of Social Psychology*, 9:25-47.

Hanfmann, Eugenia, and Helen Beier (1954), "Psychological Patterns of Soviet Citizens." Unpublished report. Cambridge: Russian Research Center.

Harris, Seymour (1948), "The Future of Higher Education in the United States," *Harvard Educational Review*, 18:183-208.

Hartmann, Hans (1952), *Der Totenkult in Irland; ein Beitrag zur Religion der Indogermanen*. Heidelberg: Winter.

Hartmann, Heinz, Ernst Kris, and Rudolph M. Loewenstein (1951), "Some Psychoanalytic Comments on 'Culture and Personality,'" in *Psychoanalysis and Culture*, ed. by G. Wilbur and W. Muensterberger. New York: International Universities Press, pp. 3-31.

Hartung, Frank E. (1954), "Cultural Relativity and Moral Judgments," *Philosophy of Science*, 21:118-126.

Hawley, Florence (1934), *The Significance of the Dated Prehistory of Chetro Ketl*. Bulletin 246, Monograph Series, Vol. 1, No. 1. Albuquerque: University of New Mexico.

Hill, W. W. (1938), *The Agricultural and Hunting Methods of the Navaho Indians*. Yale University Publications in Anthropology, 18. New Haven: Yale University Press.

———— (1944), "The Navaho Indians and the Ghost Dance of 1890," *American Anthropologist*, 46:523-527.

Hobson, Richard (1954), *Navaho Acquisitive Values*. Cambridge: Papers of the Peabody Museum of Archaeology and Ethnology, Vol. 42, No. 3.

Hollingshead, August (1949), *Elmtown's Youth: The Impact of Social Classes on Adolescents*. New York: John Wiley & Sons, Inc.

Hull, Clark L. (1945), "Moral Values, Behaviorism, and the World Crisis," *Transactions of the New York Academy of Sciences*, Section of Psychology, Series II, 7:90-94.

Joseph, Alice, Rosamond B. Spicer, and Jane Chesky (1949), *The Desert People: A Study of the Papago Indians*. Chicago: University of Chicago Press.

Kennard, E. A. (1937), "Hopi Reactions to Death," *American Anthropologist*, 39:491-496.

Kidder, A. V., and A. O. Shepard (1936), *The Pottery of Pecos*, Vol. II. New Haven: Published for Phillips Academy by the Yale University Press.

Kolb, William L. (1953), "A Social-Psychological Conception of Human Freedom," *Ethics*, 63:180-189.

Kroeber, A. L. (1949), "The Concept of Culture in Science," *Journal of General Education*, 3:182-196.

Ladd, John (1957), *The Structure of a Moral Code: A Philosophical or, Ethical Discourse Applied to the Ethics of the Navaho Indians*. Cambridge: Harvard University Press.

Lasswell, H. D. (1935), *World Politics and Personal Insecurity*. New York: McGraw-Hill Book Company, Inc.

Lee, Dorothy (1938), "Conceptual Implications of an Indian Language," *Philosophy of Science*, Vol. 5, No. 1.

―――― (1940), "A Primitive System of Values," *Philosophy of Science*, 7:355-378.

―――― (1948), "Are Basic Needs Ultimate?" *Journal of Abnormal and Social Psychology*, 43-391-395.

Leites, Nathan C. (1948), "Psycho-cultural Hypotheses about Political Acts," *World Politics*, 1:102-119.

―――― (1951), *The Operational Code of the Politburo*. New York: McGraw-Hill Book Company, Inc.

―――― (1953), *A Study of Bolshevism*. New York: The Free Press.

―――― (1954), "The Image of Betrayal: 1949-1954." [Cf. "Epilogue; The Image of Betrayal, 1949-1954," in Leites and Bernaut (1954), pp. 350-392.]

Leites, Nathan, and Elsa Bernaut (1954), *Ritual of Liquidation: The Case of the Moscow Trials*. New York: The Free Press.

Lévi-Strauss, Claude (1945), "French Sociology," in *Twentieth Century Sociology*, ed. by Georges Gurvitch and Wilbert Moore. New York: Philosophical Library, pp. 503-537.

―――― (1955), "The Structural Study of Myths," *Journal of American Folklore*, 68:428-444.

Lieb, Fritz (1945), *Russland Unterweg: der russische Mensch zwischen Christentum und Kommunismus*. Bern: A. Francke.

Linton, Ralph (1952) "Universal Ethical Principles: an Anthropological View," in *Moral Principles of Action*, ed. by Ruth N. Anshen. New York: Harper & Brothers, pp. 645-660.

―――― (1954), "The Problem of Universal Values," in *Method and Perspective in Anthropology*, ed. by Robert F. Spencer. Minneapolis: University of Minnesota Press, pp. 145-168.

Macbeath, Alexander (1952), *Experiments in Living*. London: Macmillan & Company, Ltd.

MacGregor, Gordon (1945), *Warriors without Weapons*. Chicago: University of Chicago Press.

McNair, Robert (1948), *The Ideas of the Good in the Mythology of the Navaho Indians*. Ph.D. thesis. Cambridge: Harvard University.

Malinowski, Bronislaw (1932), *The Sexual Life of Savages*, third edition. London: George Routledge & Sons, Ltd.

Maslow, A. H. (1954), "Normality, Health and Values," *Main Currents in Modern Thought*, 10:75-81.

Matthews, Washington (1899), "The Study of Ethics among the Lower Races," *Journal of American Folklore*, 44:1-9.

Mauss, Marcel (1923-1924), "Essai sur le Don," *l'Annee Sociologique*, Seconde serie, t. I. Reprinted, 1950; *Sociologie et Anthropologie*. Paris: Presses Universitaires de France.

―――― (1926), "The Nature and Significance of the Ceremony of Sacrifice."

Chicago: Open Court Publishing Co. Reprinted as "Interpretation of the Sacrificial Ceremony" by H. Hubert and Marcel Mauss in *Primitive Heritage*, ed. by Margaret Mead. New York: Random House, Inc., 1953, pp. 66-72.

Mead, Margaret (1951), *Soviet Attitudes toward Authority*. New York: McGraw-Hill Book Company, Inc.

——— (1952), *Studies in Soviet Communication*, Vol. I. Cambridge: Center for International Studies, Massachusetts Institute of Technology.

——— (1954), "The Swaddling Hypothesis: Its Reception," *American Anthropologist*, 56:395-410.

———, and Rhoda Metraux (1953), *The Study of Culture at a Distance*. Chicago: University of Chicago Press.

Money-Kyrle, R. E. (1944), "Towards a Common Aim—a Psychoanalytical Contribution to Ethics," *British Journal of Medicinal Psychology*, 20:105-118.

Murdock, G. P. (1945), "The Common Denominator of Cultures," in *The Science of Man in the World Crisis*, ed. by Ralph Linton. New York: Columbia University Press, pp. 123-142.

Newcomb, Franc J. (1940), "Origin Legend of the Navajo Eagle Chant," *Journal of American Folklore*, 53:50-78.

Niebuhr, Reinhold (1941-1943), *The Nature and Destiny of Man: A Christian Interpretation*. New York: Charles Scribner's Sons.

Opler, M. E. (1936-1937), "An Interpretation of Ambivalence of Two American Indian Tribes," *Journal of Social Psychology*, 7:82-116.

——— (1938), "Further Comparative Anthropological Data Bearing on the Solution of a Psychological Problem," *Journal of Social Psychology*, 9:477-483.

——— (1941), *An Apache Life-Way*. Chicago: University of Chicago Press.

——— (1945), "The Lipan Apache Death Complex and Its Extensions," *Southwestern Journal of Anthropology*, 1:122-141.

——— (1946), "Reaction to Death among the Mescalero Apache," *Southwestern Journal of Anthropology*, 2:454-467.

Parsons, Elsie Clews (1936), "The House Clan Complex of the Pueblos," in *Essays in Anthropology Presented to A. L. Kroeber*, ed. by R. H. Lowie. Berkeley: University of California Press, pp. 229-231.

——— (1939), *Pueblo Indian Religion*. Chicago: University of Chicago Press.

Parsons, Talcott, and Edward A. Shils (1951), *Toward a General Theory of Action*. Cambridge: Harvard University Press.

Polson, C. J., R. P. Brittain, and T. K. Marshall (1953), *The Disposal of the Dead*. London: English Universities Press.

Rapoport, Anatol (1950), *Science and the Goals of Man: a Study in Semantic Orientation*. New York: Harper & Brothers.

Rapoport, Robert N. (1954), *Changing Navaho Religious Values*. Cambridge: Papers of the Peabody Museum of Archaeology and Ethnology, Vol. 41, No. 2.

Reichard, Gladys A. (1928), *Social Life of the Navaho Indians, with Some Attention to Minor Ceremonies*. New York: Columbia University Press.

———— (1939), *Navajo Medicine Man*. New York: J. J. Augustin.

———— (1944), *Prayer: The Compulsive Word*. New York: J. J. Augustin.

———— (1950), "Navaho Religion," in *Ethics*. New York: Pantheon Books, Inc.

Reiser, Oliver (1951), "Unified Symbolism for World Understanding in Science," address to the American Association for the Advancement of Science, Philadelphia.

Riesman, David (1952), "Some Observations on the Limits of Totalitarian Power," *Antioch Review*, Summer, pp. 155-168.

Robbins, William J. (1941), "Some Aspects of Pueblo Indian Religion," *Harvard Theological Review*, 34:25-47.

Roberts, Frank H. H., Jr. (1935), "A Survey of Southwestern Archaeology," *American Anthropologist*, 37:1-35.

———— (1938a), "Chaco Canyon Masonry," *American Antiquity*, 4:60-67.

———— (1938b), Review: *The Emergence of a General Folsom Pattern*, by E. B. Howard, *American Antiquity*, 4:79-80.

Robinson, Geroid T. (1949), "The Ideological Combat," *Foreign Affairs*, 27:525-539.

Roheim, Geza (1942), "The Origin and Function of Culture," *The Psychoanalytic Review*, 29:131-164.

———— (1947), "Dream Analysis and Field Work in Anthropology," in *Psychoanalysis and the Social Sciences*. New York: International Universities Press, I: 87-130.

———— (1950), *Psychoanalysis and Anthropology*. New York: International Universities Press.

Rosenzweig, Saul, (1944), "An Outline of Frustration Theory," in *Personality and the Behavior Disorders*, ed. by J. McV. Hunt. New York: Ronald Press, pp. 379-388.

Rosmini-Serbati, Antonio (1838), *Antropologia in Servigio della Scienza Morale*. Milan: Pogliani.

Sapir, Edward (1924), "Culture, Genuine and Spurious," *American Journal of Sociology*, 29:401-429.

Sibley, Elbridge (1946), "The Liberal College in a Secular World," *Journal of Higher Education*, 17:71-82.

Steinberg, A. S. (1929), "Um das Individuum im alten und neuen Russland," in *Die Biologie der Person*, ed. by Th. Brugsch and F. W. Lewy. Berlin and Vienna: pp. 699-735.

Steward, Julian (1949), "Cultural Causality and Law," *American Anthropologist*, 51:1-27.

———— (1953), "Evolution and Process," in *Anthropology Today*, ed. by A. L. Kroeber. Chicago: University of Chicago Press, pp. 313-326.

Thompson, Laura, and Alice Joseph (1944), *The Hopi Way*. Chicago: University of Chicago Press.

Thorndike, Edward L. (1936), "Science and Values," *Science*, 83:1-8 (No. 2140).

Titiev, Mischa (1940), "A Hopi Visit to the Afterworld," *Papers of the Michigan Academy of Science, Arts, and Letters*, 26:495-504.

Tomasic, Dinko (1953), *The Impact of Russian Culture on Soviet Communism*. Glencoe: The Free Press.

Trimborn, Hermann (1949), *Das Menschliche ist gleich im Urgrund aller Kulturen* (Beiträge zum Geschichtsunterricht, No. 9). Braunschweig: Verlag Albert Limbach.

Valéry, Paul (1948) *Reflections on the World Today*, tr. by Francis Scarfe. New York: Pantheon Books, Inc.

Vogt, Evon Z. (1951), *Navaho Veterans: a Study of Changing Values*. Cambridge: Papers of the Peabody Museum of Archaeology and Ethnology, Vol. 41, No. 1.

Weaver, Warren (1948), "Science and Complexity," *American Scientist*, 36:536-544.

Wein, Hermann (1950), *Das Problem des Relativismus: Philosophie im Übergang zur Anthropologie*. Berlin: Walter De Gruyter & Co.

White, Leslie (1943), "Energy and the Evolution of Culture," *American Anthropologist*, 45:335-356.

⸺ (1949), *The Science of Culture*. New York: Farrar, Straus & Cudahy, Inc.

Whitehead, Alfred North (1933), *Adventures of Ideas*. New York: The Macmillan Company.

Wilbur, George B. (1940), Comments on paper by Aginsky, *American Imago*, June, pp. 12-18.

Wissler, Clark (1923), *Man and Culture*. New York: Thomas Y. Crowell Company.

Witmer, Helen L. (1939), "Some Parallels between Dynamic Psychiatry and Cultural Anthropology," *American Journal of Orthopsychiatry*, 9:95-101.

Wyman, L. C., W. W. Hill, and I. Osani (1942), "Navajo Eschatology," *University of New Mexico Bulletin*, Anthropological Series, Vol. 4, No. 1.

BIBLIOGRAPHY

OF CLYDE KLUCKHOHN

Compiled by Lucy Wales

FOLLOWING THE FORM set up by Professor Kluckhohn for his complete bibliography, this list presents his works chronologically by category: books, monographs, chapters, and articles are followed by review articles, reviews, forewords, and miscellaneous works. Unpublished manuscripts available in the Harvard College Library or the Peabody Museum Library, Harvard University have been included, as have other manuscripts so specified by Professor Kluckhohn. All known versions of articles as of January, 1962, have been included. Grateful acknowledgment is due the many who managed to maintain the core of this bibliography and to those whose watchful eyes spotted new reprints.

1923

ARTICLE

(1923) "The Dance of Hasjelti." *El Palacio,* 15:187-192.

1927

BOOK

(1927) *To the Foot of the Rainbow.* New York, Century. London, Nash & Grayson, 1928.

1933

BOOK

(1933a) *Beyond the Rainbow.* Boston, Christopher.

ARTICLES

(1933b) "The Great Chants of the Navaho." *Theatre Arts Monthly,* 17:639-645. [Reprinted in *Societies around the World,* ed. by Irwin T. Sanders. Lexington, University of Kentucky, 1948, pp. 171-175. *Ibid.,* 1952, pp. 229-233. *Societies around the World,* ed. by Howard Becker. New York, Dryden Press, 1956, pp. 229-232.]

(1933c) "Hopi and Navaho." *New Mexico Quarterly,* 3:56-64 [a chapter from *Beyond the Rainbow*].

REVIEW

(1933d) *Yuman Tribes of the Gila River,* by Leslie Spier. *New Mexico Historical Review,* 8:317-318.

1935

ARTICLE

(1935a) "A Note on the Sources of the Drawings in the Del Rio Volume on Palenque." *Maya Research,* 2:287-290.

MISCELLANEOUS

(1935b) The Indian Languages of North America [unpublished map]. C. S. Coon, Frederick Johnson, Clyde Kluckhohn, drawn by R. T. Smith. Cambridge, Peabody Museum of Archaeology and Ethnology.

(1935c) Sources for Linguistic Map of North America. C. S. Coon, Frederick Johnson, Clyde Kluckhohn. Cambridge, Peabody Museum of Archaeology and Ethnology. Mimeographed.

1936

ARTICLE

(1936a) "Some Reflections on the Method and Theory of the Kulturkreislehre." *American Anthropologist,* 38:157-196.

MISCELLANEOUS

(1936b) Some Aspects of Contemporary Theory in Cultural Anthropology. Typewritten Ph.D. thesis, Harvard University. Unpublished.

1937

ARTICLE

(1937) "The Field of Higher Education in the Southwest." *New Mexico Quarterly*, 7:23-30.

1938

MONOGRAPH

(1938a) *Navaho Classification of Their Song Ceremonials.* L. C. Wyman and C. Kluckhohn. Menasha, Wisc., Memoirs of the American Anthropological Association, No. 50.

ARTICLES

(1938b) "Navaho Women's Knowledge of Their Song Ceremonials." *El Palacio*, 45:87-92.

(1938c) "Participation in Ceremonials in a Navaho Community." *American Anthropologist*, 40:359-369. [Reprinted in *Personal Character and Cultural Milieu*, ed. by Douglas Haring. Syracuse, Syracuse University Press, 1948, pp. 38-49. *Ibid.*, 1949, pp. 66-75. *Ibid.*, 1956, pp. 485-512.]

REVIEW

(1938d) *Son of Old Man Hat: a Navaho Autobiography*, by Walter Dyk. *Boston Evening Transcript*, Nov. 19. [Various other reviews—e.g., of Clark Wissler's *Indian Cavalcade* and of Isaac Wistar's *Autobiography*—appeared in the Saturday book review section of the *Boston Evening Transcript*, 1938-1939.]

MISCELLANEOUS

(1938e) The American Minstrel. *Missionary Catechist*, 14:12.

1939

MONOGRAPH

(1939a) *Preliminary Report on the 1937 Excavations, Bc 50-51, Chaco Canyon, New Mexico.* Clyde Kluckhohn and Paul Reiter. University of New Mexico Bulletin, Anthropological Series 3, No. 2. [The following portions are written by the senior editor: Introduction, 7-10; The Excavation of Rooms and Kivas, 30-48; Subsistence Remains, 147-150; Discussion, 151-163; Addenda to the Chaco Canyon Bibliography, 175-177.]

ARTICLES

(1939b) "On Certain Recent Applications of Association Coefficients to Ethnological Data." *American Anthropologist*, 41:345-377.

(1939c) "The Place of Theory in Anthropological Studies." *Philosophy of Science*, 6:328-344.

(1939d) "Some Personal and Social Aspects of Navaho Ceremonial Practice." *Harvard Theological Review*, 32:67-82. Abstract in *Anthropos*, 35-36: 1002-1003, under title, "Relations between Ceremonies and Social Organization of the Navaho."

(1939e) "Theoretical Bases for an Empirical Method of Studying the Acquisition of Culture by Individuals." *Man*, 39:98-103.

REVIEWS

(1939f) *The Chaco Canyon and Its Monuments; Pajarito Plateau and Its Ancient Peoples; Ancient Andean Life*, by E. L. Hewett. *Boletin Bibliografico de Antropologia Americana*, 3:50-51.

(1939g) *The High Priest's Grave*, by J. E. Thompson. *Boletin Bibliografico de Antropologia Americana*, 3:52-53.

(1939h) *Navaho Life*, by Katharine Luomala; *A Brief History of Navaho Silversmithing*, by Arthur Woodward; *The Agriculture and Hunting Methods of the Navaho Indians*, by W. W. Hill. *American Anthropologist*, 41: 310-313.

FOREWORDS

(1939i) *The Cultural Historical Method in Ethnology*, by Wilhelm Schmidt [English translation]. New York, Fortunys, pp. v-viii.

(1939j) *The Economic Botany of the Kiowa Indians*, by Paul A. Vestal and Richard E. Schultes. Cambridge, Botanical Museum, pp. ix-x.

MISCELLANEOUS

(1939k) What They Do—Those Anthropologists. *Gallup* [N.M.] *Gazette* (Ceremonial Edition), Aug. 18 [preliminary statement later developed into *Mirror for Man* (1949a)].

(1939l) List of References on the Physical Anthropology of the Eskimo and the American Indian. Cambridge, Peabody Museum of Archaeology and Ethnology, 22 pp. Mimeographed. March.

1940

BOOK

(1940a) *A Bibliography of the Navaho Indians*. Clyde Kluckhohn and Katherine Spencer. New York, J. J. Augustin.

MONOGRAPH

(1940b) *An Introduction to Navaho Chant Practice with an Account of the Behaviors Observed in Four Chants*. Clyde Kluckhohn and Leland C.

Wyman. Menasha, Wisc., Memoirs of the American Anthropological Association, No. 53.

CHAPTER

(1940c) "The Conceptual Structure in Middle American Studies." In *The Maya and Their Neighbors*, ed. by C. L. Hay, R. L. Linton, and others. New York, D. Appleton-Century, pp. 41-51.

MISCELLANEOUS

(1940d) Navaho Ceremonialism. *Gallup* [N.M.] *Gazette* (Ceremonial Edition), Aug. 15.

1941

CHAPTER

(1941a) "Patterning as Exemplified in Navaho Culture." In *Language, Culture, and Personality*, ed. by Leslie Spier. Menasha, Wisc., Sapir Memorial Publication Fund, pp. 109-130. [Reprinted 1960, Bobbs-Merrill Reprint Series in the Social Sciences, ed. by Erving Goffman, *et al.* Indianapolis, No. 147.]

ARTICLES

(1941b) "Notes on Navajo Eagle Way." *New Mexico Anthropologist*, 5:6-14.
(1941c) "The Way of Life." *Kenyon Review*, 3:160-179.

REVIEWS

(1941d) *National Unity and Disunity*, by G. K. Zipf. *American Anthropologist*, 43:667-668.
(1941e) *Pioneers in American Anthropology*, by Leslie White. *Hispanic-American Historical Review*, 21:325-330.
(1941f) *Race, Language, and Culture*, by Franz Boas. *Journal of American Folklore*, 54:218-220.
(1941g) *Religion in Primitive Society*, by W. D. Wallis. *American Oxonian*, 28:171-173.

MISCELLANEOUS

(1941h) Navajo Witchcraft. *Gallup* [N.M.] *Gazette* (Ceremonial Edition), Aug. 12 [part of early draft of *Navaho Witchcraft* (1944a)].
(1941i) The Socialization of Forty-eight Navaho Indian Children. [Reports from Recipients of Grants from the Research Funds. Grant No. 544 (1941), $700.] Year Book of the American Philosophical Society, pp. 216-217.
(1941j) Toward a Common Language for the Area of Social Science. T. Parsons, J. T. Dunlop, M. P. Gilmore, C. Kluckhohn, and O. H. Taylor. Cambridge, Mimeographed. [Central section of this paper is published in *Essays in Sociological Theory* by Talcott Parsons. Glencoe, The Free Press, 1949, pp. 42-52.]

1942

ARTICLES

(1942a) "Myths and Rituals: a General Theory." *Harvard Theological Review*, 35:45-79. [Reprinted (abridged) in *A Reader in Comparative Religion*, ed. by William Lessa and E. Z. Vogt. Evanston, Row, Peterson, 1958, pp. 135-151.

(1942b) "The Navahos in the Machine Age." *Technology Review*, 44:2-6. [Reprinted in *Societies around the World*, ed. by Irwin T. Sanders. Lexington, University of Kentucky, 1948, pp. 196-203. *Ibid.*, 1952, pp. 249-253. *Societies around the World*, ed. by Howard Becker. New York, Dryden Press, 1956, pp. 245-247.]

REVIEW

(1942c) *The Social Life of Primitive Man*, by S. A. Sieber and F. H. Mueller. *Social Forces*, 20:407-408.

MISCELLANEOUS

(1942d) Comment in Chapter: "The Comparative Study of Culture," by Margaret Mead. In *Science, Philosophy, and Religion*. New York, Harper & Bros., pp. 72-76.

1943

ARTICLES

(1943a) "Bronislaw Malinowski, 1884-1942." *Journal of American Folklore*, 56:208-219.

(1943b) "Covert Culture and Administrative Problems." *American Anthropologist*, 45:213-227.

REVIEWS

(1943c) *And Keep Your Powder Dry*, by Margaret Mead. Florence and Clyde Kluckhohn. *American Anthropologist*, 45:622-625.

(1943d) *Man's Most Dangerous Myth: the Fallacy of Race*, by M. F. Ashley Montagu. *Isis*, 34:419-420.

(1943e) *Origin Legend of the Navaho Flintway*, by Berard Haile. *American Anthropologist*, 45:611-612.

(1943f) *The Role of Conjuring in Saulteaux Society*, by A. I. Hallowell. *Crozer Quarterly*, 20:165-166.

(1943g) *Smoke from Their Fires*, by C. S. Ford. *Social Research*, 10:127-128.

(1943h) *Sun Chief*, by Leo Simmons. *American Anthropologist*, 45:267-270.

MISCELLANEOUS

(1943i) Anent Patterns and "Flexible Methods." *American Anthropologist*, 45:328-329.

(1943j) On the Use of Cultural Contact Situations in Regional Training. In collaboration with the Council of Inter-cultural Relations. New York. Mimeographed. 16 pp.

1944

MONOGRAPH

(1944a) *Navaho Witchcraft.* Cambridge, Papers of the Peabody Museum of Archaeology and Ethnology, Harvard University. Vol. 22, No. 2. [Portions reprinted in *Personal Character and Cultural Milieu,* ed. by Douglas Haring. Syracuse, Syracuse University Press, 1948, pp. 389-417. *Religion, Society and the Individual,* ed. by J. Milton Yinger. New York, Macmillan Company, 1957, pp. 359-371 (under title "Functions and Disfunctions of Witchcraft").]

CHAPTERS

(1944b) "Anthropological Research and World Peace." In *Approaches to World Peace.* ed. by Lyman Bryson, Louis Finkelstein, and Robert M. MacIver. New York, Harper & Bros., pp. 143-152. [Reprinted in *Readings in Social Psychology,* ed. by T. M. Newcomb. New York, Henry Holt, 1947, pp. 657-664. Translation: Japanese, in *Collections of the Japanese Ethnological Society,* Journal of the Japanese Society of Ethnology, 1:135-149. 1949.]

(1944c) "Dynamic Theory of Personality." O. H. Mowrer and Clyde Kluckhohn. In *Personality and the Behavior Disorders,* ed. by J. McV. Hunt. New York, Ronald Press, pp. 69-135.

(1944d) "The Influence of Psychiatry on Anthropology in America during the Past One Hundred Years." In *One Hundred Years of American Psychiatry,* ed. by J. K. Hall, G. Zilboorg, and E. A. Bunker. New York, Columbia University Press, pp. 589-617. [Translation: Japanese, in *Collections of the Japanese Ethnological Society,* Journal of the Japanese Society of Ethnology, 1:18-68, 1949. Reprinted in *Personal Character and Cultural Milieu,* ed. by Douglas Haring. Syracuse, Syracuse University Press, 1956. pp. 485-512.]

ARTICLE

(1944e) "Culture and Personality, A Conceptual Scheme." Clyde Kluckhohn and O. H. Mowrer. *American Anthropologist,* 46:1-29. [Reprinted in *Contributions toward Medical Psychology,* ed. by Arthur Weider and David Wechsler, New York, Ronald Press, 1953, pp. 105-135 (under title "Determinants and Components of Personality").]

REVIEWS

(1944f) *The Character and Derivation of the Jicarilla Holiness Rites,* by Morris Opler. *Acta Americana,* 2:401-402.

(1944g) *Emotions and Memory,* by David Rapaport. *American Anthropologist,* 46:410.

FOREWORD

(1944h) *The Navajo and Pueblo Silversmiths,* by John Adair. Norman, University of Oklahoma Press, pp. xv-xvii.

1945

MONOGRAPH

(1945a) *The Personal Document in History, Anthropology, and Sociology.* Louis Gottschalk, Clyde Kluckhohn, and Robert Angell. New York, Social Science Research Council, Bulletin 53, pp. 79-174. Fourth printing, 1960.

CHAPTERS

(1945b) "The Concept of Culture." Clyde Kluckhohn and W. H. Kelly. In *The Science of Man in the World Crisis,* ed. by Ralph Linton. New York, Columbia University Press, pp. 78-105. [Translation: Japanese, by M. Namba. Osaka, Sogensha. 1949. Mimeographed, 1944, copy of which this is only part.]

(1945c) "Group Tensions: Analysis of a Case History." In *Approaches to National Unity,* ed. by Lyman Bryson, Louis Finkelstein, and Robert M. MacIver. New York, Harper & Bros., pp. 222-231.

(1945d) "The Myth of Race," In *Religion in the Post-War World,* ed. by Willard Sperry, Cambridge, Harvard University Press, Vol. III, pp. 3-28.

ARTICLE

(1945e) "A Navaho Personal Document with a Brief Paretian Analysis." *Southwestern Journal of Anthropology,* 1:260-283. [Reprinted in *Personal Character and Cultural Milieu,* ed. by Douglas Haring. Syracuse, Syracuse University Press, 1949, pp. 449-472. *Ibid.,* 1956, pp. 513-533.]

REVIEW

(1945f) *Kota Texts,* Part I, by M. B. Emeneau. *American Oxonian,* 32:183.

MISCELLANEOUS

(1945g) Comment on papers by H. Overstreet, P. Sorokin, W. Albright, T. Das, K. Shridharani, and C. Friedrich, in *Approaches to National Unity,* ed. by Lyman Bryson, Louis Finkelstein, and Robert M. MacIver. New York, Harper & Bros., pp. 82-84, 215-217, 272-274, 297-300, 312-314, 628-634.

(1945h) Editing, by C. Kluckhohn and L. C. Wyman, of "A Comparison of Navaho and White Mountain Apache Ceremonial Forms and Categories," by Grenville Goodwin. *Southwestern Journal of Anthropology,* 1:498-506.

(1945i) The Psychiatry-Anthropology Relationship. C. Kluckhohn and R. H. Lowie. *American Journal of Psychiatry,* 102:414-416.

1946

BOOK

(1946a) *The Navaho.* Clyde Kluckhohn and Dorothea Leighton. Cambridge, Harvard University Press. Subsequent printings: 2nd, 1947; 3rd, 1948;

4th, 1951; 5th, 1956; 6th, 1958. [Reprinted: Chapter 8 in *The Language of Wisdom and Folly*, ed. by I. J. Lee. New York, Harper & Bros., 1949, pp. 266-273. Chapter 9, in *Sociological Analysis*, ed. by Logan Wilson and W. L. Kolb. New York, Harcourt Brace, 1949, pp. 130-142. Pp. 19-23, 29-30, 32-33 (Navaho Economy) in *Societies around the World*, ed. by Irwin T. Sanders. Lexington, University of Kentucky Press, 1952, pp. 161-164; and in *Societies around the World*, ed. by Howard Becker. New York, Dryden Press, 1956, pp. 169-172. Excerpt in *Exploring the Ways of Mankind*, by Walter Goldschmidt (see 1960g). Paperback edition (revised). New York, Doubleday, in press, 1962.]

ARTICLE

(1946b) "Personality Formation among the Navaho Indians." *Sociometry*, 9:128-132.

REVIEW ARTICLE

(1946c) *Configurations of Culture Growth*, by A. L. Kroeber. *American Journal of Sociology*, 51:336-341.

REVIEWS

(1946d) *Dynamics of Culture Change*, by Bronislaw Malinowski. *American Journal of Sociology*, 51:571-573.

(1946e) *Handbook of South American Indians*, Vol. I: *The Marginal Tribes;* Vol II: *The Andean Civilizations*, ed. by J. H. Steward. *Science*, 104:212-213.

(1946f) *Human Nature, the Marxian View*, by Vernon Venable. *Kenyon Review*, 8:149-154.

MISCELLANEOUS

(1946g) Letter to the Editor: The Social Scientist's Responsibility. *Commentary*, 2:186-187.

1947

BOOK

(1947a) *Children of the People*. Dorothea Leighton and Clyde Kluckhohn. Cambridge, Harvard University Press. Subsequent printing: 2nd, 1948.

CHAPTERS

(1947b) "American Culture: Generalized Orientations and Class Patterns." Clyde Kluckhohn and Florence R. Kluckhohn. In *Conflicts of Power in Modern Culture*, ed. by Lyman Bryson. New York, Harper & Bros., pp. 106-128. [Translation: Japanese (in Iwanami New Library, No. 11, Tokyo, Iwanami Publishing Company, 1949, pp. 1-42.]

(1947c) "Some Aspects of Navaho Infancy and Early Childhood." In *Psychoanalysis and the Social Sciences*, Vol. I, ed. by Geza Roheim. New York, International Universities Press, pp. 37-86. [Reprinted (in part) in

Societies around the World, ed. by Irwin T. Sanders. Lexington, University of Kentucky Press, 1948, pp. 149-160. *Ibid.,* 1952, pp. 206-217. *Societies around the World,* ed. by Howard Becker, New York, Dryden Press, 1956, pp. 210-219. *Personal Character and Cultural Milieu,* ed. by Douglas Haring. Syracuse, Syracuse University Press, 1949, pp. 472-487. *Readings in Child Development,* ed. by W. E. Martin and Celia B. Stendler. New York, Harcourt, Brace, 1954, pp. 177-193.]

ARTICLE

(1947d) "Some Remarks on the Branches of Anthropology and on Anthropology's Relation to Other Disciplines." *Central States Bulletin,* 2:2-9. [Translation: Japanese, in *Collections of the Japanese Ethnological Society, Journal of the Japanese Society of Ethnology,* 14:1-6, 1949. Reprinted in *Southwestern Lore,* 16:40-47, 1950.]

REVIEWS

(1947e) *Men out of Asia,* by Harold Gladwin. *New York Herald Tribune Book Review,* Dec. 14, p. 10.

(1947f) *The Story of the Navajo Hail Chant,* by Gladys Reichard. *American Anthropologist,* 49:95-97.

MISCELLANEOUS

(1947g) "Statement on Human Rights, Submitted to the Commission on Human Rights, United Nations." With other members of the Executive Board of the American Anthropological Association. *American Anthropologist,* 49:539-543.

(1947h) "What Modern Parents Can Learn from the Navajos." *American Indian,* 4:11-13.

(1947i) Unity in Diversity: Some Questions and Affirmations. Address given at the first annual meeting of the Institute of Ethnic Affairs, Washington, D.C., May 29, 1946. Mimeographed. 8 pp.

1948

BOOK

(1948a) *Personality in Nature, Society, and Culture.* Clyde Kluckhohn and Henry A. Murray (editors and coauthors). New York, Alfred Knopf. London, Jonathan Cape, 1949. [Introduction: "A Conception of Personality"; "The Determinants of Personality Formation" written by the editors. Translation (in part only): *Personligheten: natur. samhälle, och kultur,* Stockholm, Kooperativa förbundets bokförlag. 1953. Revised edition: Clyde Kluckhohn, Henry A. Murray, and David Schneider. New York, Alfred Knopf, 1953 (see 1953a).]

CHAPTER

(1948b) "As an Anthropologist Views It." In *Sex Habits of American Men: a Symposium on the Kinsey Report,* ed. by Albert Deutsch. New York,

Grosset and Dunlap, pp. 88-104. [Reprinted in *Sexual Behavior in American Society*, ed. by Jerome Himelhoch and S. F. Fava. New York, W. W. Norton, 1955, pp. 332-345 (under title "Sexual Behavior in Cross-cultural Perspective").]

ARTICLES

(1948c) "An Anthropologist Looks at Psychology." *American Psychologist*, 3:439-442.

(1948d) "Conceptions of Death among the Southwestern Indians" (Ingersoll Lecture on the Immortality of Man for the academic year 1947-1948, Harvard University). *Divinity School Bulletin*, 66:5-19.

REVIEWS

(1948e) *The American People: a Study in National Character*, by Geoffrey Gorer. *Psychosomatic Medicine*, 10:304-305.

(1948f) *The Heathens: Primitive Man and His Religion*, by W. W. Howells, *Saturday Review of Literature*, 31 (no. 19):27-28.

(1948g) *Magic, Science, and Religion*, by Bronislaw Malinowski. *Crozer Quarterly*, 25:353-354.

(1948h) *Man and His Works*, by Melville J. Herskovits. *Saturday Review of Literature*, 31 (no. 38):11-12.

(1948i) *The Proper Study of Mankind*, by Stuart Chase. *New York Herald Tribune Book Review*, Oct. 3, p. 2.

(1948j) *Sexual Behavior in the Human Male*, by A. C. Kinsey and others. *American Anthropologist*, 50:322-324.

(1948k) *The Ways of Men*, by John Gillin. *Social Forces*, 27:98-99.

MISCELLANEOUS

(1948l) Comment on *The Limitations of Anthropological Methods in Sociology*, by Robert Bierstedt. *American Journal of Sociology*, 54:30.

1949

BOOK

(1949a) *Mirror for Man*. New York, McGraw-Hill. [Translations: *Antropologia*. Mexico City, Libreria Robredo, 1949. Corrected edition, 1957. *Specchiati, Uomo!* Milan, Aldo Garzanti, 1952. *Spiegel der Menschheit*. Zurich, Pan Verlag, 1951. *Människans spegel*. Stockholm, Tiden Forlag, 1951. Reprinted: London, Harrap, 1950. New York, Premier Books, 1957. Chapter 1 in *Form and Idea*, by Morton W. Bloomfield and E. W. Robbins. New York, Macmillan, 1955 (c. 1953), pp. 106-119. Chapter 2 in *Outside Readings in Sociology*, ed. by Edgar A. Schuler and others. New York, Crowell, 1952, pp. 57-70. Second edition, under title *Readings in Sociology*, 1960. Chapter 6 in *General College Readings*, New York, Dryden, 1955. Chapter 9 in *Form and Thought in Phrase*, by Wilfred H. Stone and Robert Hoopes. New York, Ronald Press, 1954. Chapter 2 in a Syllabus of Social Science Material, Haverford College, 1954. Pp. 1-14 in *Readings in Anthropology*, ed. by E.

Adamson Hoebel. New York, McGraw-Hill, 1955, pp. 1-4. Pp. 17-27 in *Man and Society*, ed. by Jerome G. Manis and Samuel I. Clark, as chapter entitled "Cultural Differences" (see 1960b). Pp. 17-36 in *Introductory Sociology*. Norman Press, 1958. Pp. 170-178 in *A Psychological Warfare Casebook*, ed. by William E. Dougherty. Bethesda, Johns Hopkins Press (Operations Research Office), 1958, pp. 512-514. Pp. 230-237, 246-248 in *Contemporary Social Issues*, ed. by R. L. Lee. New York, Crowell, 1955. Excerpts in *Gateway to the Social Sciences*, by Arthur W. Thompson. New York, Henry Holt & Co., revised edition, 1959. *Readings in Educational Sociology*. Crowell, 1958. *Sociology of American Life*, by Harold C. Hoffsommer, Englewood Cliffs, N.J., Prentice-Hall, 1958. *Exploring the Ways of Mankind*, by Walter Goldschmidt, as chapter entitled "The Educational Process" (see 1960c).]

CHAPTERS

(1949b) "The Limitations of Adaptation and Adjustment as Concepts for Understanding Cultural Behavior." In *Adaptation*, ed. by John Romano. Ithaca, Cornell University Press, pp. 99-113.

(1949c) "Needed Refinements in the Biographical Approach." In *Culture and Personality*, ed. by S. S. Sargent and M. W. Smith. New York, Viking Fund, pp. 75-92.

(1949d) "The Philosophy of the Navaho Indians." In *Ideological Differences and World Order*, ed. by F. S. C. Northrop. New Haven, Yale University Press, pp. 356-384. [Reprinted in *Readings in Anthropology*, ed. by Morton H. Fried. New York, Crowell, Vol. II, 1959, pp. 424-449.]

(1949e) "Variations in the Human Family." In *The Family in a Democratic Society*. New York, Columbia University Press, pp. 3-11. [Reprinted in *A Modern Introduction to the Family*, ed. by Norman W. Bell and Ezra F. Vogel. Glencoe, The Free Press, 1960, pp. 45-51.]

ARTICLES

(1949f) "Russian Research at Harvard." *World Politics*, 1:267-272.

(1949g) "Two Navaho Children over a Five-year Period." Clyde Kluckhohn and Janine C. Rosenzweig. *American Journal of Orthopsychiatry*, 19:266-278.

REVIEW

(1949h) *They Came Here First*, by D'Arcy McNickle. *New York Herald Tribune Book Review*, Nov. 13, p. 30.

MISCELLANEOUS

(1949i) How Can We Find Personal Peace and Security in Today's World? Town Meeting of the Air Broadcast: George V. Denny, moderator, K. A. Menninger, S. S. Ackerly, Roy Burkhart, and Clyde Kluckhohn. *Town Meeting*, 14:3-18.

(1949j) "The Ramah Project." In *Gregorio, the Hand-Trembler*, by A. H. and Dorothea Leighton. Papers of the Peabody Museum of Archaeology and Ethnology, Cambridge, Harvard University, Vol. 40, No. 1, pp. v-x.

(1949k) Rejoinder: "Sociological Mirror for Cultural Anthropologists" by Jessie Bernard, same issue. *American Anthropologist*, 51:677-678.

(1949l) *Ruth Fulton Benedict: A Memorial.* New York, Viking Fund, Inc., pp. 18-19.

1950

CHAPTERS

(1950a) "Midcentury Manners and Morals." In *Twentieth Century Unlimited*, ed. by Bruce Bliven. New York, J. B. Lippincott, pp. 303-315. [See Article. Expanded version of "Manners and Morals: A.D. 1950."]

(1950b) "Population Genetics and Social Anthropology." Clyde Kluckhohn and Charles Griffith. In *Origin and Evolution of Man.* Cold Spring Harbor Symposia on Quantitative Biology, 15:401-408.

(1950c) "The Special Character of Integration in an Individual Culture." In *The Nature of Concepts. Their Inter-Relation and Role in Social Structure.* Proceedings of Stillwater Conference sponsored by Foundation for Integrated Education and Oklahoma A. & M. College. Stillwater, Oklahoma A. & M. College, pp. 78-87.

ARTICLE

(1950d) "Manners and Morals: A.D. 1950." *New Republic*, 122:10-14. [Reprinted in *Twentieth Century Unlimited*, pp. 303-315. See Chapters.]

REVIEW ARTICLE

(1950e) "Anthropology Comes of Age," *American Scholar*, 19:241-256.

REVIEWS

(1950f) *The Folk Lore of Chios*, by Philip Argenti and H. J. Rose. *American Anthropologist*, 52:404-405.

(1950g) *Human Behavior and the Principle of Least Effort*, by George Zipf. *American Anthropologist*, 52:268-270.

(1950h) *The Indians of the Southwest*, by E. E. Dale. *Annals* of the American Academy of Political and Social Science, 267:242.

(1950i) *Patterns and Ceremonials of the Southwest*, by John Collier. *New York Herald Tribune Book Review*, Jan. 8, p. 7.

(1950j) *A Plan for Peace*, by Grenville Clark, *New York Times Book Review*, Nov. 5, p. 4.

FOREWORDS

(1950k) *Masked Gods*, by Frank Waters. Albuquerque, University of New Mexico Press, pp. 7-8.

(1950l) *Public Opinion in Soviet Russia: a Study in Mass Persuasion*, by Alex Inkeles. Cambridge, Harvard University Press, pp. vii-ix.

(1950m) *Soviet Politics: The Dilemma of Power*, by Barrington Moore, Jr. Cambridge, Harvard University Press, pp. ix-xi.

MISCELLANEOUS

(1950n) The Dynamics of American Democracy. Babson Institute of Business Administration, *Bulletin*, 2:8-10.

(1950o) Social Anthropology. In *Proceedings of the First National Conference of Cardiovascular Diseases*. New York, American Heart Association, pp. 206-207.

(1950p) Tension in Family Life. *Child Study*, 27:68-69.

1951

BOOK

(1951a) *Navaho Means People*. Leonard McCombe, E. Z. Vogt, and Clyde Kluckhohn. Cambridge, Harvard University Press. London, Oxford University Press.

CHAPTERS

(1951b) "Some Fundamental Categories in the Theory of Action." Introductory statement by T. Parsons, E. A. Shils, G. W. Allport, C. Kluckhohn, *et al.*, in *Toward a General Theory of Action*, ed. by Talcott Parsons and Edward Shils. Cambridge, Harvard University Press, pp. 3-29. [Translation: Chinese, by Hsu Tao-lin, in *Contemporary Philosophy and Social Sciences*, Hong Kong, Vol. 1, No. 1, November, 1956.]

(1951c) "Some Notes on Navaho Dreams." Clyde Kluckhohn and William Morgan. In *Psychoanalysis and Culture*, ed. by G. B. Wilbur and Warner Muensterberger. New York, International Universities Press, pp. 120-131.

(1951d) "Student-Teacher." In *The People in Your Life*, ed. by Margaret Hughes. New York, Alfred Knopf, pp. 158-181.

(1951e) "The Study of Culture." In *The Policy Sciences*, ed. by Daniel Lerner and Harold Lasswell. Stanford, Stanford University Press, pp. 86-101. [Translation: "Le Concept de Culture" (tr. Francois Bourricaud). In *Les "Science de la Politique" aux Etats-Unis*. Paris, Librairie Armand Colin (Cahiers de la Fondation Nationale des Sciences Politiques, 19) pp. 133-152. Reprinted in *Sociological Theory: A Book of Readings*, ed. by Lewis A. Coser and Bernard Rosenberg. New York, Macmillan, 1957, pp. 49-63.]

(1951f) "Values and Value-Orientations in the Theory of Action." In *Toward a General Theory of Action*, ed. by Talcott Parsons and Edward Shils. Cambridge, Harvard University Press, pp. 388-433. [Translation: Chinese, in *Contemporary Philosophy and Social Sciences*. Hong Kong. 1:65-79. October, 1957. (This contains an amplification requested by the Editor of *Contemporary Philosophy and Social Sciences* on the subject of "Conscience" and is printed as a letter from Clyde Kluckhohn to the Editor.)]

REVIEWS

(1951g) *Good Will and Ill Will, A Study in Moral Judgments*, by F. C. Sharp. *American Anthropologist*, 53:119-120.

(1951h) *The Moral Life and the Ethical Life*, by Eliseo Vivas. *American Anthropologist*, 53:568-569.

(1951i) *The Nature of Natural History*, by Marston Bates. *American Anthrolopogist*, 53:121-122.

FOREWORDS

(1951j) *The Ethnobotany of the Kayenta Navaho: an Analysis of the John and Louisa Wetherill Ethnobotanical Collection*, by L. C. Wyman and S. K. Harris. Albuquerque, University of New Mexico Press, pp. 3-4.

(1951k) *Navaho Veterans*, by E. Z. Vogt. Papers of the Peabody Museum of Archaeology and Ethnology, Cambridge, Harvard University, Vol. 41, No. 1, pp. vii-xii (under title "A Comparative Study of Values in Five Cultures").

(1951l) *Three Navaho Households*, by J. M. Roberts. Papers of the Peabody Museum of Archaeology and Ethnology, Cambridge, Harvard University, Vol. 40, Nov. 3, p. vii.

MISCELLANEOUS

(1951m) "American Culture and Military Life." Clyde Kluckhohn, Kaspar Naegele, and Ralph Patrick. Appendix 106, Report of the Working Group on Human Behavior under Conditions of Military Service, Office of the Secretary of Defense. Duplicated. [Reprinted (in part) in *Human Factors in Military Operations*, ed. by Richard Williams, Operations Research Office, Johns Hopkins University, Chevy Chase, Md., 1954, pp. 90-127.]

(1951n) An Anthropological Approach to the Study of Values. *Communication* (Bulletin of the American Academy of Arts and Sciences), 4:2-3.

(1951o) The Harvard Project on the Soviet Social System. Cambridge, Harvard University Russian Research Center. A. Schedules 1951, 37 vols.; B. Schedules 1950-1954, 24 vols.; Survey of Research Objectives, 26 pp. Duplicated.

(1951p) Preview: *Navaho Means People*. E. Z. Vogt and Clyde Kluckhohn. *Psychological Book Previews*, 1:71-74.

1952

MONOGRAPH

(1952a) *Culture: a Critical Review of Concepts and Definitions*. A. L. Kroeber and Clyde Kluckhohn. Papers of the Peabody Museum of Archaeology and Ethnology, Cambridge, Harvard University, Vol. 47, No. 1. [Translation: Chinese, in part, in *Contemporary Philosophy and Social Sciences*. Hong Kong. 2:12-54. 1958.]

CHAPTER

(1952b) "Universal Values and Anthropological Relativism." In *Modern Education and Human Values*. Pittsburgh, University of Pittsburgh Press, pp. 87-112.

388   CULTURE AND BEHAVIOR

REVIEW

(1952c) *Heritage of Conquest,* by Sol Tax and others. *New York Times Book Review,* Feb. 24, p. 30.

FOREWORD

(1952d) *The Sandpaintings of the Kayenta Navaho: an Analysis of the Louisa Wade Wetherill Collection,* by L. C. Wyman. Albuquerque, University of New Mexico Press, pp. 3-4.

MISCELLANEOUS

(1952e) Editing of "Social and Psychological Factors in the Resettlement of Refugees." Cambridge, Center for International Studies, Massachusetts Institute of Technology. Duplicated.

MISCELLANEOUS

(1952f) Getting behind the Iron Curtain. *ABC Weekly* (Journal of the Australian Broadcasting Commission). Vol. 14, No. 40, pp. 7, 9.

(1952g) The Meaning of Good Behavior. *Main Currents,* 9:81-82.

(1952h) Western Civilization Needs New Ideas. *ABC Weekly* (Journal of the Australian Broadcasting Commission). Vol. 14, No. 39, pp. 7, 9.

1953

BOOK

(1953a) *Personality in Nature, Society, and Culture.* Clyde Kluckhohn, Henry A. Murray, and David Schneider. New York, Alfred Knopf. Revised edition. [Original edition, 1948.] Subsequent printings: January, 1954, June, 1955; November, 1956.

CHAPTER

(1953b) "Universal Categories of Culture." In *Anthropology Today,* ed. by A. L. Kroeber. Chicago, University of Chicago Press. pp. 507-523. [Translation: Arabic, by Farwq Abd-il-qadir for *Readings in the Social Sciences,* Winter 1958-1959, No. 1:9-34, UNESCO Middle East Science Corporation Office, 1959. Reprinted in *Readings in Cross-cultural Methodology,* ed. by Frank W. Moore. New Haven, Human Relations Area Files Press, 1961, pp. 89-105.]

ARTICLE

(1953c) "Inbreeding Coefficients of the Ramah Navaho Population." J. N. Spuhler and Clyde Kluckhohn. *Human Biology,* 25:295-317.

REVIEWS

(1953d) *Cultural Sciences,* by Florian Znaniecki. *American Anthropologist,* 55:421-422.

(1953e) *Franz Boas: The Science of Man in the Making,* by M. J. Herskovits. *New York Herald Tribune Book Review,* Dec. 20, p. 4.

(1953f) *Indian Tales*, by Jaime de Angulo. *New York Herald Tribune Book Review*, April 19, p. 4.

(1953g) *The Second Sex*, by Simone de Beauvoir. *New York Times Book Review*, Feb. 22, pp. 3, 33.

(1953h) *Sexual Behavior in the Human Female*, by A. C. Kinsey *et al*. *New York Times Book Review*, Sept. 13, pp. 3, 38.

(1953i) *The World of Primitive Man*, by Paul Radin. *New York Herald Tribune Book Review*, Nov. 8, p. 15.

FOREWORD

(1953j) *The World's Rim: Great Mysteries of the North American Indians*, by Hartley Burr Alexander. Lincoln, University of Nebraska Press, pp. v-vii.

MISCELLANEOUS

(1953k) Anthropology. *Saturday Review*, Apr. 4, 36:25, 49-50.

(1953l) The Concept of Culture for Psychiatric Theory and Practice. *Digest of Neurology and Psychiatry*, 21:153.

(1953m) Anthropological Studies of Human Relations. Rockefeller Foundation. Conference on Research in Human Relations. Mimeographed. February, 48 pp.

1954

CHAPTERS

(1954a) "Application of Anthropology in the United States." [Translation: Japanese, in *Review of Contemporary America: Public Lectures at the American Studies Seminar, 1954*, ed. by S. Suetsugu. Tokyo, University of Tokyo Press, pp. 53-77.]

(1954b) "Culture and Behavior." In *Handbook of Social Psychology*, ed. by Gardner Lindzey. Cambridge, Addison-Wesley, pp. 921-976.

(1954c) "Social Science Principles and the Indian Reorganization Act." Clyde Kluckhohn and Robert A. Hackenberg. In *Indian Affairs and the Indian Reorganization Act*, ed. by W. H. Kelly. Tucson, University of Arizona, pp. 29-34. Mimeographed.

ARTICLES

(1954d) "Methods of Study at the Russian Research Center, Harvard University." *Civilizations* (Revue d'Institut International des Civilisations Différentes), 4:199-206.

(1954e) "Moral Apathy or Moral Growing Pains?" *The Humanist*, 14:124-128.

(1954f) "Science as a Possible Source of New Moral Values." *The Humanist*, 14:211-214. [This is the continuation of the article "Moral Apathy or Moral Growing Pains?"]

(1954g) "Southwestern Studies of Culture and Personality." *American Anthropologist*, 56:685-708.

REVIEWS

(1954h) *For a Science of Social Man*, ed. by John Gillin. *Science*, 120:888-889.

(1954i) *The Primitive World and Its Transformations*, by Robert Redfield. *American Anthropologist*, 56:295-297.

(1954j) *The Savages of America*, by Roy H. Pearce; *Theoretical Anthropology*, by David Bidney; *The World of Primitive Man*, by Paul Radin. *Isis*, 45:107-109.

(1954k) *Sexual Behavior in the Human Female*, by A. C. Kinsey and others; *The Second Sex*, by Simone de Beauvoir. *Perspectives USA*, 7:144-147.

(1954l) *The Story of Man*, by Carleton S. Coon. *New York Times Book Review*, Nov. 7, pp. 3, 52-53.

FOREWORDS

(1954m) *Enemy Way Music*, by David McAllester. Papers of the Peabody Museum of Archaeology and Ethnology, Cambridge, Harvard University, Vol. 41, No. 3, p. v.

(1954n) *A Study of Rorschach Responses in Four Cultures*, by Bert Kaplan. Papers of the Peabody Museum of Archaeology and Ethnology, Cambridge, Harvard University, Vol. 42, No. 2, p. v.

MISCELLANEOUS

(1954o) Obituary of Earnest Albert Hooton. Clyde Kluckhohn, J. O. Brew, and William Langer. Harvard University *Gazette*, Oct. 30, pp. 39-40.

(1954p) Obituary of Earnest Albert Hooton (1887-1954). Year Book of the American Philosophical Society, pp. 418-422.

(1954q) Obituary of Paul Reiter (1909-1953). *American Anthropologist*, 56:1085-1087.

(1954r) History and Anthropology. Unpublished manuscript, substantial portions of which are quoted in *The Social Sciences in Historical Study*, Social Science Research Council Bulletin 64:36-41.

(1954s) Strategic, Psychological, and Sociological Strength and Vulnerabilities of the Soviet Social System. Clyde Kluckhohn, Alex Inkeles, and Raymond A. Bauer. Cambridge, Russian Research Center, Harvard University. Duplicated, 406 pp.

1955

CHAPTER

(1955a) "Anthropology." In *What is Science?* ed. by James R. Newman. New York, Simon and Schuster, pp. 319-357. [Reprinted: New York. Paperback, 1958.]

ARTICLES

(1955b) "Ethical Relativity: *Sic et Non*." *Journal of Philosophy*, 52:663-677.

(1955c) "Implicit and Explicit Values in the Social Sciences Related to Human Growth and Development." *Merrill-Palmer Quarterly*, 1:131-140.

(1955d) "Indian Americans in a White Man's World: a Study of Indian American Values and Culture Change." *Advance* (Congregational Christian Journal), 147:13-15.

(1955e) "Moencopi Variations from Whorf's Second Mesa Hopi." Clyde Kluckhohn and Kenneth MacLeish. *International Journal of American Linguistics*, 21:150-156.

(1955f) "Physical Anthropology." *American Anthropologist*, 57:1280-1295.

(1955g) "Recent Studies of the 'National Character' of Great Russians." *Human Development Bulletin*, papers presented at the Sixth Annual Symposium, Feb. 5, 1955. Chicago, pp. 39-60. [Reprinted, 1959, Cambridge, Russian Research Center, Harvard University.]

REVIEW ARTICLE

(1955h) "Politics, History, and Psychology." *World Politics*, 8:112-123. [Translation of Section II, review of *A Study of Bolshevism* by Nathan Leites, appeared under title "Geist und Standort der Sowjetelite" in *Ost-Probleme*. 8:141-143.]

REVIEWS

(1955i) *Aspects of Culture and Personality*, ed. by F. L. K. Hsu. *Scientific Monthly*, 80:204-205.

(1955j) *Eros and Civilization: a Philosophical Inquiry into Freud*, by Herbert Marcuse. *New York Times Book Review*, Nov. 27, p. 30.

(1955k) *Interrelations of Cultures*, by Richard McKeon, *et al. Psychological Bulletin*, 52:357.

(1955l) *Property Concepts of the Navaho Indians*, by Berard Haile. *Ethnohistory*, 2:386-387.

(1955m) *The Tree of Culture*, by Ralph Linton. *New York Times Book Review*, Sept. 18, pp. 6, 36.

MISCELLANEOUS

(1955n) Obituary, "The Son of Many Beads, 1866-1954." Clyde Kluckhohn and Evon Z. Vogt. *American Anthropologist*, 57:1036-1037.

(1955o) Are There Unifying Concepts That Can Be Applied across Various Disciplines? Association of Princeton Graduate Alumni, Report of Fifth Conference, December 30-31, 1955, pp. 28-32.

(1955p) A Study of the Need for a New Cyclopedic Treatment of the Social Sciences. Kingsley Davis, Clyde Kluckhohn, W. Allen Wallis, *et al.*, under the auspices of the University of Chicago. Staff director, Bert F. Hoselitz. Mimeographed. 239 pp.

1956

BOOK

(1956a) *How the Soviet System Works*. Raymond A. Bauer, Alex

Inkeles, and Clyde Kluckhohn. Cambridge, Harvard University Press. Subsequent printings: 2nd, 1957; 3rd, 1959. [English edition, Oxford University Press. Reprinted: paperback, 1960, Vintage Russian Library R-1004.]

CHAPTERS

(1956b) "Aspects of the Demographic History of a Small Population." In *Estudios Anthropologicos* publicados en homenaje al doctor Manuel Gamio. Mexico, D.F., Dirreccion General de Publicaciones, pp. 359-381.

(1956c) "Navaho Morals." In *Encyclopedia of Morals,* ed. by Vergilius Ferm. New York, Philosophical Library, pp. 383-390.

(1956d) "New Uses for 'Barbarians.'" In *Frontiers of Knowledge in the Study of Man,* ed. by Lynn White, Jr. New York, Harper & Bros., pp. 33-47.

(1956e) "Toward a Comparison of Value-Emphases in Different Cultures." In *The State of the Social Sciences,* ed. by Leonard D. White. Chicago, University of Chicago Press, pp. 116-132.

ARTICLES

(1956f) "Biological and Cultural Evolution: Some Analogies and Explorations." R. W. Gerard, Clyde Kluckhohn, and Anatol Rapoport. *Behavioral Science,* 1:6-34.

(1956g) "The Impact of Freud on Anthropology." *Bulletin of the New York Academy of Medicine,* Second Series, 32:903-907.

(1956h) "Some Navaho Value Terms in Behavioral Context." *Language,* 32:140-145.

(1956i) "Suppose Columbus Had Stayed Home." *Saturday Review,* Sept. 22, 39:9, 10, 37-39. [Reprinted in revised and abridged form, under title "If Columbus Had Not Discovered America." *Boston Sunday Globe,* Oct. 7, 1956.]

REVIEW ARTICLES

(1956j) *Culture and Human Fertility,* by Frank Lorimer. *American Journal of Physical Anthropology,* 14 n.s.:527-532.

(1956k) *Language in Culture: Proceedings of a Conference on the Interrelations of Language to Other Aspects of Culture,* ed. by Harry Hoijer. *American Anthropologist,* 58:569-574. [Also duplicated, original version, with note that published review had certain small changes which altered meaning.]

REVIEWS

(1956l) *Great Men: Psychoanalytic Studies,* by Edward Hitschmann. *New York Times Book Review,* June 17, p. 6.

(1956m) *Hungarian and Vogul Mythology,* by Geza Roheim. *The Psychoanalytic Quarterly,* 25:99-100.

(1956n) *The Navajos,* by Ruth M. Underhill. *The Pacific Historical Review,* 25:401-402.

(1956o) *New Lives for Old,* by Margaret Mead. *Saturday Review,* May 12, 39:16.

(1956p) *Other Men's Skies,* by Robert Bunker. *New York Herald Tribune Book Review,* Nov. 11, p. 11.

(1956q) *A Pictorial History of the American Indian,* by Oliver La Farge. *New York Herald Tribune Book Review,* Dec. 23, p. 3.

MISCELLANEOUS

(1956r) Obituary of Alfred Marston Tozzer (1877-1954). Year Book of the American Philosophical Society, pp. 128-131.

(1956s) The Behavioral Sciences on TV. Summary of Talk at NAEB Program Planning Seminar, University of Wisconsin, Aug. 26-Sept. 1, 1956, Madison, pp. 36-60. Mimeographed.

1957

BOOK

(1957a) *Les Navajos,* Lausanne, Nouvelles Editions S.A.

CHAPTER

(1957b) "Cultures, Values, and Education." In *Bulletin of the Research Institute of Comparative Education and Culture,* English edition, No. 1, March, pp. 44-61. [Published simultaneously in Japanese translation.]

ARTICLES

(1957c) "Developments in the Field of Anthropology in the Twentieth Century." *Journal of World History,* 3:754-777.

(1957d) "General Semantics and 'Primitive' Languages." Alfred Korzybski Memorial Lecture. *General Semantics Bulletin.* Nos. 20 and 21.

REVIEWS

(1957e) *Beautyway: A Navaho Ceremonial,* ed. by Leland C. Wyman. *Boston University Graduate Journal,* slightly altered, 6:11-12. *Review of Religion,* 22:63-65.

(1957f) *Culture, Psychiatry, and Human Values: the Methods and Values of a Social Psychiatry,* by Marvin K. Opler. *American Anthropologist,* 59:192-194.

(1957g) *The Seven Caves,* by Carleton S. Coon. *Saturday Review,* Jan. 5, p. 11.

(1957h) *Some Uses of Anthropology: Theoretical and Applied,* ed. by Joseph B. Casagrande and Thomas Gladwin. *Annals* of the American Academy of Political and Social Science (Current Issues in International Labor Relations), 310:198.

FOREWORDS

(1957i) *Cultural Foundations of Education, An Interdisciplinary Exploration,* by Theodore Brameld. New York, Harper & Bros., pp. xi-xiii.

(1957j) *The Structure of a Moral Code: a Philosophical Analysis of Ethical Discourse Applied to the Ethics of the Navaho Indians,* by John Ladd. Cambridge, Harvard University Press, pp. xiii-xv.

MISCELLANEOUS

(1957k) Biographical essay: A. L. Kroeber. To accompany his recording of lecture "The Concept of Culture in Science," New York, Walden Records.

(1957l) Navajo or Navaho Indians. *Encyclopedia Americana.*

(1957m) Reply of Professor Clyde Kluckhohn, former Director of the Russian Research Center, Harvard University, Jan. 14, 1957. In *Control and Reduction of Armaments. Attitudes of Soviet Leaders toward Disarmament. Replies from Experts on the Soviet Union to Subcommittee Questionnaire.* Staff Study No. 8, Subcommittee on Disarmament of the Committee on Foreign Relations. Washington, D.C., U.S. Government Printing Office, pp. 56-58.

(1957n) Short one-paragraph reviews of various publications. *Key Reporter,* various issues.

1958

CHAPTERS

(1958a) "Have There Been Discernible Shifts in American Values during the Past Generation?" In *The American Style,* ed. by Elting Morison, New York, Harper & Bros., pp. 145-217.

(1958b) "Ralph Linton (1893-1953)." In *Biographical Memoirs of the National Academy of Sciences,* New York, Columbia University Press, 31:236-253.

ARTICLES

(1958c) "The Evolution of Contemporary American Values." *Daedalus,* 87-78-109 [a portion of 1958a].

(1958d) "The Scientific Study of Values and Contemporary Civilization." *Proceedings of the American Philosophical Society,* 102:469-476.

REVIEW

(1958e) *Young Man Luther,* by Erik H. Erikson. *New York Herald Tribune Book Review,* Nov. 16, p. 4.

FOREWORD

(1958f) *A Reader in Comparative Religion,* by William Lessa and Evon Z. Vogt. Evanston, Ill. Row, Peterson, pp. v-vi.

1959

CHAPTERS

(1959a) "Anthropology and Psychology." In *Proceedings of the*

Fifteenth International Congress of Psychology, Brussels, 1957. Amsterdam, North Holland Publishing Company, pp. 63-75.

(1959b) "Franz Boas: Influences during the Formative Years." Clyde Kluckhohn and Olaf Prufer. In *The Anthropology of Franz Boas,* ed. by Walter Goldschmidt. *Memoir* No. 89 of the American Anthropological Association. Vol. 61, No. 5, Part 2, pp. 4-28. [Reprinted, paperback. San Francisco, Chandler Publishing Company, 1960.]

(1959c) "Common Humanity and Diverse Cultures." In *The Human Meaning of the Social Sciences,* ed. by Daniel Lerner. New York, Meridian, pp. 245-284. [Translations: French (in part): *Esprit,* January, 1959, pp. 98-112; Chinese, by P. C. Chun, in *Contemporary Philosophy and Social Sciences,* Hong Kong, Vol. 2, No. 1, 1958.]

(1959d) "The Role of Evolutionary Thought in Anthropology." In *Evolution and Anthropology: a Centennial Appraisal.* Anthropological Society of Washington. Washington, D.C., pp. 144-157.

(1959e) "The Scientific Study of Values." In *Three Lectures* (University of Toronto Installation Lectures, 1958). Toronto, University of Toronto Press, pp. 25-54.

ARTICLES

(1959f) "Frontiers of Anthropological Research." *Colorado Quarterly,* 7:271-286.

(1959g) "Recurrent Themes in Myths and Mythmaking." *Daedalus,* 88:268-279. [Translation: Japanese, *Americana,* USIS, pp. 23-34. December, 1959. Reprinted in *Myth and Mythmaking,* ed. by Henry A. Murray. New York, George Braziller, 1960, pp. 46-60.]

REVIEW ARTICLE

(1959h) "Shifts in American Values." Review of *America as a Civilization: Life and Thought in the United States Today,* by Max Lerner. *World Politics,* 11:251-261. [Reprinted in *American History: Recent Interpretations,* Book II, ed. by Abraham S. Eisenstadt. New York, Thomas Y. Crowell Company, 1962, pp. 507-529.]

REVIEWS

(1959i) *An Anthropologist at Work, Writings of Ruth Benedict,* by Margaret Mead. *Basic Book News,* 15. *New York Times Book Review Section,* May 31, p. 12.

(1959j) *Five Families: Mexican Case Studies in the Culture of Poverty,* by Oscar Lewis. *New York Herald Tribune Book Review,* June 28, p. 6.

(1959k) *Freud: The Mind of the Moralist,* by Philip Rieff. *The Unitarian Register,* 138:17-18.

(1959l) *The Freudian Ethic. An Analysis of the Subversion of American Character,* by Richard La Piere. *New York Herald Tribune Book Review,* Dec. 20, p. 12.

(1959m) *The Inland Whale,* by Theodora Kroeber. *New York Herald Tribune Book Review,* May, 3, p. 6.

396 CULTURE AND BEHAVIOR

(1959n) *Man's Way: a Preface to the Understanding of Human Society*, by Walter Goldschmidt. *American Anthropologist*, 61:1098-1099.

(1959o) *Naven: A Survey of the Problems Suggested by a Composite Picture of the Culture of a New Guinea Tribe Drawn from Three Points of View*, by Gregory Bateson. *Contemporary Psychology*, 4:41-42.

(1959p) *The Sacred and the Profane*, by Mircea Eliade. *Religious Education*, 54:541-542.

(1959q) *Social Anthropology as Science and as Art*, by Raymond Firth. *American Anthropologist*, 61:512-513.

(1959r) *Taboo*, by Franz Steiner. *Psychoanalytic Quarterly*, 28:540-541.

(1959s) *Die Wiener Schule der Völkerkunde*, ed. by J. Haekel, A. Hohenwart-Gerlachstein, and A. Slawik. *American Anthropologist*, 61:515-517.

MISCELLANEOUS

(1959t) Abstract: "On Values in Cross-cultural Perspective." In *Proceedings of the Fifteenth International Congress of Psychology, Brussels, 1957*. Amsterdam, North Holland Publishing Company, pp. 82-84.

(1959u) Introduction: *Navaho Art and Culture*, by George Mills. Colorado Springs, The Taylor Museum of the Colorado Springs Fine Arts Center, pp. xi-xii.

(1959v) "Anthropology in Harvard College." Harvard Foundation for Advanced Study and Research *Newsletter*, Dec. 31, pp. 4-6.

(1959w) "The Library's New Program in American Indian Linguistics and Ethnohistory." *Proceedings of the American Philosophical Society*, Philadelphia, 103:768-769.

1960

BOOK

(1960a) *A Selected Bibliography on Values, Ethics, and Esthetics in the Behavioral Sciences and Philosophy, 1920-1958*. Ethel M. Albert and Clyde Kluckhohn with the assistance of Robert LeVine, Warren Seulowitz and Miriam Gallaher. Glencoe, The Free Press. c. 1959.

CHAPTERS

(1960b) "Cultural Differences." In *Man and Society*, ed. by Jerome G. Manis and Samuel I. Clark. Book I, reading 7. New York, Macmillan, pp. 122-126. [A selection from *Mirror for Man*, 1949a.]

(1960c) "The Educational Process." In *Exploring the Ways of Mankind*, ed. by Walter Goldschmidt. New York, Holt, Rinehart, and Winston, pp. 179-187. [A selection from *Mirror for Man*, 1949a.]

(1960d) "The Moral Order in the Expanding Society." In *The City Invincible*, ed. by Carl H. Kraeling and Robert M. Adams. Chicago, University of Chicago Press, pp. 391-404.

(1960e) "Navaho Categories." In *Culture in History: Essays in Honor of*

Paul Radin, ed. by Stanley Diamond. New York, published for Brandeis University by Columbia University Press, pp. 65-98.

(1960f) "A Navaho Politician." In *In the Company of Man: Twenty Portraits by Anthropologists*, ed. by Joseph B. Casagrande. New York, Harper & Bros., reading 17, pp. 439-465.

(1960g) "The Religious World of the Navaho." Clyde Kluckhohn and Dorothea Leighton. In *Exploring the Ways of Mankind*, ed. by Walter Goldschmidt. New York, Holt, Rinehart, and Winston, pp. 508-520. [A selection from *The Navaho*, 1946a.]

(1960h) "Social and Cultural Evolution." In *Issues in Evolution*, Vol. 3 of *Evolution after Darwin*, ed. by Sol Tax. Chicago, University of Chicago Press, pp. 207-243.

(1960i) "The Use of Typology in Anthropological Theory." In *Men and Cultures*, Selected Papers of the Fifth International Congress of Anthropological and Ethnological Sciences, Philadelphia, Sept. 1-9, 1956, ed. by Anthony F. C. Wallace. Philadelphia, University of Pennsylvania Press, pp. 134-140.

REVIEWS

(1960j) *Cochiti: A New Mexico Pueblo, Past and Present*, by Charles H. Lange. *Annals* of the American Academy of Political and Social Science, 331:140-141.

(1960k) *Culture and History: Prolegomena to the Comparative Study of Civilizations*, by Philip Bagby. *American Anthropologist*, 62:1058-9.

(1960l) *Hellenism: The History of a Civilization*, by Arnold J. Toynbee. *American Sociological Review*, 25:122-123.

(1960m) Miscellaneous reviews, paperback section, *New York Herald Tribune Book Review*.

MISCELLANEOUS

(1960n) Historical consultant for *We Were There with Charles Darwin on the H. M. S. Beagle*, by Philip Eisenberg. New York, Grosset & Dunlap.

(1960o) Notes on Some Anthropological Aspects of Communication. Paper prepared for symposium, "Comparative Aspects of Human Communication," Wenner-Gren Foundation for Anthropological Research. Manuscript. 25 pp. [Published 1961, see 1961d.]

1961

BOOK

(1961a) *Anthropology and the Classics*. Brown University Colver Lectures, 1960. Providence, Brown University Press.

CHAPTERS

(1961b) "The Rimrock Navaho." Clyde Kluckhohn and A. Kimball Romney. In *Variations in Value Orientations*, ed. by Florence R. Kluckhohn and Fred Strodtbeck. Evanston, Row, Peterson, pp. 318-339.

(1961c) "The Study of Values." In *Values in America*, ed. by Donald N. Barrett. Notre Dame, University of Notre Dame Press, pp. 17-45.

ARTICLE

(1961d) "Notes on Some Anthropological Aspects of Communication" (1960). *American Anthropologist*, 63:895-910.

MISCELLANEOUS

(1961e) Encyclopedia articles: Navaho, for *Encyclopaedia Britannica*. Navaho, for Funk and Wagnalls *Encyclopedia*. Witchcraft, for *Encyclopaedia Britannica*.

1962

BOOK

(1962a) *Culture and Behavior*. The Collected Essays of Clyde Kluckhohn. Ed. by Clyde Kluckhohn and Richard Kluckhohn. New York, The Free Press.

CHAPTERS

(1962b) Two chapters for a high-school textbook, *Problems and Promise of American Democracy*, ed. by Donald H. Riddle. Chapter 1, "The Individual, Society, and Culture," by Clyde Kluckhohn; Chapter 2, "The Achievement of Social Order: Cultural Patterns in Informal Groups," by Clyde Kluckhohn and Florence R. Kluckhohn. New York, McGraw-Hill, 1963.

INDEX